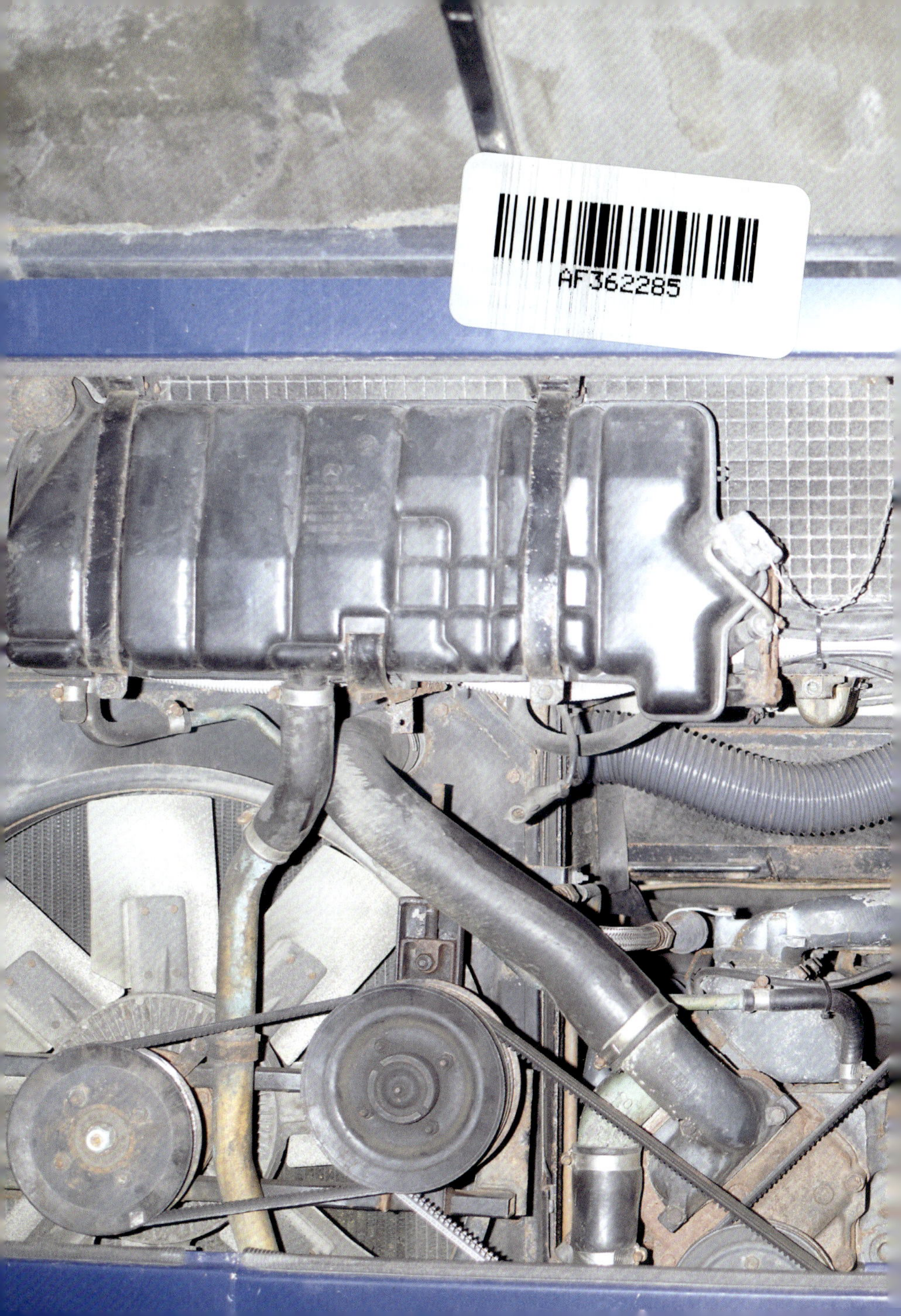

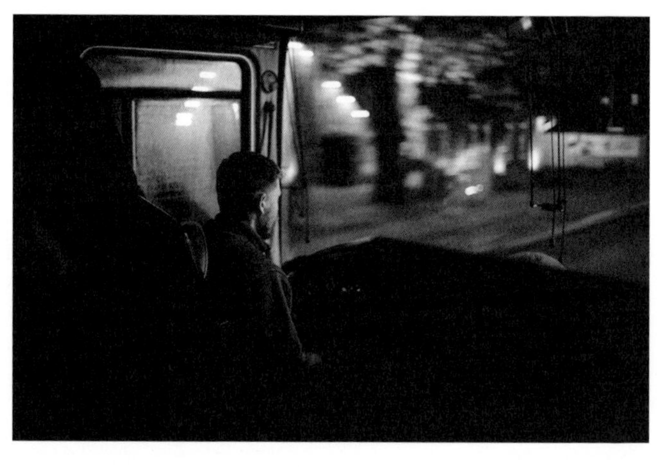

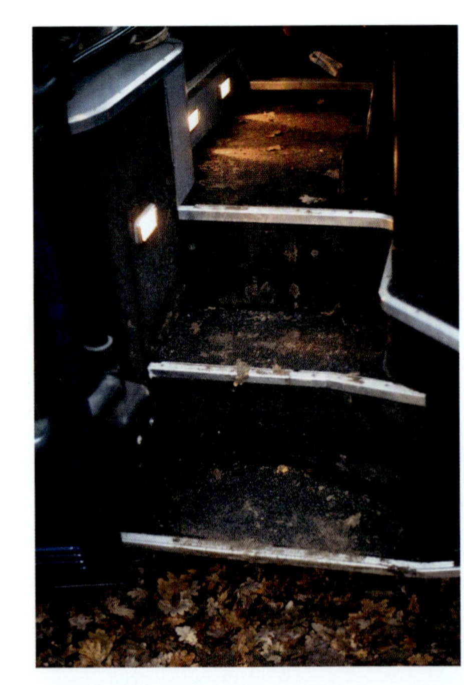

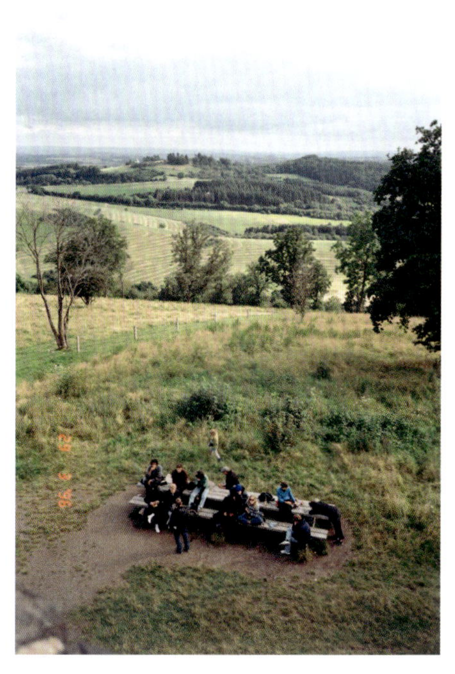

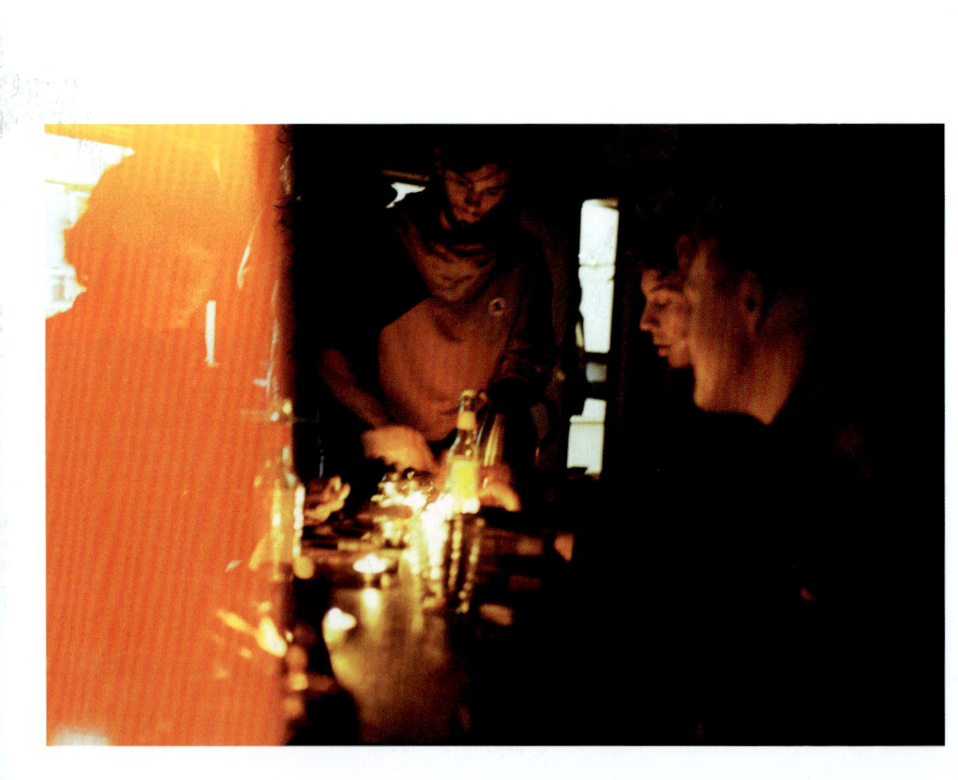

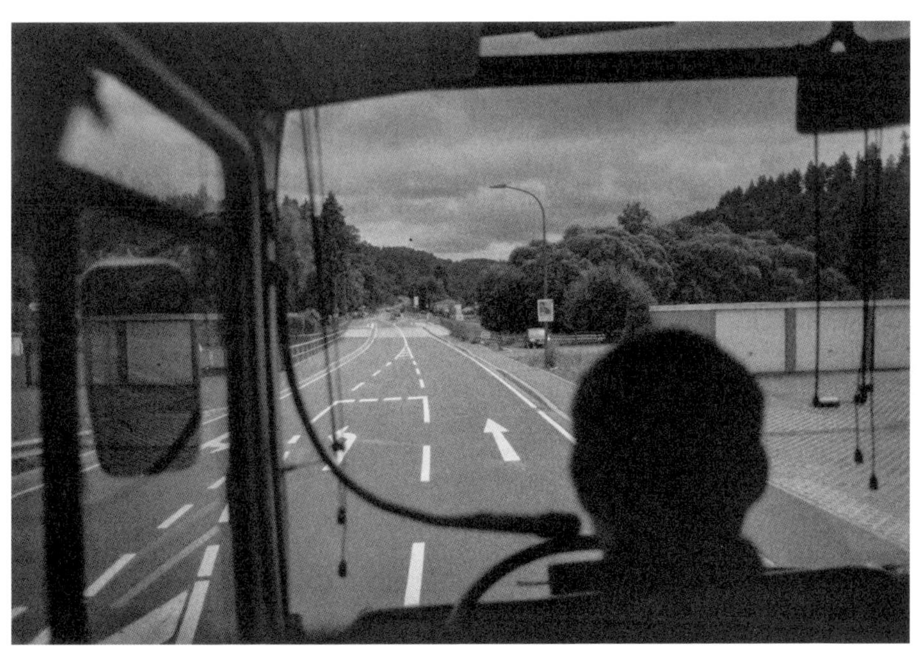

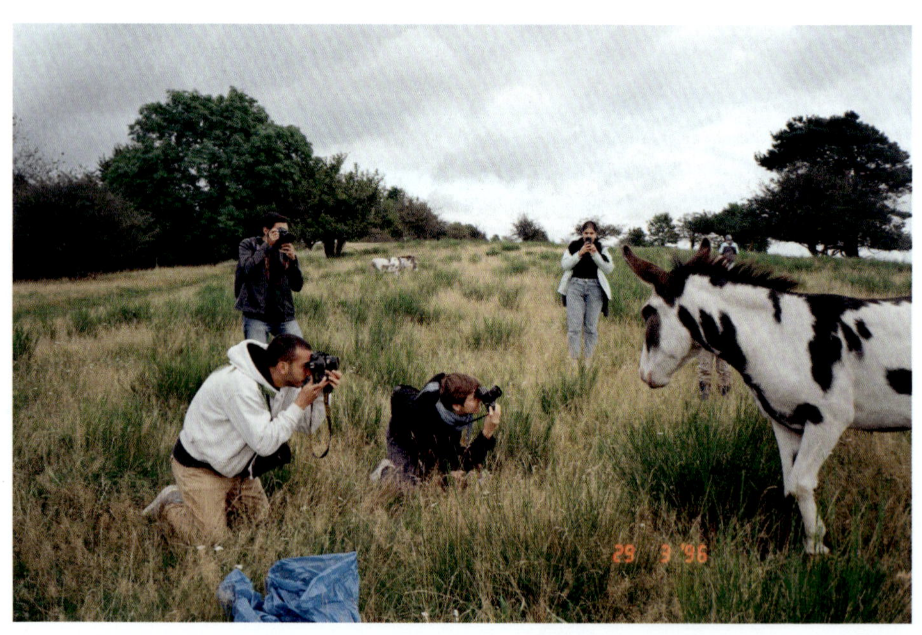
29 3 '96

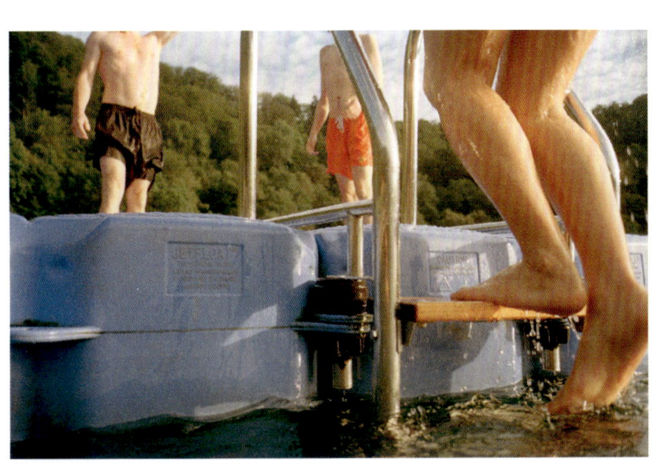

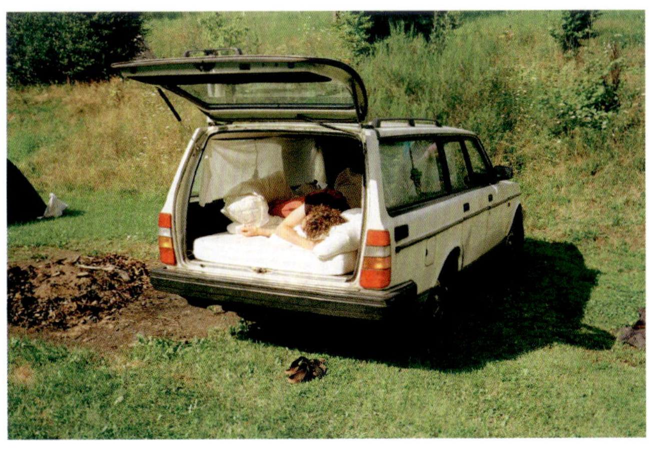

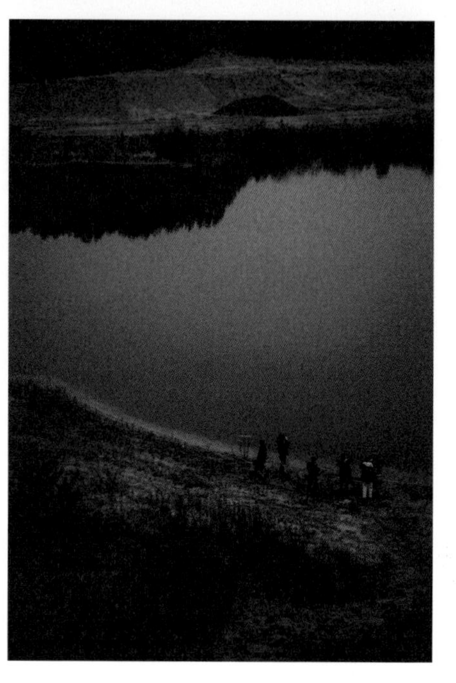

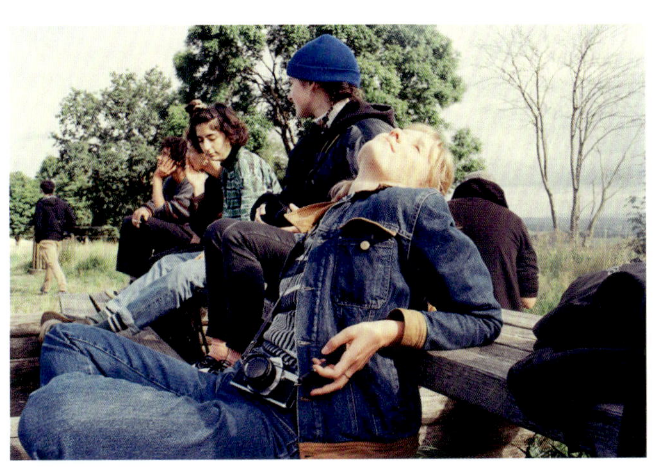

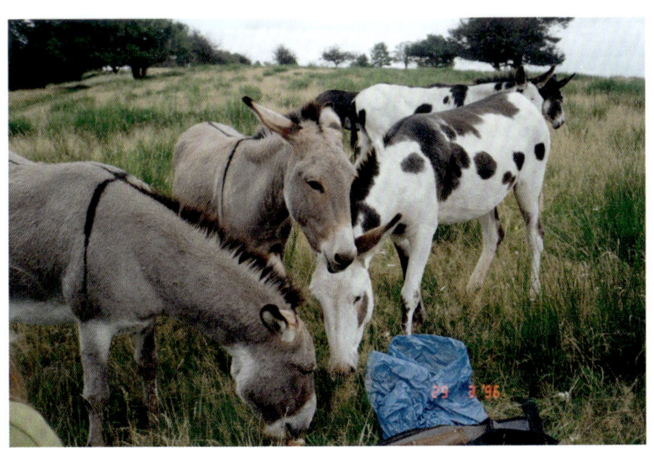
29 3 '96

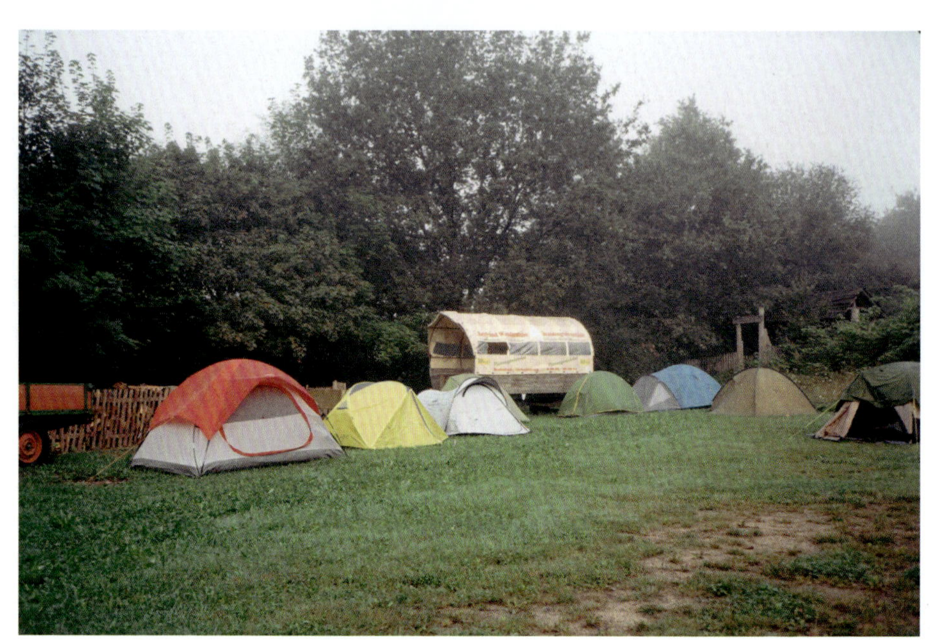

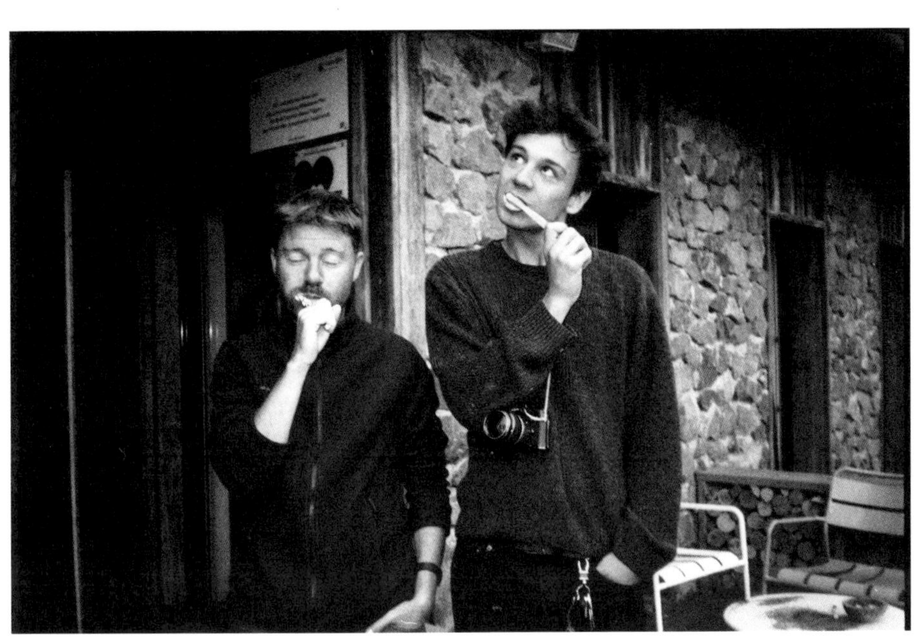

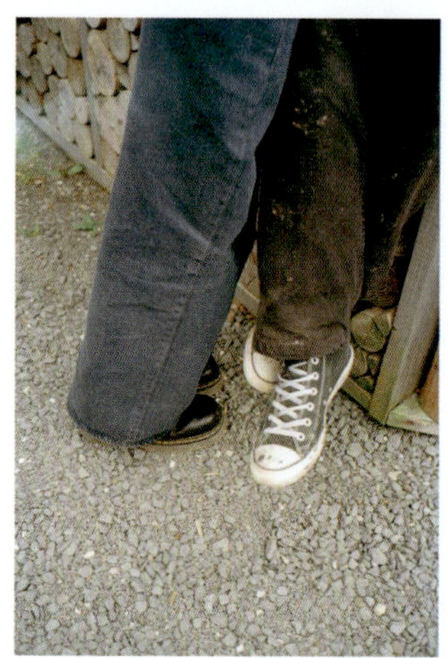

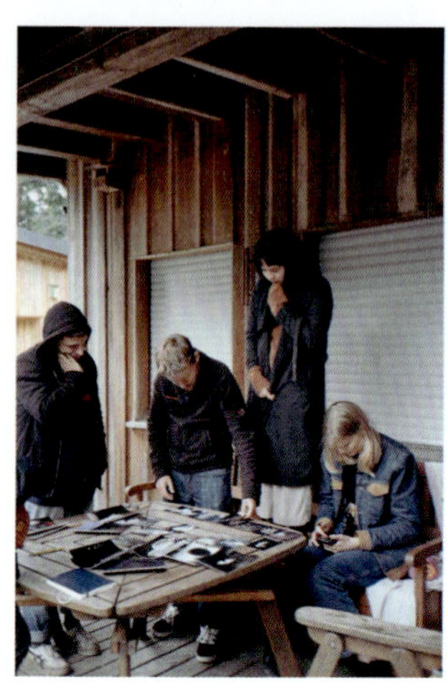

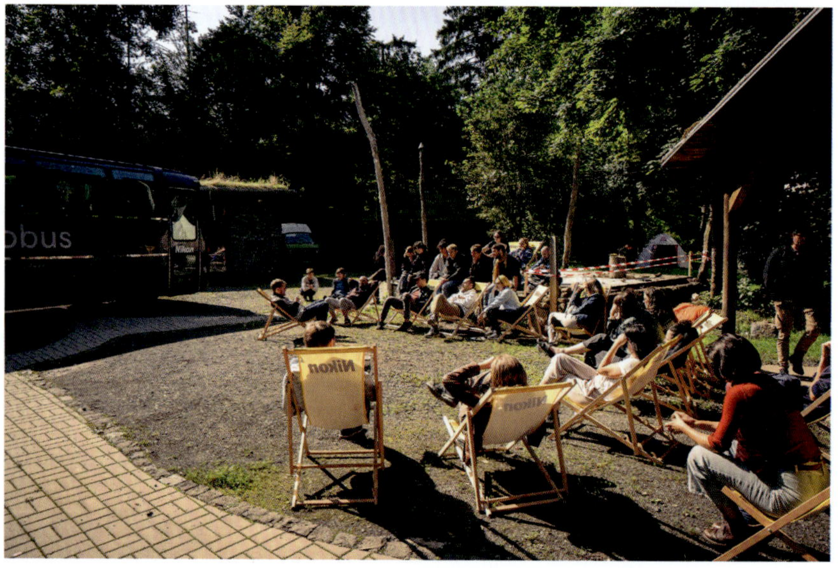
obus

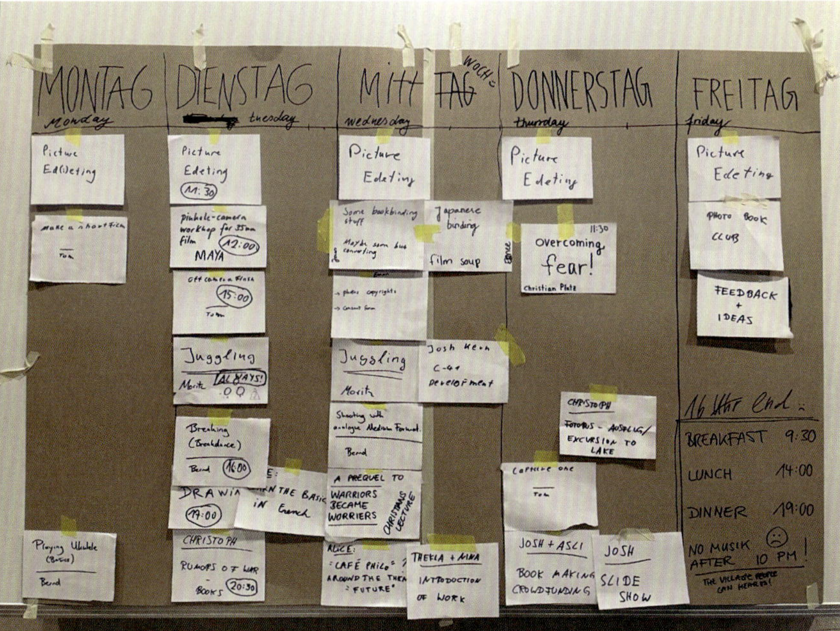

MONTAG
monday
DIENSTAG
tuesday
wednesday
DONNERSTAG
thursday
FREITAG
friday
Picture Edeting
11:30
pinhole-camera workshop for 35mm film
12:00
MAYA
15:00
Juggling
Moritz
ALWAYS!
Breaking (Breakdance)
Bernd
16:00
19:00
CHRISTOPH
RUMORS OF WAR - BOOKS
20:30
Playing Ukulele (Basics)
Bernd
Some bookbinding stuff
Japanese binding
film soup
photos copyrights
Juggling
Moritz
Josh Keon
Shooting with analogue Medium Format.
Bernd
A PREQUEL TO WARRIORS BECAME WORRIERS
CHRISTMAS LECTURE
ALICE:
"CAFÉ PHILO"
THEKLA + NINA
INTRODUCTION OF WORK
11:30
Overcoming fear!
Christian Platz
CHRISTOPH
EXCURSION TO LAKE
Capture One
JOSH + ASLI
BOOK MAKING
CROWDFUNDING
JOSH
SLIDE SHOW
PHOTO BOOK CLUB
FEEDBACK + IDEAS
BREAKFAST 9:30
LUNCH 14:00
DINNER 19:00
NO MUSIK AFTER 10 PM!

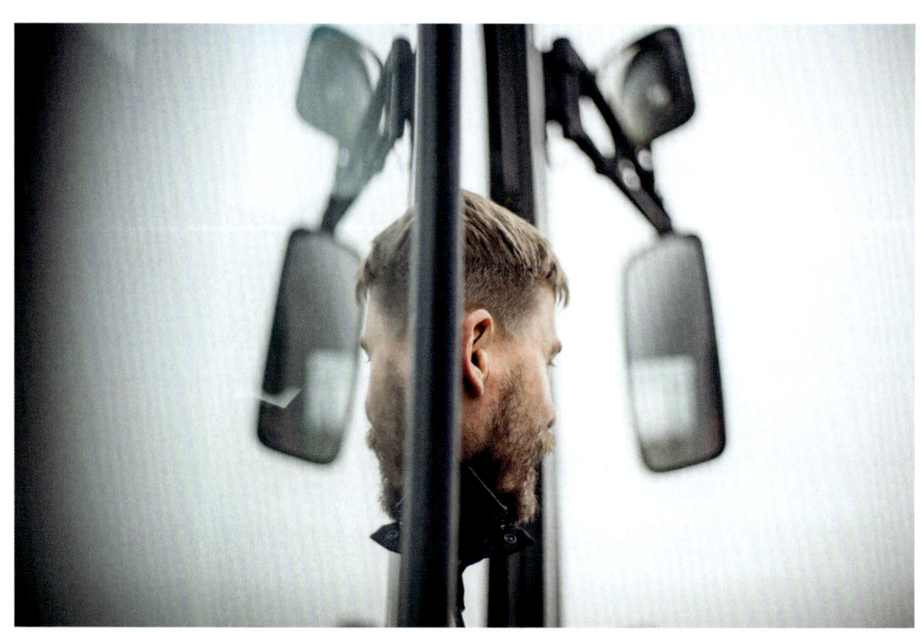

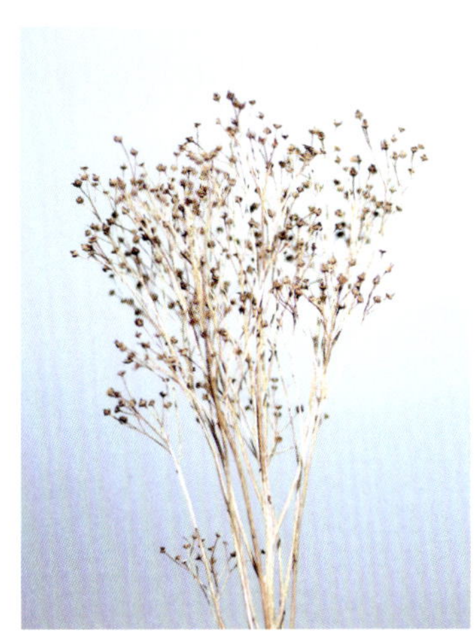

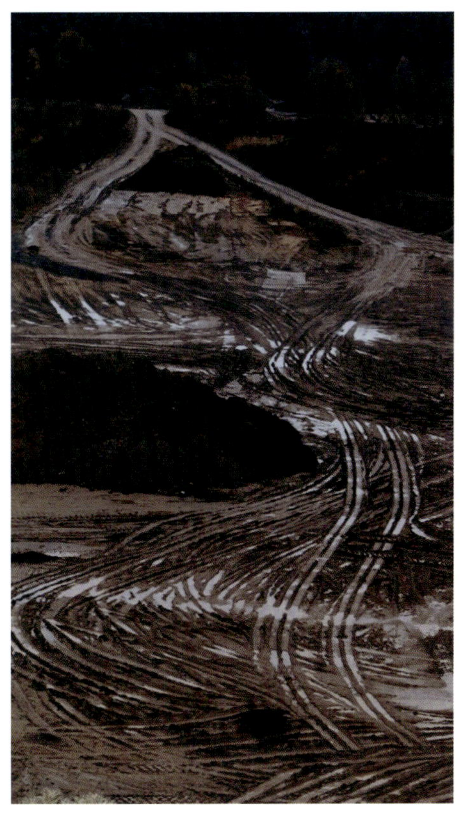

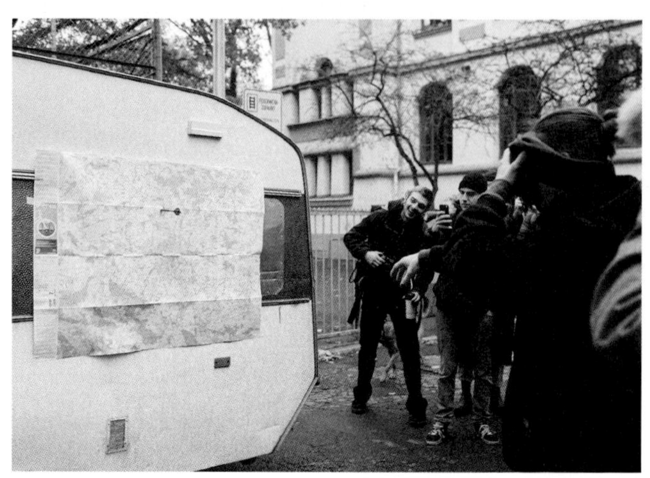

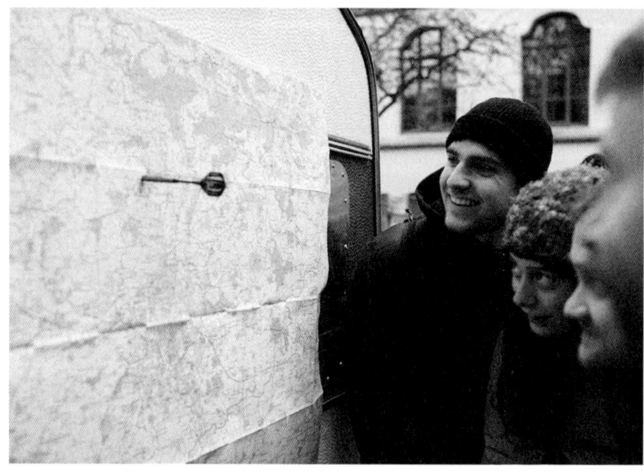

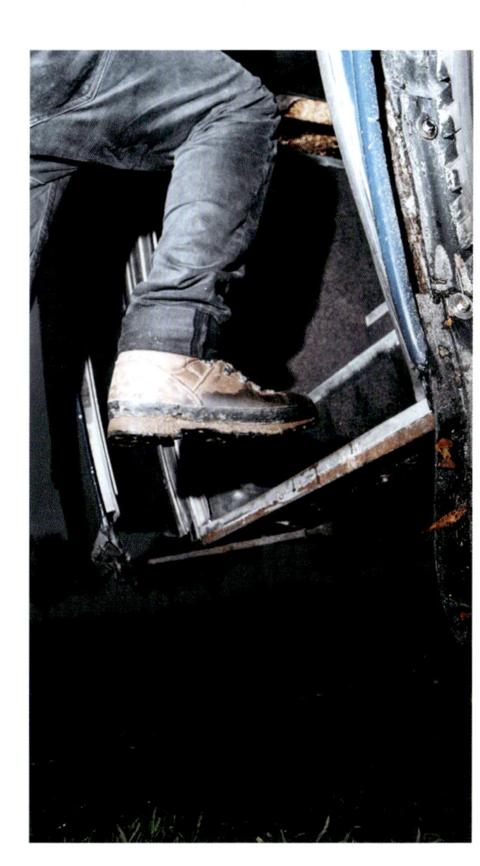

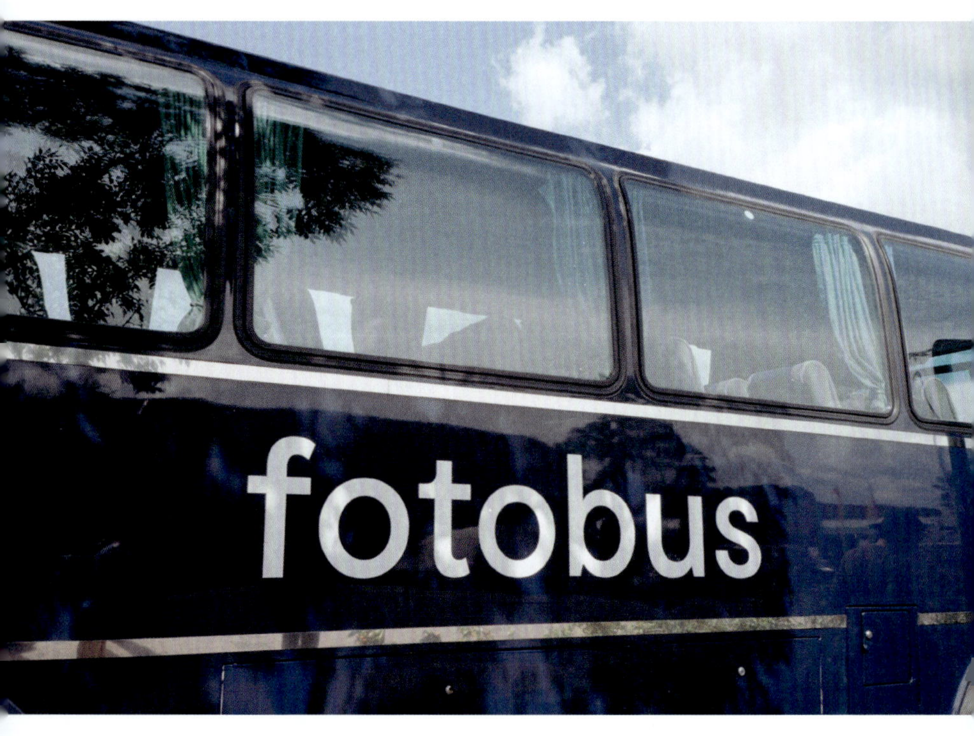
fotobus

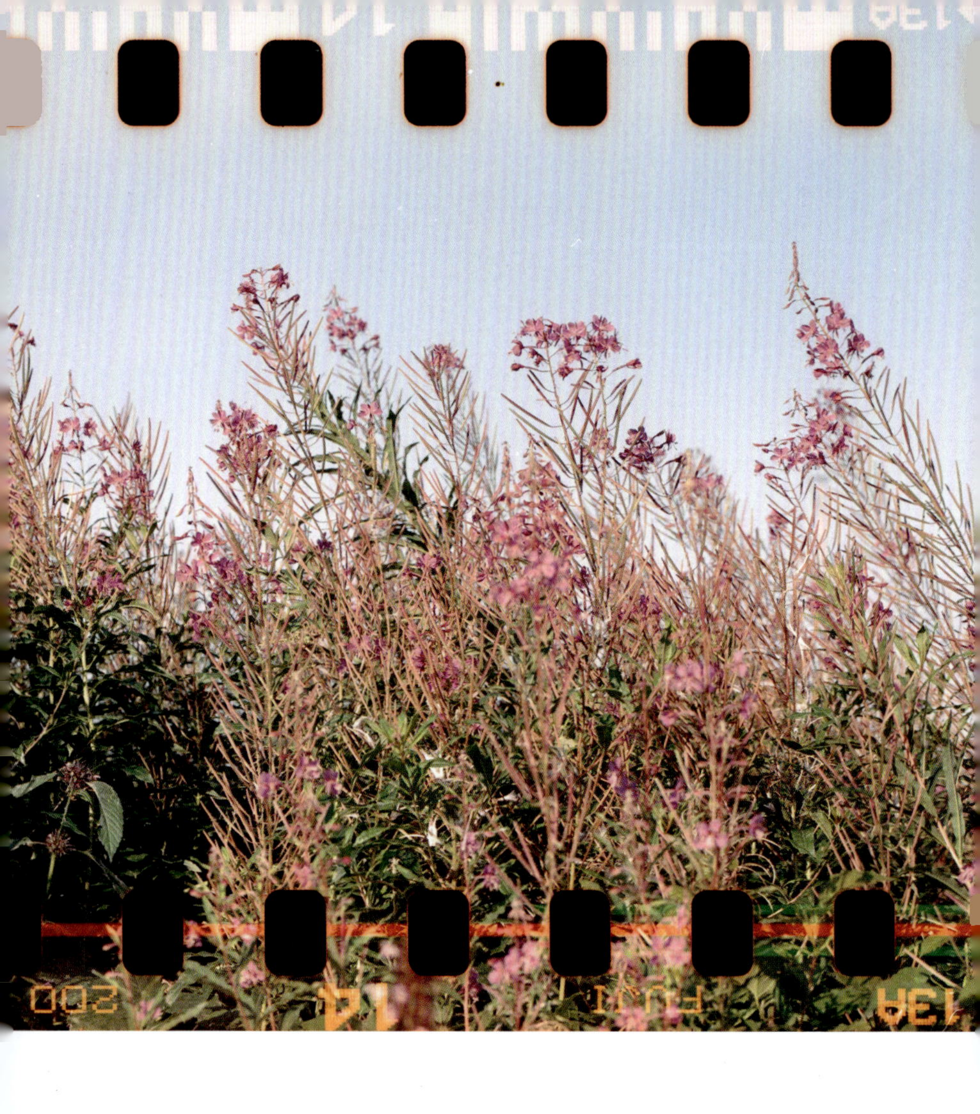

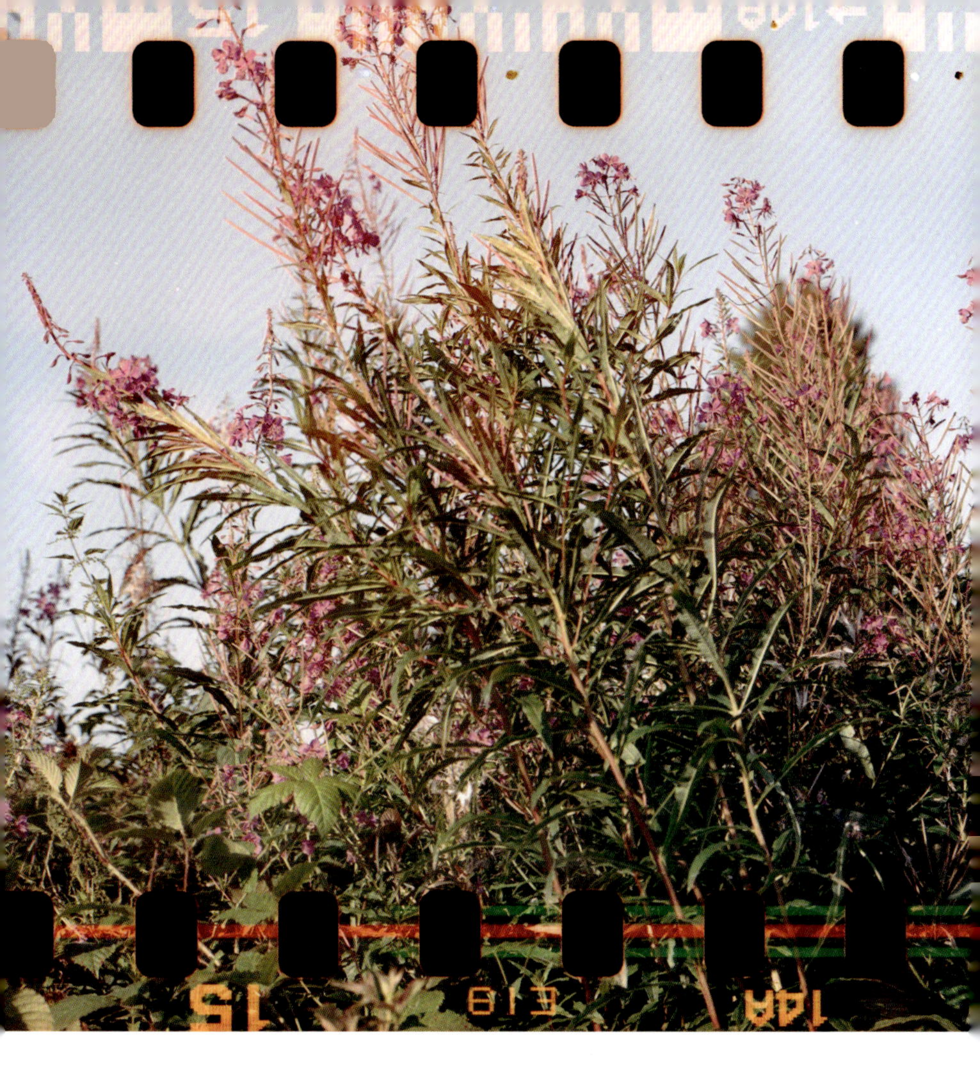

Photography, by nature of the medium, is a snippet from the past. Somewhen, somewhere, someone saw what is depicted in the image. In the present, we as the viewer get invited to glimpse into this past. When we look at photography, we forget about the medium, we don't mind that the pictures traveled through space and time to get here. If the images speak to us, they bridge the time between past and present—and thus allow a glimpse into the future.

This year's edition of further aims to do just that: picturing the future. It does so by showing images and telling stories from a time in the world where the old answers don't seem to work anymore and the new answers don't seem to work yet.

The stories shown depict everything from mundane daily life to extraordinary events. They offer space for reflection and resonance. Some show violence, against one self, against others and against our planet. Others question the role of images in a world where communication is dominated by them. They turn inward and show both individuals struggling with their everyday life, as well as groups and societies working on ever changing challenges together. They show freedom, hope and love—and the lack thereof.

They do what photography does best: invite you to another point of view, to see parts of the world that you would never get to see otherwise. Photography can provide you with an overview effect to allow you to see that we all share the same basic fears, doubts, joys and dreams. Photography captures the past to talk about the future.

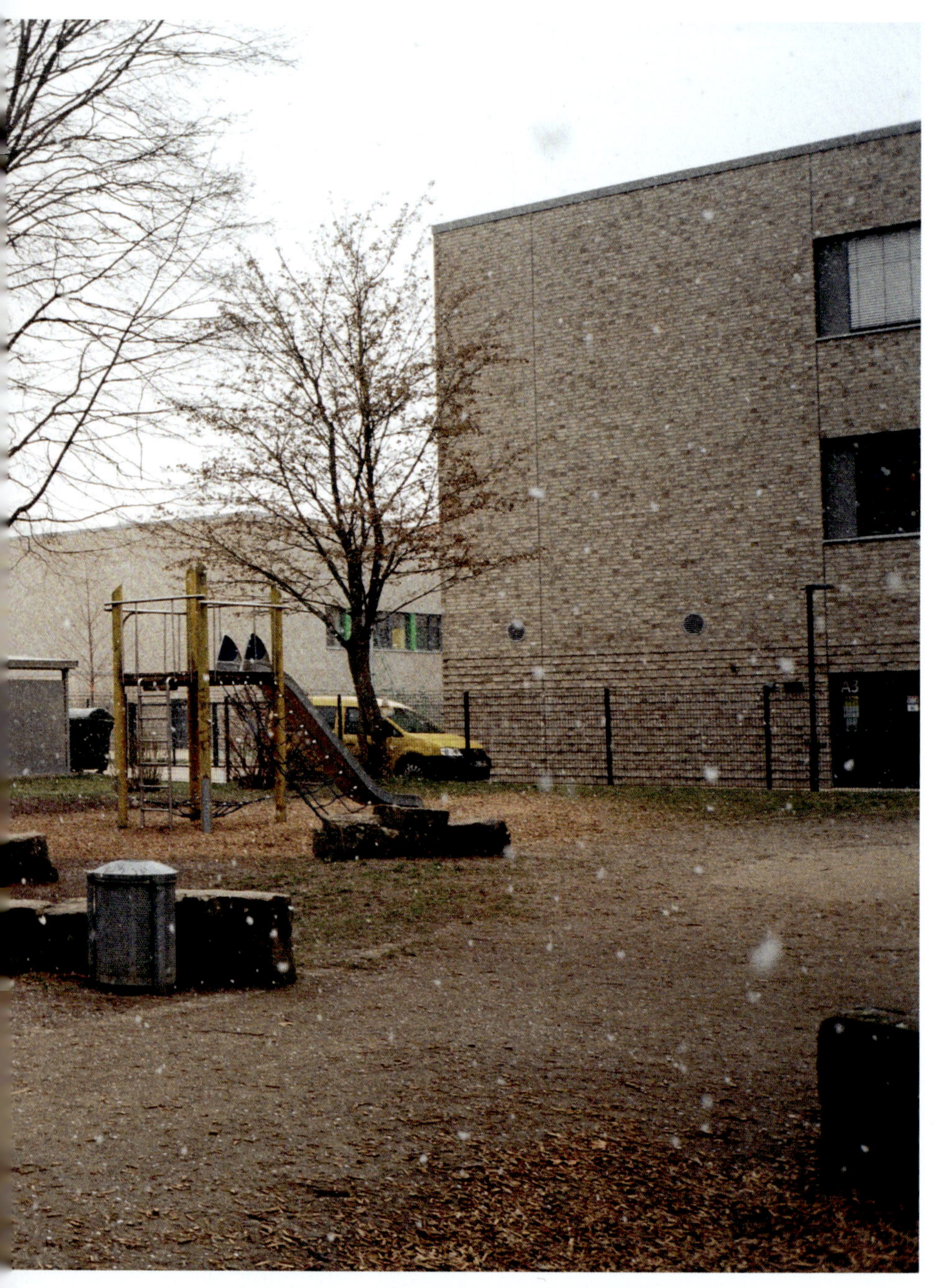
A3

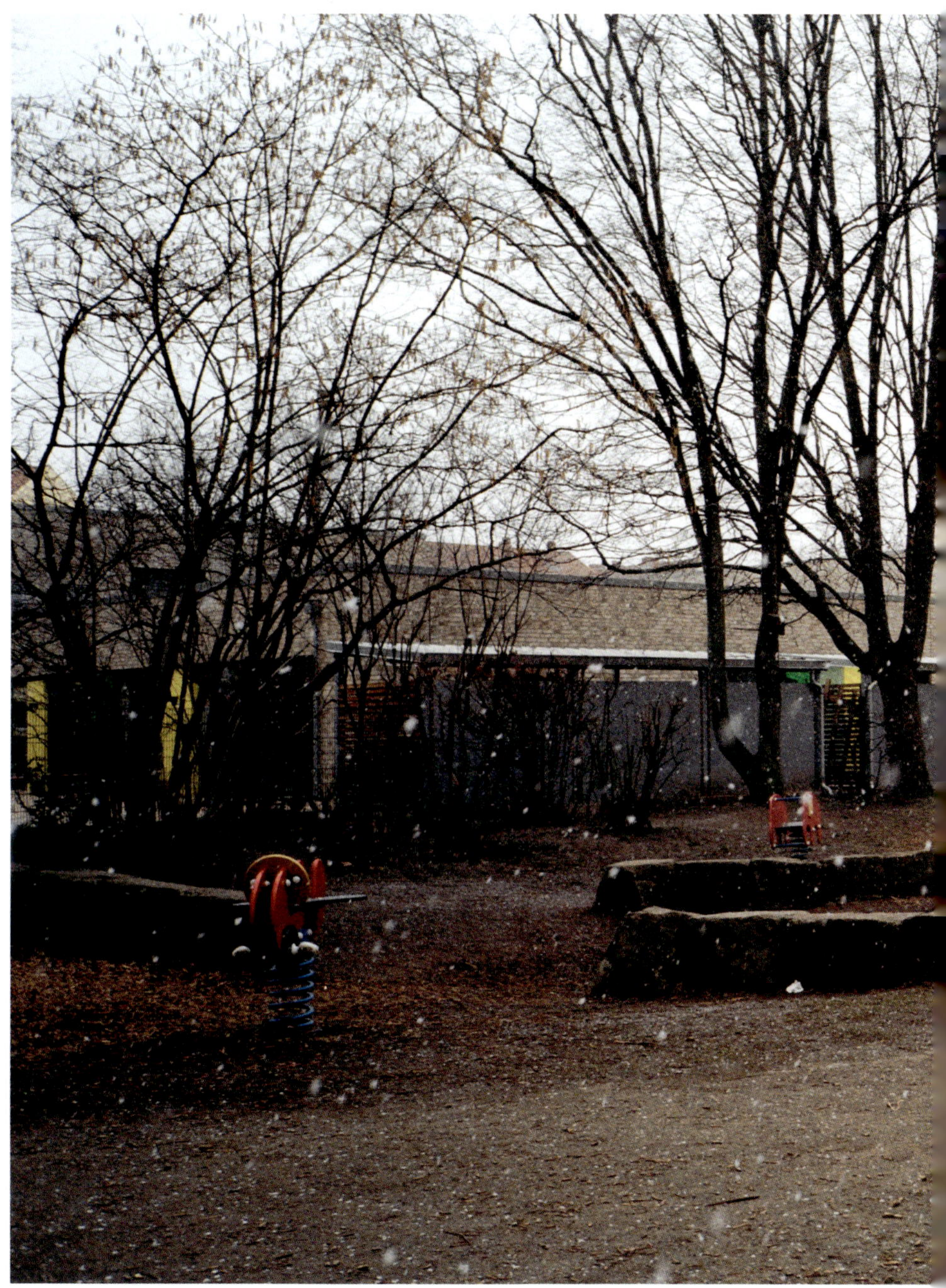

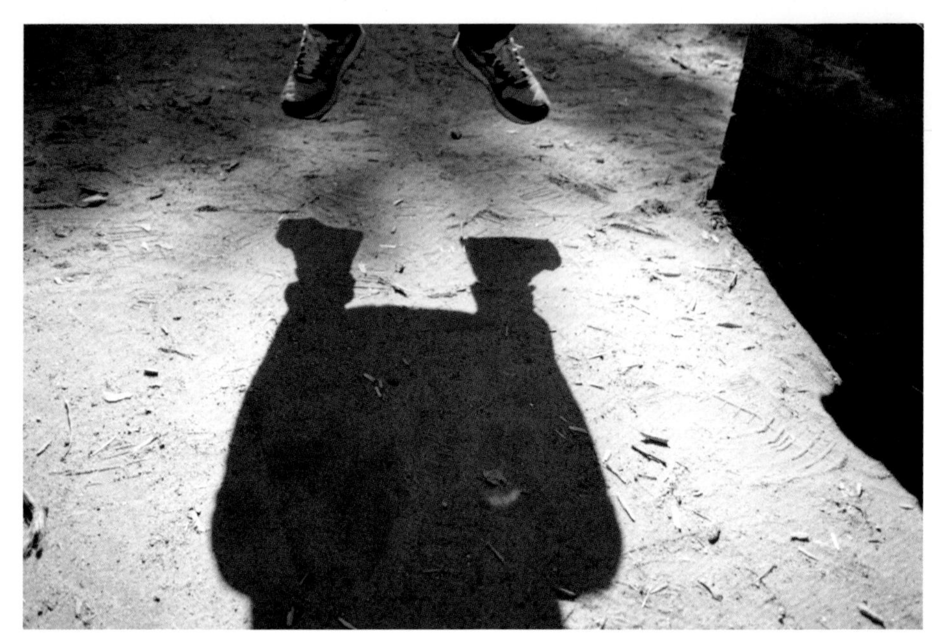

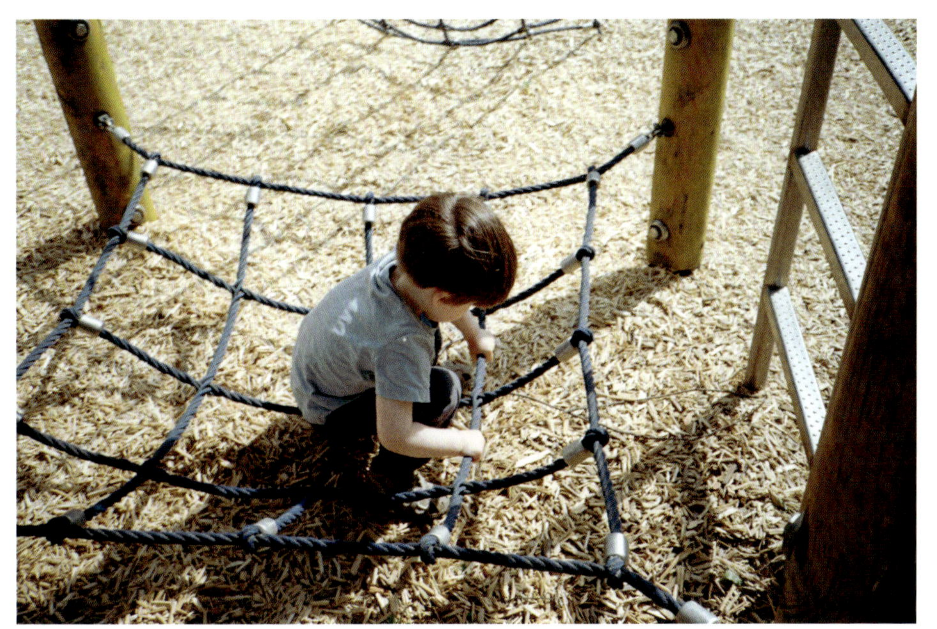

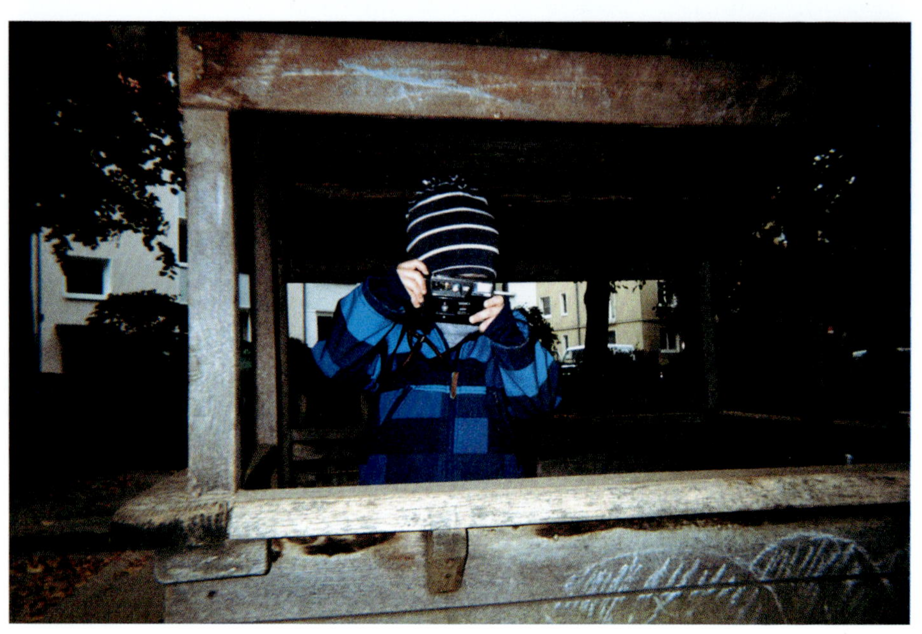

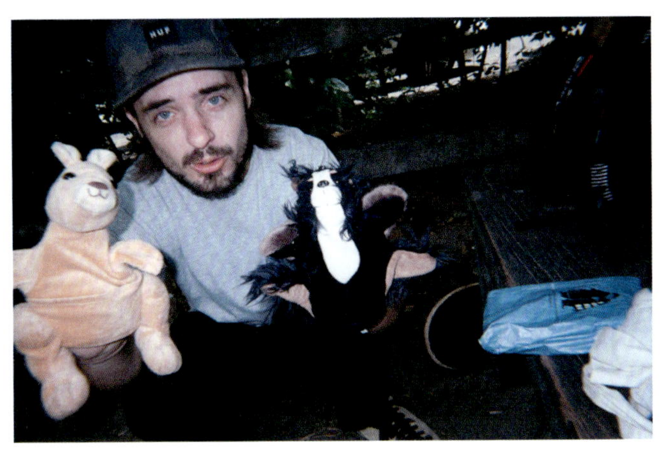
HUF

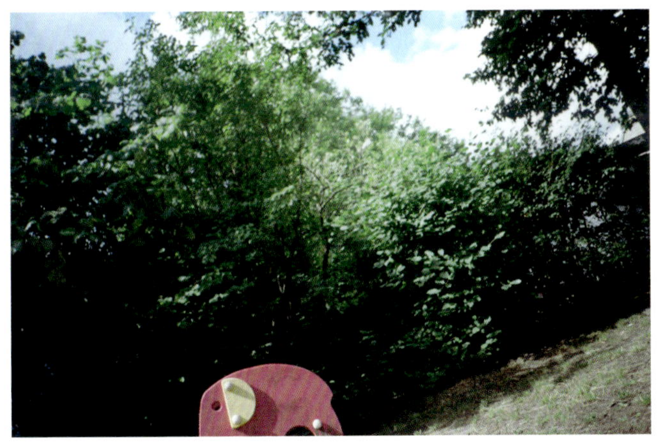

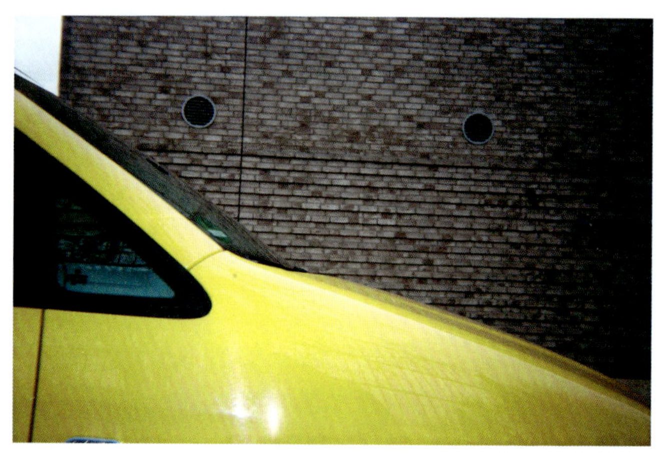

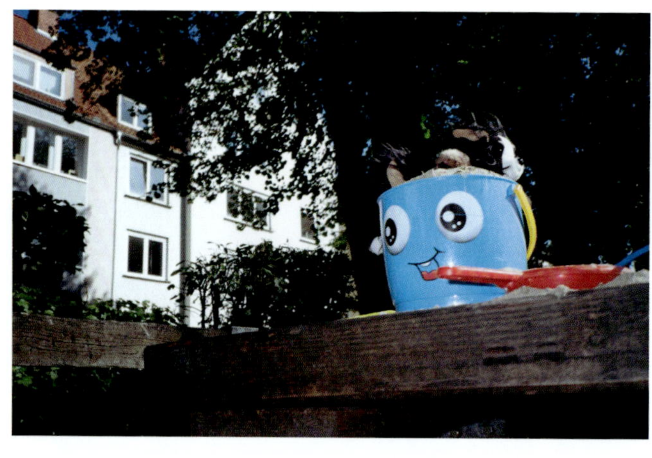

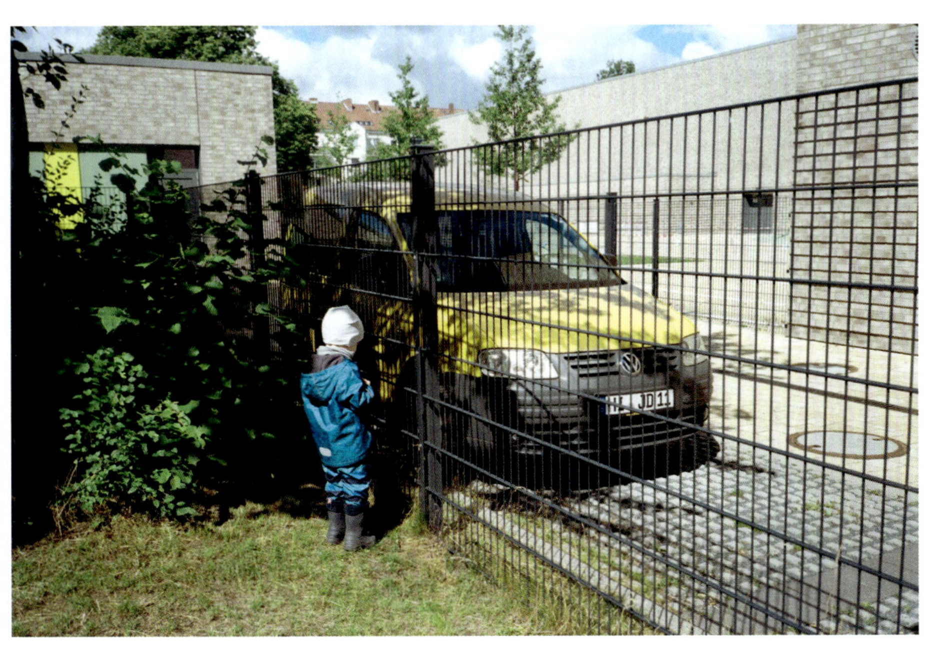

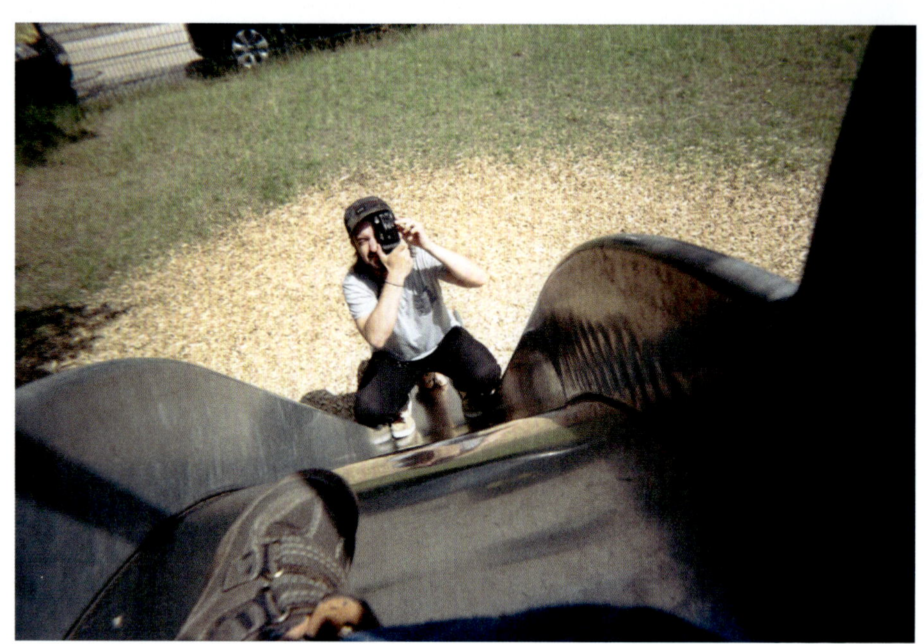

Those were the words I once heard from my son when we were spending time together on a play-ground. I immediately yelled bravo back, but my son didn‘t show any res-ponse. I felt I had to fight for my recognition and acceptance as a father. In fact, my fatherhood is a very tough one. I‘m a seperated father and spending time with my son has become very limited —for over two years we met for one hour every two weeks on a Saturday morning at a playground that became something like our home.

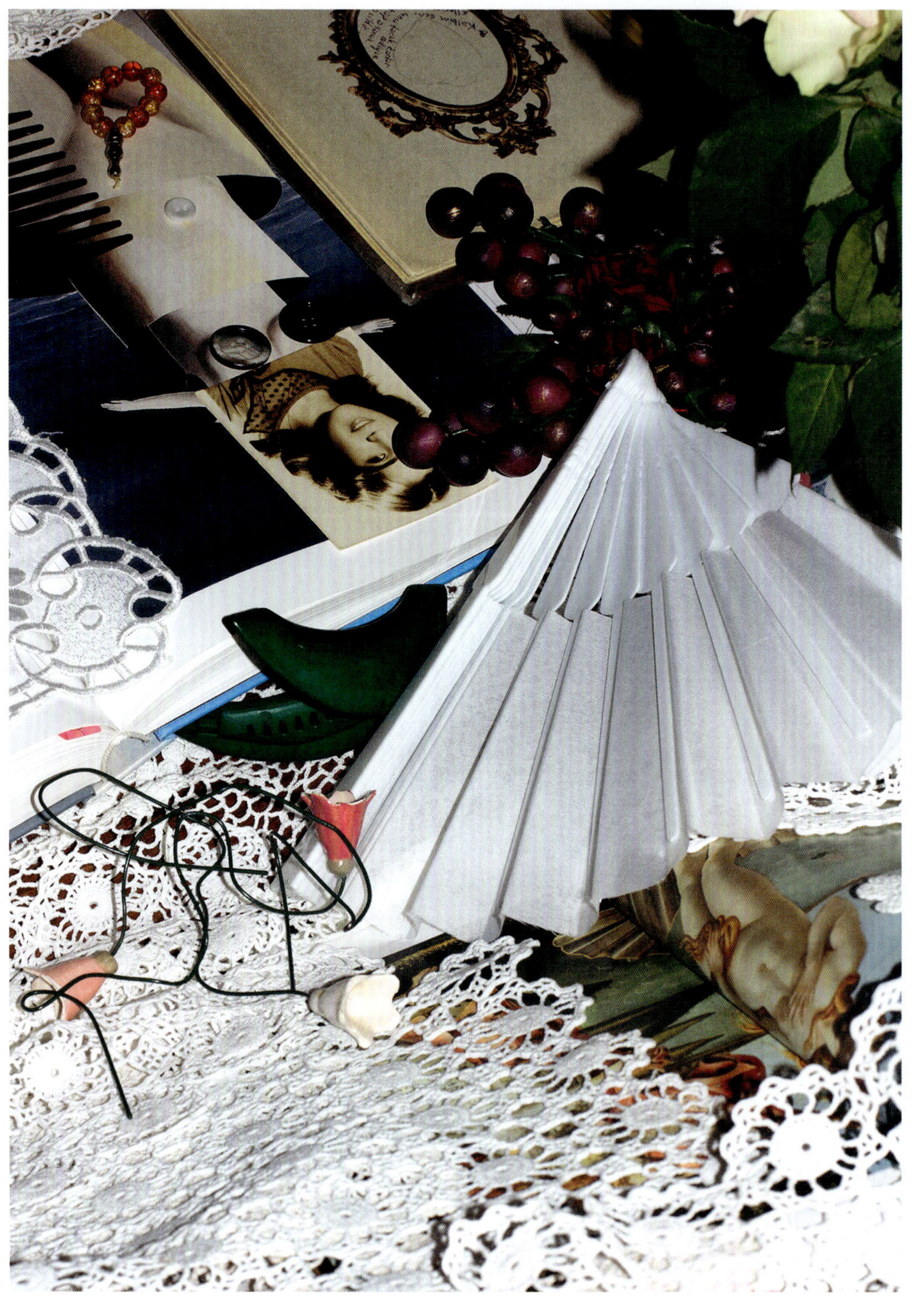

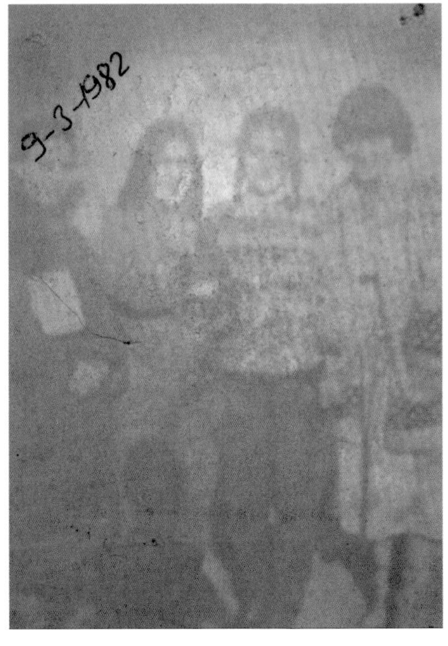
9-3-1982

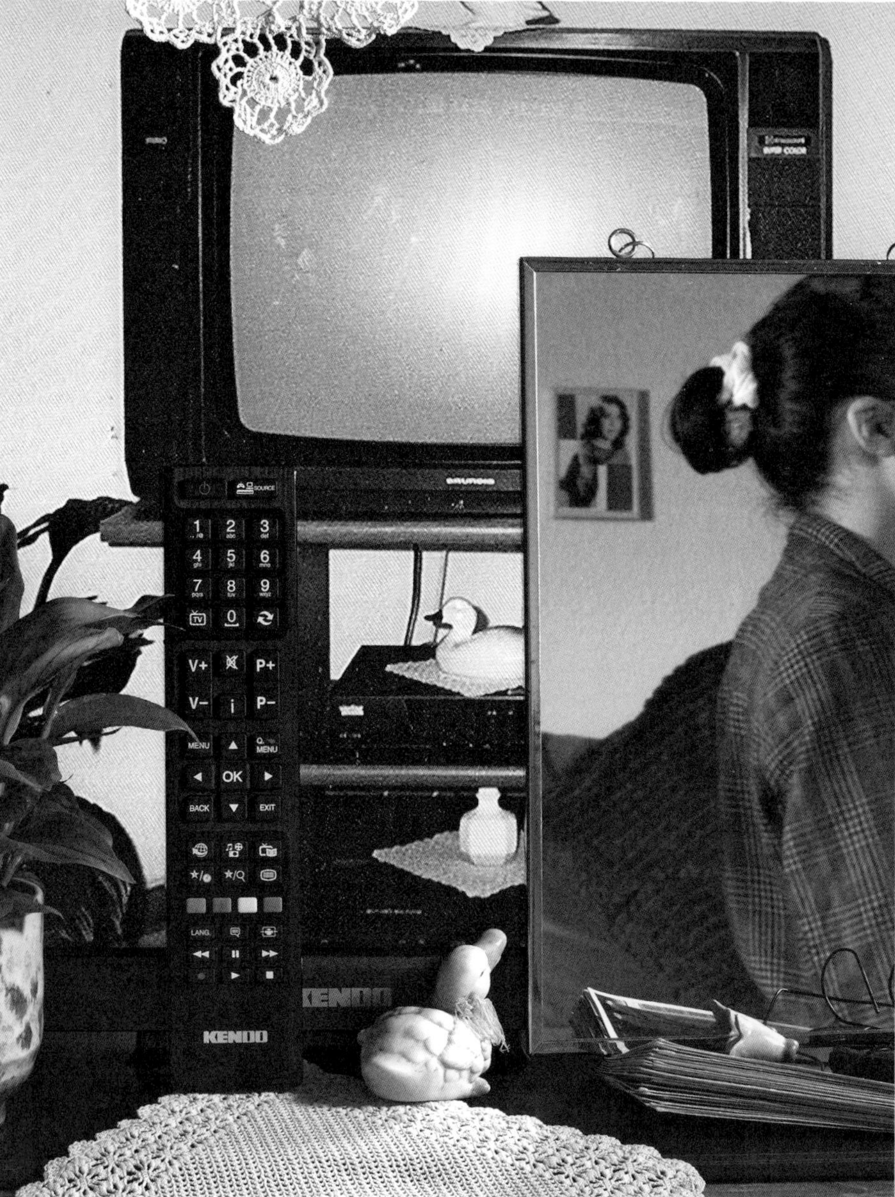
SOURCE
1
2
3
4
5
6
7
8
9
0
V+
P+
V–
i
P–
MENU
MENU
OK
BACK
EXIT
LANG.
KENDO
KENDO

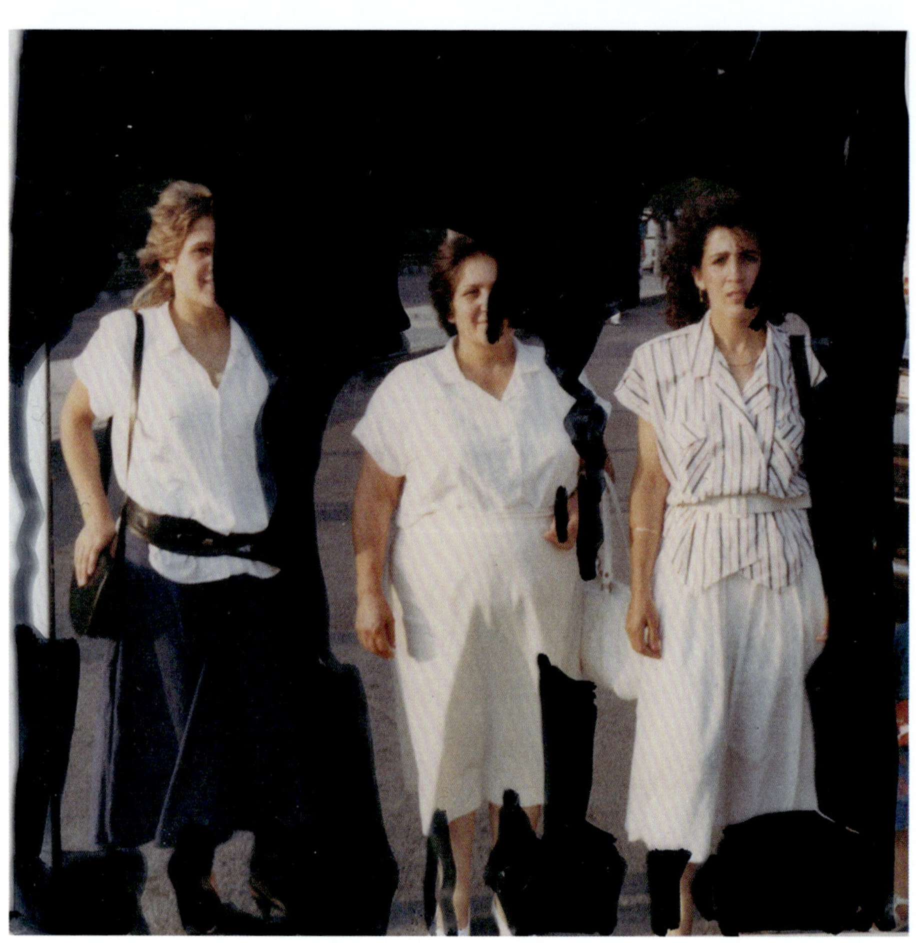

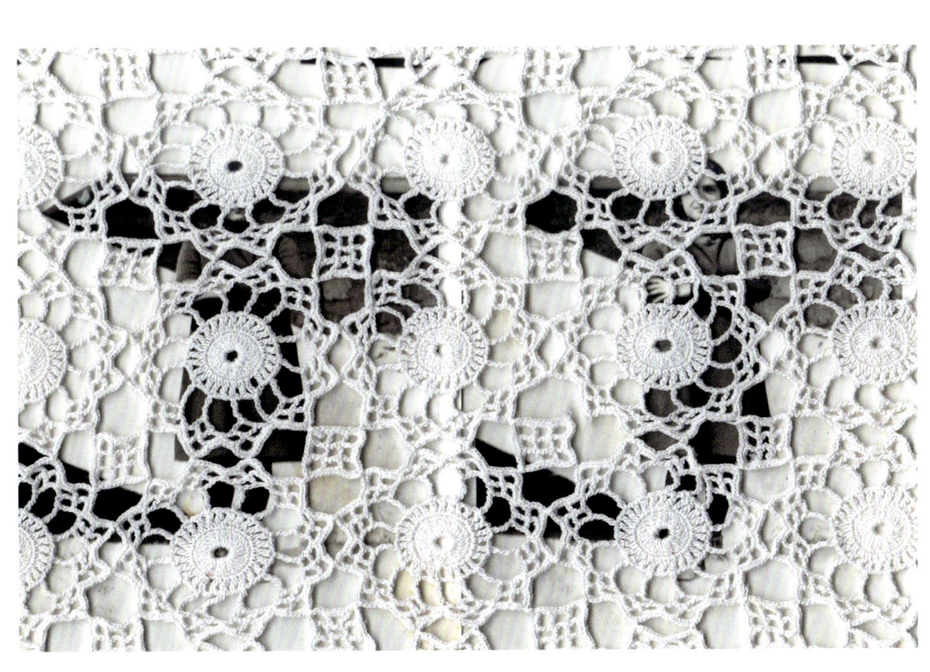

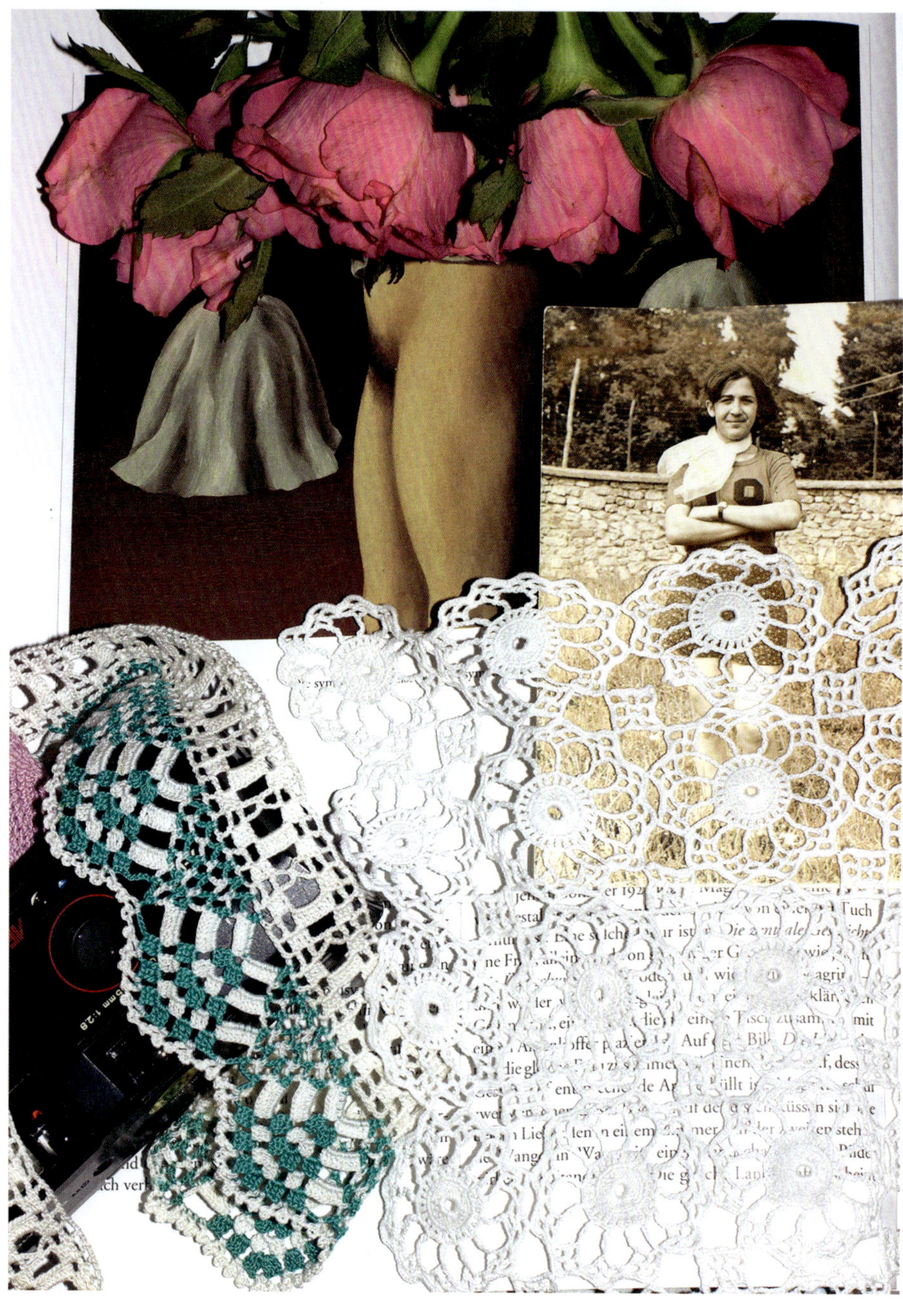

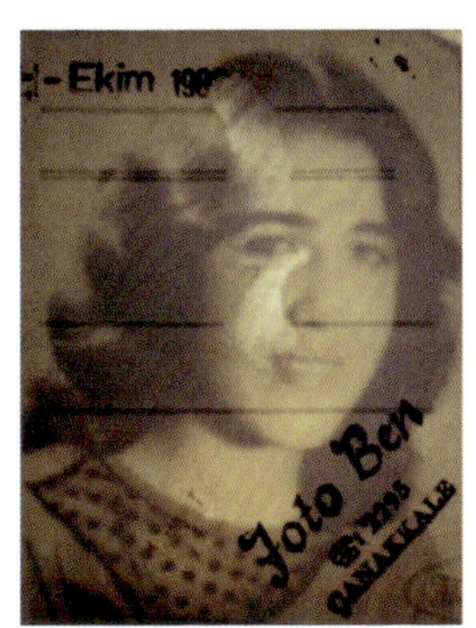
-Ekim
Foto Ben
ÇANAKKALE

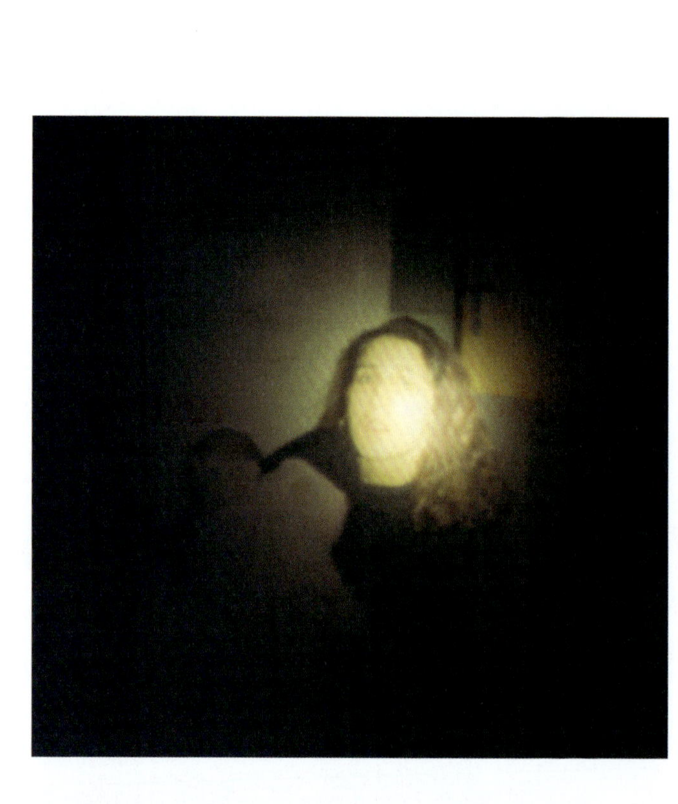

Aslı embarks on a metaphorically journey into the image of her mother as a young woman. She does so by searching for the time contained within the photographic objects found, examining their materiality and staging them in her mother's house. Thus, she intertwines the past with the present through the daughter's gaze and the mother's absent presence.

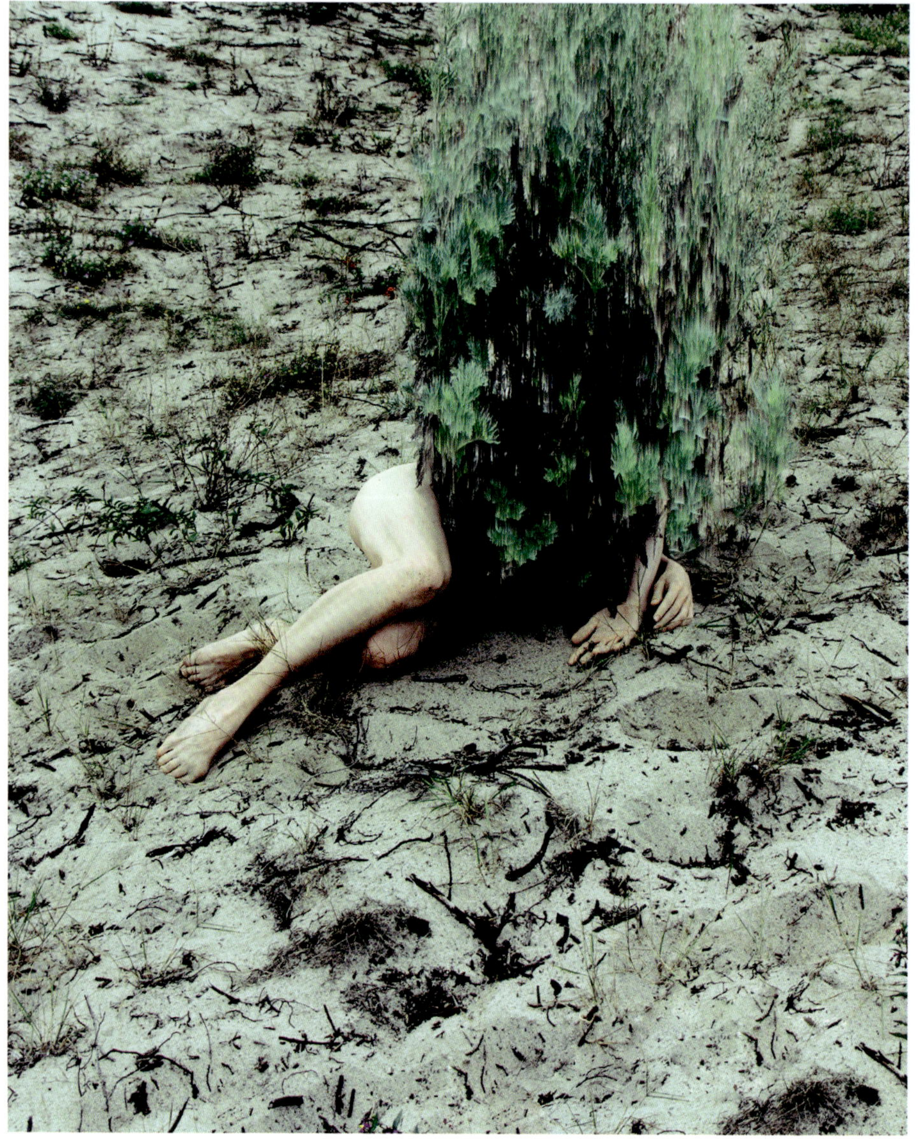

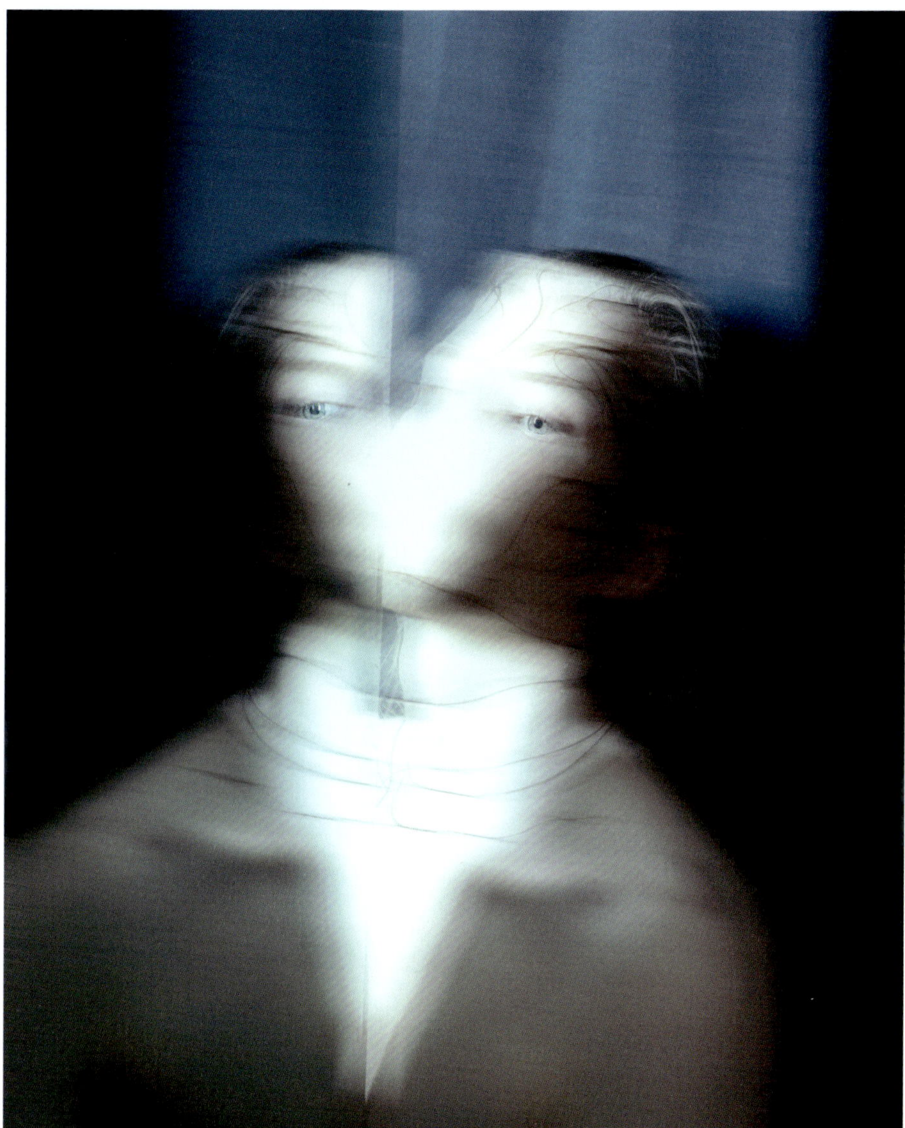

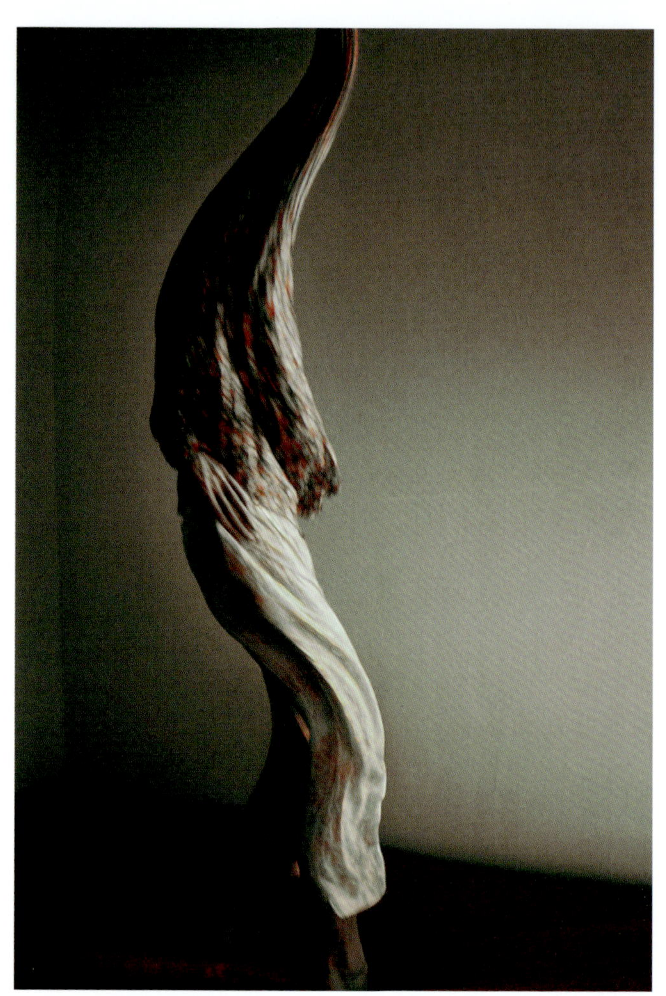

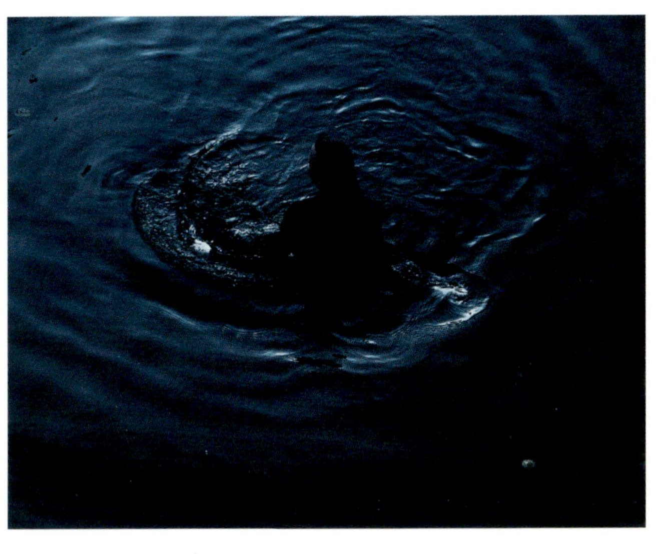

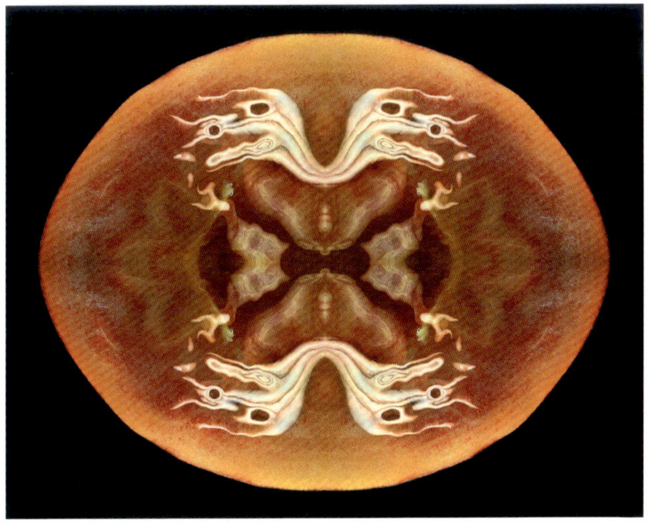

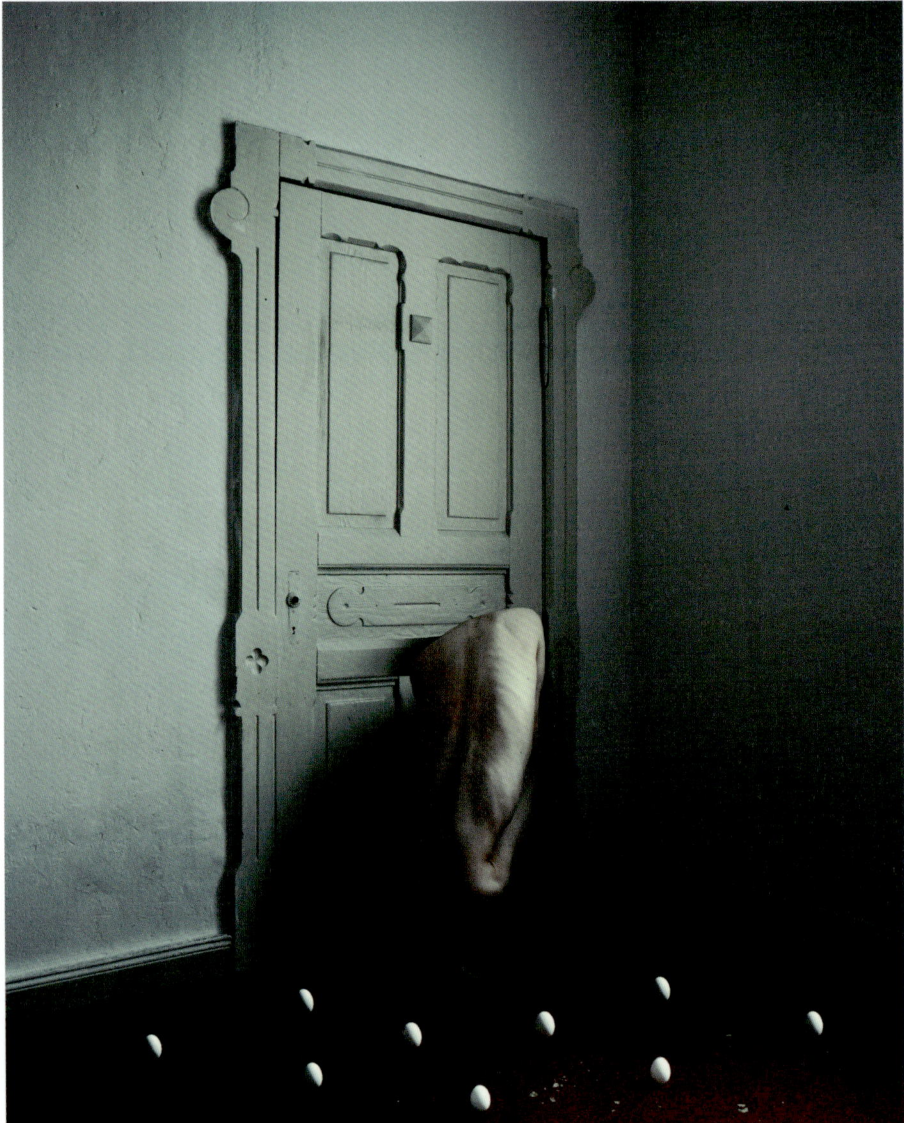

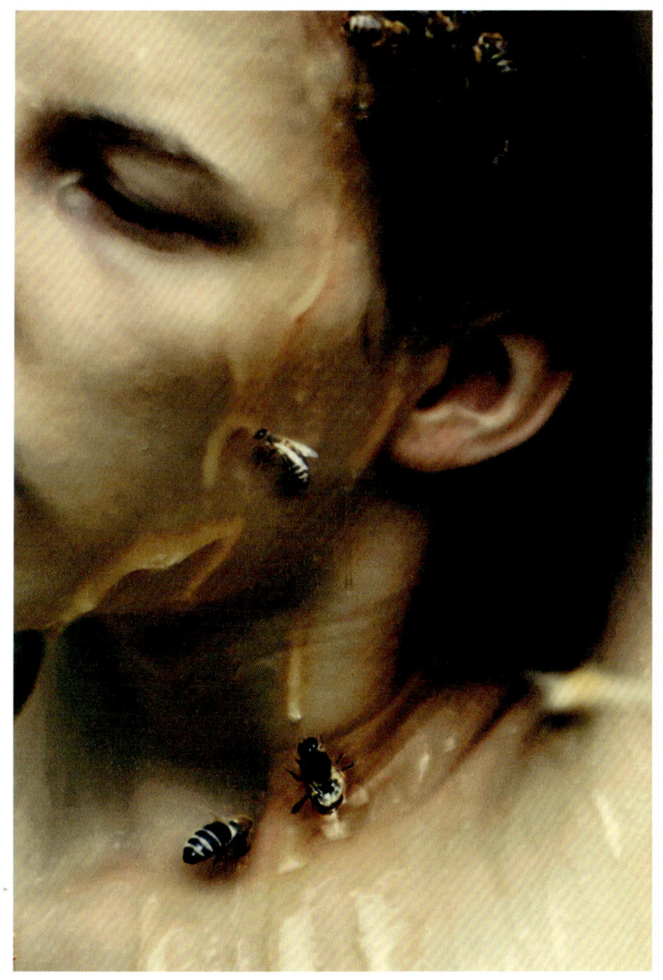

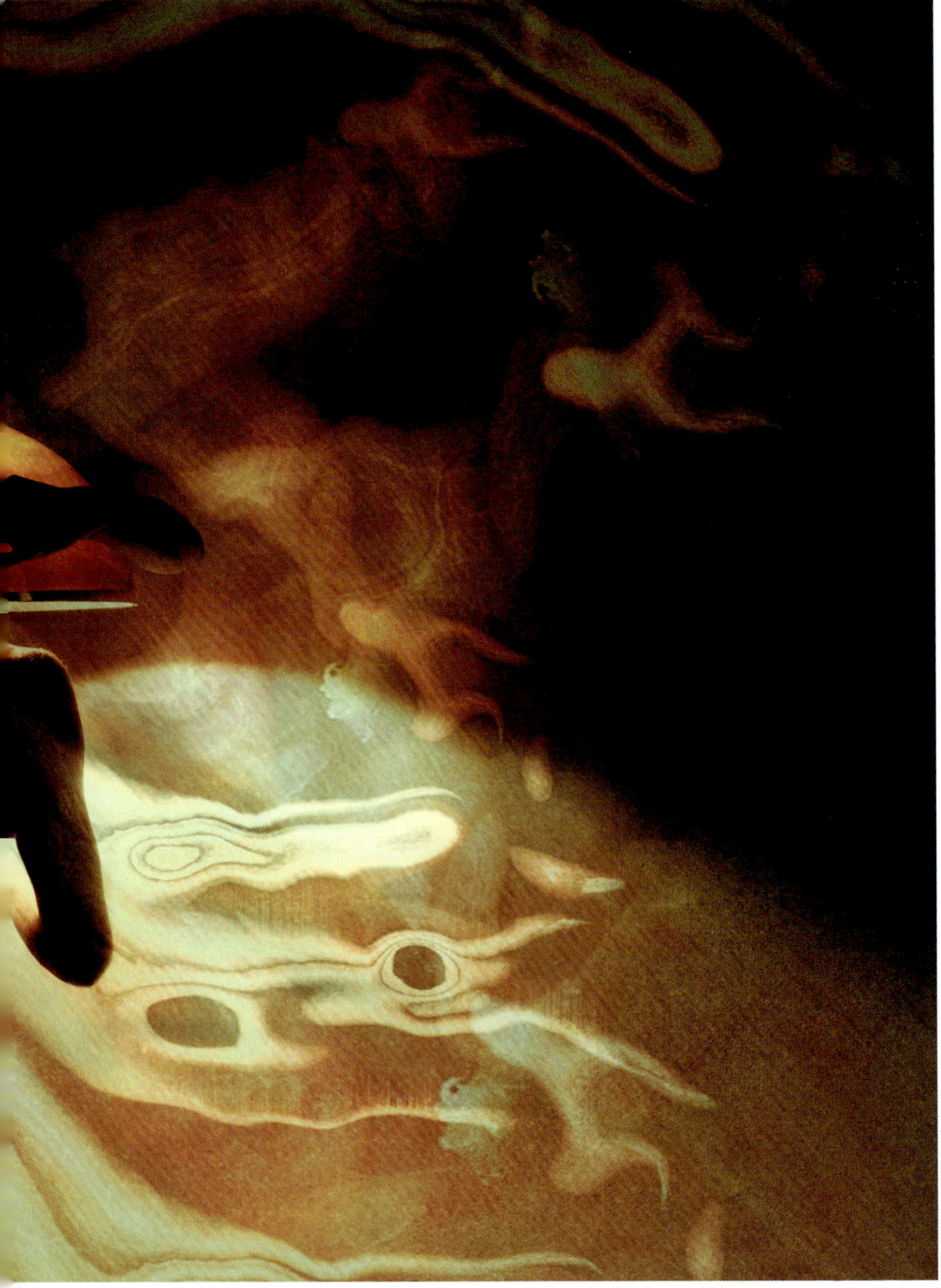

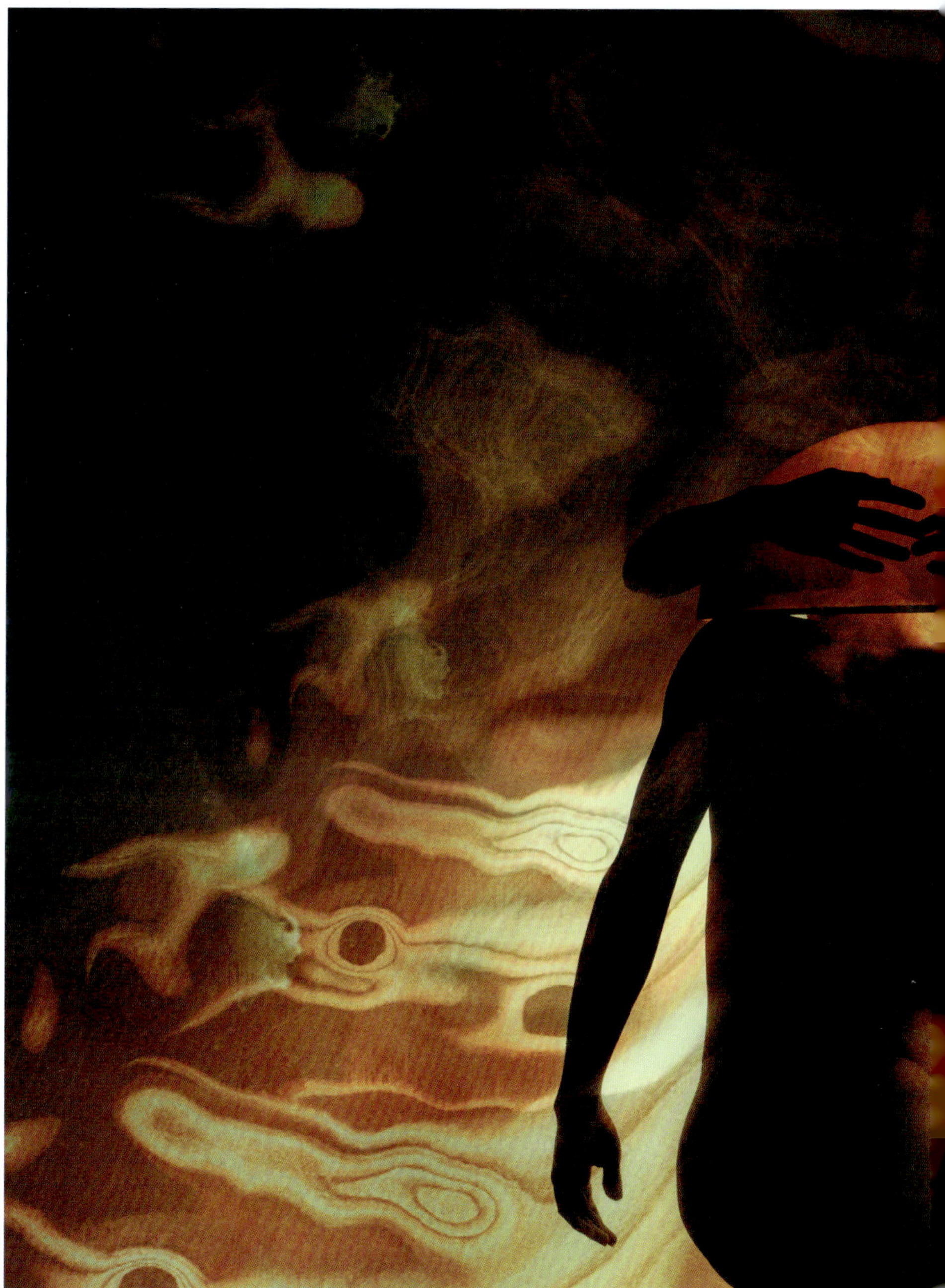

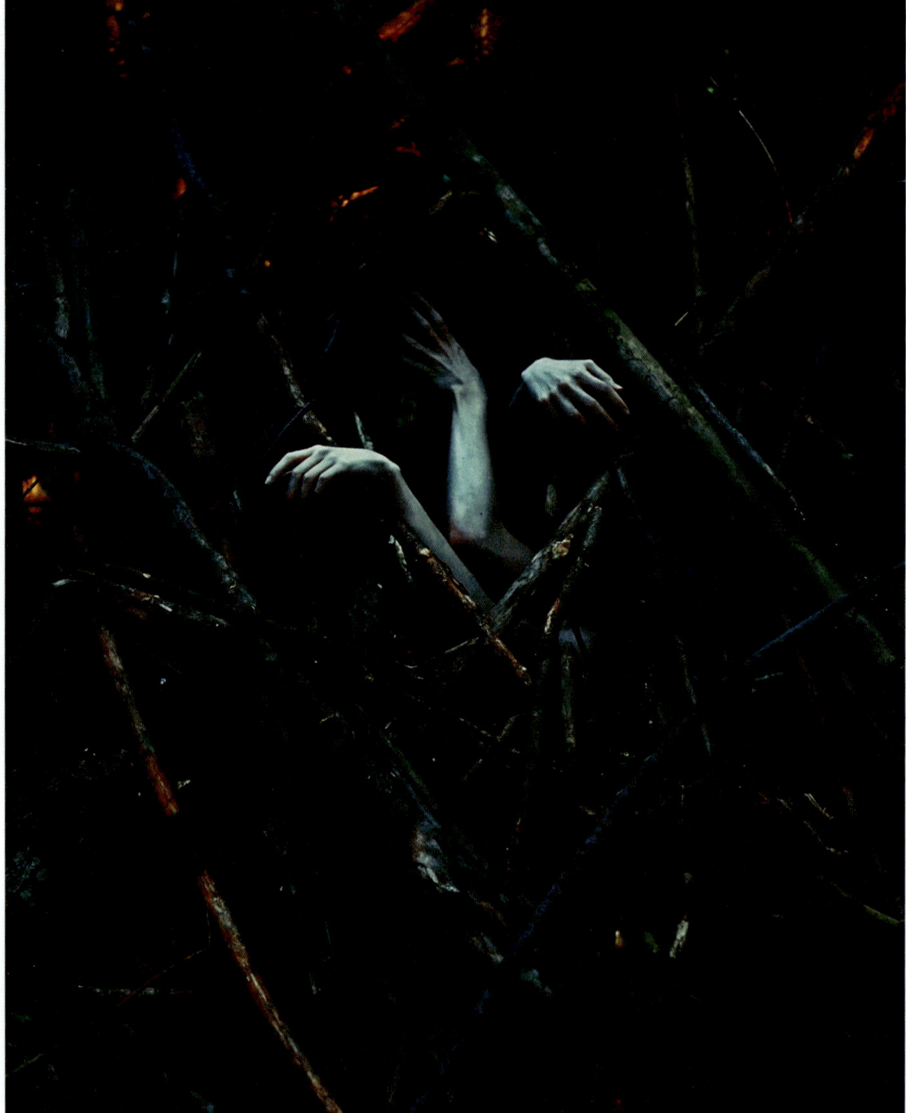

My inner self if confronting it's being and it's from. Sometimes it reminds me of warm honey, sometimes of sturdy wood. To anchor myself in this overflow of dreams, fantasy and madness, I create new universes in photography. Here I can play by my own rules and approach my lies and my truths. They depict fragments of myself, my senses and my consciousness.

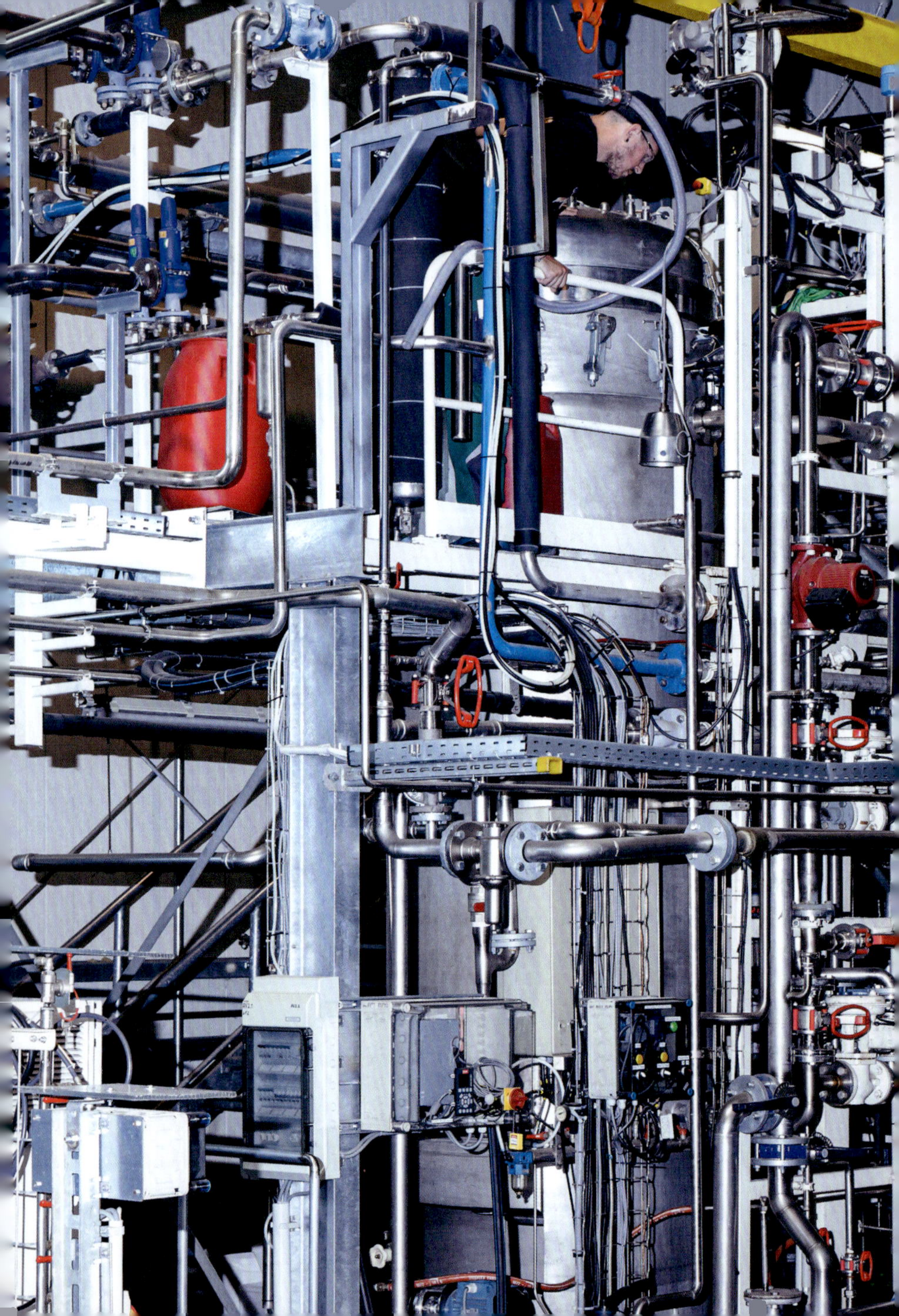

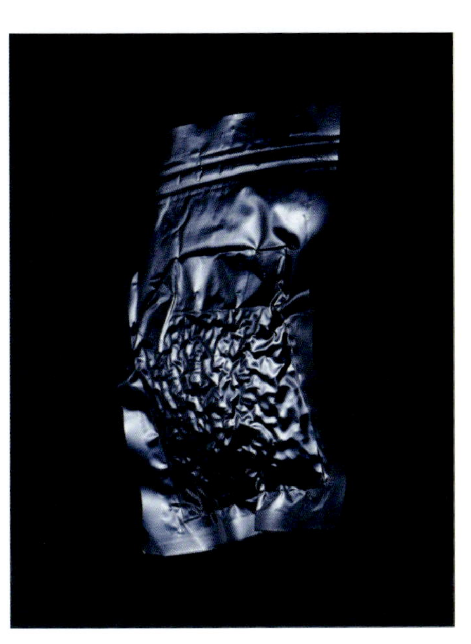

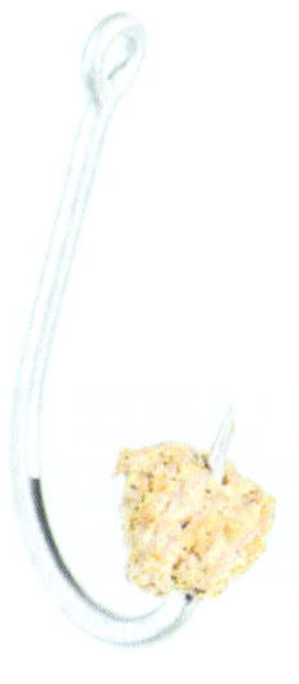

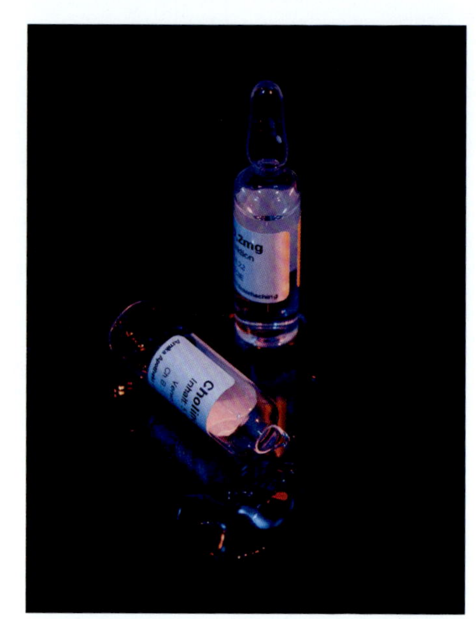

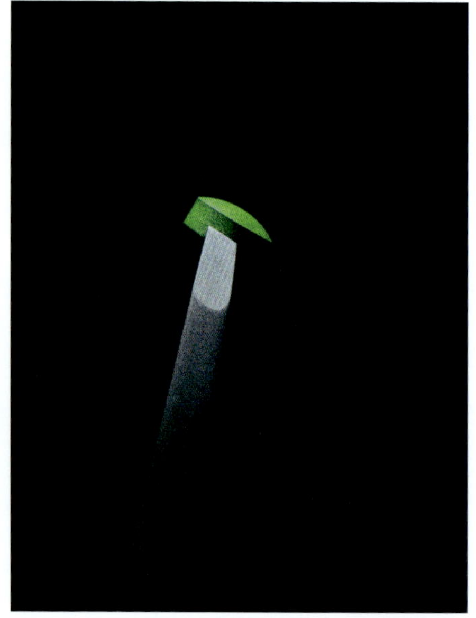

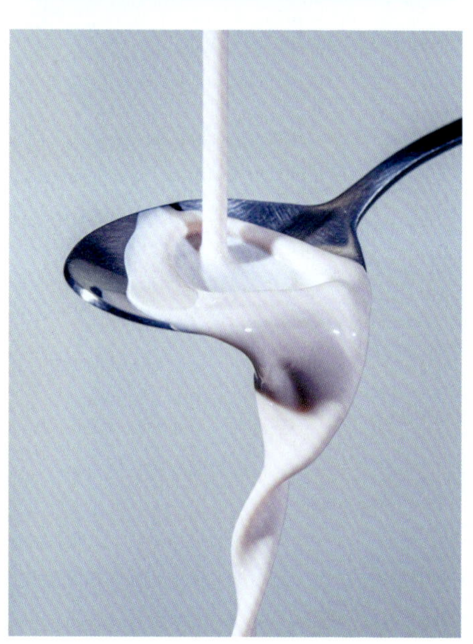

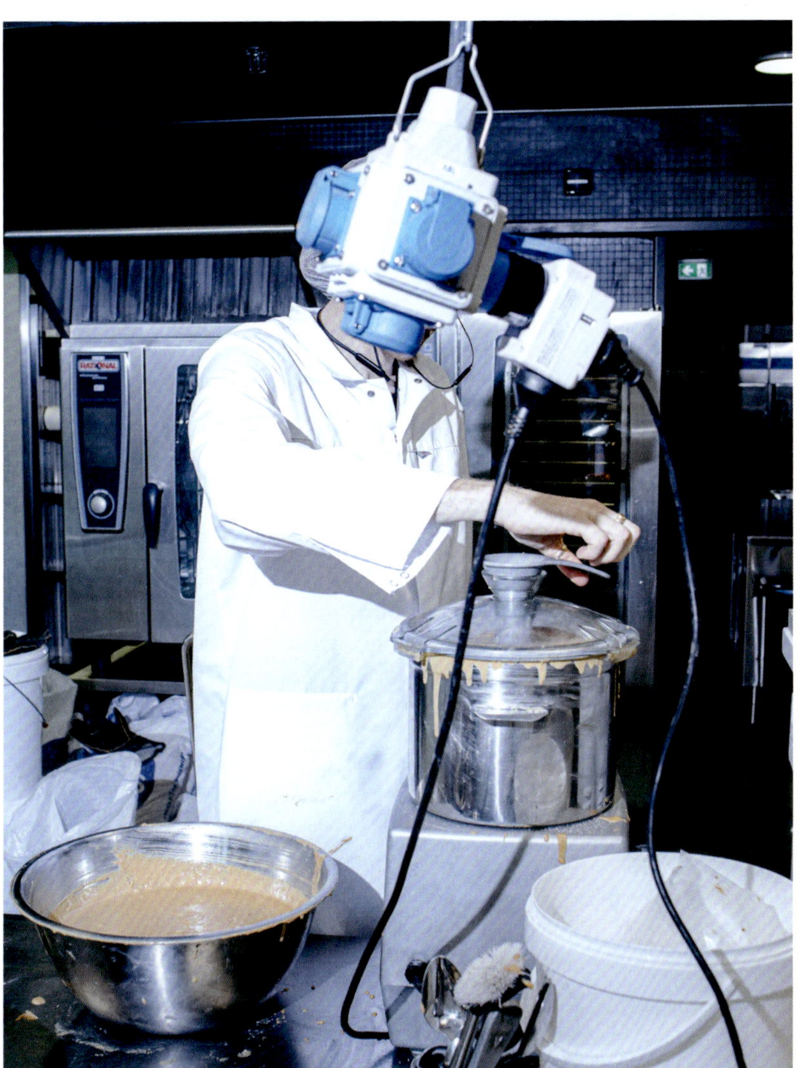
RATIONAL

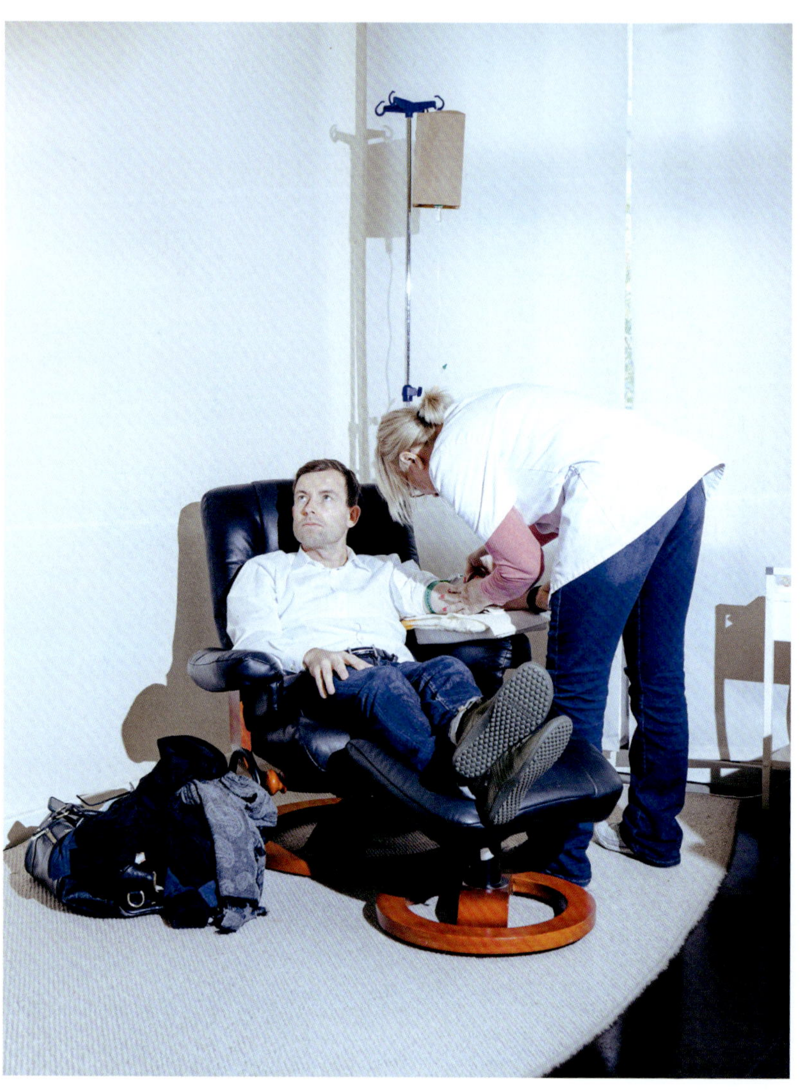

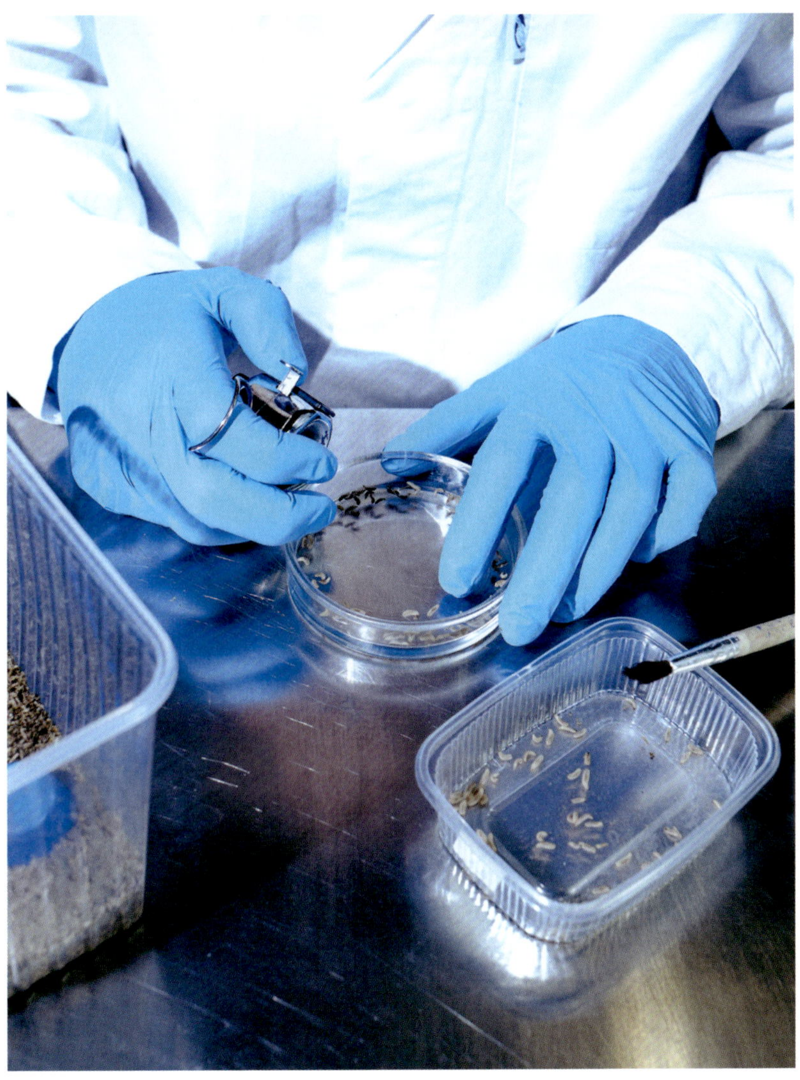

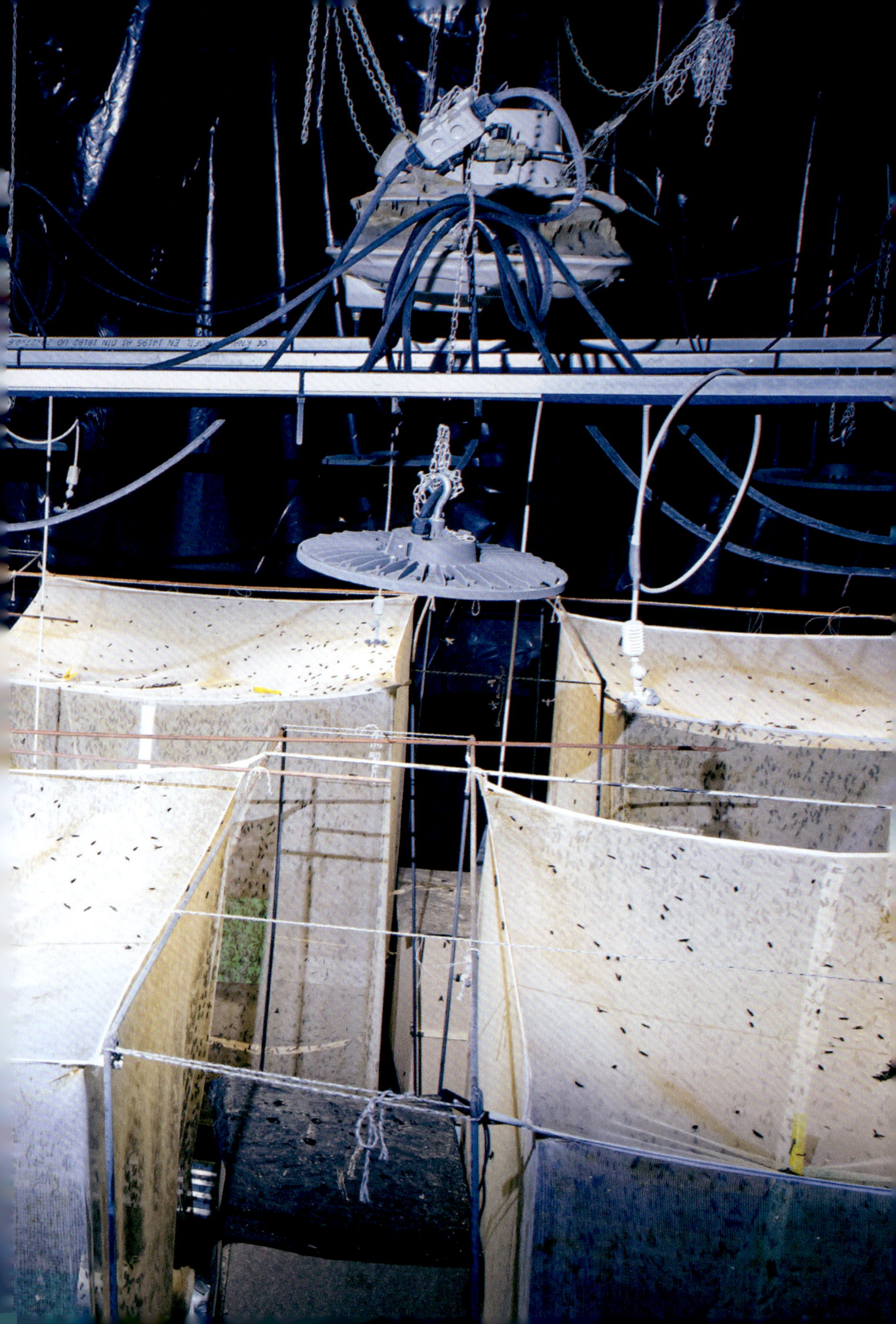

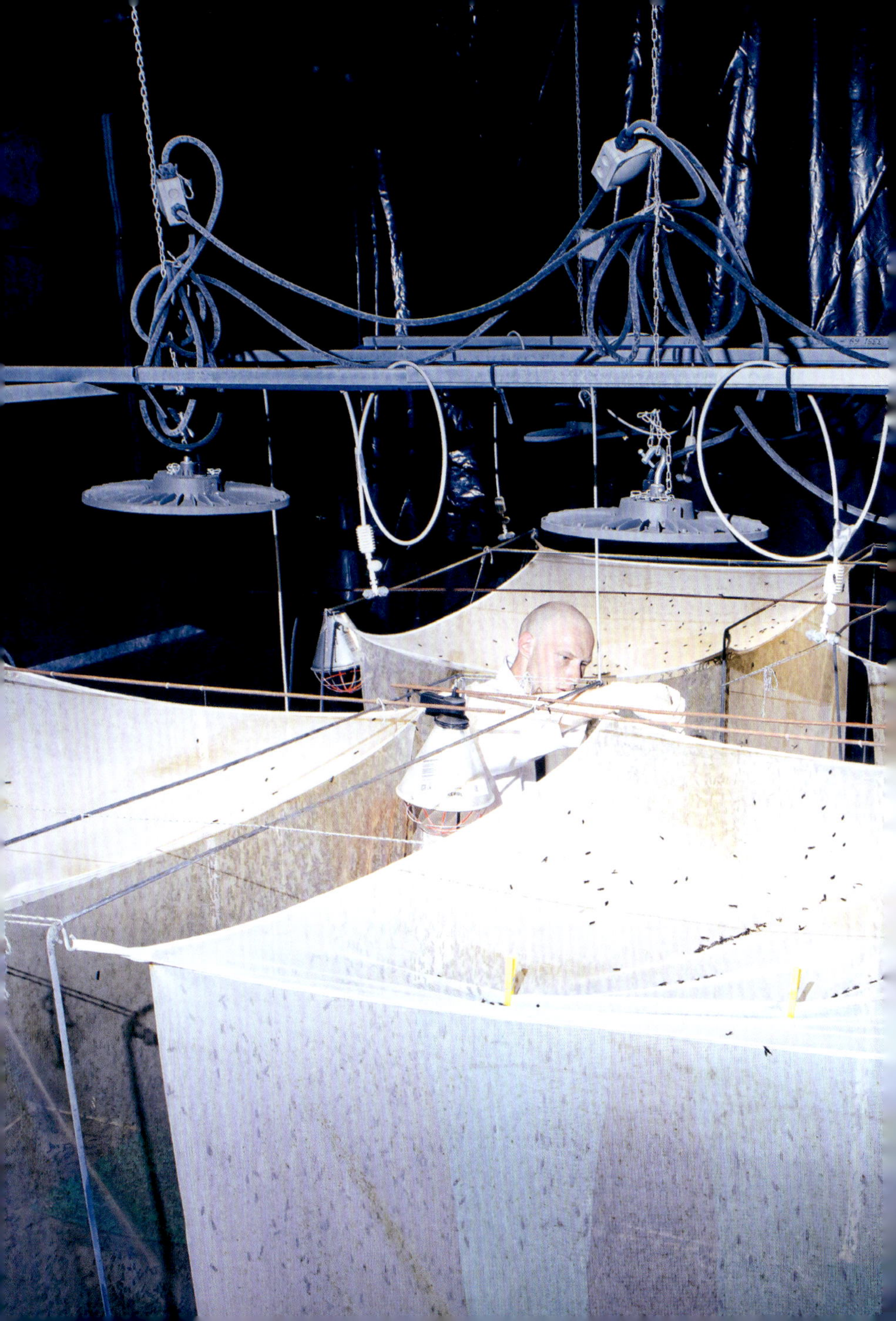

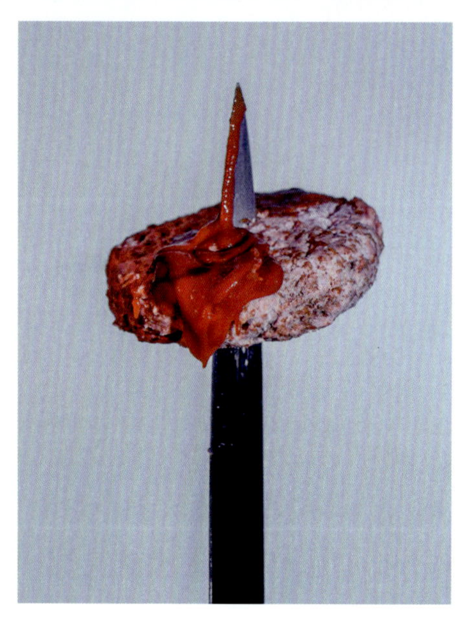

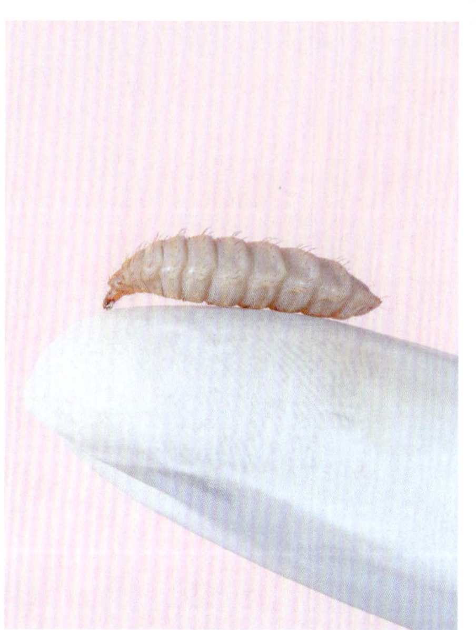

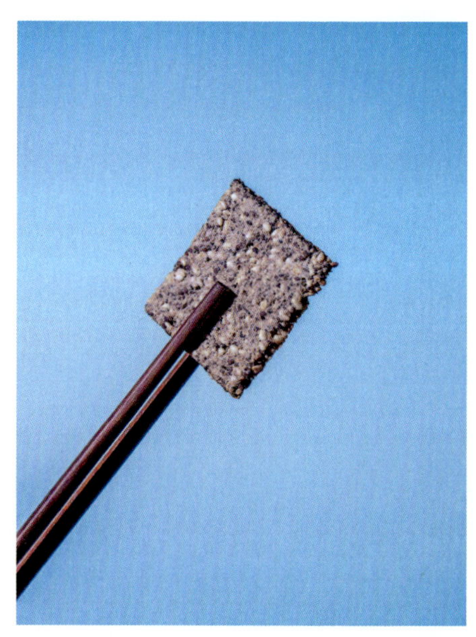

The food system transformation is just as important as the energy transition and the transportation transition. Start-ups and companies around the world are researching how to use innovative technology to reduce the resources required for food production and reduce food waste. They work on projects like microbial mushrooms that have a higher protein content than chicken meat or cultivate microalgae in kilometer-long glass tubes, producing hundreds of times more biomass than conventional grain fields.

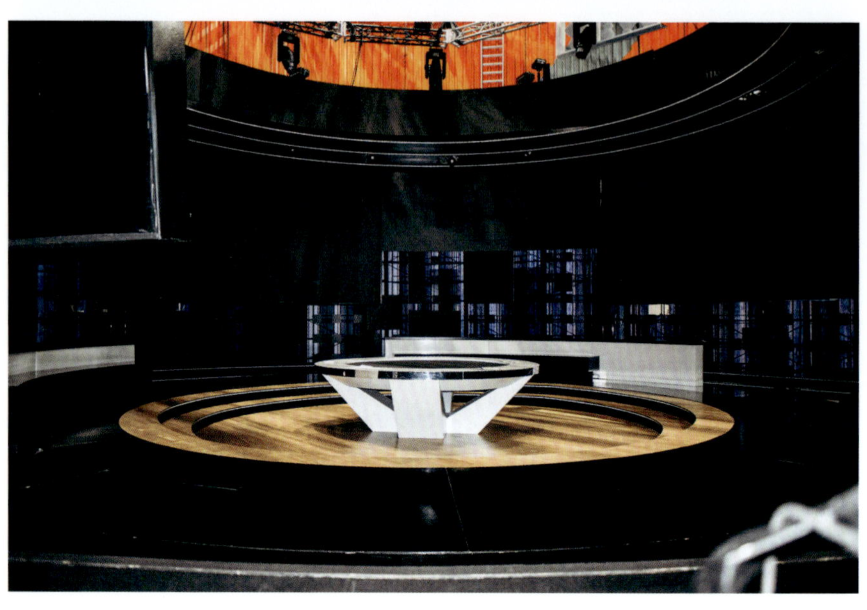

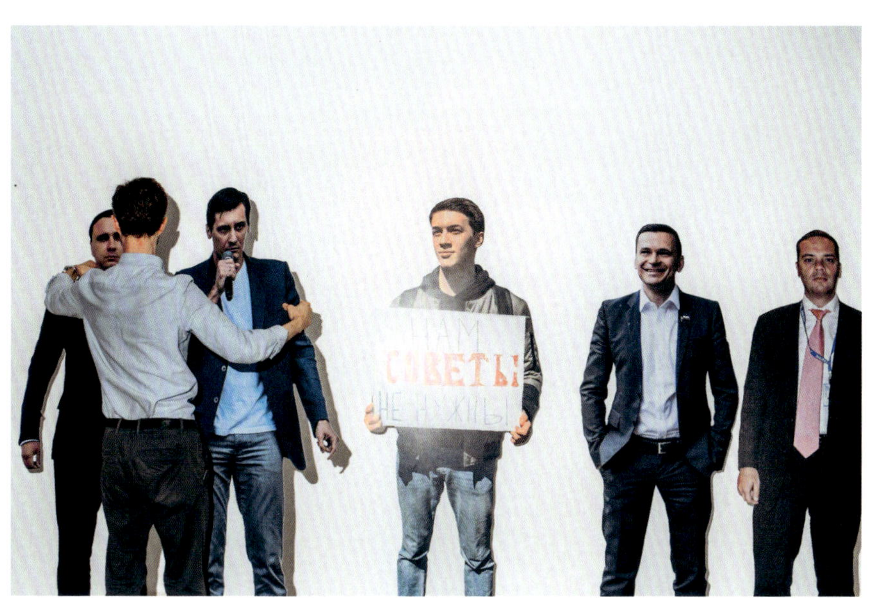
НАМ
СОВЕТЫ
НЕ НУЖНЫ

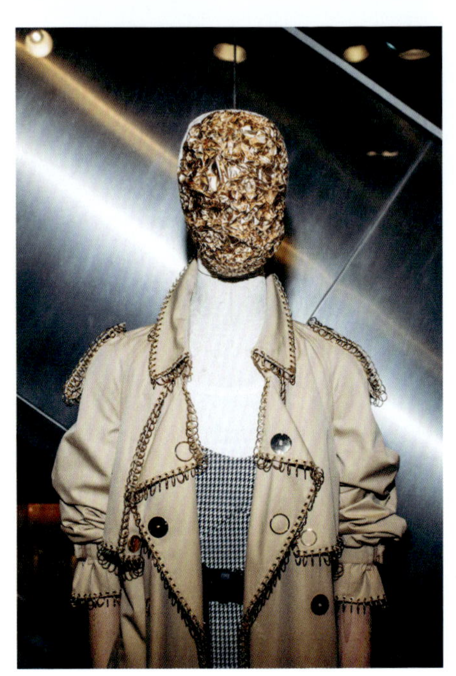

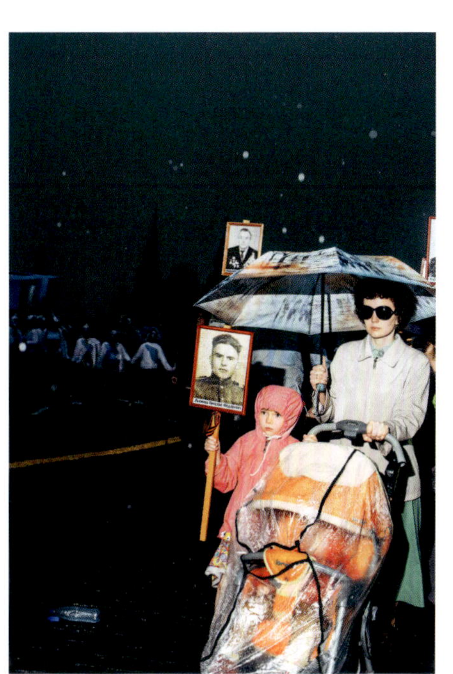

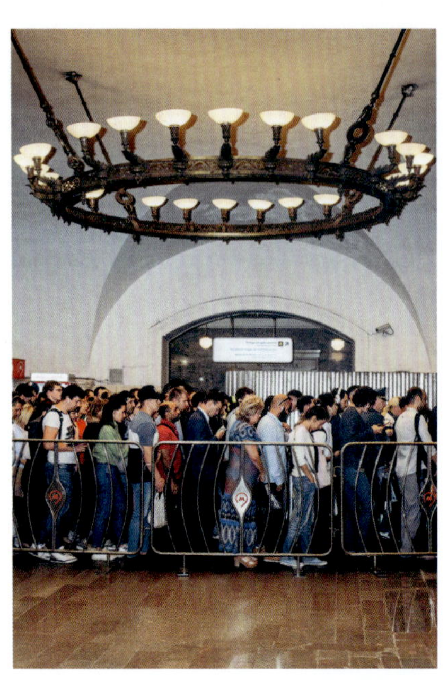

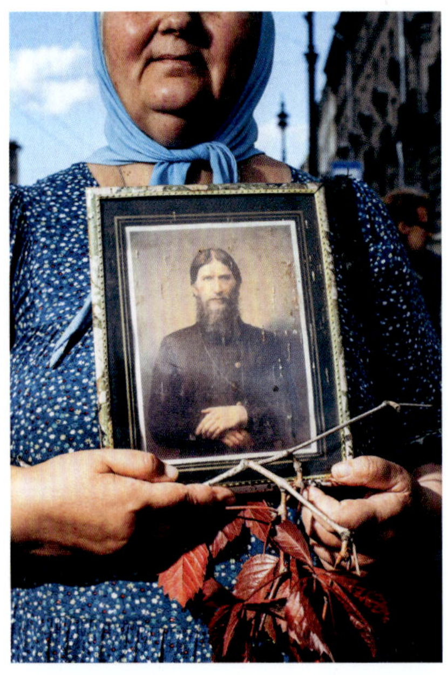

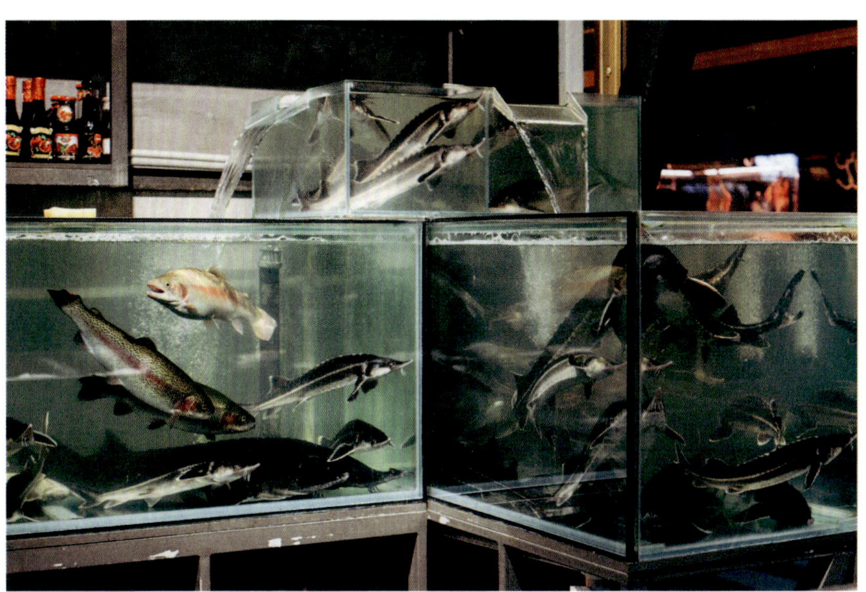

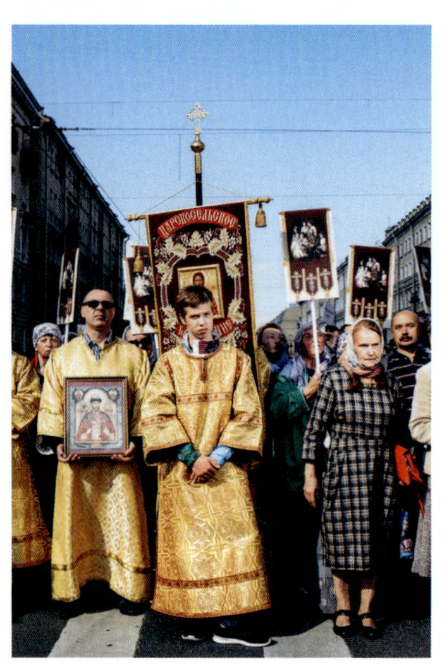
ЦАРСКОСЕЛЬСКОЕ

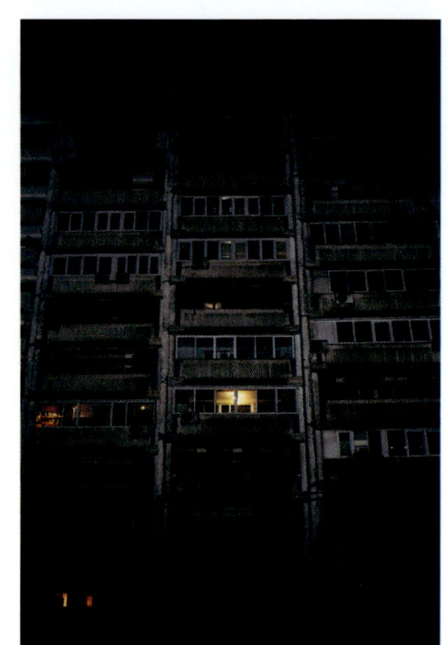

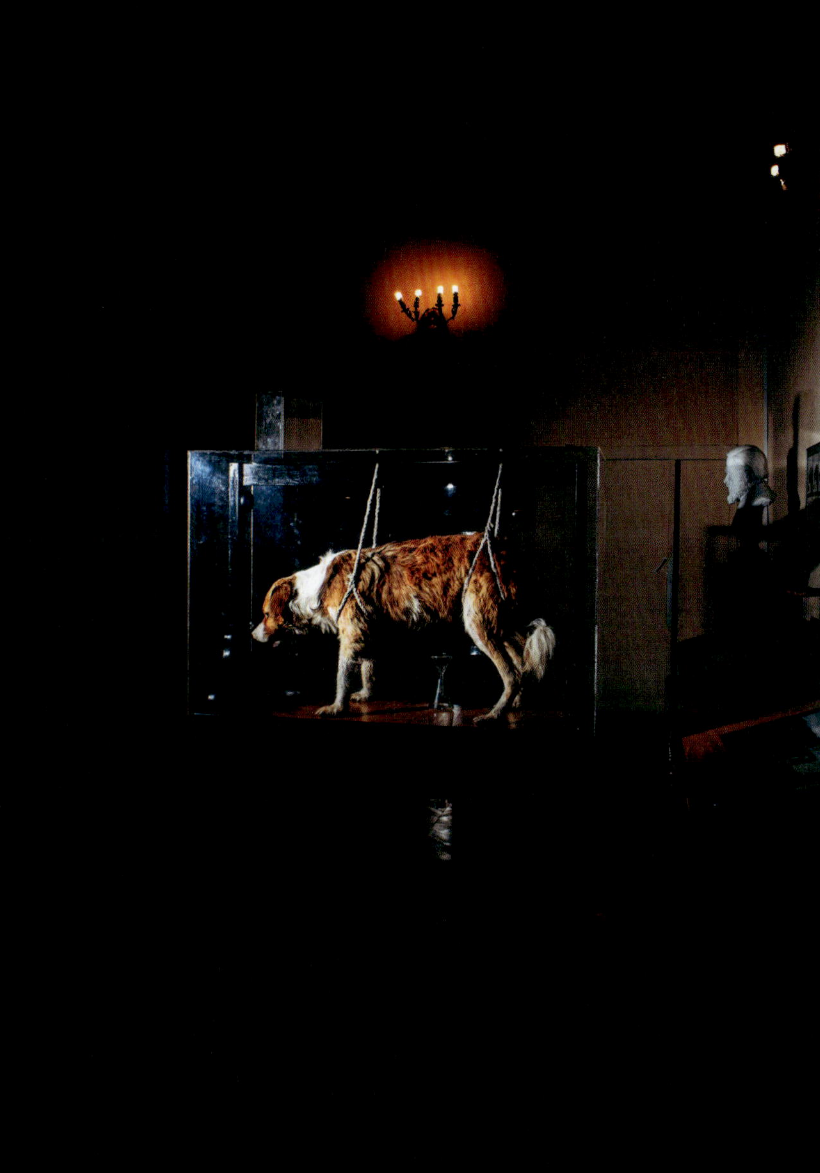

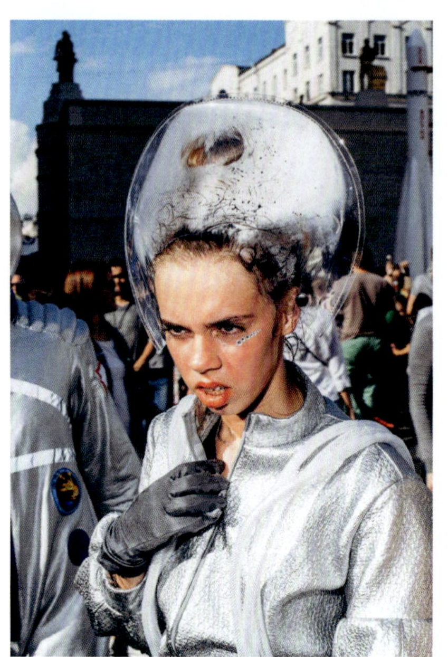

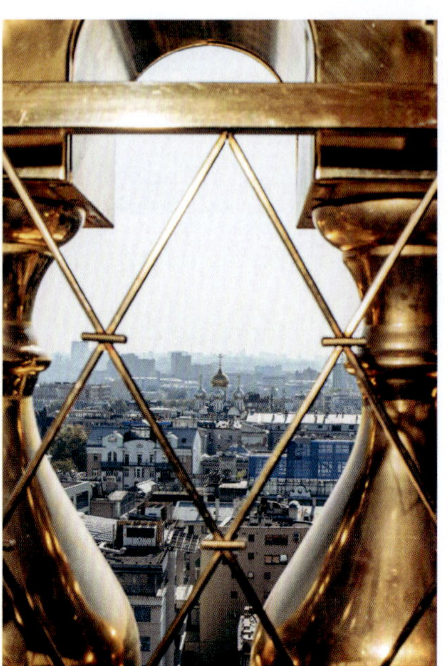

I left St. Petersburg and Russia nearly 20 years ago to live abroad. Last year I visited Moscow for the first time. What I found was a city playing the role of a potemkin village. Mass events, ceremonies, marches and parades distract from the rest of the world's largest country. Governmental stagings condition the masses and reminded me to continue to discover my home country through photography.

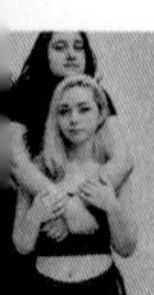

o und Dilo, 16

C-Print, Fine-Art-Papier, 50 x 70 cm, und Originaldokument

Die Pille wird von 100 Millionen Frauen weltweit eingenommen. In den letzten Jahren ist ein Rückgang der Verschreibungen zu beobachten. 2013 wurde sie in Deutschland an 60 Prozent der Mädchen zwischen 16 und 19 Jahren verschrieben, 2018 noch an 48 Prozent.

„Zunächst schien es eine Wunderpille. Dann haben, gerade die Feministinnen, Anfang der 70er Jahre angefangen darüber zu informieren, dass sie viele Nebenwirkungen hat und dass der Preis, den wir Frauen körperlich zahlen, sehr hoch ist.

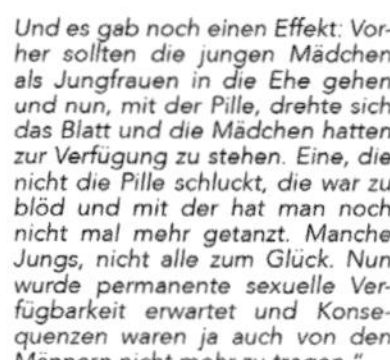

Ilayda, 20

Und es gab noch einen Effekt: Vorher sollten die jungen Mädchen als Jungfrauen in die Ehe gehen und nun, mit der Pille, drehte sich das Blatt und die Mädchen hatten zur Verfügung zu stehen. Eine, die nicht die Pille schluckt, die war zu blöd und mit der hat man noch nicht mal mehr getanzt. Manche Jungs, nicht alle zum Glück. Nun wurde permanente sexuelle Verfügbarkeit erwartet und Konsequenzen waren ja auch von den Männern nicht mehr zu tragen."

*Alice Schwarzer, *1942 Wuppertal, Journalistin und Feministin*

Isa, 22

lle: *Schwarzer, Alice: Schattenseiten der Antibaby- in: ZEITZEUGEN Portal, o. J., https://www.zeitzeu-portal.de/videos/L5Y9kr8L70U (Zugriff: 04.08.2020) 0:00–00:01:19].*

ly, Maria: Warum jede Pille anders wirkt. Über Nut- und Risiken verschiedener Verhütungspräparate, in: kompakt.de, 01.10.2015, https://www.geo.de/ma-ie/geo-kompakt/946-rtkl-verhuetung-warum-jede-anders-wirkt (Zugriff: 24.07.2020).

emitteilung: Tag der Antibabypille: Verordnungen n deutlich zurück, in: Die Techniker Krankenkasse, .2019, https://www.tk.de/presse/themen/arzneimit-g-der-antibabypille-2069966 (Zugriff: 05.07.2020).

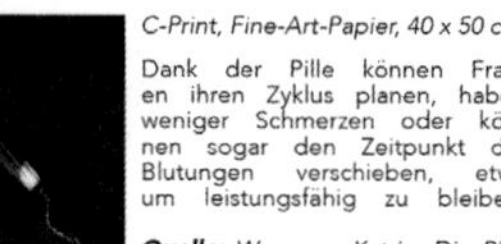

C-Print, Fine-Art-Papier, 40 x 50 cm

Dank der Pille können Frauen ihren Zyklus planen, haben weniger Schmerzen oder können sogar den Zeitpunkt der Blutungen verschieben, etwa um leistungsfähig zu bleiben.

Quelle: *Wegener, Katrin: Die Pille und ich. Vom Symbol der sexuellen Befreiung zur Lifestyle-Droge. Beck, München, 2015, S. 169 ff.*

Die Pille durchgehend einnehmen, in: familienpla-.de, 10.05.2016, https://www.familienplanung.de/uetung/verhuetungsmethoden/pille-und-minipille/ille-durchgehend-einnehmen/ (Zugriff: 01.08.2020).

C-Print, Fine-Art-Papier, 90 x 105 cm

Nebenwirkungen

OP-Narbe einer Betroffenen von Nebenwirkungen durch Einnahme der Antibabypille. Doppelte Lungenembolie.

Über die Jahrzehnte wurde die Pille optimiert. Es ist heute eine viel gere Dosierung möglich als noch in den 1960er n. Aber was einigen Frauen nicht bewusst ist: Viele der neuen Generation führen zu einem doppelt so n Thromboserisiko wie Pillen der alten Generation.

ohl die älteren Pillen wesentlich besser verträgnd, werden die neuen, mit 75 Prozent Marktanteil, ch öfter von Ärzten in Deutschland verschrieben, ert Prof. Dr. Gerd Glaeske, *1945, Pharmakologe rzneimittelexperte.

e: *Wegener, Katrin: Die Pille und ich. Vom Symbol exuellen Befreiung zur Lifestyle-Droge. C.H.Beck, hen, 2015, S.11/S. 132.*

ssen2go, Funk: Anti-Baby-Pille: Gefährlich für Frau- Unmöglich für Männer?, in: YouTube, 06.03.2019, //www.youtube.com/watch?v=qSA6YiHAIFw (Zu- 01.04.2020) [06:10–7.00].

C-Print, Fine-Art-Papier, 40 x 50 cm

Bayer HealthCare AG

Mit Verhütungspillen setzte Bayer 2017 etwa 648 Millionen Euro um.

Für die Pharmaindustrie stellen gerade die neuen Antibabypillen, mit „Beauty-Effekt", aber höherem Thromboserisiko, ein lukratives Geschäft dar. Diese Produkte stehen unter Patentschutz und können somit doppelt bis dreimal so teuer verkauft werden wie die Pillen der ersten und zweiten Generation.

Quelle: *Dittrich, Monika: Pille unter Beobachtung. Verhütung oder Verhängnis, in: Deutschlandfunk.de, 17.10.2018, https://www.deutschlandfunk.de/pille-unter-beobachtung-verhuetung-oder-verhaengnis.724.de.html?dram:article_id=430782 (Zugriff: 05.07.2020).*

Wegener, Katrin: Die Pille und ich. Vom Symbol der sexuellen Befreiung zur Lifestyle-Droge. C.H.Beck, München, 2015, S. 10/S. 119.

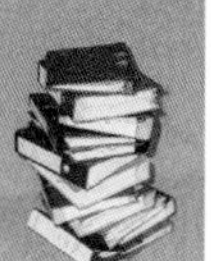

C-Print, Fine-Art-Papier, 40 x 50 cm

Klage gegen Bayer

Wegen möglicher Nebenwirkungen der Verhütungspille *Yasminelle* muss sich der Konzern *Bayer Pharma AG* vor einem deutschen Gericht verantworten. Den ersten Prozess gegen den Pharmariesen in Deutschland führt Felicitas Rohrer. Sie wäre 2009 beinahe an einer Lungenembolie gestorben, einer der möglichen Nebenwirkungen von Antibabypillen. Rohrer verlangt von *Bayer* Schadensersatz und Schmerzensgeld in Höhe von mindestens 200.000 Euro. *Bayer* hält die Ansprüche für „unbegründet".

In den USA sah sich *Bayer* 2016 wegen ähnlicher Vorwürfe einer Prozesswelle ausgesetzt und willigte ein, 10.600 Frauen mit 2,1 Millionen US-Dollar zu entschädigen – allerdings außergerichtlich und ohne Anerkennung einer juristischen Verantwortung.

Der Prozess von Felicitas Rohrer zieht sich bereits seit zehn Jahren.

Quelle: *Berres, Irene: 31-Jährige verklagt Bayer wegen Antibabypille, in: Spiegel Gesundheit, 16.12.2015, https://www.spiegel.de/gesundheit/sex/antibabypille-yasminelle-31-jaehrige-verklagt-bayer-a-1068186.html (Zugriff: 05.07.2020).*

dpa: Im Streit um Pille „Yasminelle" ruft das Gericht zur Einigung auf, in: Berufsverband Deutscher Internisten e.V., 22.10.2018, https://www.bdi.de/politik-und-presse/nachrichten/ansicht/article/im-streit-um-pille-yasminelle-ruft-das-gericht-zur-einigung-auf/ (Zugriff: 05.07.2020).

Rohrer, Felicitas: Felicitas Rohrer spricht vor den Bayer-Aktionären 2010, in: Risiko Pille, 2010, https://www.risiko-pille.de/felicitas-rohrer-bayer-aktionaere-2010/ (Zugriff: 01.07.2020).

C-Print, Fine-Art-Papier, 40 x 50 cm

Verpackung der *Yasminelle*

Optimierung von Haut, Haar und Gewicht, größere Brüste: Die Nebenwirkungen der Pille werden in den Mittelpunkt der Werbung gestellt. Die neuen Generationen der Antibabypille richten sich insbesondere an junge Frauen. Die Verhütung scheint nebensächlich.

Beim Kauf der Verhütungspille *Yasminelle* der *Bayer Pharma AG* erhielten die Mädchen das Medikament in einer silbernen Metallschachtel, mit eingelassenem Spiegel. Als Geschenk mit in der Box war ein kleiner Schminkpinsel mit *Yasminelle* Logo. Die Packungsbeilage war mit bunten Blumen verziert. Mittlerweile haben sich die Pharmakonzerne in Deutschland einem Kodex verschrieben, der Werbegeschenke verbietet.

Quelle: *Dittrich, Monika: Pille unter Beobachtung. Verhütung oder Verhängnis, in: Deutschlandfunk.de, 17.10.2018, https://www.deutschlandfunk.de/pille-unter-beobachtung-verhuetung-oder-verhaengnis.724.de.html?dram:article_id=430782 (Zugriff: 05.07.2020).*

MrWissen2go, Funk: Anti-Baby-Pille: Gefährlich für Frauen? Unmöglich für Männer?, in: YouTube, 06.03.2019, https://www.youtube.com/watch?v=qSA6YiHAIFw (Zugriff: 01.04.2020).

Wegener, Katrin: Die Pille und ich. Vom Symbol der sexuellen Befreiung zur Lifestyle- Droge. C.H.Beck, München, 2015, S. 12/S. 104/S. 119.

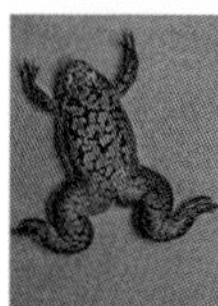

C-Print, Fine-Art-Papier, 90 x 105 cm

Umweltverschmutzung

Das Östrogen 17-alpha-Ethinylestradiol, der Hauptwirkstoff der Antibabypille, gelangt durch ungenügend angepasste Kläranlagen in Seen und Flüsse. Anstatt Spermien produzieren viele der in den belasteten Gewässern lebenden Amphibien Eier; sie verweiblichen. Auf dem Foto ist ein Afrikanischer Krallenfrosch zu sehen. Er wird für Forschungszwecke in Berlin am Leibniz-Institut für Gewässerökologie und Binnenfischerei gezüchtet.

Zu den Kosten der sexuellen Freiheit gehören auch Ausgaben für bessere Kläranlagen. Denn das Östrogen aus der Pille ist zu einem bedeutsamen Schadstoff in Gewässern geworden.

Quelle: *Pressemitteilung IGB: Bislang unbemerkte Geschlechtsumkehr bei Amphibien durch Pillen-Östrogen, in: IGB, 04.04.2016, https://www.igb-berlin.de/news/bislang-unbemerkte-geschlechtsumkehr-bei-amphibien-durch-pillen-oestrogen (Zugriff: 09.04.2020).*

Rögener, Wiebke: Antibabypille im Fluss, in: sueddeutsche.de, 14.06.2012, https://www.sueddeutsche.de/wissen/wasserverschmutzung-antibabypille-im-fluss-1.1381340 (Zugriff: 07.04.2020).

Buchkonzept *(siehe Videobeitrag)*

Smile Effekt ist ein Buchobjekt und kann, weil es ohne Bindung auskommt, auch eine Pop-up-Ausstellung an der Wand sein. Smile Effekt eignet sich als Gesprächsgrundlage im Aufklärungsunterricht.

Fotobuch **Smile Effekt**
14,8 x 21,0 cm | 25 Einzelteile | 80–300g, DIN A5–A2 | ohne Bindung, dafür Kreuzgummiband | 5 Kapitel

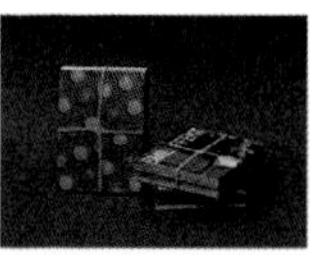

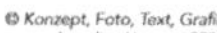

Smile Effekt erscheint anlässlich 60 Jahren Antibabypille.

Ausstellung in der *Galerie für Fotografie*, Eisfabrik Hannover

Smile Effekt

Impressum

Angelina Vernetti
Fotografie, Berlin

Tel.: +49 157 55961399
www.angelinavernetti.de
mail@angelinavernetti.de

Diese Packungsbeilage wurde zuletzt überarbeitet 01/2021.

GEBRAUCHSINFORMATION: INFORMATION FÜR DIE ANWENDER

Smile Effekt

Lesen Sie die gesamte Packungsbeilage sorgfältig durch, um das Projekt *Smile Effekt* in seiner Gänze zu verstehen, denn sie enthält wichtige Informationen.

- Heben Sie die Packungsbeilage auf. Vielleicht möchten Sie diese später nochmals lesen.
- Wenn Sie weitere Fragen haben, wenden Sie sich an einen Experten, wie beispielsweise Ihren Arzt oder Apotheker.
- Wenn es um konkrete Fragen zur Verhütung geht, wenden Sie sich bitte an den Arzt Ihres Vertrauens.
- Geben Sie *Smile Effekt* gerne an Dritte weiter.

Was in dieser Packungsbeilage steht
Hintergrundinformationen, Bildunterschriften und Quellenangaben von:

1. exemplarischen Verhütungsmythen
2. der Einführung der Pille
3. persönlichen Erfahrungsberichten
4. ausgewählten Fakten rund um die Pille
5. dem Buchobjekt *Smile Effekt*

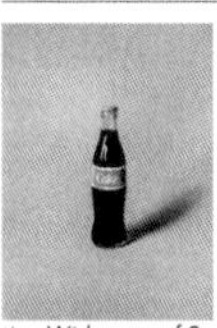

C-Print auf Alu-Dibond, 25 x 35 cm

Verhütungsmethode Scheidenspülung

Bis in die 1950er Jahre wurde – besonders von amerikanischen Teenagern – als Scheidenspülung nach dem Geschlechtsverkehr Coca-Cola verwendet. Ohne Wirkung. Weder Cola noch Pepsi oder ähnliche Softdrinks haben eine negative Wirkung auf Spermien. Im Gegenteil: Sie enthalten viel Zucker, den Spermien brauchen und lieben.

Quelle: *o.V.: Coca-Cola. Plakat, in: Museum für Verhütung und Schwangerschaftsabbruch, 2020, http://de.muvs.org/verhuetung/vergebliche-versuche/coca-cola-id2522/ (Zugriff: 24.07.2020).*

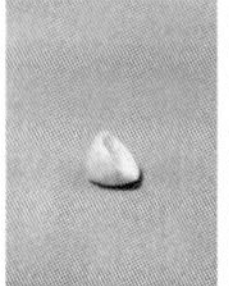

C-Print auf Alu-Dibond, 25 x 35 cm

Verhütungsmethode Scheidenbarrieren

Casanova soll im 18. Jahrhundert die Verwendung von Zitronen als Verhütungsmittel erfunden haben: Eine halbierte Zitrone wird ausgepresst und die umgedrehte Schale wie eine Kappe über den Muttermund gestülpt.

Quelle: *o.V.: Zitronenhälfte, in: Museum für Verhütung und Schwangerschaftsabbruch, 2020, http://de.muvs.org/verhuetung/scheidenbarrieren/zitronenhaelfte-id2518/ (Zugriff: 24.07.2020).*

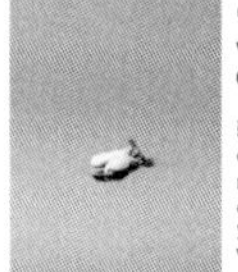

C-Print auf Alu-Dibond, 25 x 35 cm

Verhütungsmethode Chemische Substanzen

Im 4. Jahrhundert nach Christus empfahl ein griechischer Arzt erstmals auch Männern den Gebrauch chemischer Substanzen, um eine Schwangerschaft zu vermeiden. Vor dem Beischlaf sollte das Glied dafür mit dem Saft eines Hahnenkopfes oder mit einer Mischung aus Granatapfelsaft und Essig oder Alaun bestrichen werden.

Quelle: *o.V.: Wie Frauen in der Antike verhüteten. Amulette und Schwämmchen. Griechenland und Rom, in: Museum für Verhütung und Schwangerschaftsabbruch, 2020, http://de.muvs.org/topic/wie-frauen-in-der-antike-verhueteten/ (Zugriff: 24.07.2020).*

C-Print auf Alu-Dibond, 25 x 35 cm

Verhütungsmethode Aberglaube

Verzweiflung und Not waren groß, wenn es darum ging, die Kinderzahl einzuschränken. Bis ins 19. Jahrhundert brachten Frauen aus Wachs geformte Gurken als Votivgaben in die Kirche und hofften, dadurch nach dem siebten Kind nicht mehr zu empfangen. „Beim Siebenten, o Herr, hör auf mit deinem Segen!" Im Original waren die ausgehöhlten Wachsgurken mit sieben kleinen Püppchen verziert.

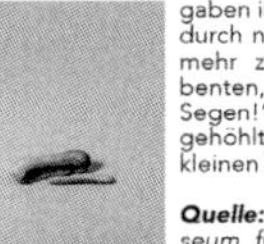

Quelle: *o.V.: Wachsgurke, in: Museum für Verhütung und Schwangerschaftsabbruch, 2020, http://de.muvs.org/verhuetung/vergebliche-versuche/wachsgurke-id2536/ (Zugriff: 24.07.2020).*

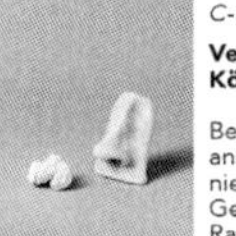

C-Print auf Alu-Dibond, 25 x 35 cm

Verhütungsmethode Körperliche Übungen

Beim Koitus den Atem anhalten, anschließend direkt aufstehen, sich niederhocken, heftig niesen und die Geschlechtsteile waschen. Diesen Rat für Frauen gab Soranos, der Verfasser der wohl bedeutendsten gynäkologischen Schrift der Antike. Manche Überlieferungen rieten außerdem dazu, nach dem Geschlechtsakt kräftig auf- und abzuspringen und etwas Kaltes zu trinken.

Quelle: *o.V.: Wie Frauen in der Antike verhüteten. Amulette und Schwämmchen. Griechenland und Rom, in: Museum für Verhütung und Schwangerschaftsabbruch, 2020, http://de.muvs.org/topic/wie-frauen-in-der-antike-verhueteten/ (Zugriff: 24.07.2020).*

Albat, Daniela: In die Hocke gehen und niesen. Die Anfänge der Verhütung, in: scinexx das Wissensmagazin, 03.03.2017, https://www.scinexx.de/dossierartikel/in-die-hocke-gehen-und-niesen/ (Zugriff: 24.07.2020).

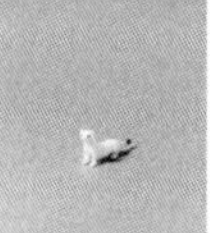

C-Print auf Alu-Dibond, 25 x 35 cm

Verhütungsmethode Enthaltsamkeit

Kein Sex ist zu 100 Prozent sicher. Im Mittelalter, in dem Kirchenlehrer die Enthaltsamkeit predigten, soll ein weißes Hermelin als Keuschheitssymbol gegolten haben. „Safer Sex" dagegen kündigte sich erst mit einer Entwicklung im 16. Jahrhundert an. Damals erfand ein italienischer Arzt in Flüssigkeit getränkte Leinensäcke für den Penis. Er wollte damit die ansteckende Syphilis eindämmen, die Seefahrer aus Amerika mitgebracht hatten. Das erste Kondom war geboren.

Quelle: *Albat, Daniela: In die Hocke gehen und niesen. Die Anfänge der Verhütung, in: scinexx das Wissensmagazin, 03.03.2017, https://www.scinexx.de/dossierartikel/in-die-hocke-gehen-und-niesen/ (Zugriff: 24.07.2020).*

Rothenfluh, Anna: Kommen wir nun zu den Sex-Wieseln ..., in: watson.ch, 07.06.2020, https://www.watson.ch/wissen/kunst/679625970-sex-wiesel-was-die-tierchen-auf-renaissance-gemaelden-verloren-haben (Zugriff: 24.07.2020).

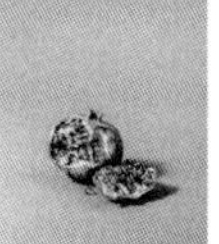

C-Print auf Alu-Dibond, 25 x 35 cm

Verhütungsmethode Spermizide

Weit verbreitet in der Antike war der Einsatz kontrazeptiver Substanzen: Schwämmchen wurden mit ihnen getränkt und in die Scheide eingeführt. Beliebt waren beispielsweise Granatapfelkerne, Ingwer, Olivenöl, Honig, Essig, Salzlake und diverse Harze. Sie konnten die Säuren-Basen-Ausgewogenheit in Scheide und Gebärmutter so beeinflussen, dass die Spermien auf ungünstige Aufnahmebedingungen trafen.

Quelle: *o.V.: Wie Frauen in der Antike verhüteten. Griechenland und Rom, in: Museum für Verhütung und Schwangerschaftsabbruch, 2020, https://muvs.org/de/themen/verhuetung/wie-frauen-in-der-antike-verhueteten/ (Zugriff: 02.02.2021).*

Ohne Verhütung würden Frauen in ihren 35 fruchtbaren Jahren durchschnittlich 12 bis 15 Schwangerschaften durchleben. Die ältesten uns bekannten Methoden zur Empfängnisverhütung sind nahezu 4.000 Jahre alt.

Quelle: *Dr. Fiala, Christian/Parzer, Elisabeth: Österreichischer Verhütungsreport, in: verhuetungsreport.at, 2019, http://verhuetungsreport.at/ (Zugriff: 07.07.2020), S. 46.*

Müller-Landgraf, Ingrid: Von der Verhütung mit Granat- und Gallapfel zur hormonalen Kontrazeption. Kunstgriffe aus der Antike, in: Staupe, Gisela/Vieth, Lisa/Deutsches Hygiene-Museum (Hrsg.): Die Pille. Von der Lust und von der Liebe. Rowohlt, Berlin, 1996, S. 101.

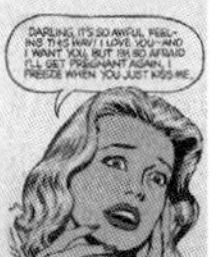

Tapetendruck, 130 x 178 cm

Escape from Fear. For Adults O

Ausschnitt aus einem amerika schen Aufklärungscomic von 19 In diesem geht es um Joan u Ken Harper. Das junge Paar l in einer glücklichen Ehe. Die Glück gerät durch die rasch wa sende Kinderzahl ins Ungleich wicht. Joan lebt in der ständig Angst, erneut schwanger zu werden. Aufgrund ih Überforderung zieht sie schweren Herzens in Er gung, ihren Ehemann zu verlassen. Ken möchte ni kampflos aufgeben und sucht nach Lösungen. Ein A kann dem Paar helfen: Er verschreibt ihnen die Anti bypille.

Quelle: *Persoff, Ethan: Comics with Proble 1956/1962 Planned Parenthood Comic Book on B Control. Issue No. 17, in: http://www.ep.tc, 18.06.20 http://www.ep.tc/problems/seventeen/index.html (griff: 01.07.2020), S. 1/S. 2/S. 10.*

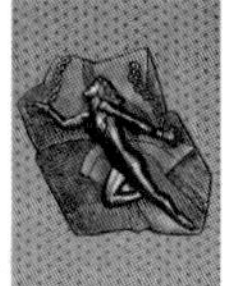

C-Print, Fine-Art-Papier, 40 x 50

Collage *Enovid* Werbemateria

Goldfarbene Plakette für das P dukt *Enovid* von *Searle* – d Hersteller der ersten zugelasse Antibabypille in Amerika.

Dargestellt ist Andromeda, e Frau aus der griechischen My logie. Diese befreit sich von Ketten, in die sie gelegt war. Material: Kunststoff, e jekt in cm: 14,7 x 10,5 x 2,5, Datierung: 1961.

Hintergrundmotiv Originale Werbe- und Infobrosch über das amerikanische Produkt *Enovid* von *Searle*, zember 1964.

Quelle: *o.V.: Enovid-Plakette. Werbemittel für die erste Enovid, in: Museum für Verhütung und Schwangerschaft bruch, 2013, http://de.muvs.org/verhuetung/v-media/e vid-plakette-id2333/?media_id=5232 (Zugriff: 07.11.2019*

o.V.: Beiheft zur Antibabypille Enovid. Planing your fa in: Museum für Verhütung und Schwangerschaftsabbr 2020, https://muvs.org/de/bib/document/details/a1736 arch=a1736 (Zugriff: 07.11.2019).

Zeitgleich mit der Antibabypille wurde auch an eir Pille für den Mann geforscht. Jahrelange Anläu Abbrüche und Versprechen: Auf dem weltweit Markt sind mehr als 250 Pillenpräparate für die F erhältlich, doch kein einziges für den Mann. „D Witz ist: Wir sind seit 40 Jahren immer nur fünf Jah entfernt von der Pille für den Mann", bemerkt d Physiologe John Amory 2019 in einem Interview.

Selbst Carl Djerassi – der sich ironisch „Mutter d Pille nennt" – sprach sich 1990 bereits für den B darf einer „Pille für den Mann" aus. Heute gibt es s kaufen kann man sie aber nicht.

Quelle: *Jütte, Robert: Lust ohne Last. Geschich der Empfängnisverhütung. C.H.Beck, Münche 2003, S. 328.*

Esch, Kirsten/ARTE: 60 Jahre Pille: Wo bleibt d Pille für den Mann?, in: YouTube, 2019, https www.youtube.com/watch?v=2ePCs3lLwO4 (Zugr 05.06.2020) [00:00:50/00:14:20/00:23:50].

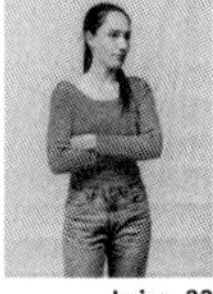

Luisa, 22

C-Print, Fine-Art-Papier, 50 x cm, und Originaldokument

Straßenporträts

Die Porträts und Erfahrungsbe te entstanden im Sommer 2 in Berlin (Neukölln, Schöneb Kreuzberg, Prenzlauer Berg).

Editorische Notiz: Zum Schutz der befragten Personen wurde im Layout mit den Texten und Fotos frei umgegangen. Die handschriftlichen Notizen sind keiner Person zuordenbar.

C-Print, Fine-Art-Papier, 50 x 70 cm, und Originaldokument

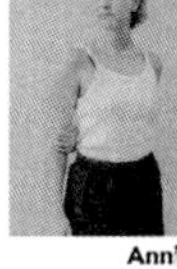

Ann

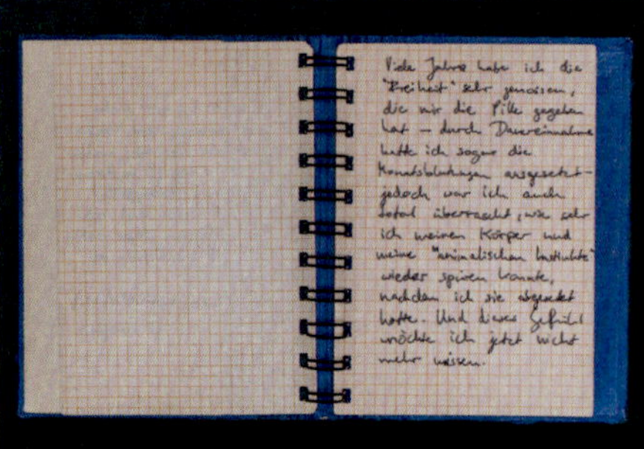
Viele Jahre habe ich die
"Freiheit" sehr genossen,
die mir die Pille gegeben
hat – durch Dauereinnahme
hatte ich sogar die
Monatsblutungen ausgesetzt –
jedoch war ich auch
total überrascht, wie sehr
ich meinen Körper und
meine "animalischen Instinkte"
wieder spüren konnte,
nachdem ich sie abgesetzt
hatte. Und dieses Gefühl
möchte ich jetzt nicht
mehr missen.

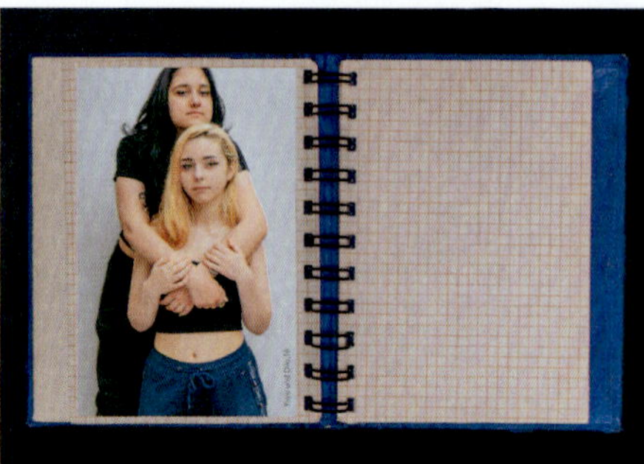

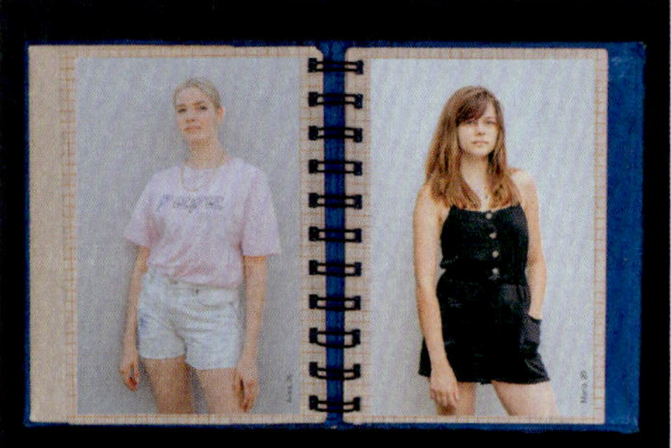

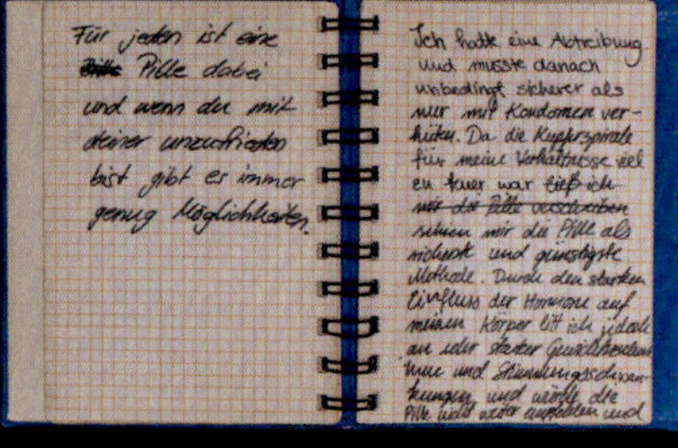
Für jeden ist eine
Pille dabei
und wenn du mit
deiner unzufrieden
bist gibt es immer
genug Möglichkeiten.
Ich hatte eine Abtreibung
und musste danach
unbedingt sicherer als
nur mit Kondomen ver-
hüten. Da die Kupferspirale
für meine Verhältnisse viel
zu teuer war
schien mir die Pille als
sicherste und günstigste
Methode. Durch den starken
Einfluss der Hormone auf
meinen Körper litt ich jedoch
an sehr starken Gewichtsschwan-
kungen und Stimmungsschwan-
kungen und würde die
Pille nicht mehr empfehlen und

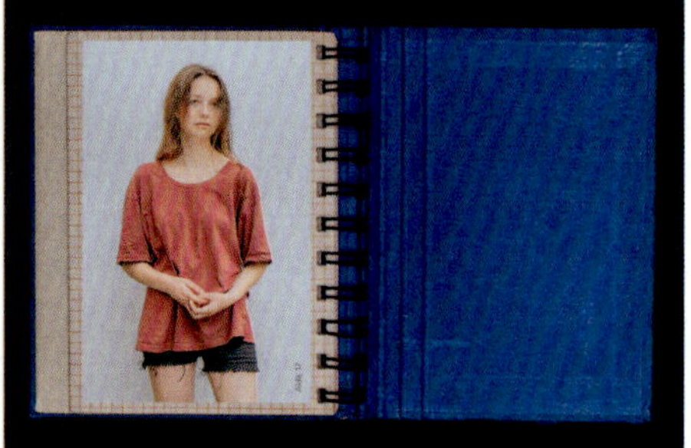

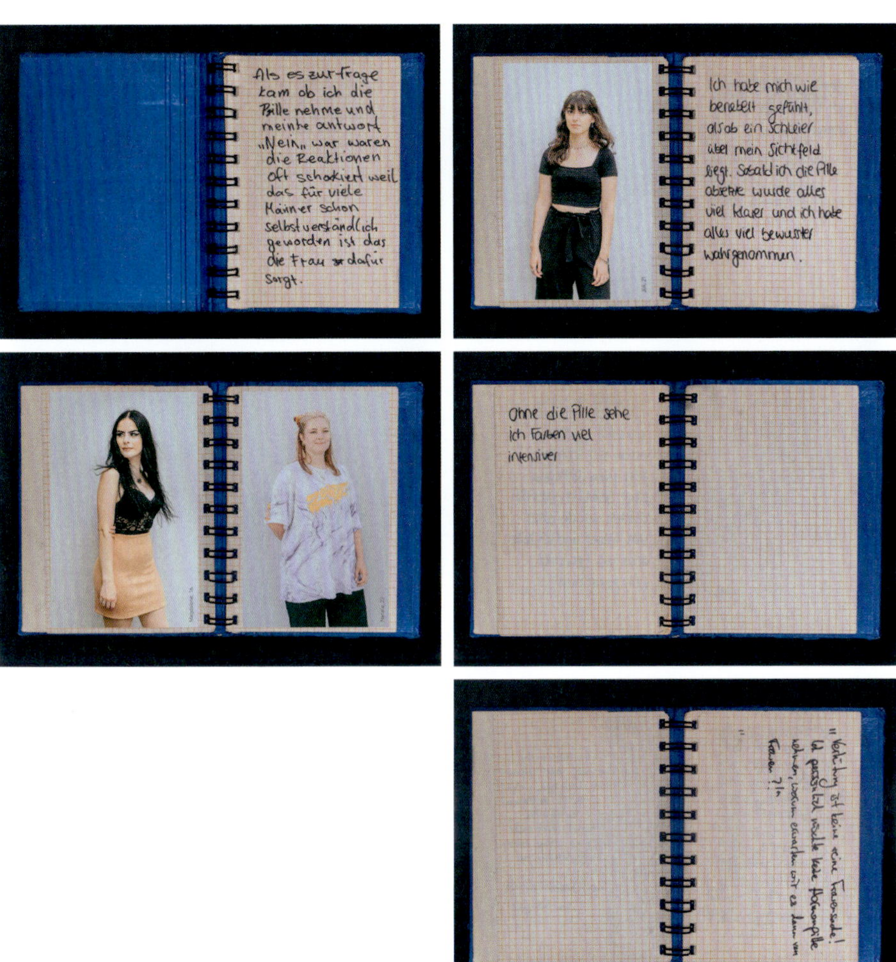
Als es zur Frage kam ob ich die Pille nehme und meine antwort „Nein" war waren die Reaktionen oft schokiert weil das für viele Männer schon selbstverständlich geworden ist das die Frau dafür sorgt.
Ich habe mich wie benebelt gefühlt, als ob ein Schleier über mein Sichtfeld liegt. Sobald ich die Pille absetzte wurde alles viel klarer und ich habe alles viel bewusster wahrgenommen.
Ohne die Pille sehe ich Farben viel intensiver
„Verhütung ist keine reine Frauensache! Ich persönlich würde keine Hormonpille nehmen, warum erwarten wir es dann von Frauen?!"

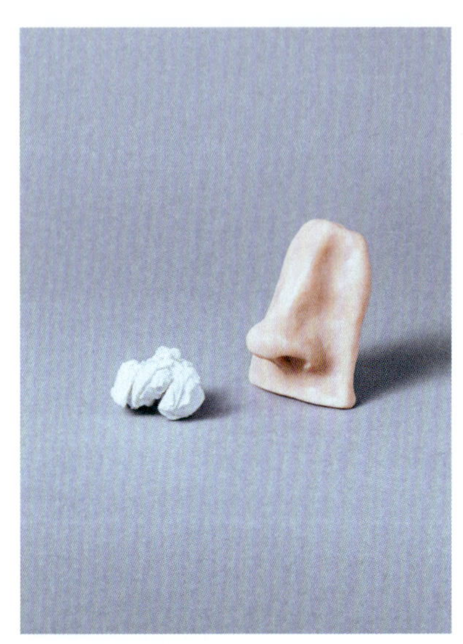

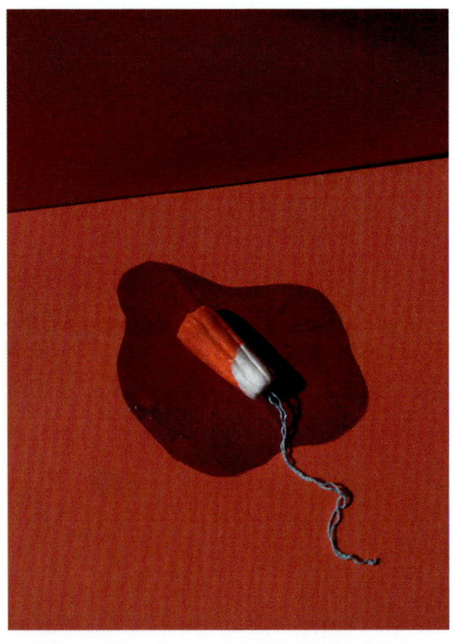

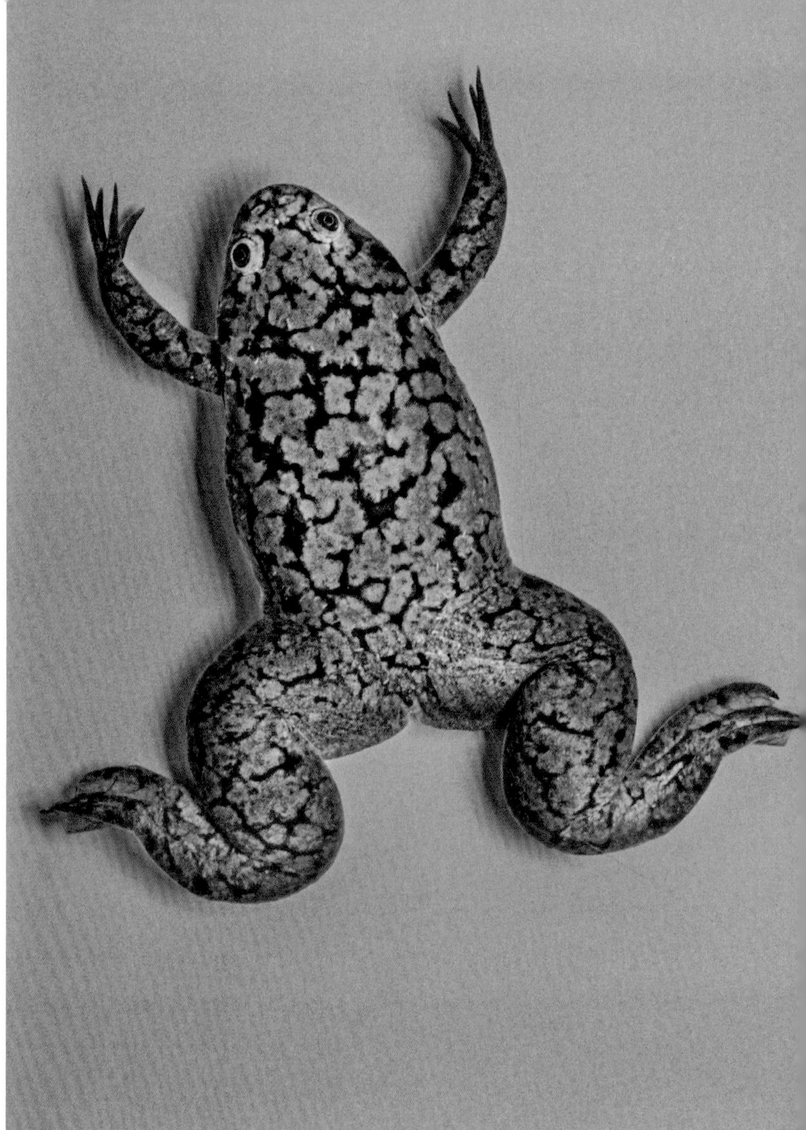

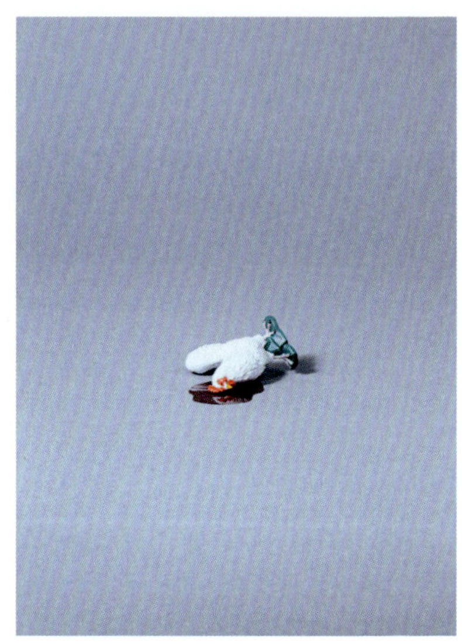

Chemische Substanzen

Im 4. Jahrhundert nach Christus empfahl ein griechischer Arzt erstmals auch Männern den Gebrauch chemischer Substanzen, um eine Schwangerschaft zu vermeiden. Vor dem Beischlaf sollte das Glied dafür mit dem Saft eines Hahnenkopfes oder mit einer Mischung aus Granatapfelsaft mit Essig oder Alaun bestrichen werden.

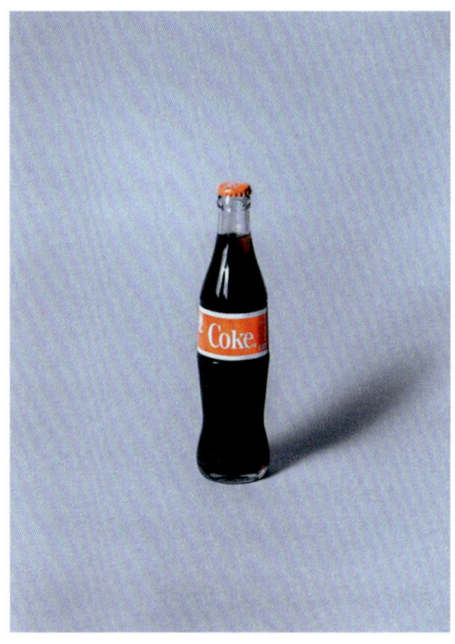

Scheidenspülung

Bis in die 1950er Jahre wurde - besonders von amerikanischen Teenagern - als Scheidenspülung nach dem Geschlechtsverkehr Coca-Cola verwendet. Ohne Wirkung. Weder Cola noch Pepsi oder ähnliche Softdrinks haben eine negative Wirkung auf Spermien. Im Gegenteil: Sie enthalten viel Zucker, den Spermien brauchen und lieben.

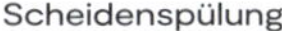

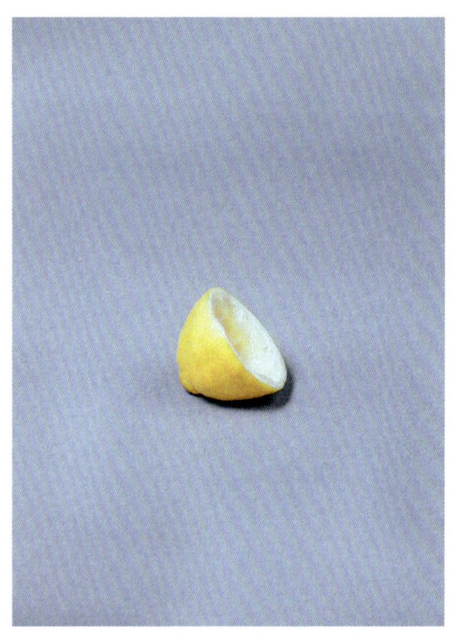

Scheidenbarrieren

Casanova soll im 18. Jahrhundert die Verwendung von Zitronen als Verhütungsmittel erfunden haben: Eine halbierte Zitrone wird ausgepresst und die umgedrehte Schale wie eine Kappe über den Muttermund gestülpt. Die im Zitronensaft enthaltene Zitronensäure soll Spermien in ihrer Bewegung bremsen.

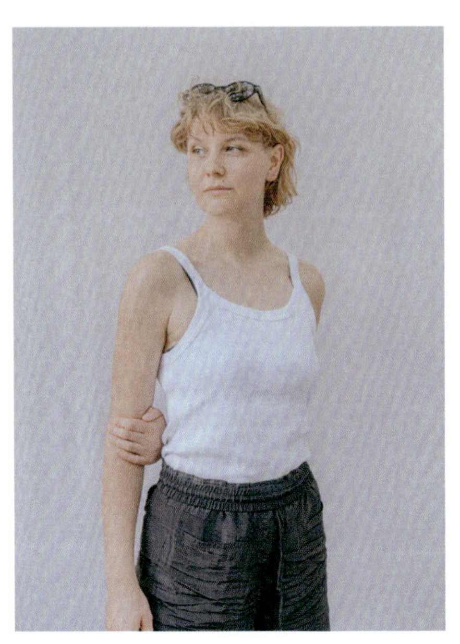

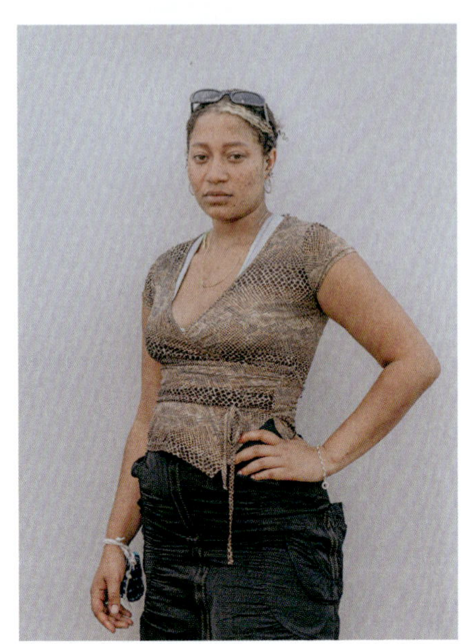

Every second woman in Germany takes the birth control pill. Manufacturers convey the image of a »Lifestyle product«: better skin, beautiful hair, less weight, separating sexuality from fertility. However, side effects include a tendency towards a decreasing hormonal contraception. As common as the drug is, its sociocultural status and health effects are rarely consciously discussed.

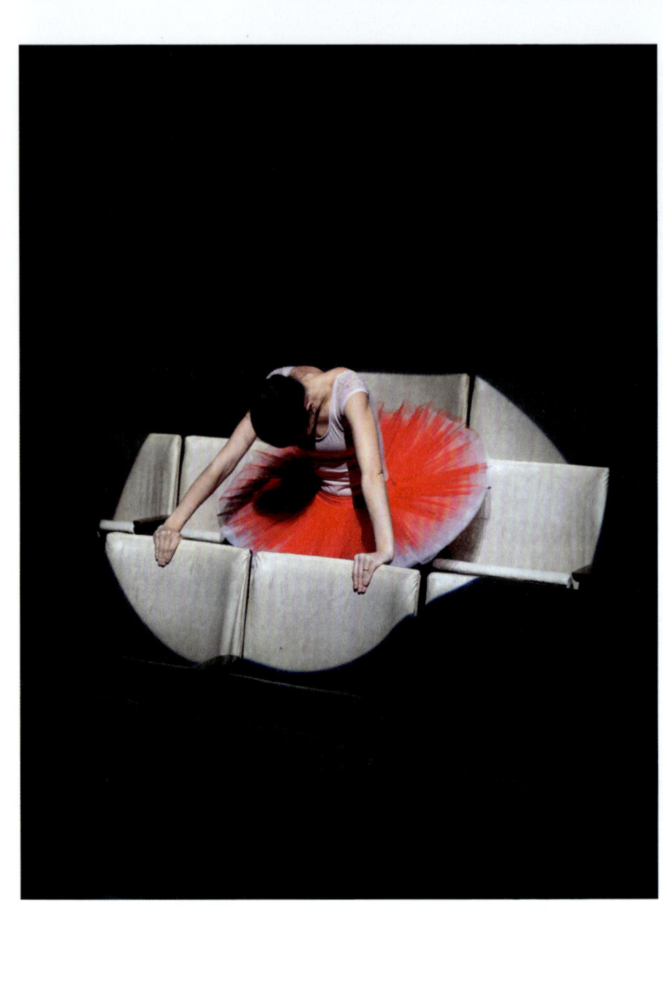

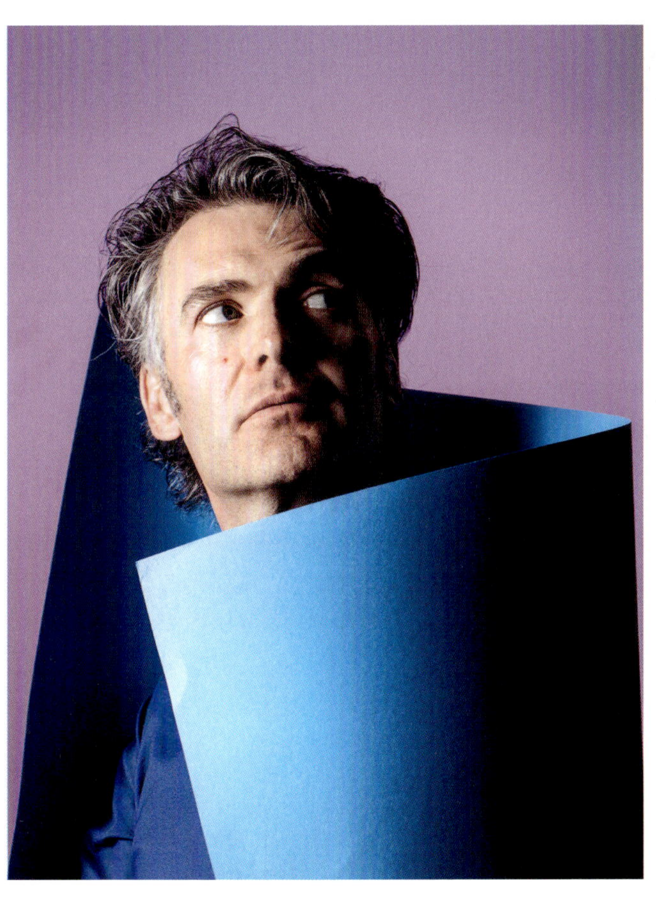

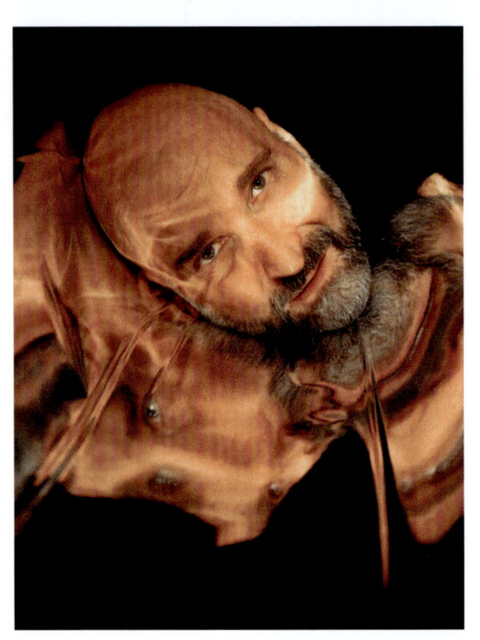

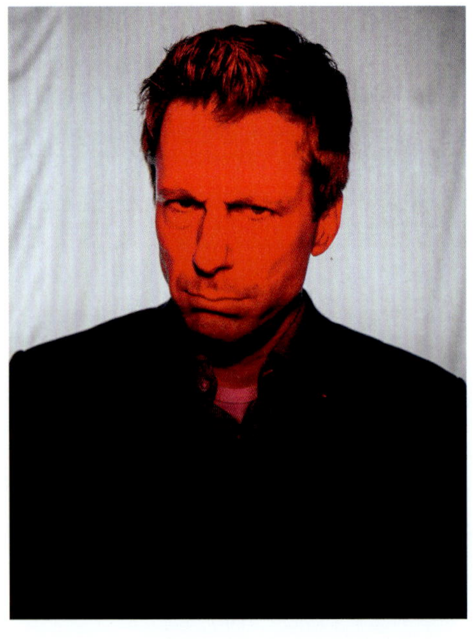

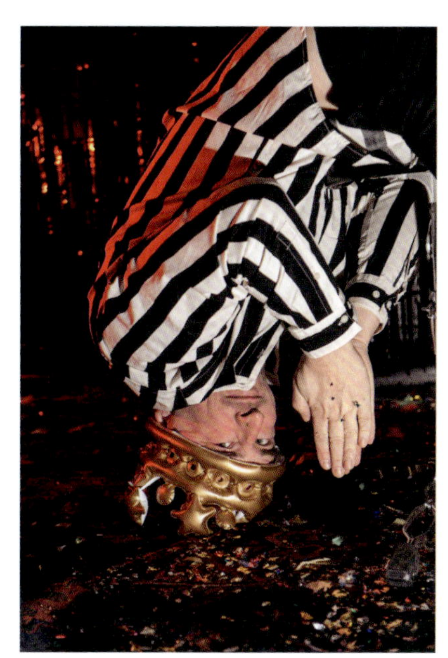

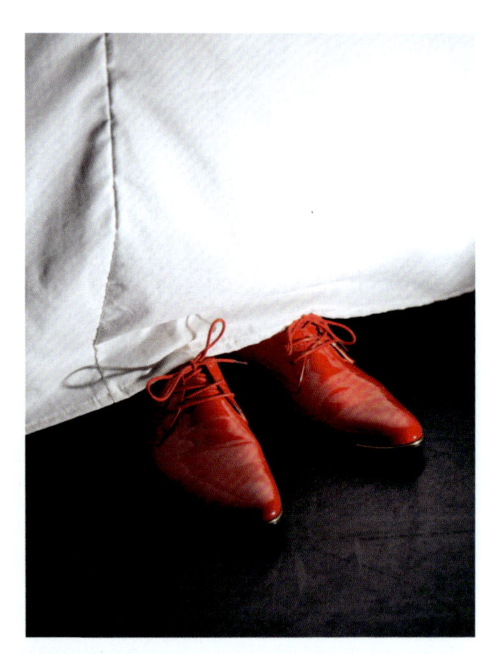

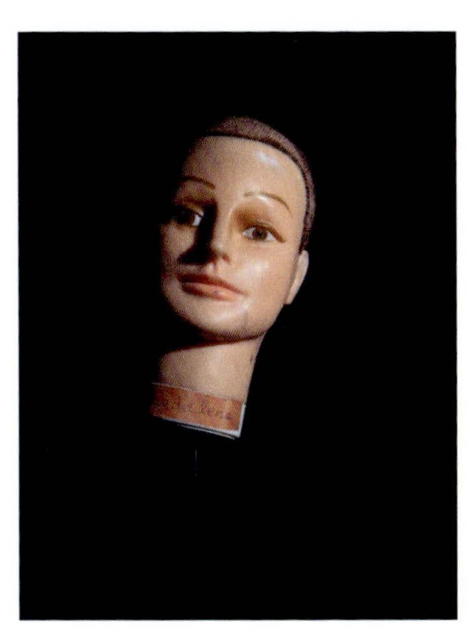

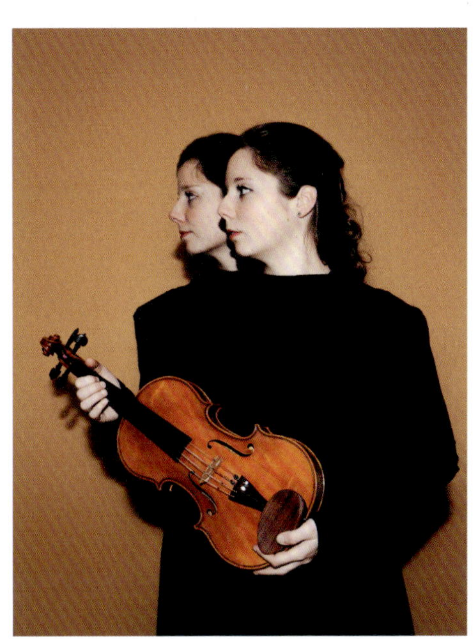

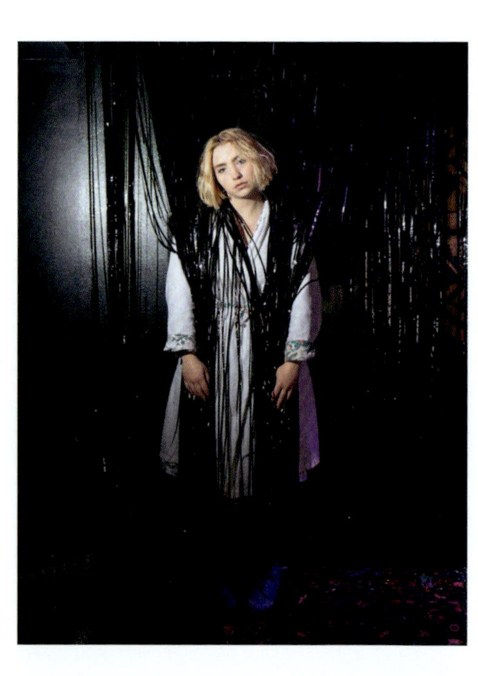

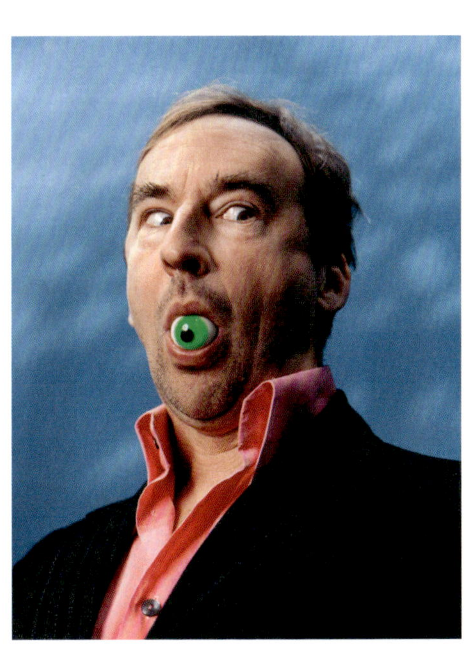

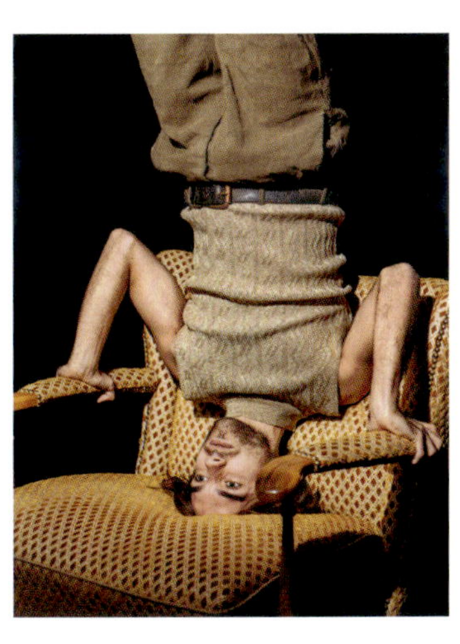

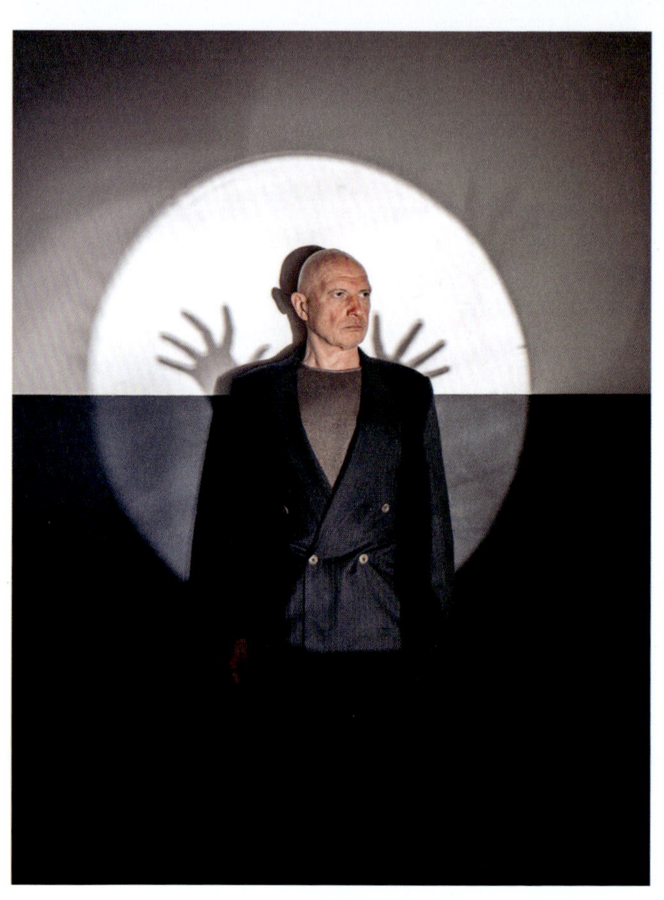

Excitement paired with anticipation. It’s about to start —the tension rises! But it doesn’t start, it stays quiet. There is no applause, the halls remain empty and the props gather dust. Usually, art and culture turn the world upside down, but now a virus has claimed that role for itself.

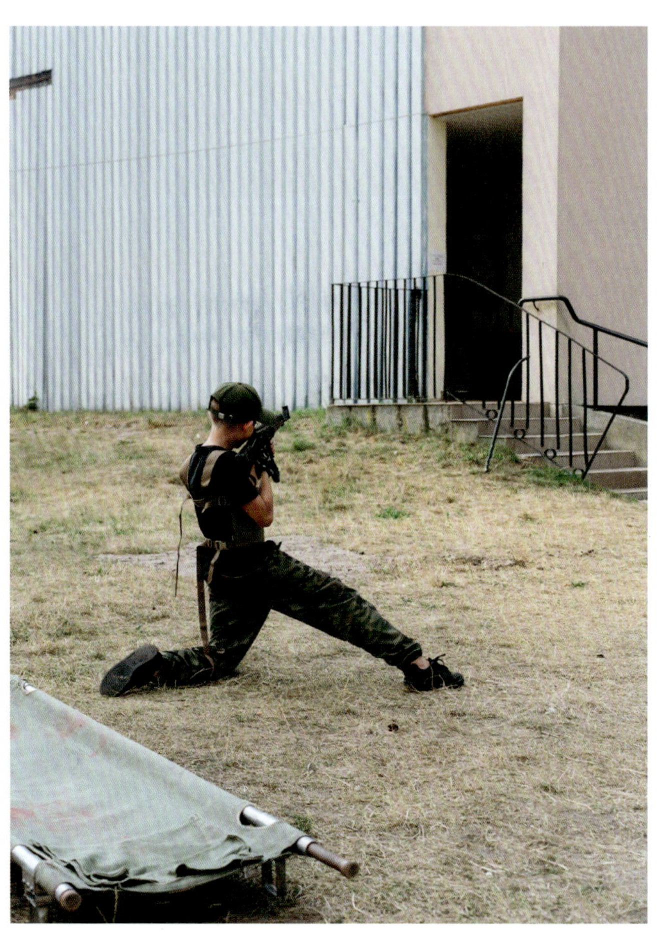

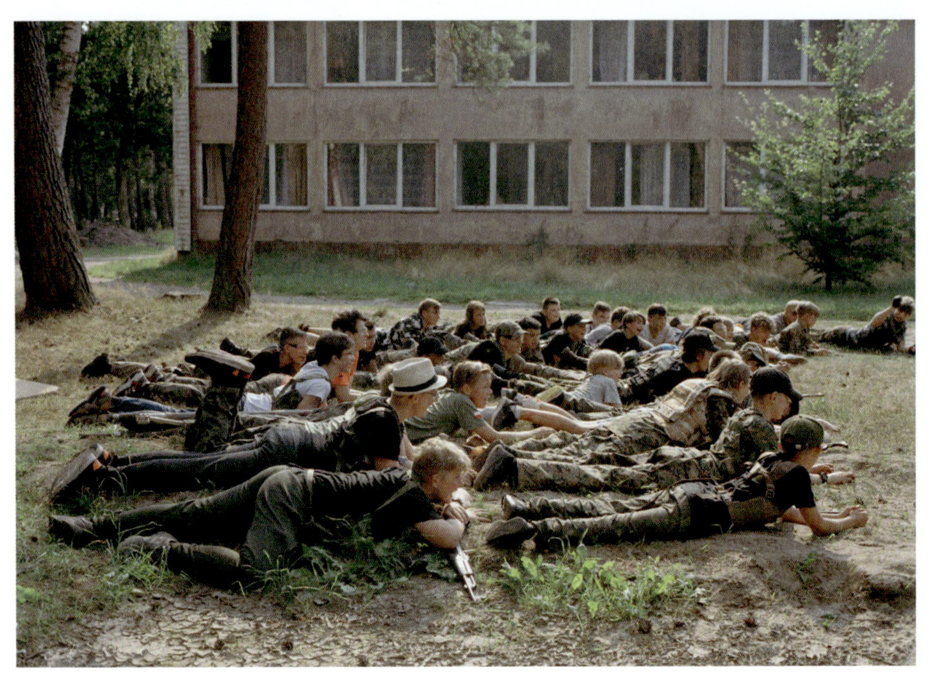

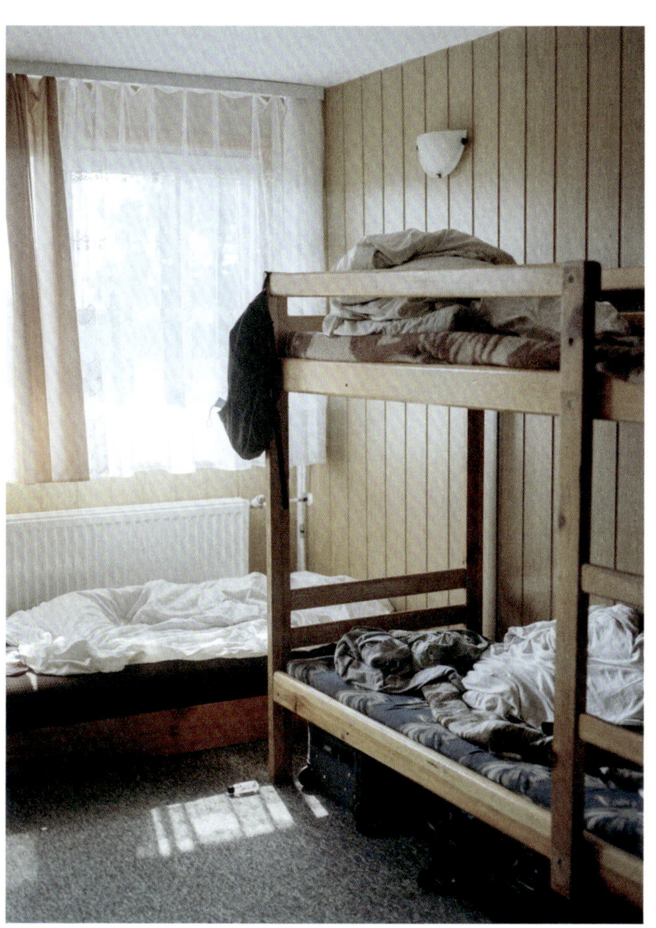

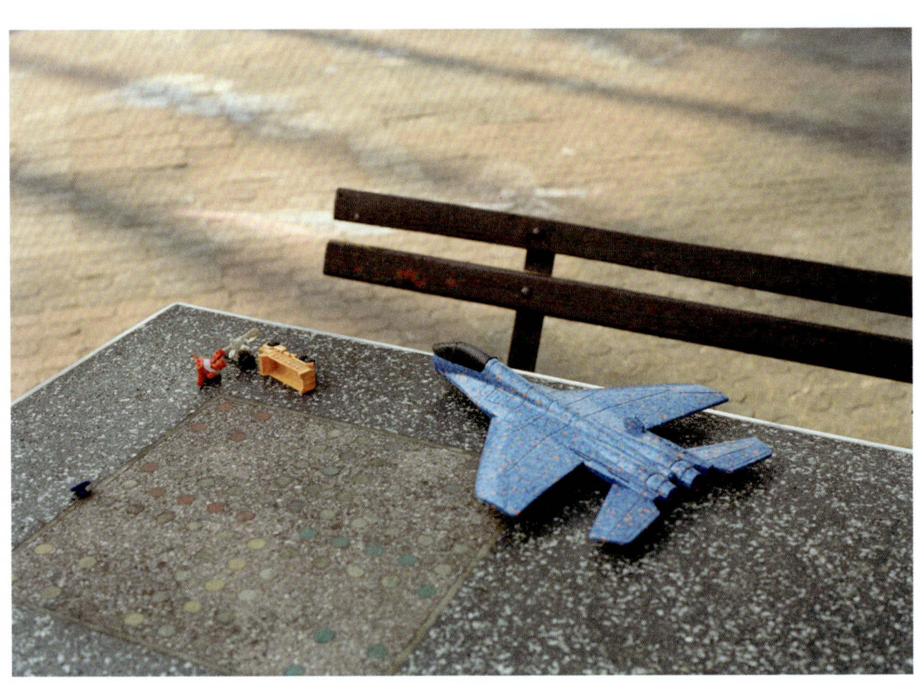

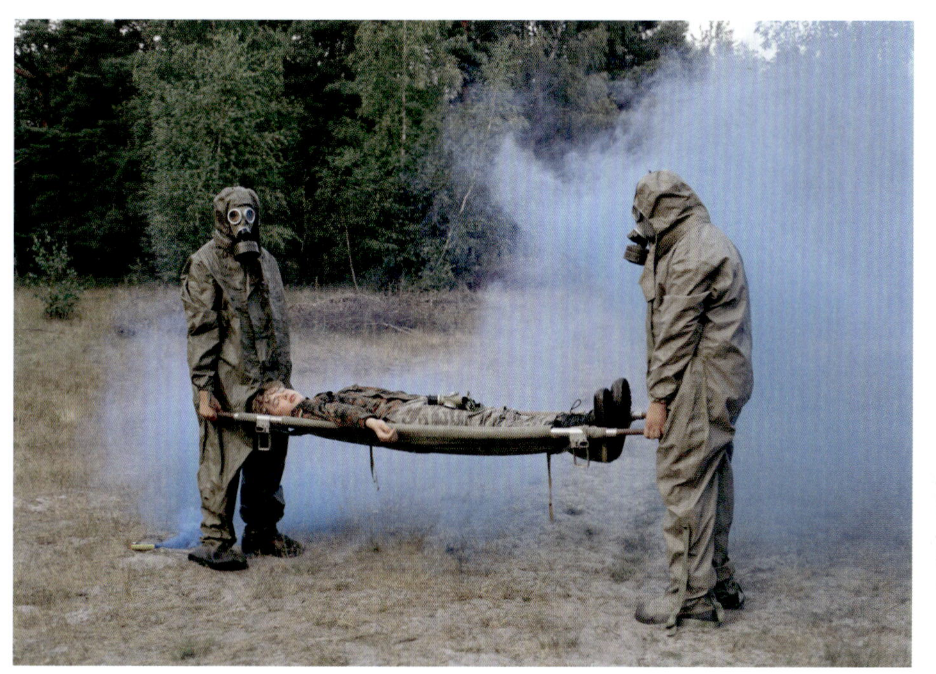

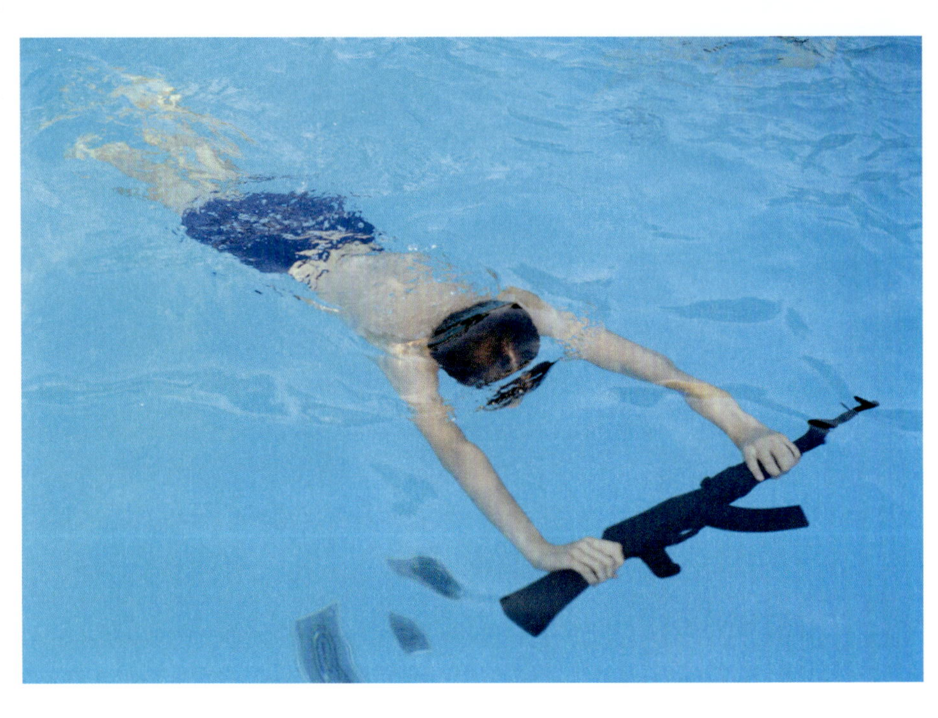

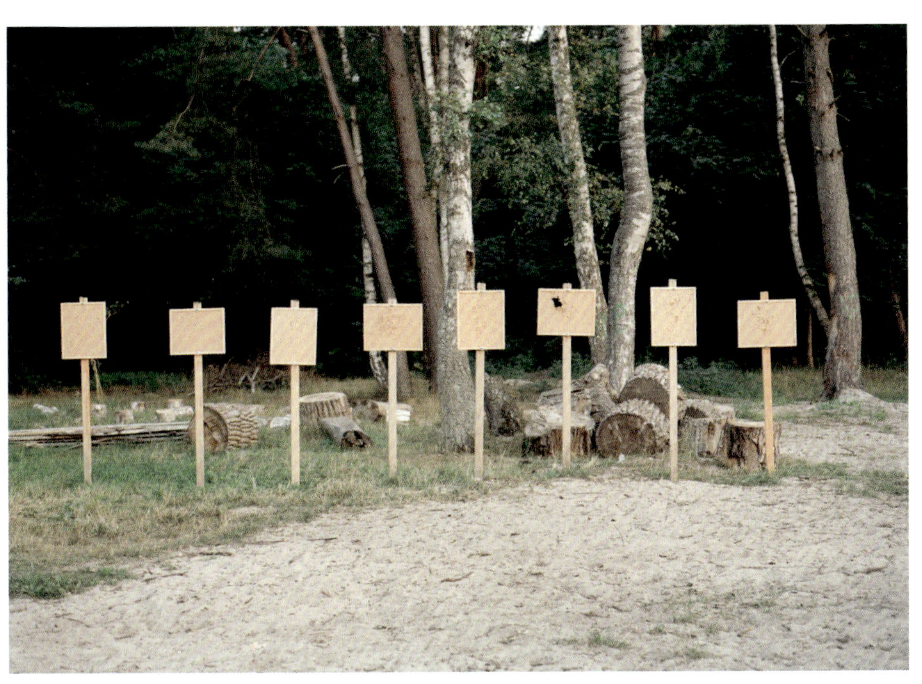

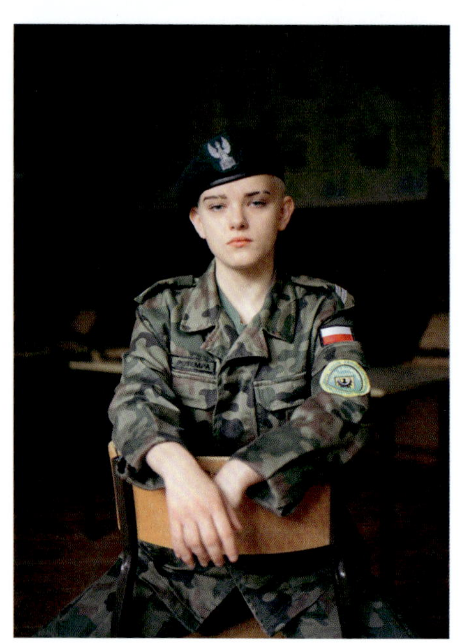

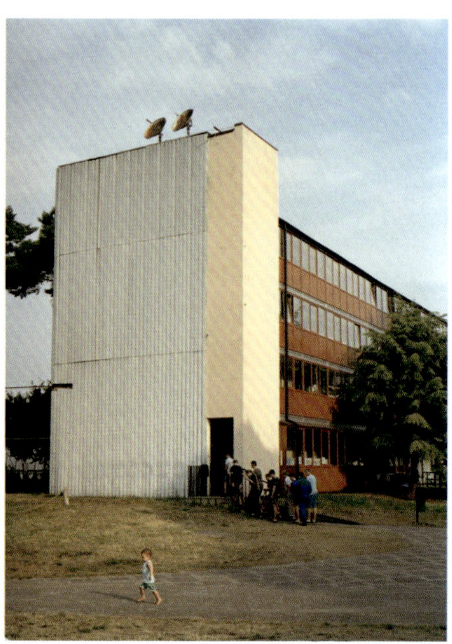

Military camps are a phenomenon that has experienced a massive influx in Poland in recent years. In addition to being taught military basics, children and young people are playfully indoctrinated in obedience, fearlessness and patriotism. Between fake blood, drill and the unreserved use of weapons, the emotional effects of military education are often overlooked.

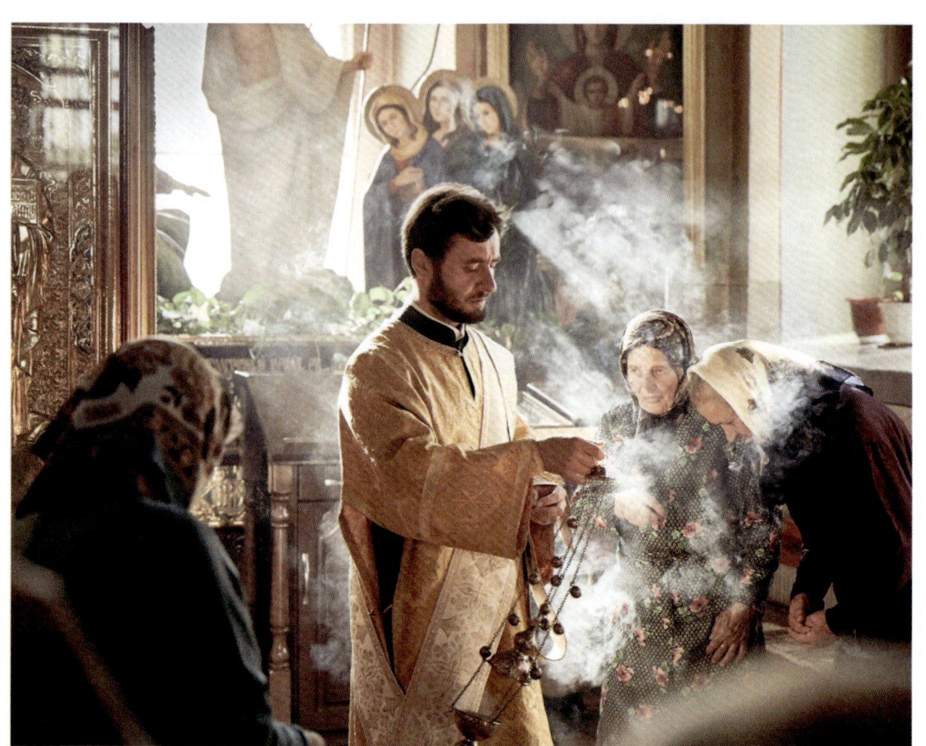

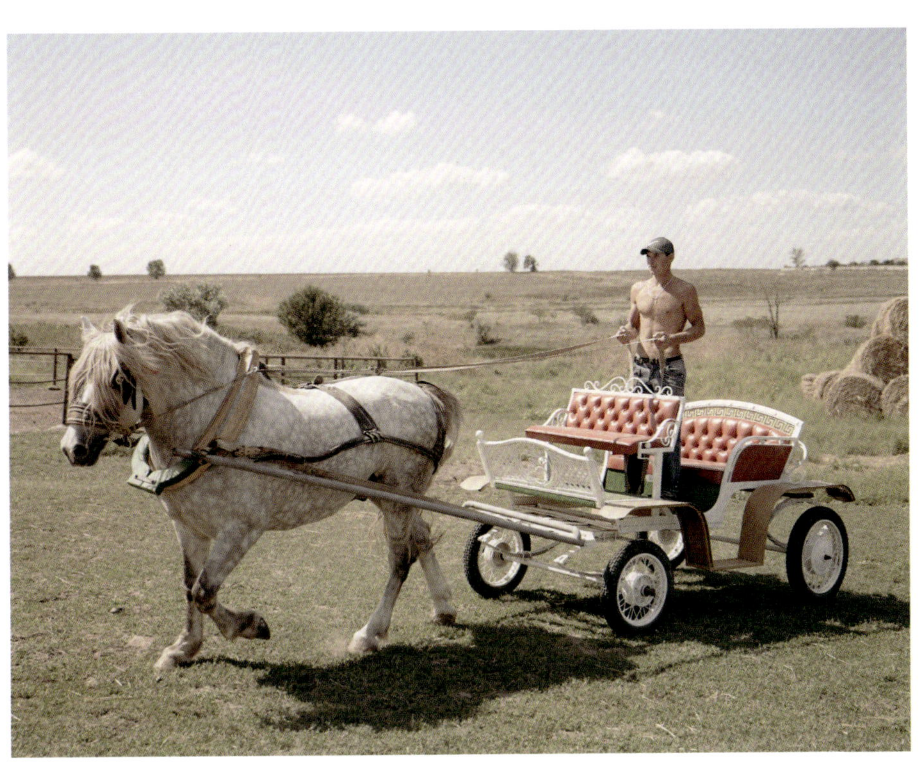

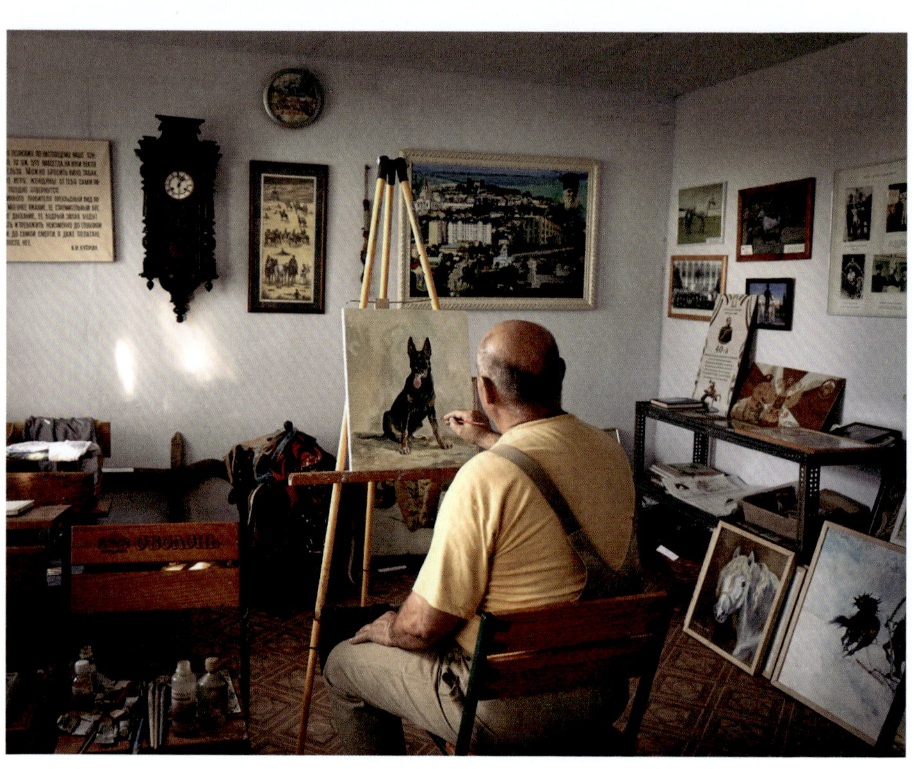
ОБОЛОНЬ

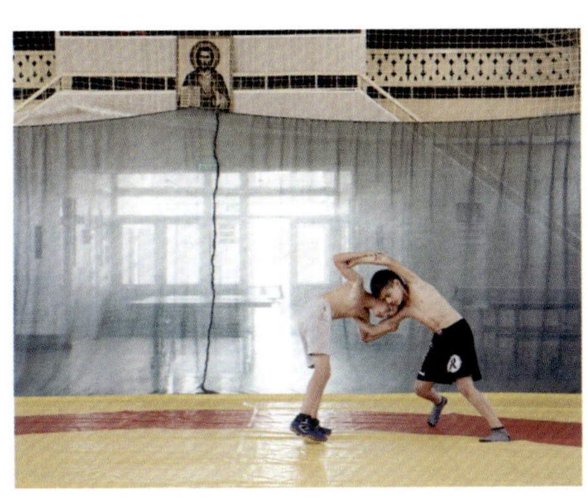

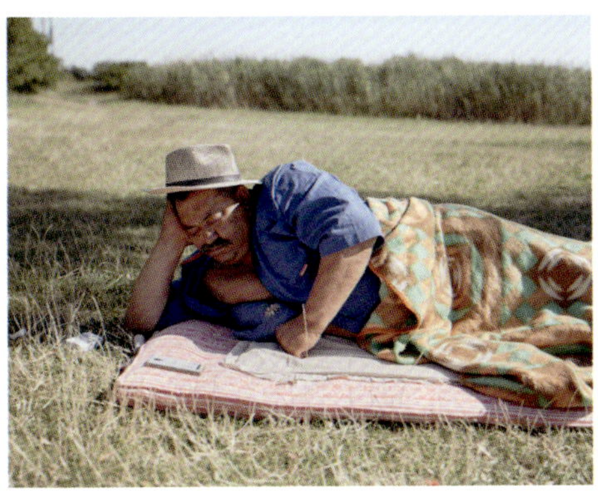

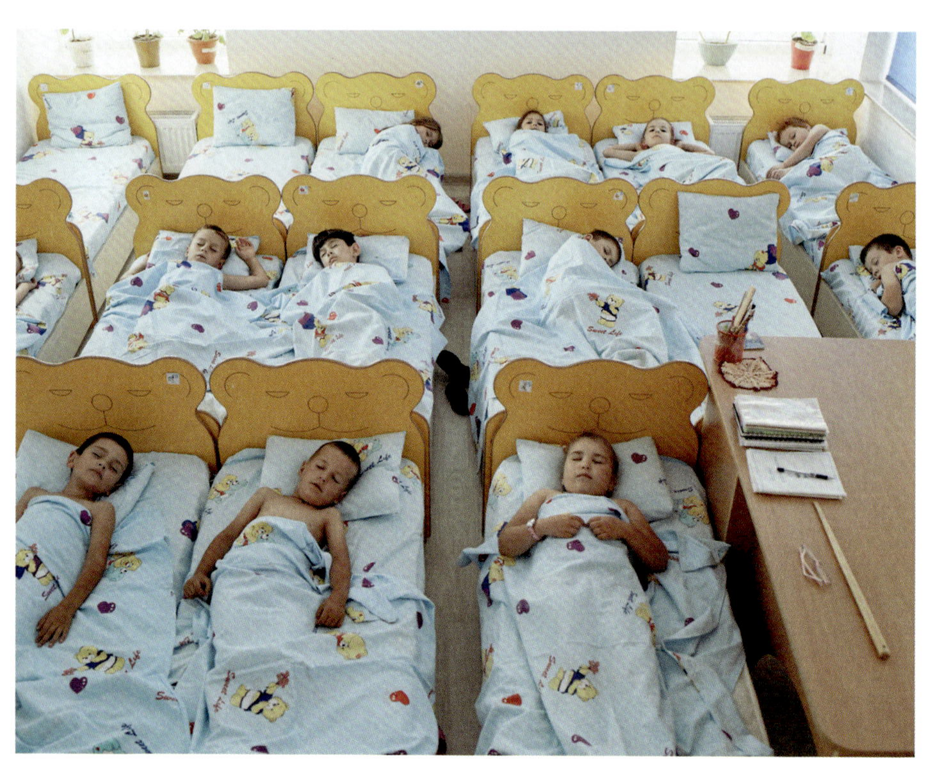

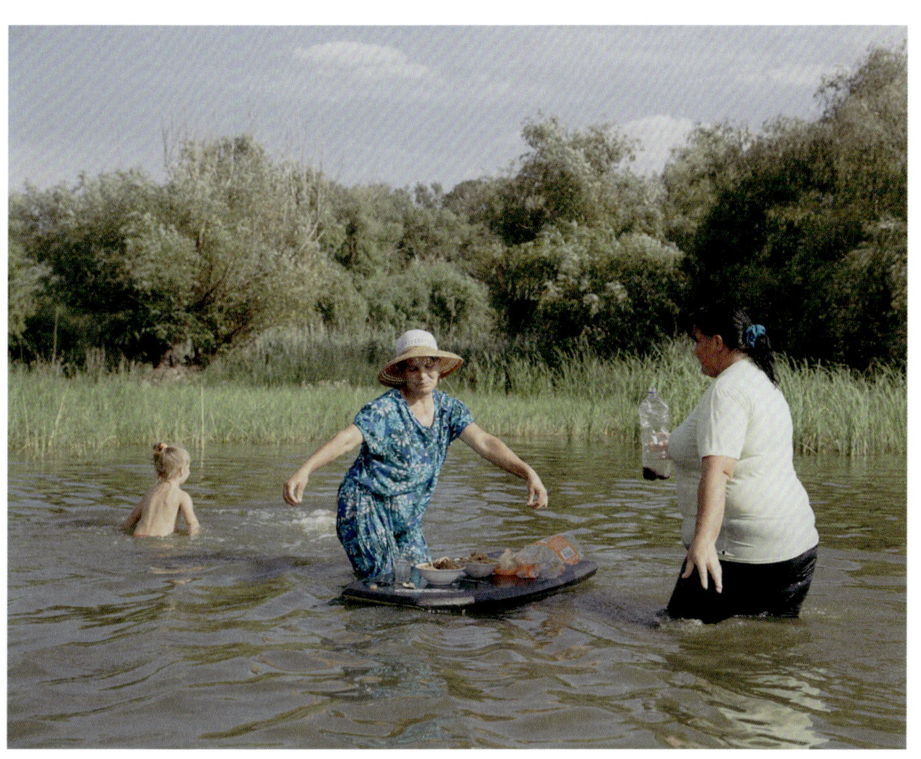

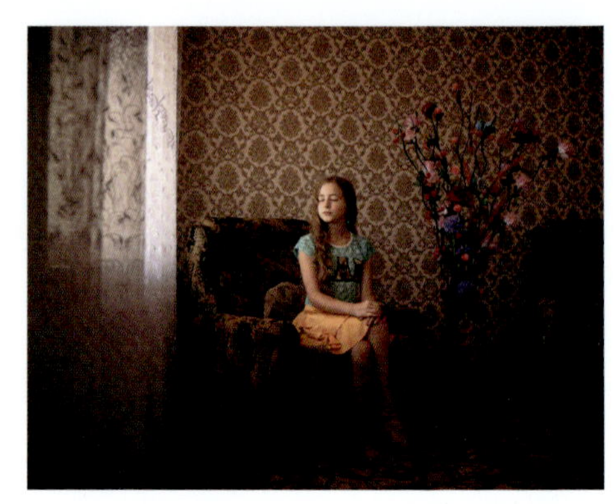

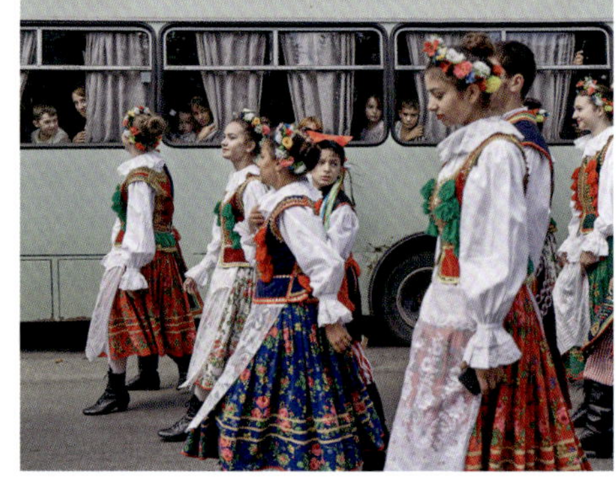

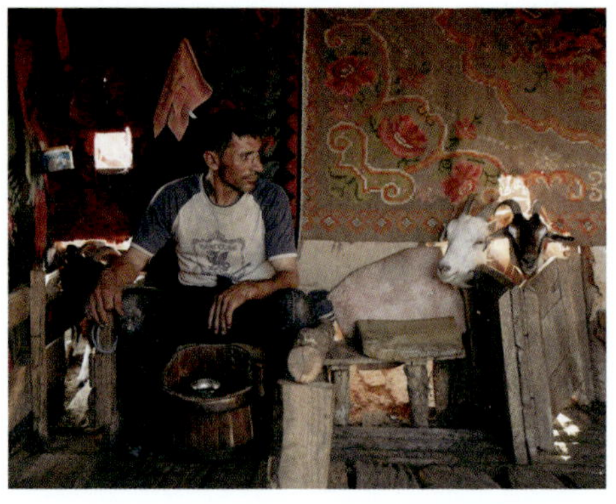

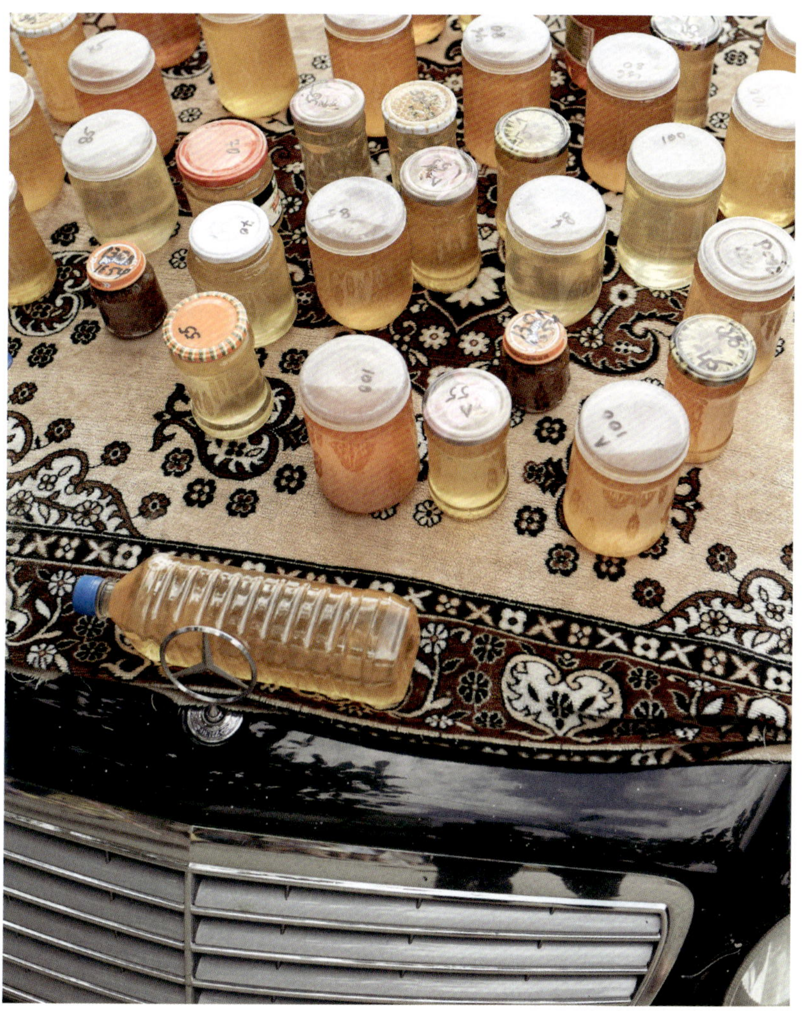

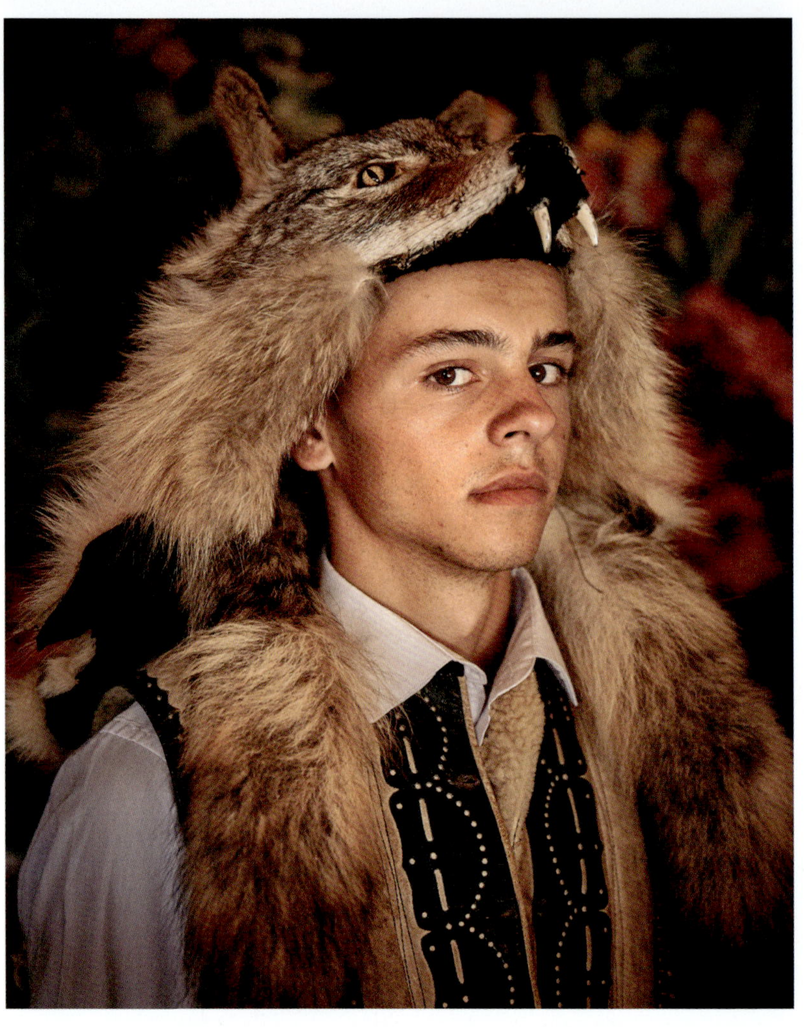

According to legend, a she-wolf discovered a little boy after a hostile raid, who had miraculously survived in the forest, and cared for him. This boy became the ancestor of the Gagauz, a minority of ethnic Turks with Christian Orthodox faith, that now live in a small autonomous region in the south of the Republic of Moldova. Today, as influence by the Moldavian capital increases and a growing number of young people leave home to find work abroad, they struggle with remaining their identity and keeping their traditions.

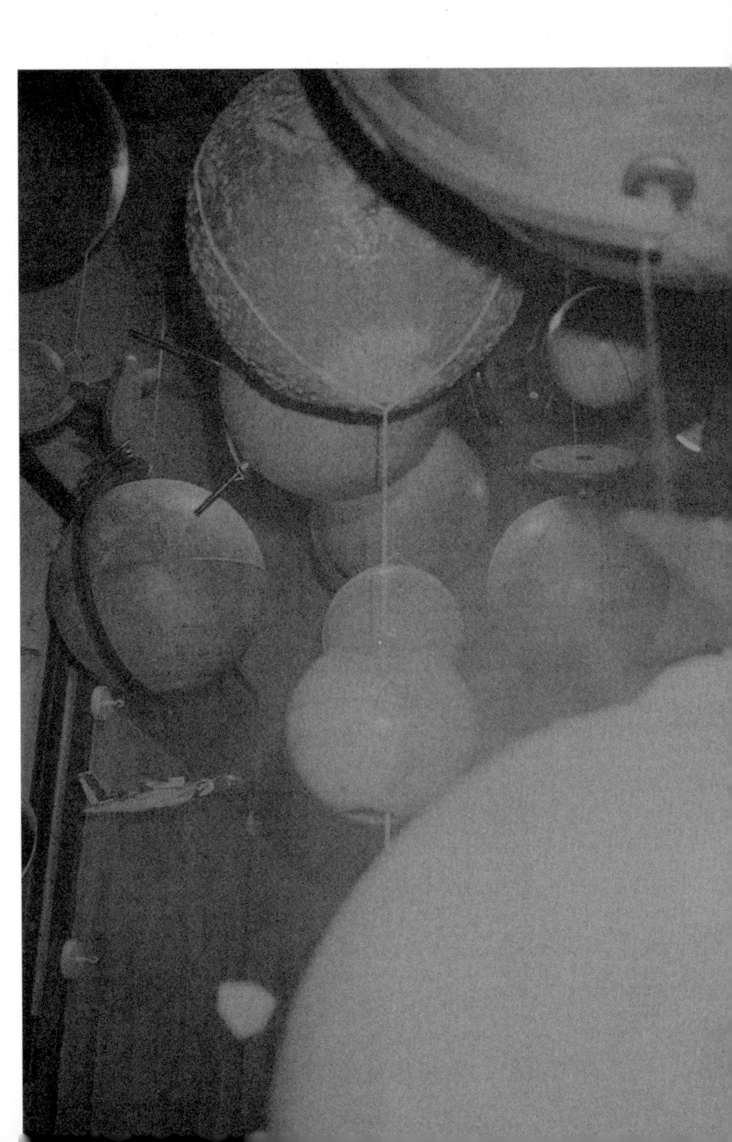

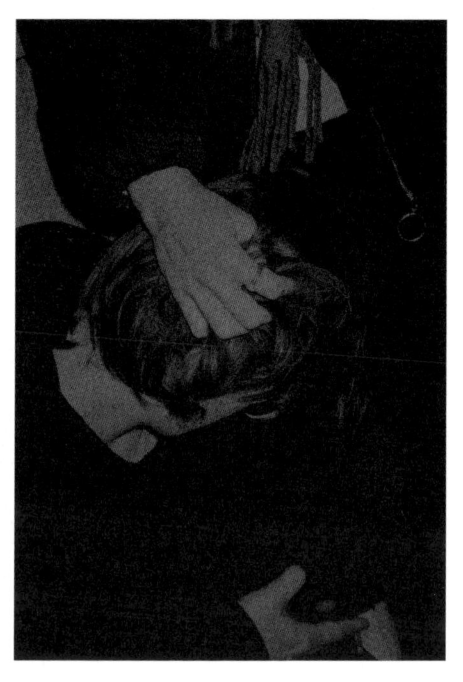

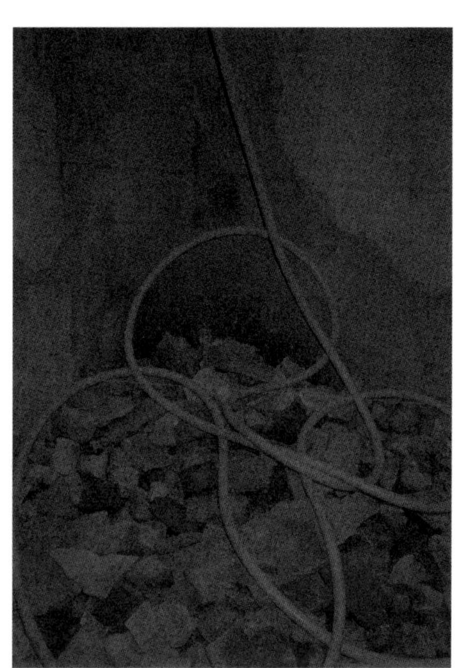

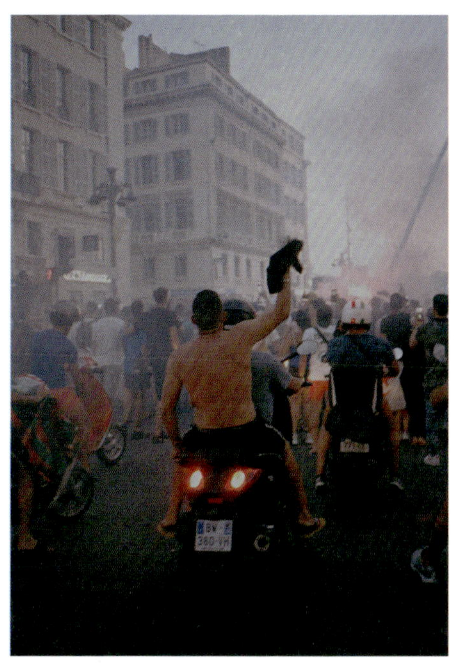

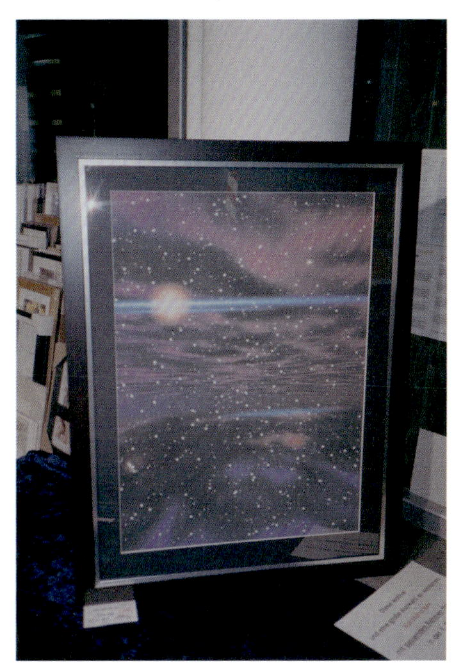

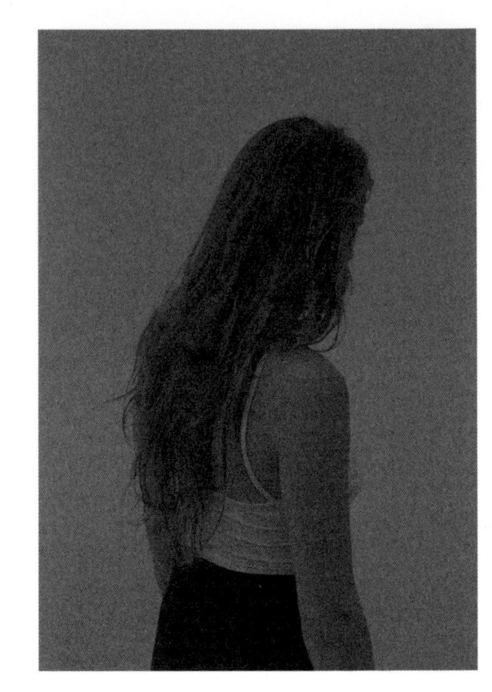

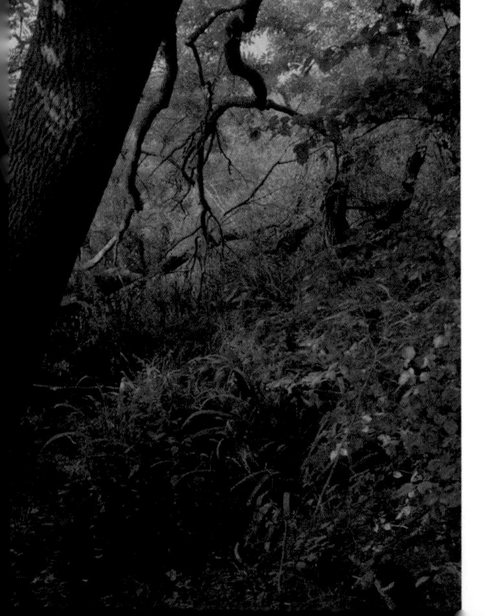

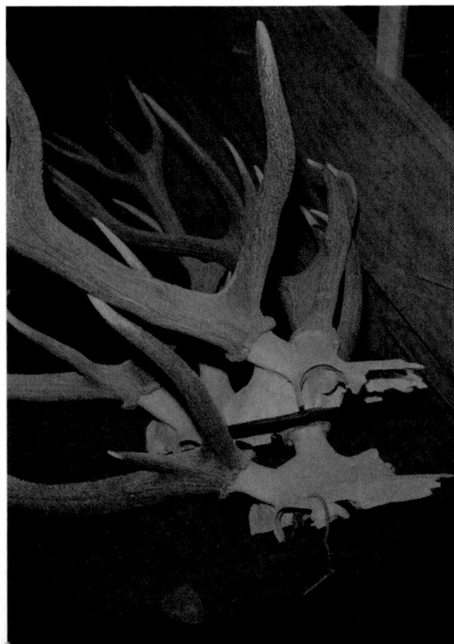

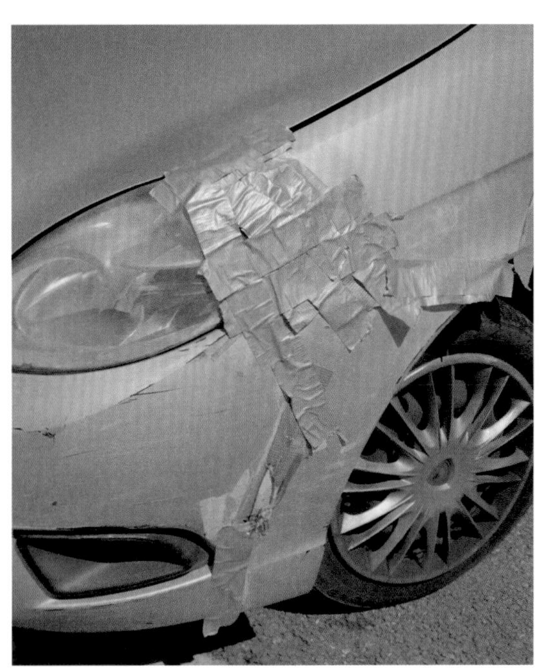

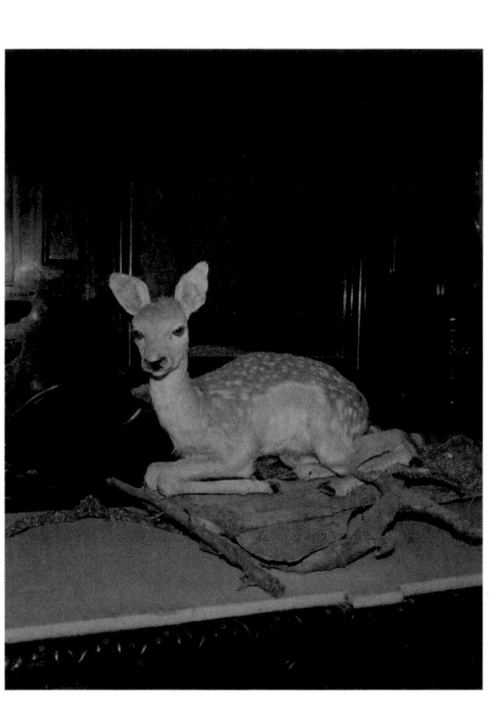

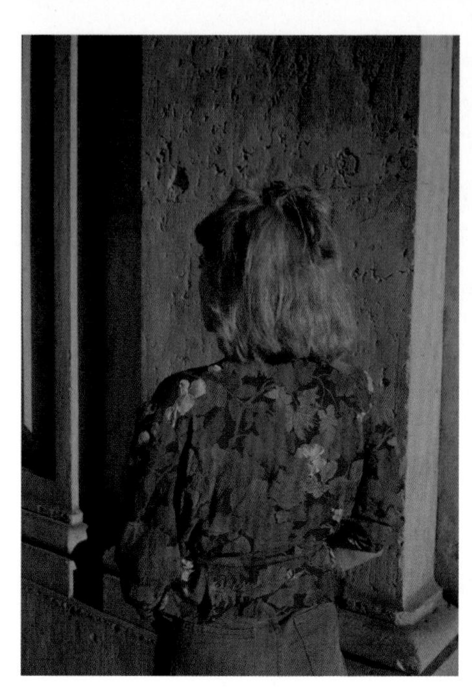

I was here the whole time. While I escape into a state of emotional floating, the feeling of Nostalgia crashes down upon me with an unpleasant force. This unattached, free sense of being alone, might never come back. Even though I am chasing longings that can't be caught and remembering memories that never existed, I know that I am home for now. Being so stuck in the present, and lost to the past, feels as if one is continuously stumbling and then catches oneself again, shortly before falling, only to continue stumbling again.

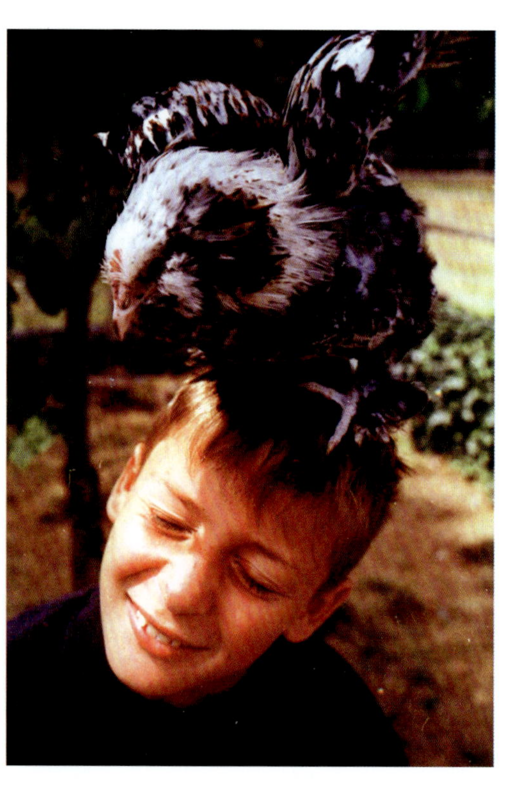

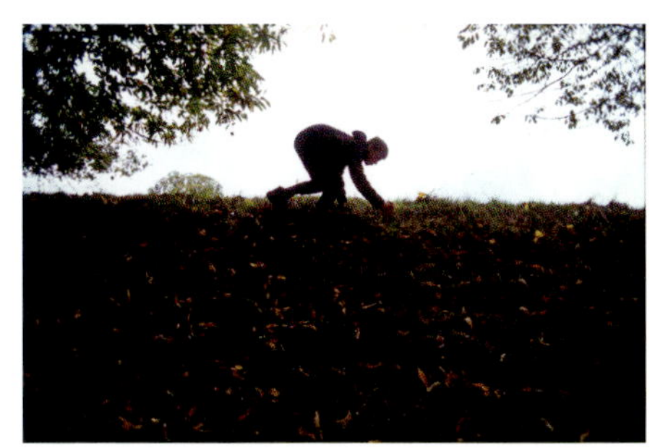

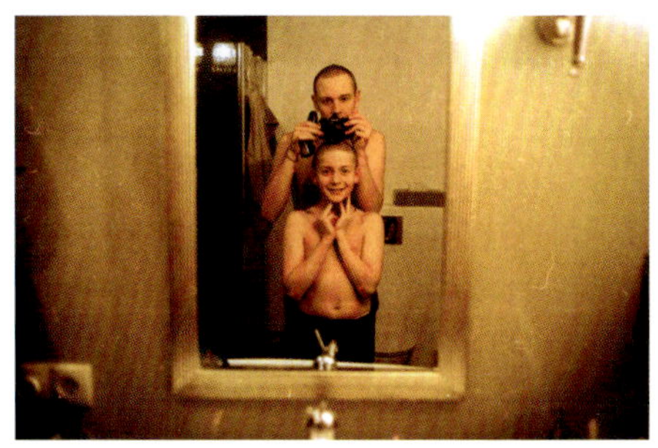

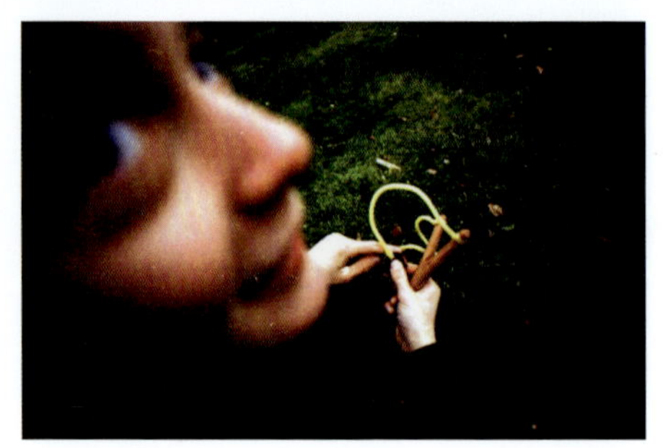

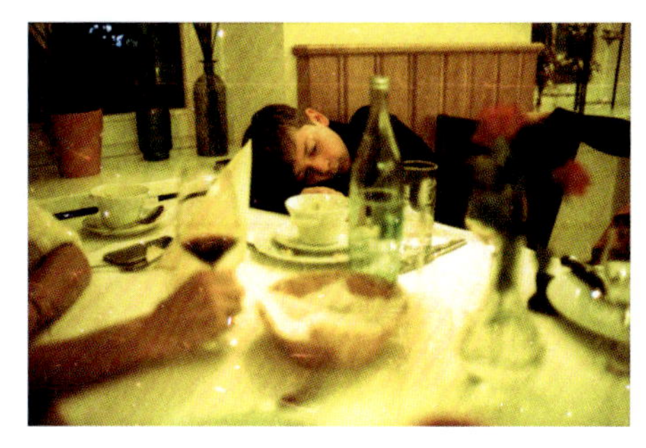

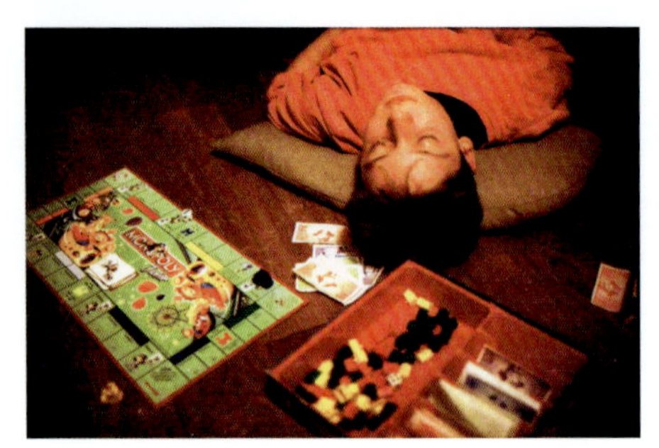

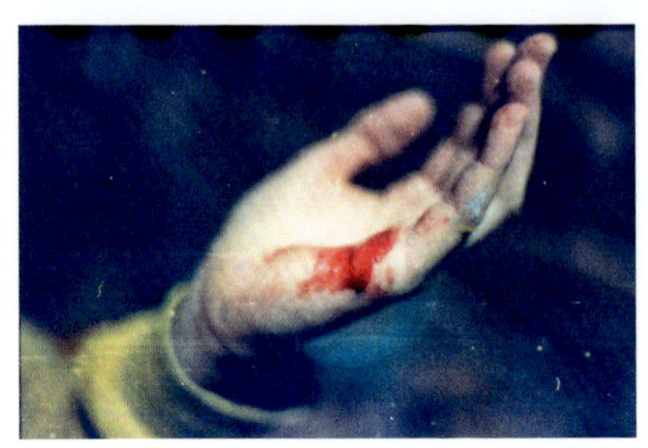

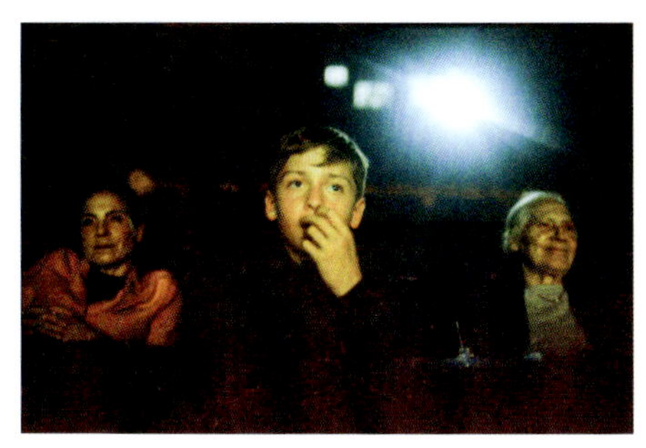

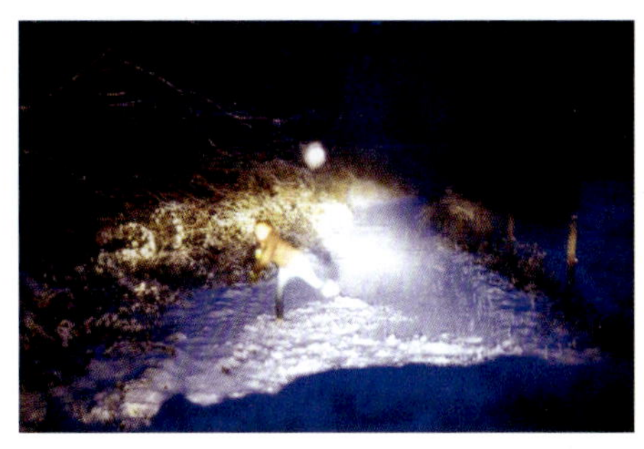

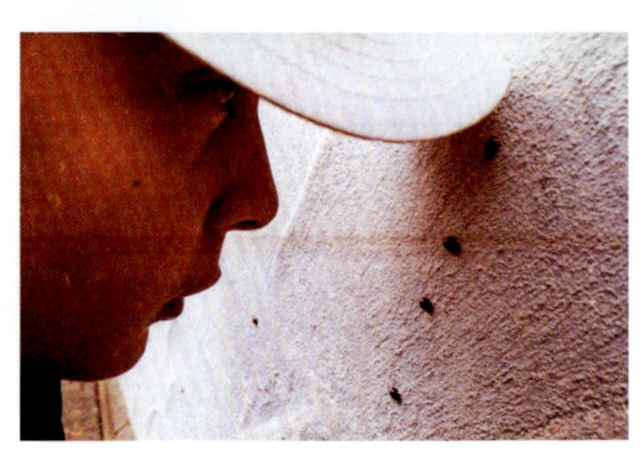

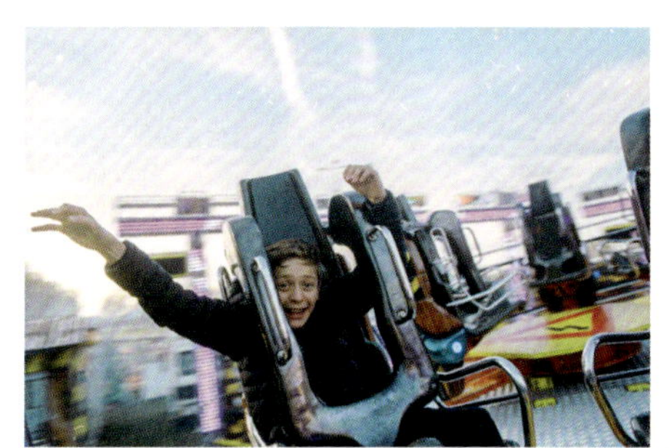

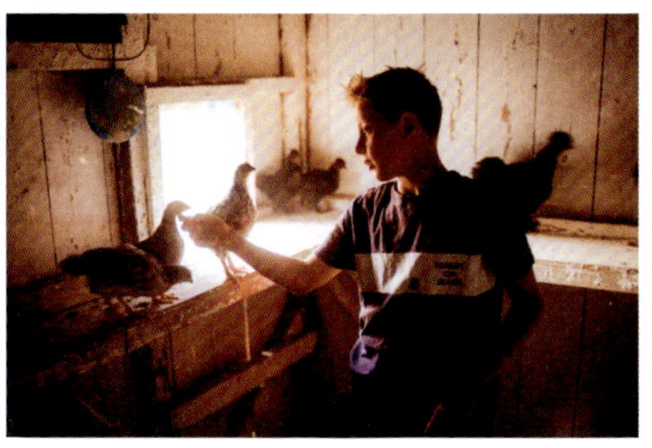

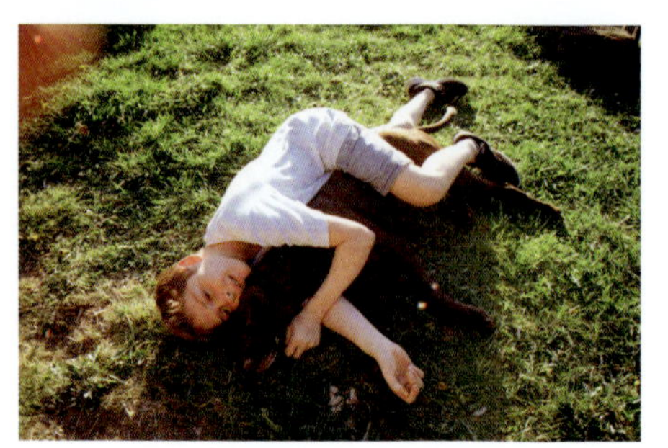

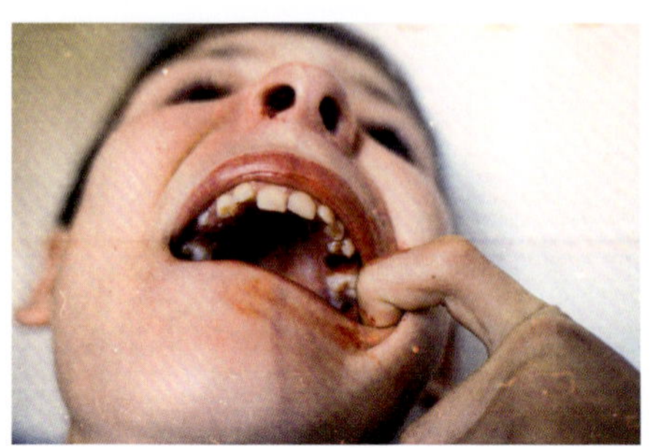

Räuber is a project about my younger brother Jascha. We are quite far apart in age, so I had already moved out when Jascha was still very young. As the project was unfolding I realized that it was simply a way of getting to know each other whilst reminiscing on my own child-hood.

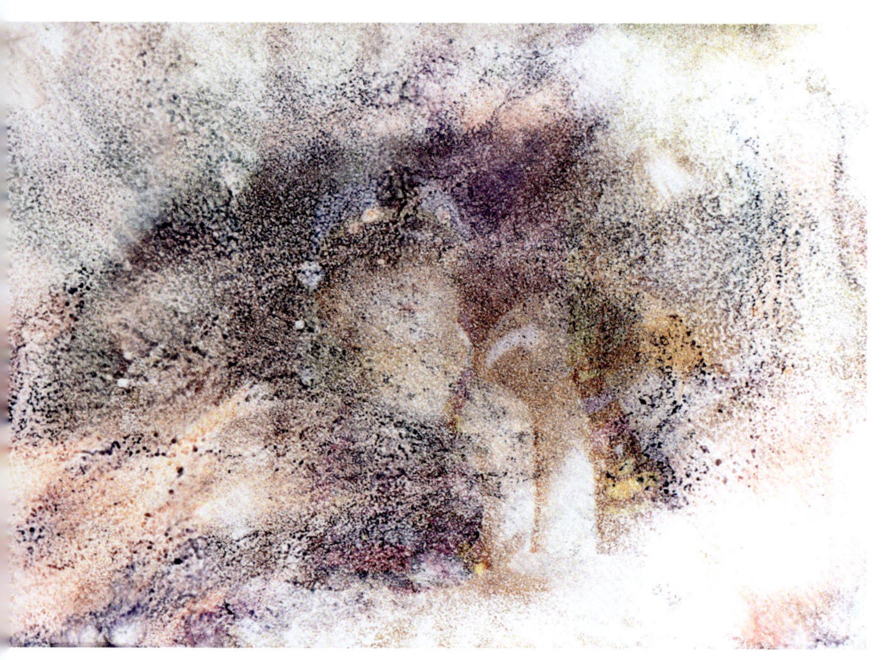

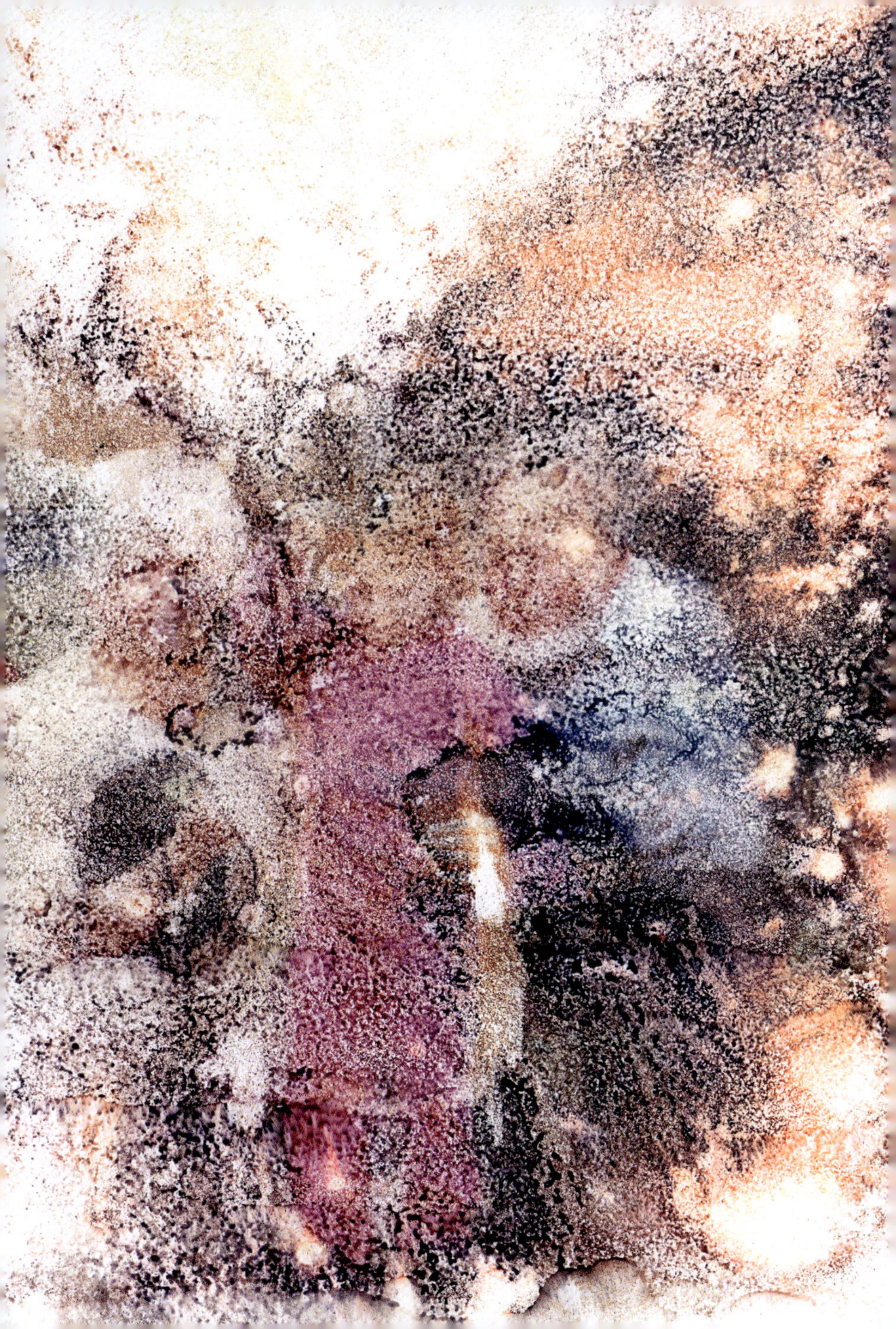

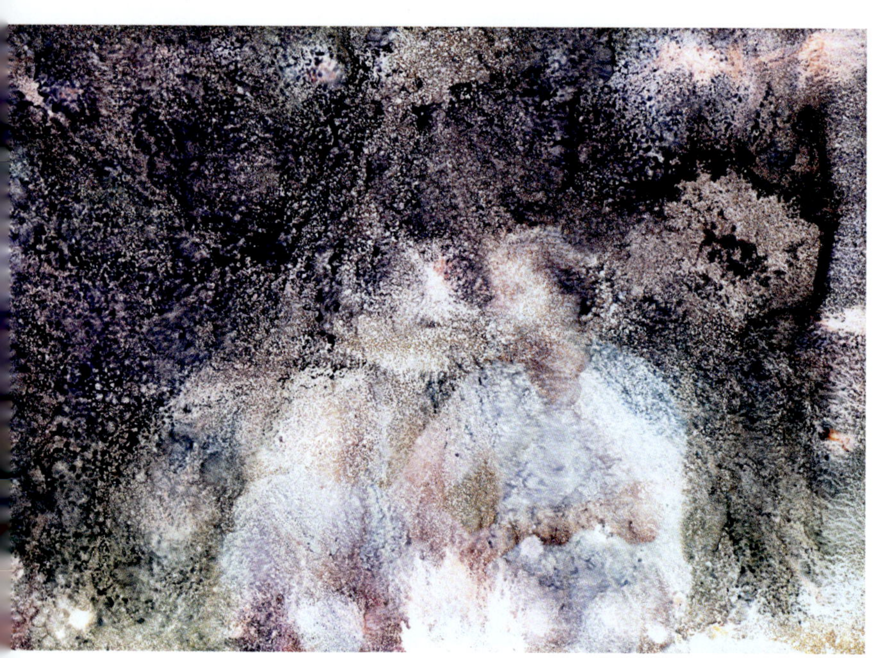

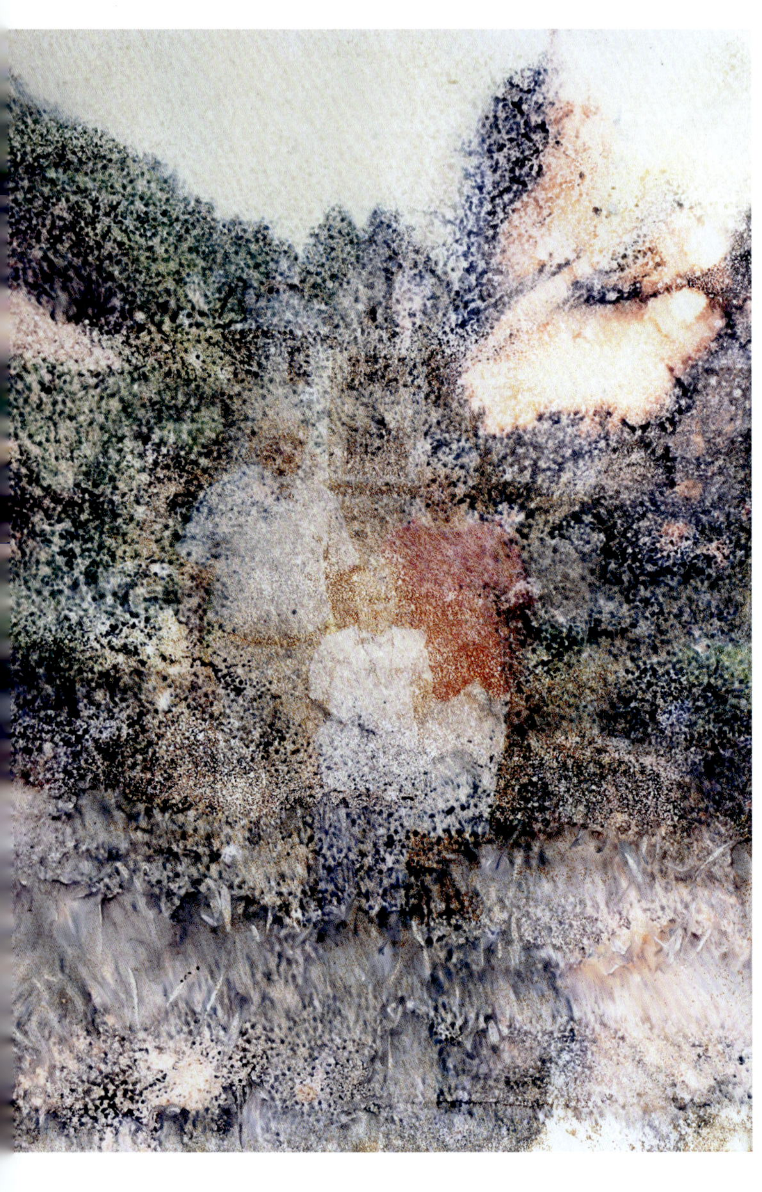

Photography can be seen as an externalisation of memory. But prints on paper, pixels and hard-drives can be just as vulnerable as our mind. Here too, people, places and events can fade. We often subconsciously resort to making up our own fictionalized pasts if parts of our memory fade, mixing our own realities with that of movies we've seen or stories we've heard. Johanna aims at visualizing this loss of memory and shows us the ghosts that live in every mind.

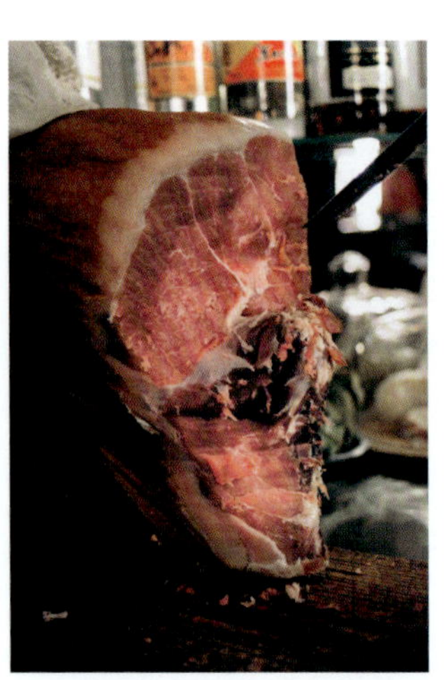

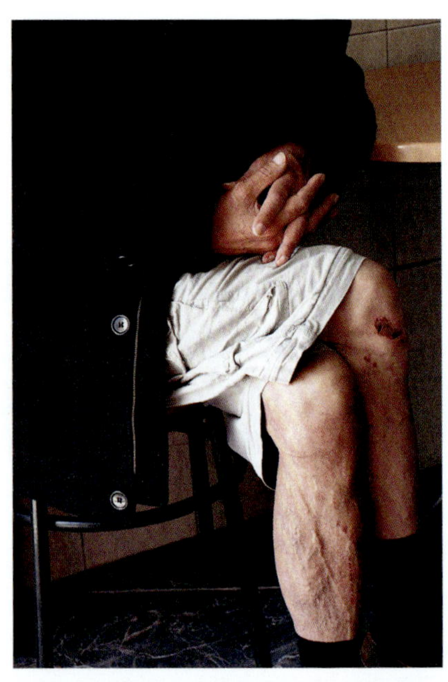

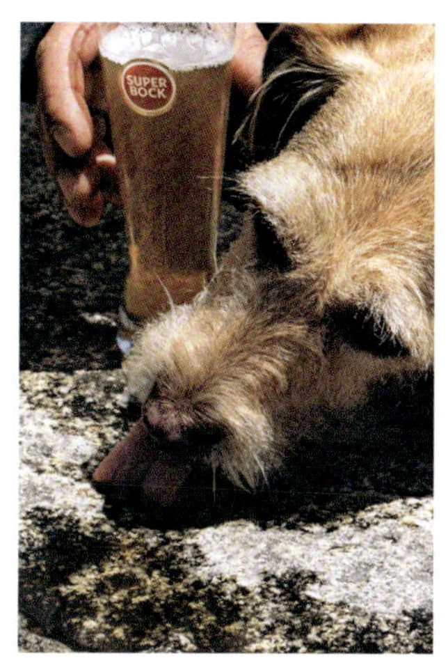
SUPER
BOCK

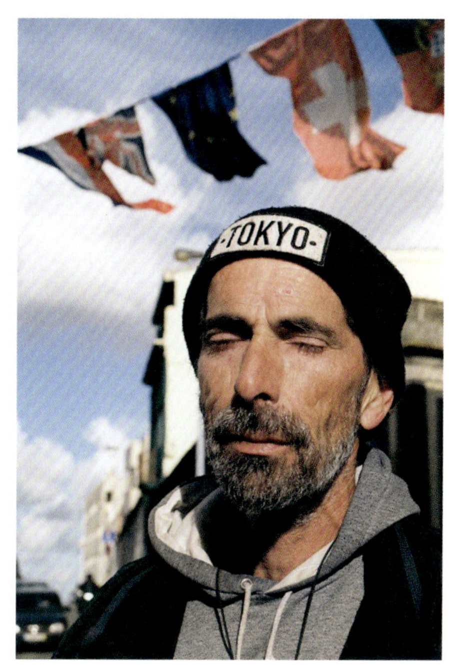
·TOKYO·

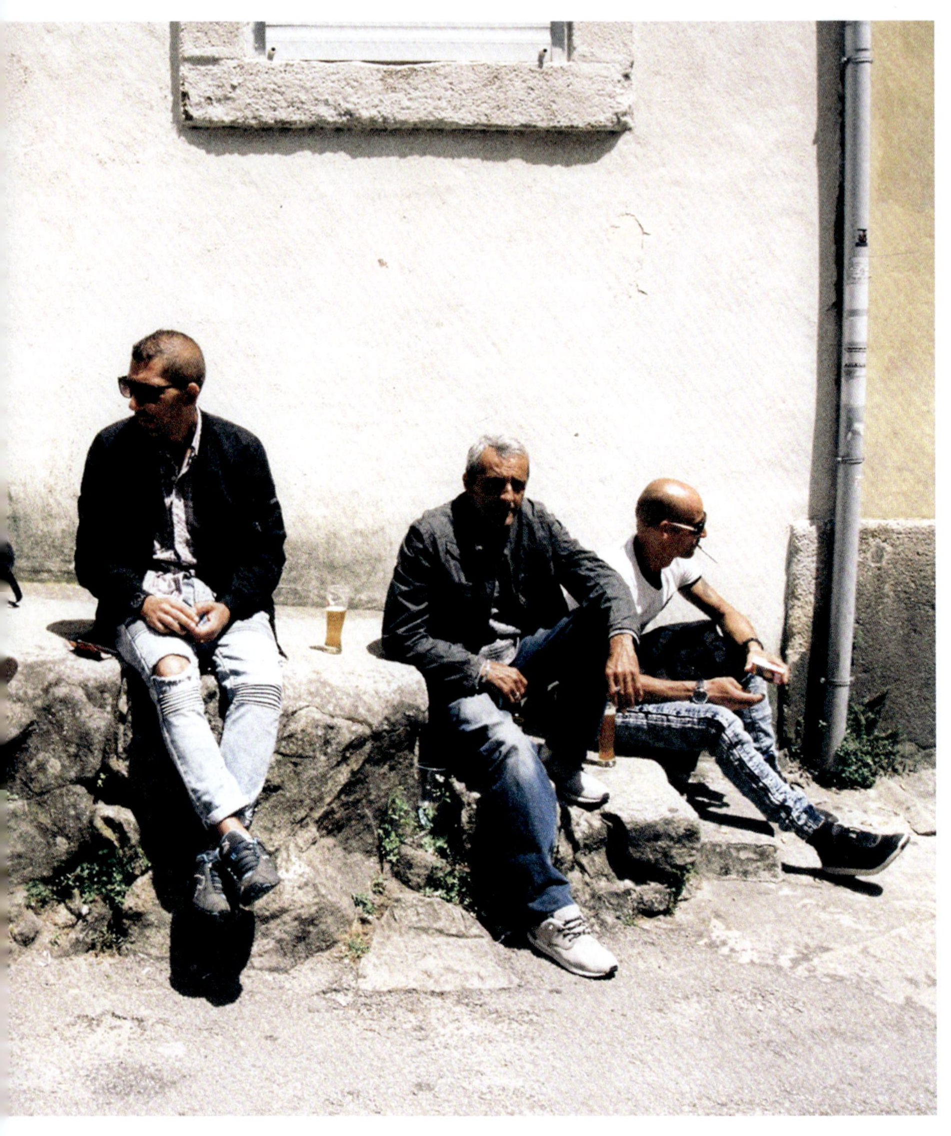

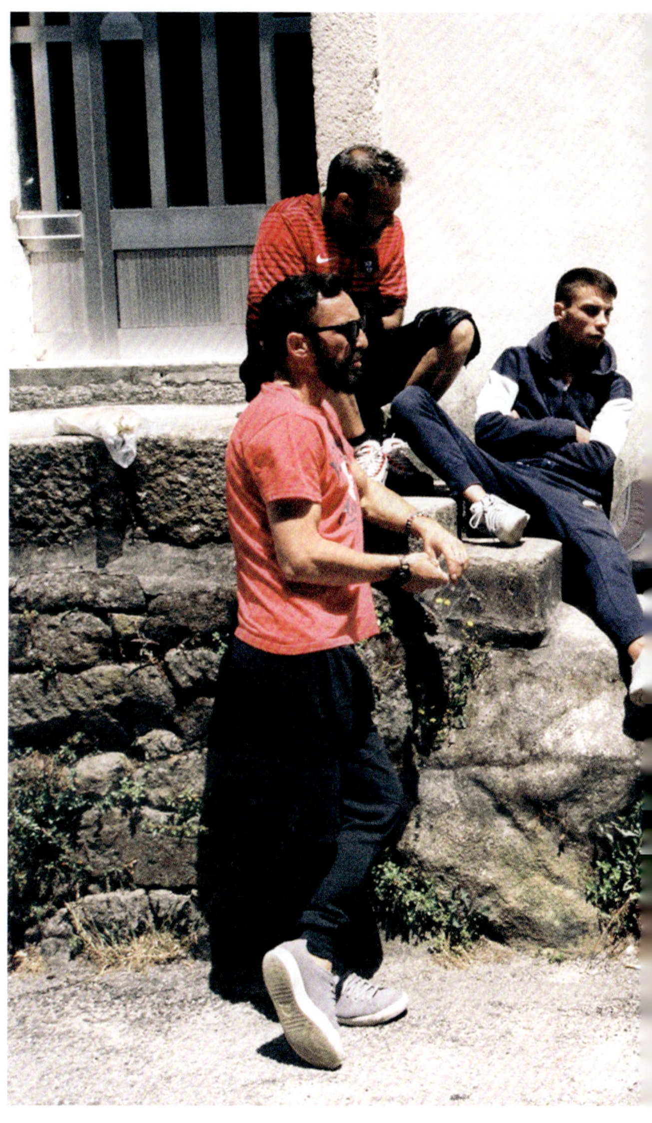

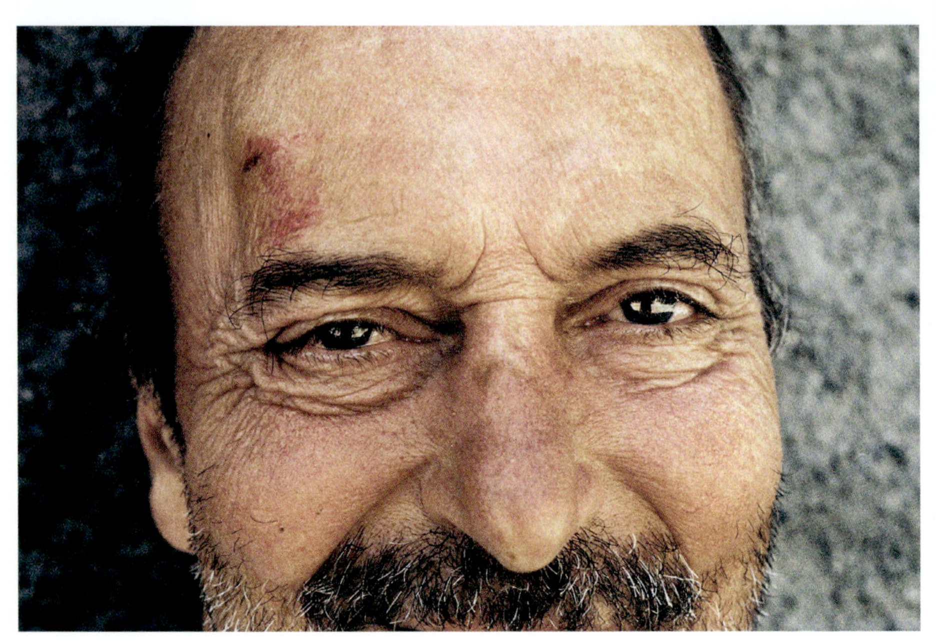

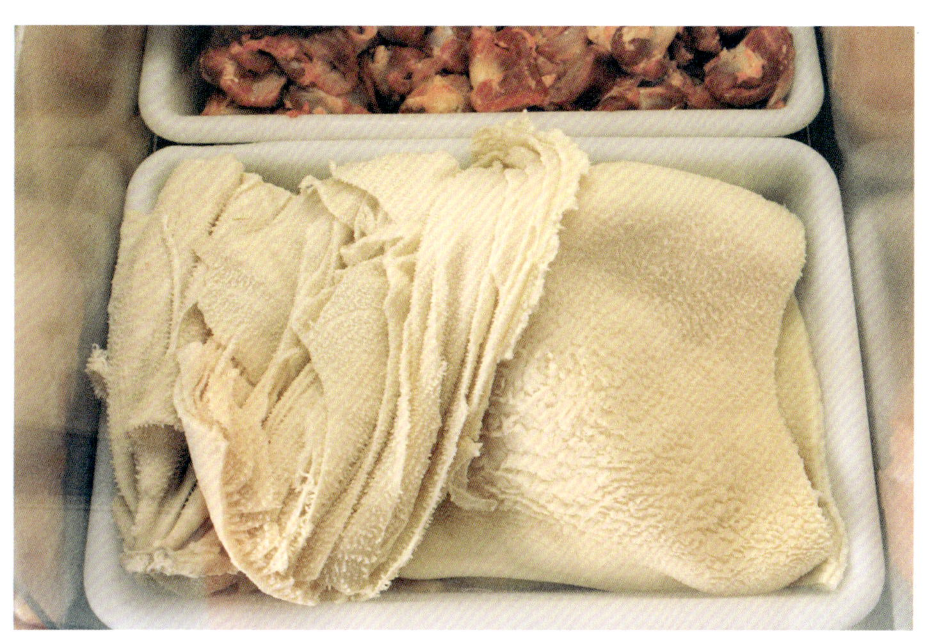

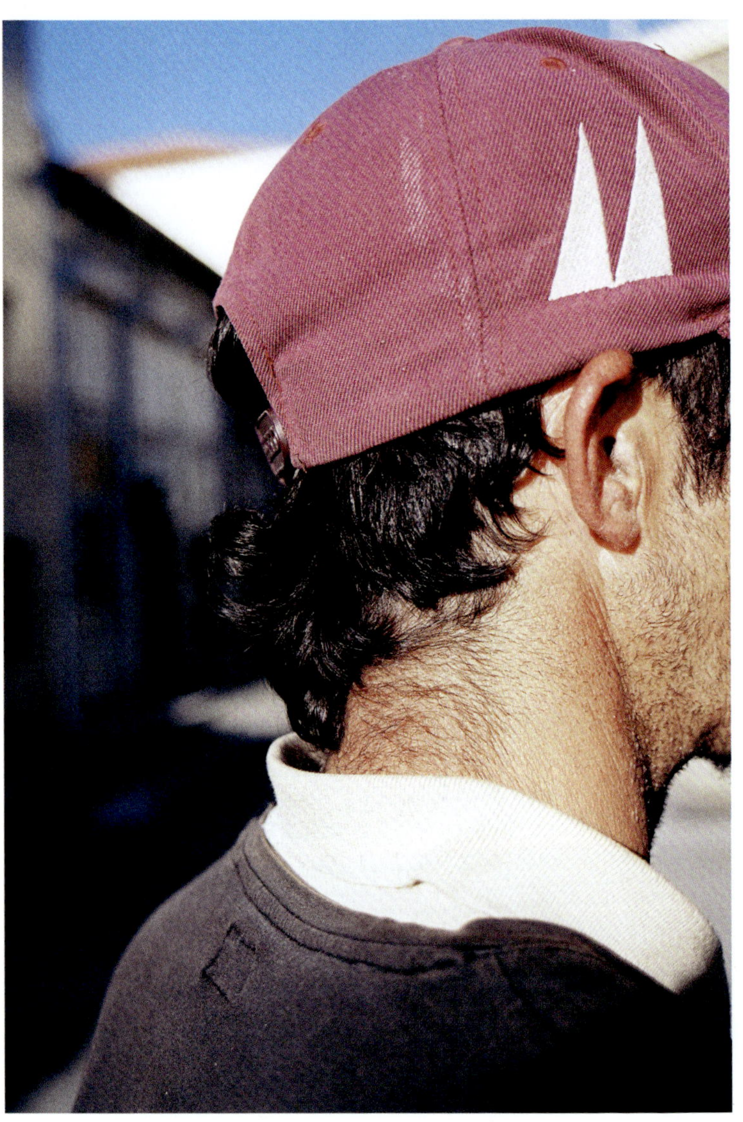

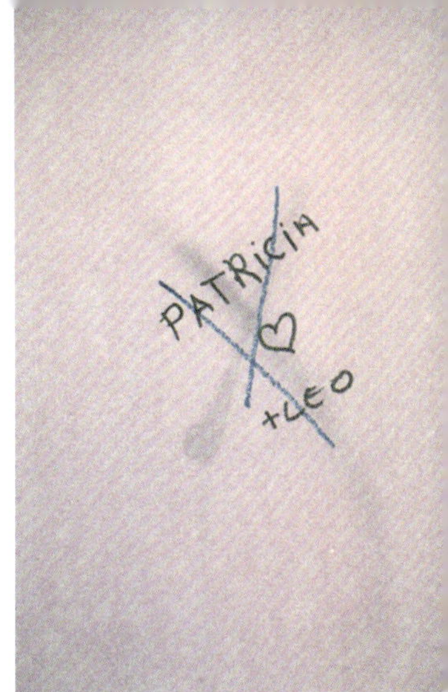
PATRICIA
+LEO

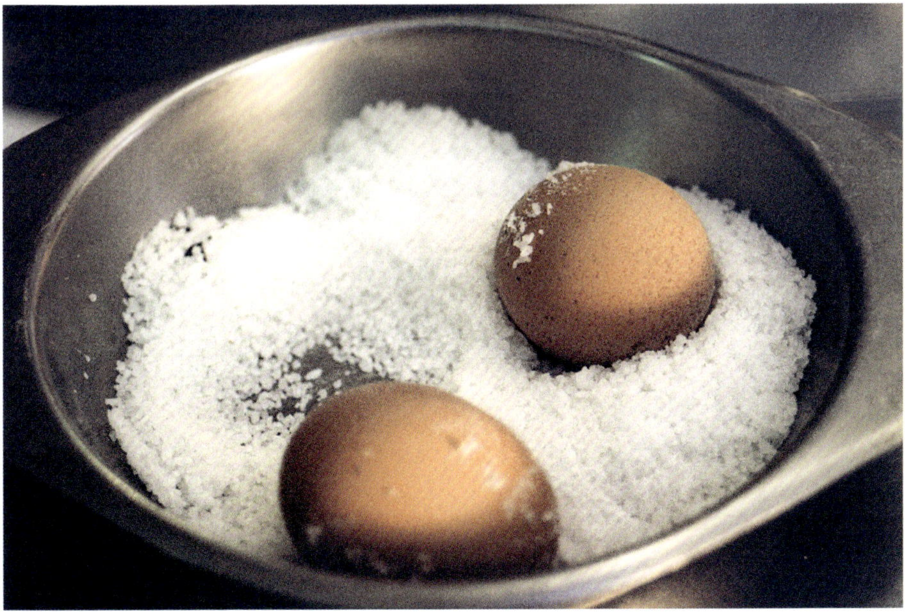

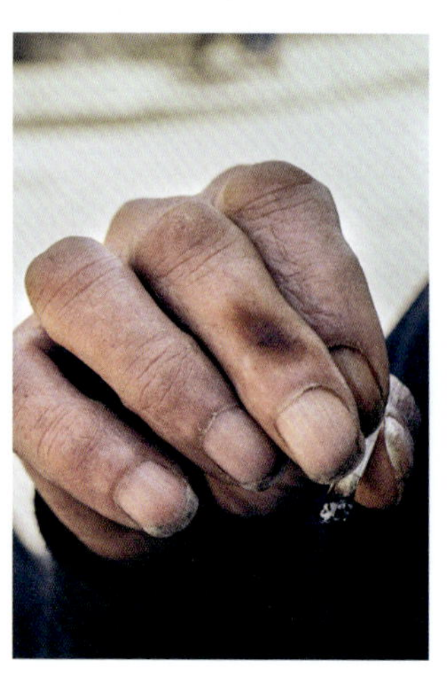

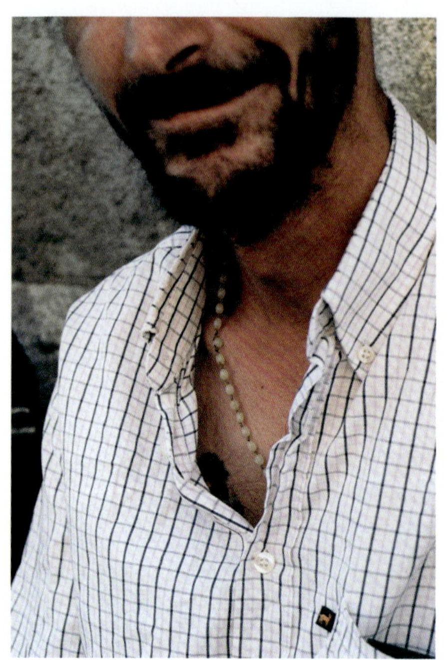

The male universe in the city of Porto is representative of traditional and conservative values still very present in Portuguese culture. Wandering through its streets and bars and squares, you pass by words, characters and things that build up layers of raw reality and beautiful banality. As affection and familiarity started to develop, what was intended to portray a preconceived idea of masculinity developed into a more delicate approach that takes shape through contrast, ambiguity, and minimalist images.

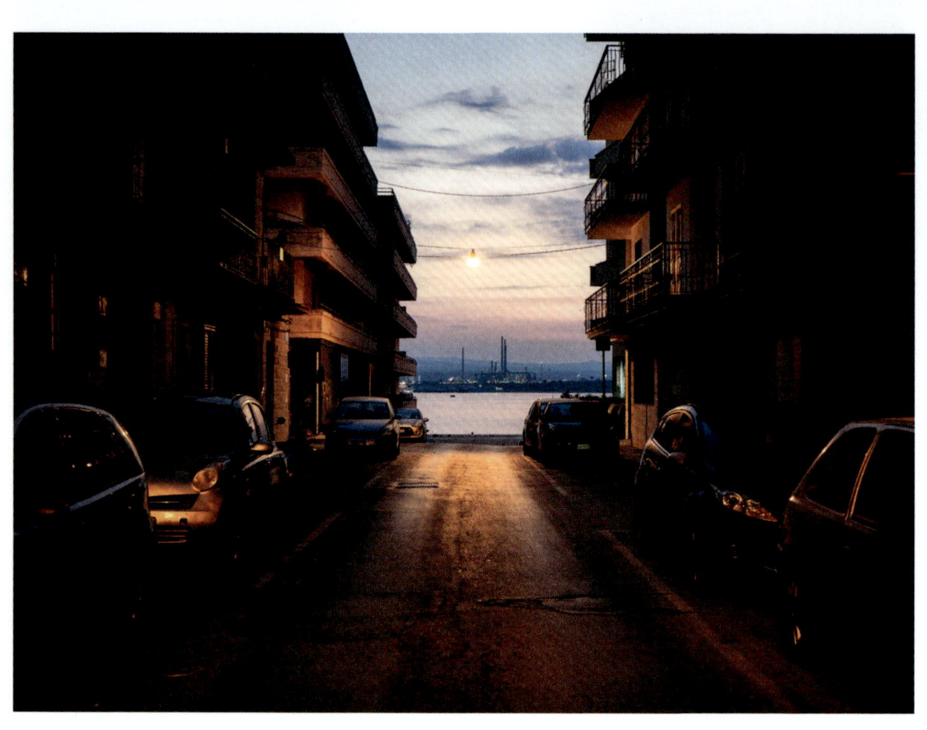

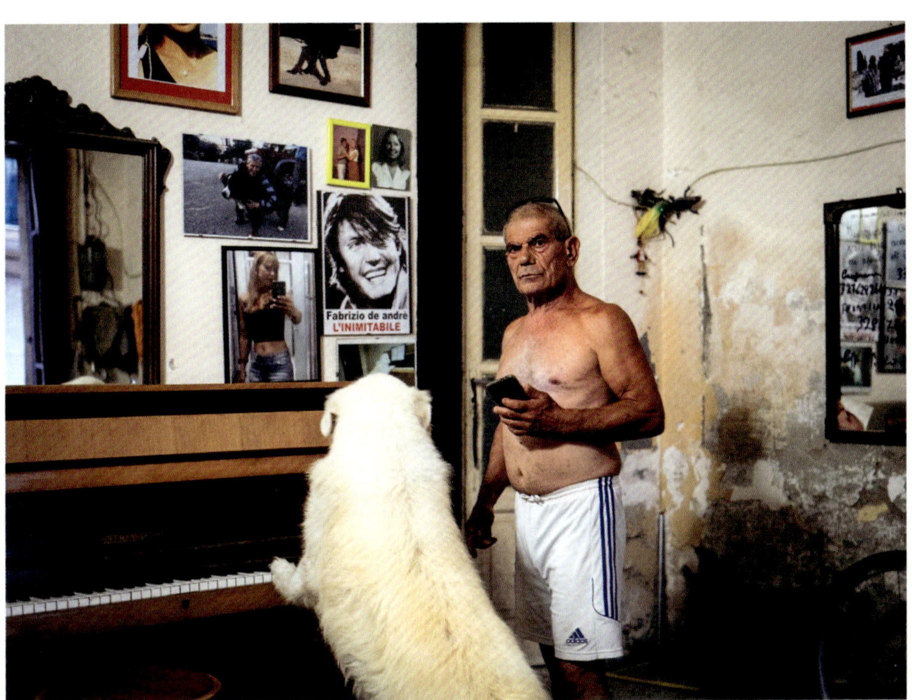
Fabrizio de andre
L'INIMITABILE
adidas

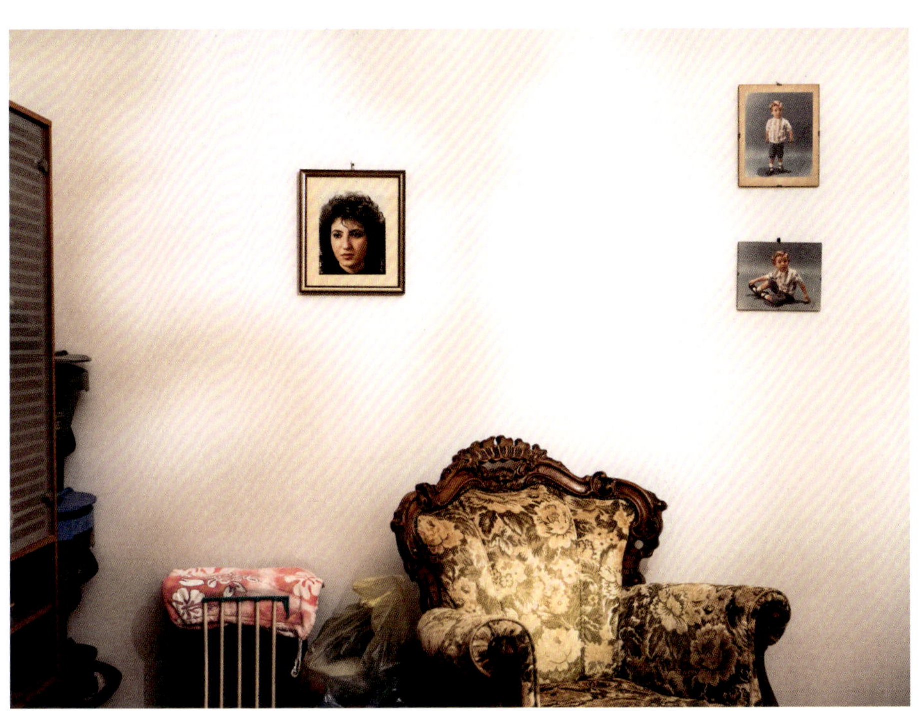

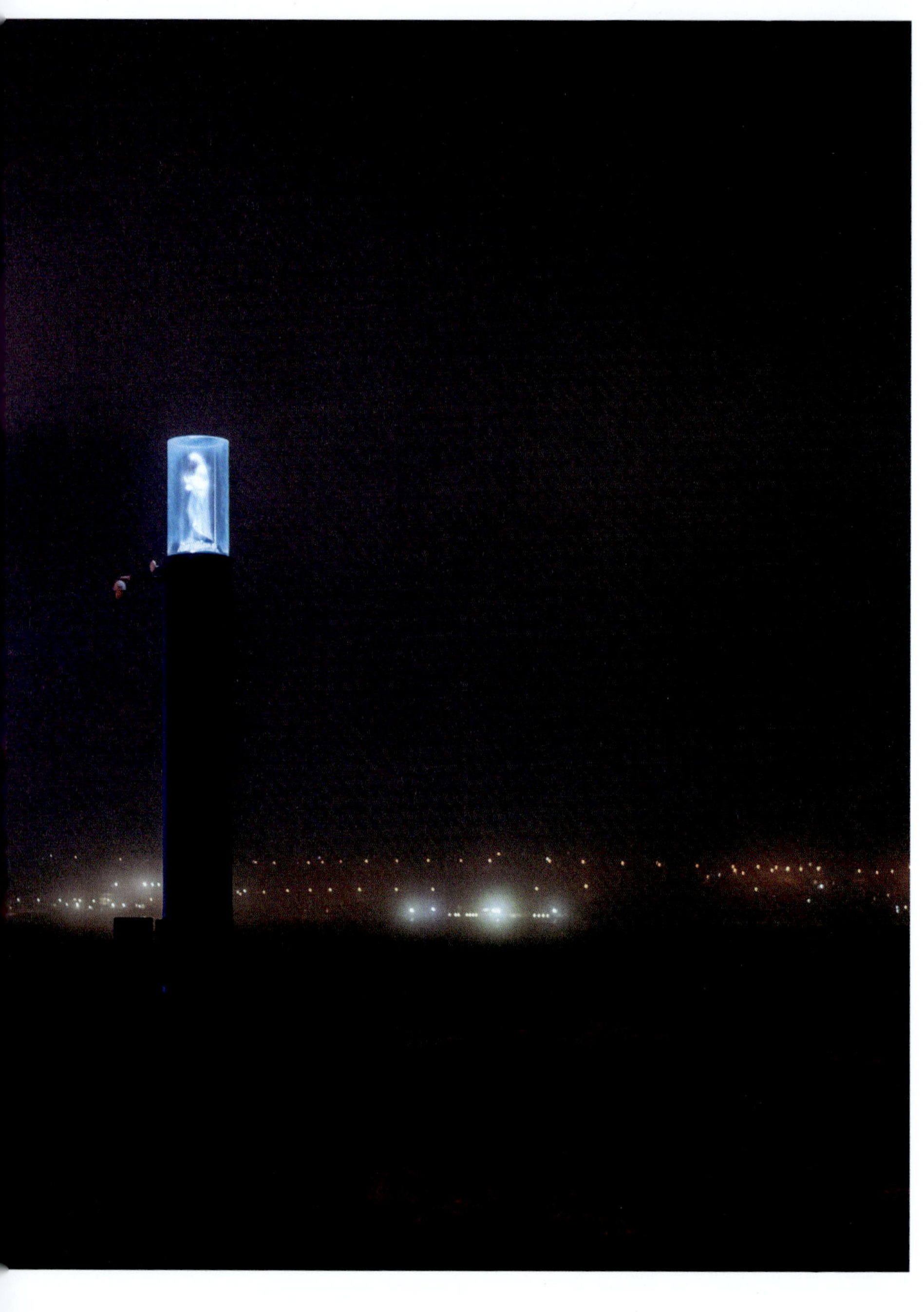

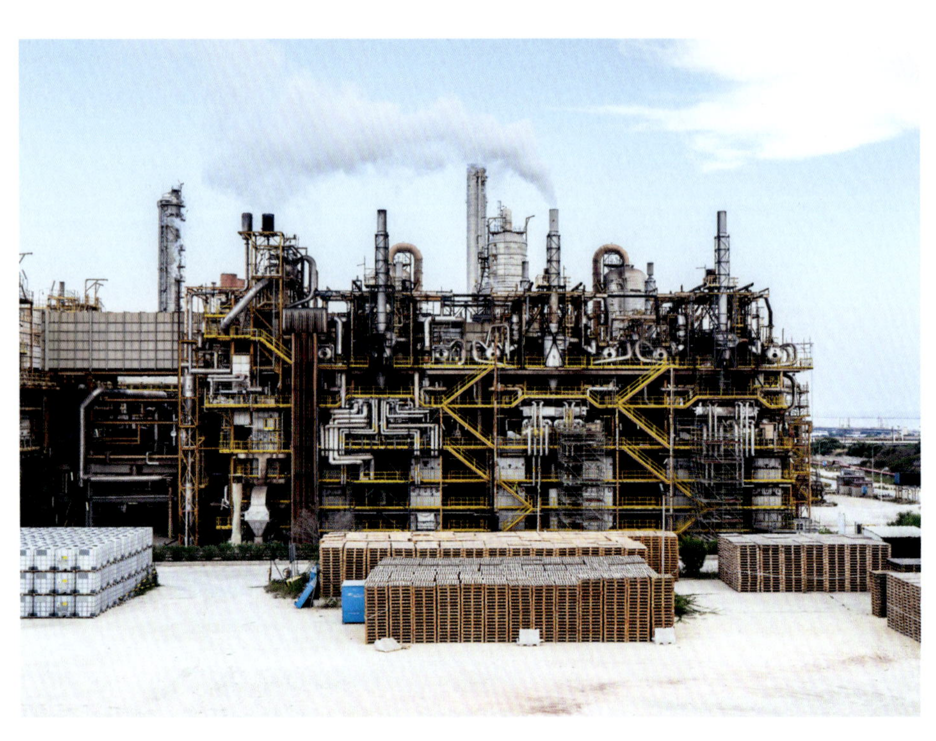

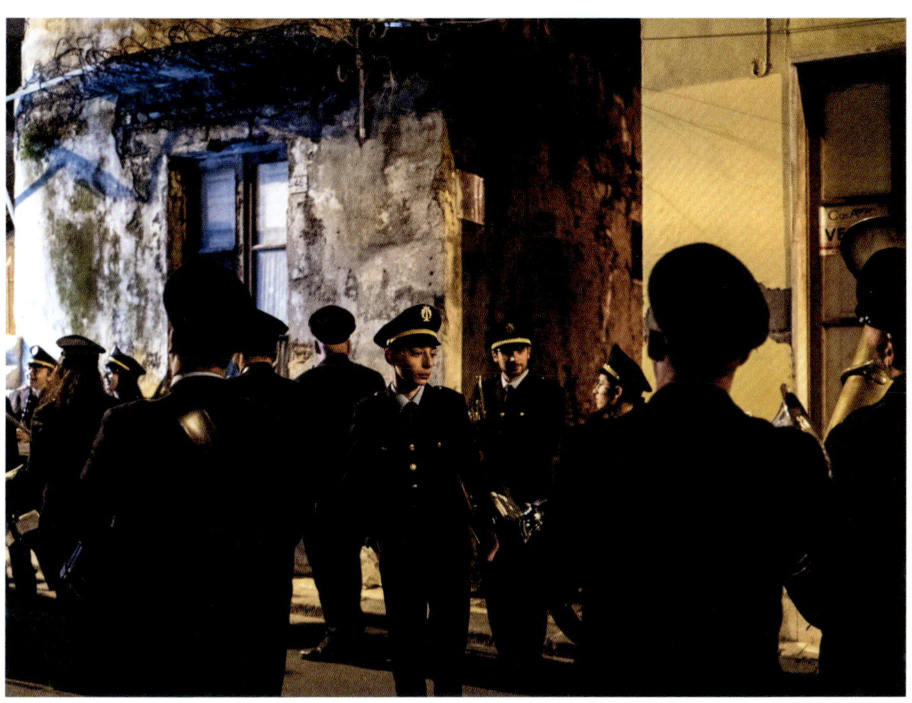

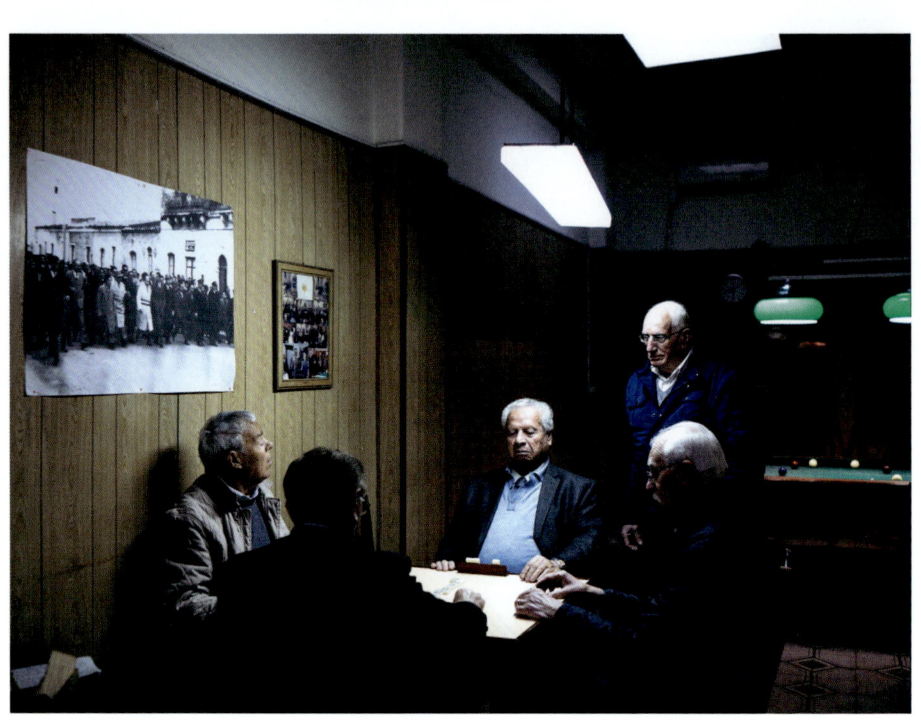

One oil refinery after another is lined up on the Bay of Augusta, a thirty-kilometer-long coastal strip in south-eastern Sicily. The water, air, and soil are polluted. Rates of cancer and miscarriages are alarmingly high. Instead of twenty thousand jobs, as there were at the peak of the oil processing industry in the 1980s, there are now only seven thousand. Corruption is as omnipresent as the distrust of authority.

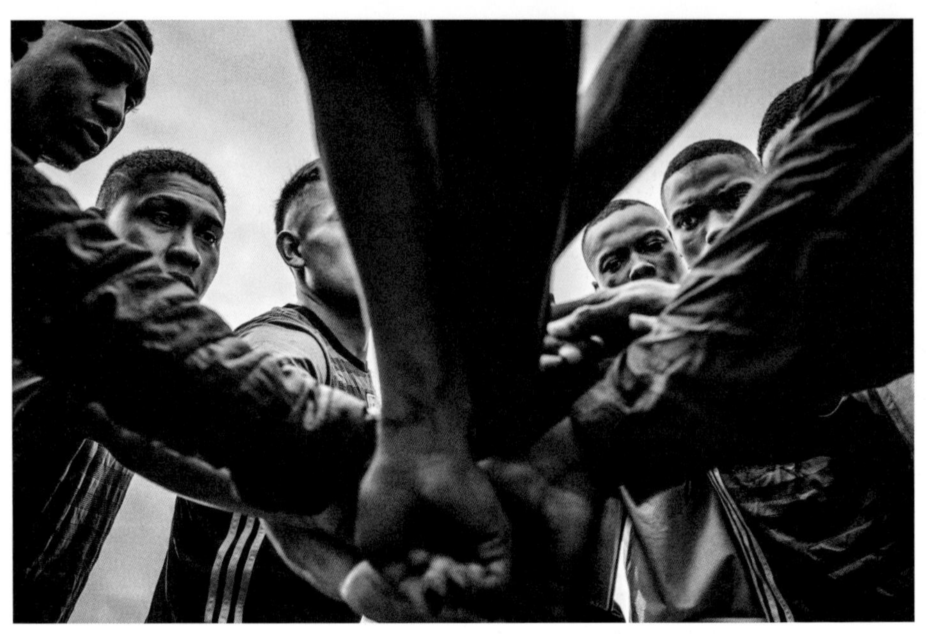

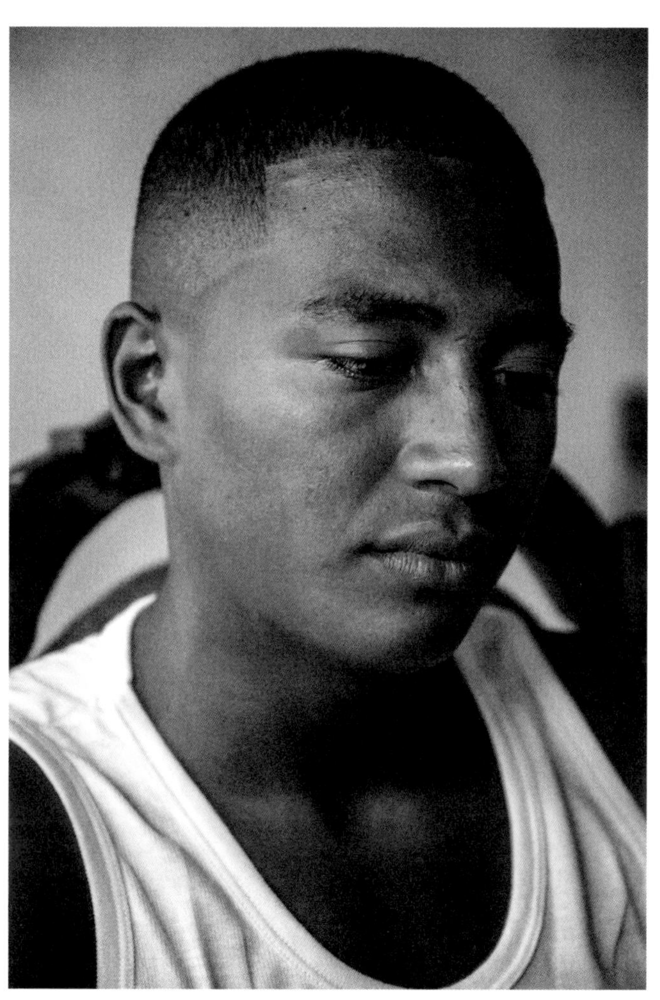

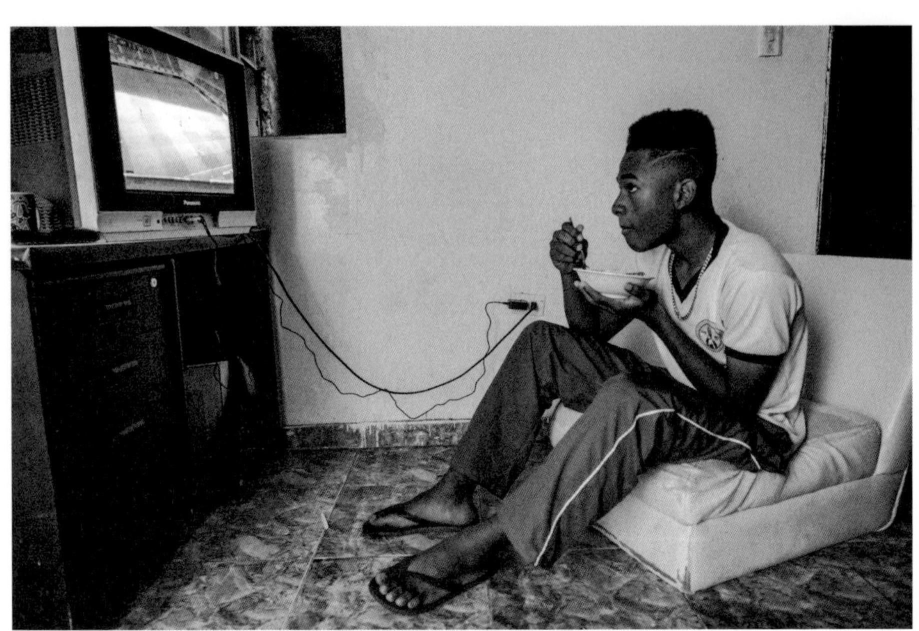

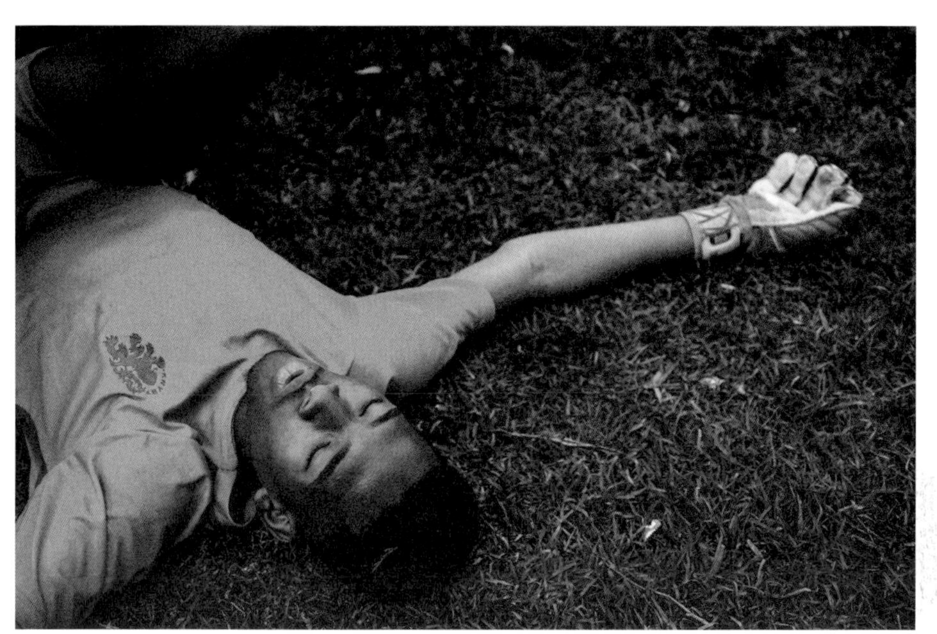

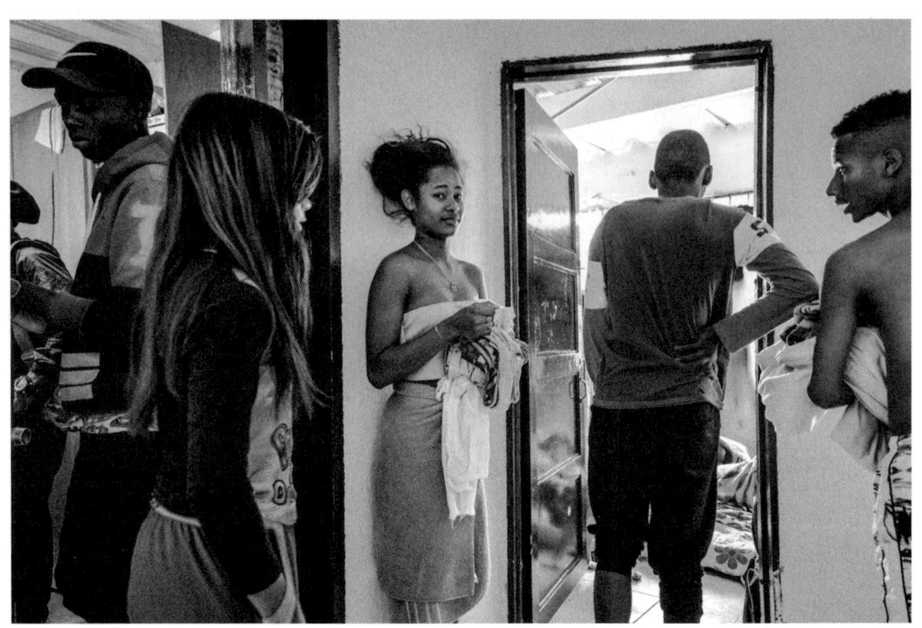

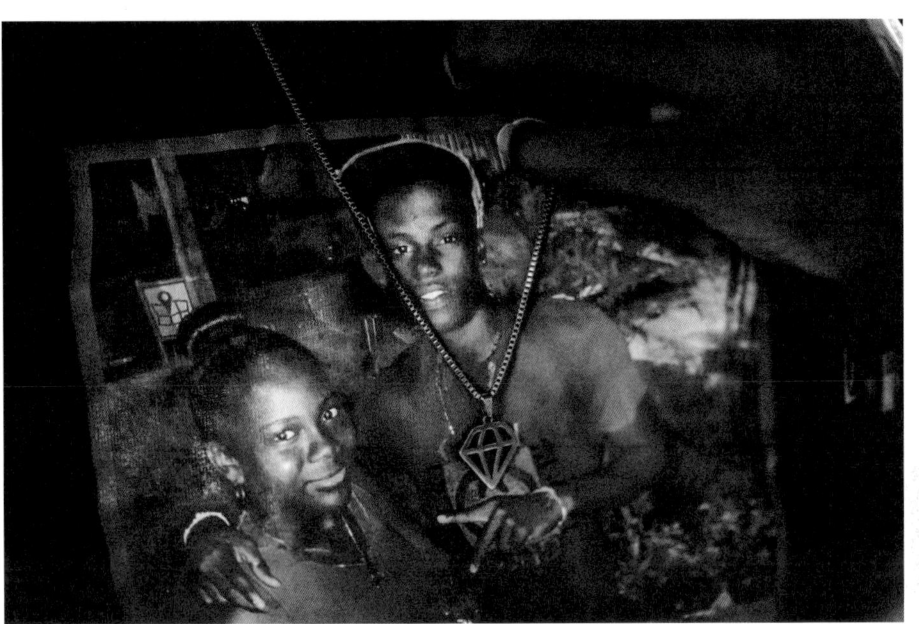

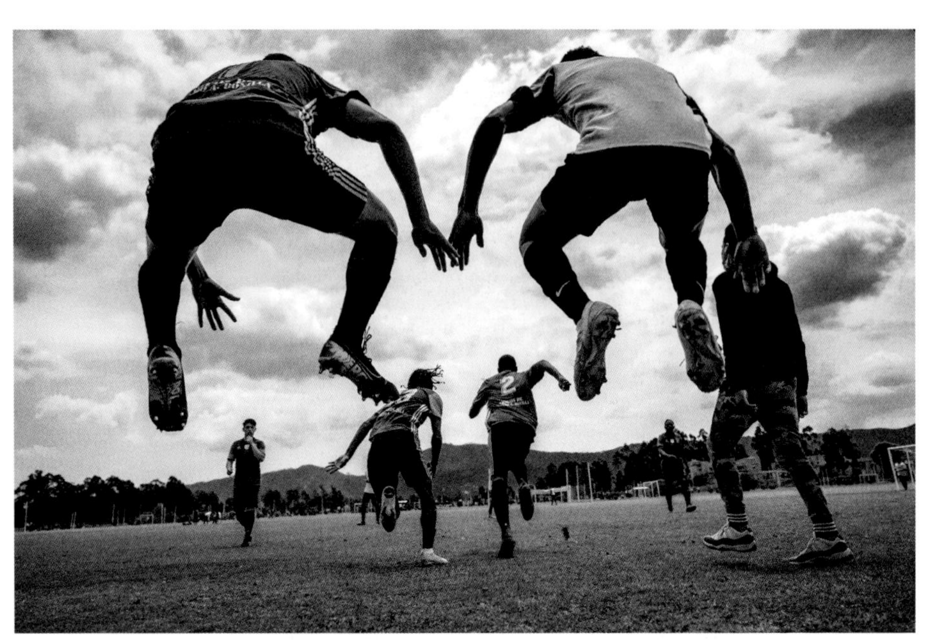
2

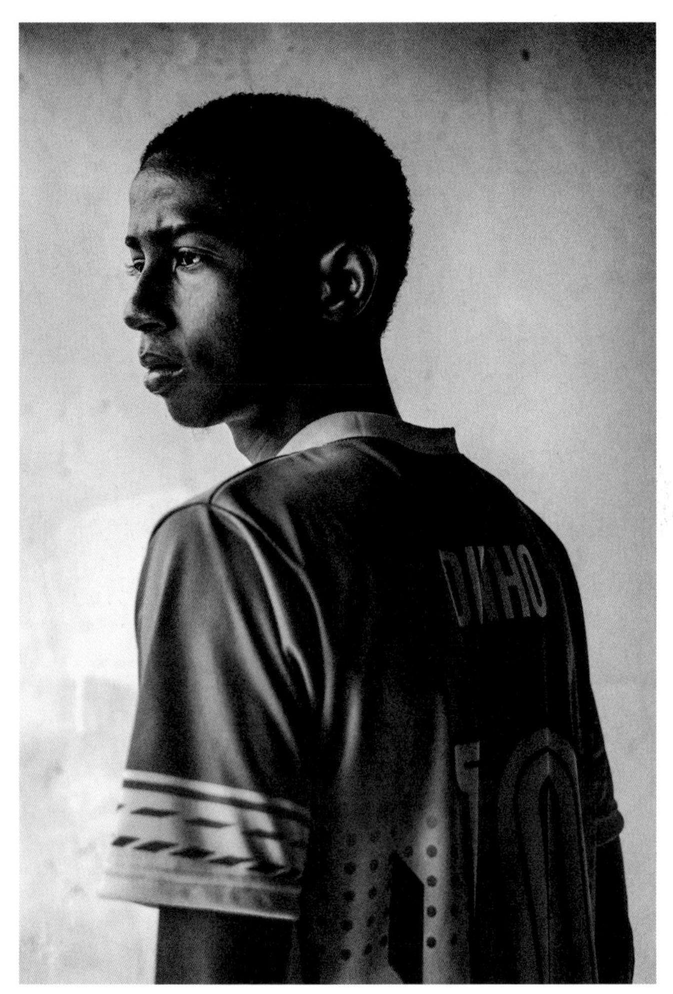

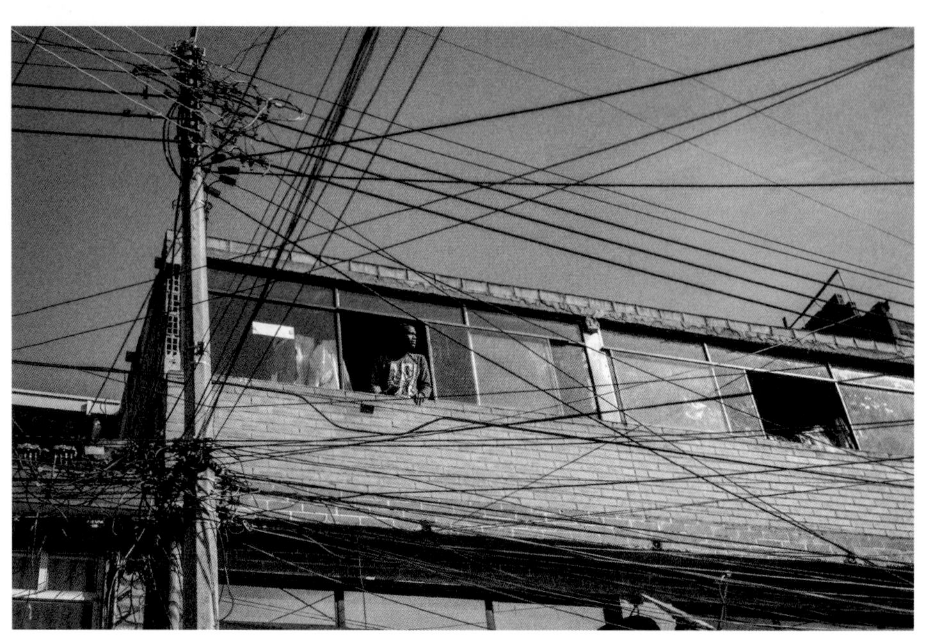

The youth in Buenaventura, Colombia's most important port city, face poverty, governmental neglect and gang violence. To break out of this cycle, some dream of becoming a professional football player. They join a football school, which causes further financial struggles, and share a house with 30 of their teammates in hopes to make it to the capital Bogotá. There, the teenagers will face the same struggle for recognition again, only on a much bigger stage.

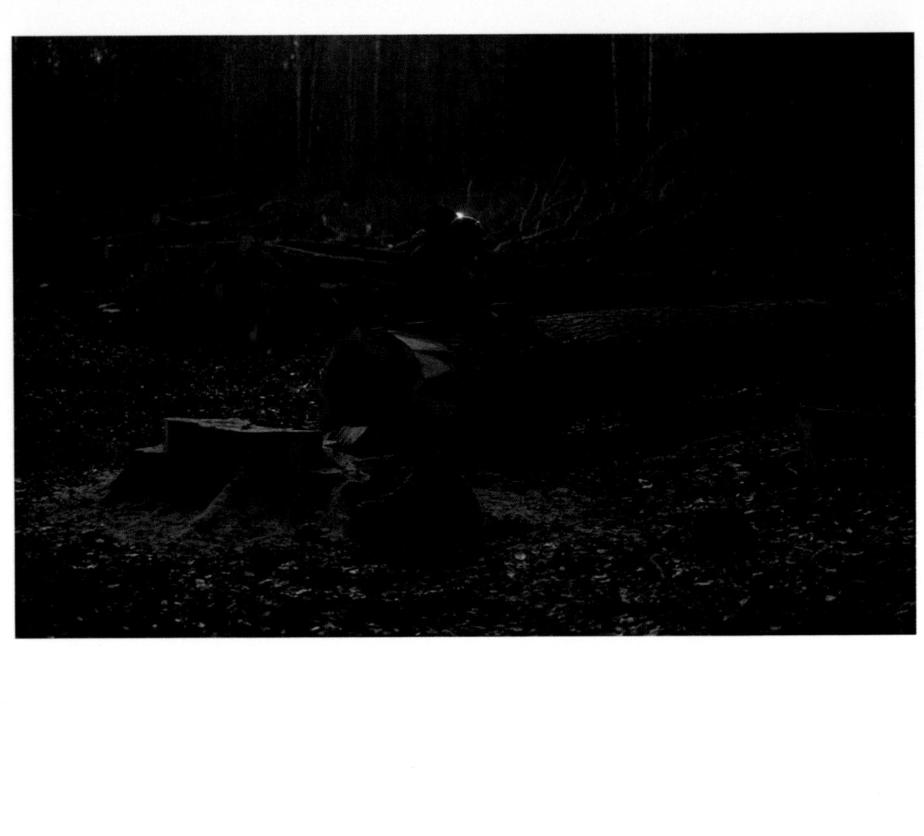

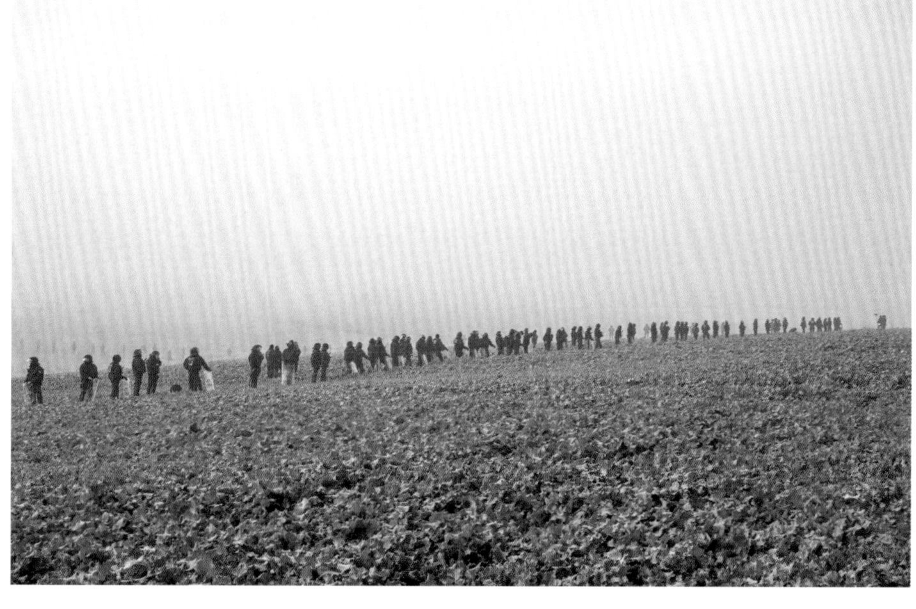

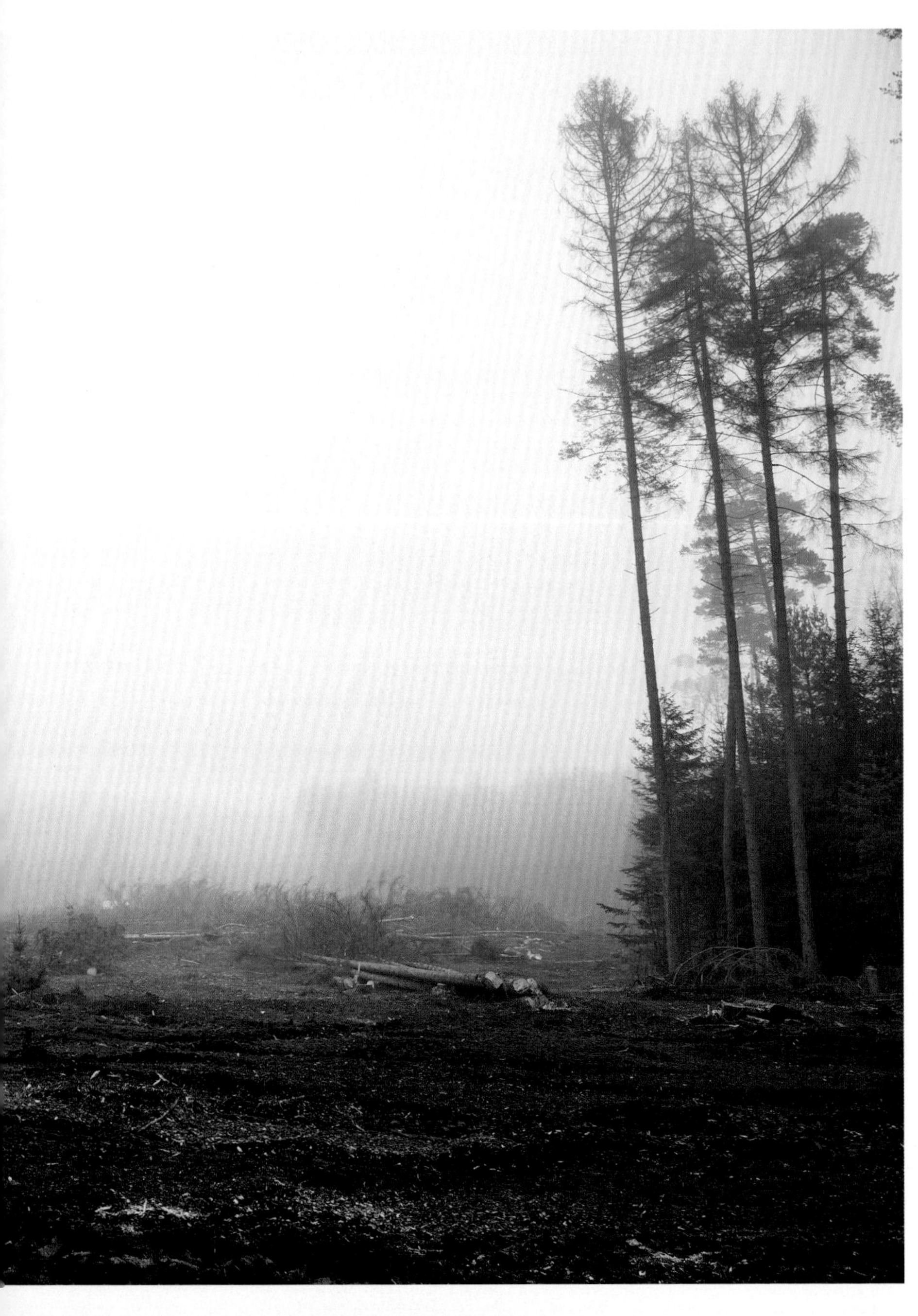

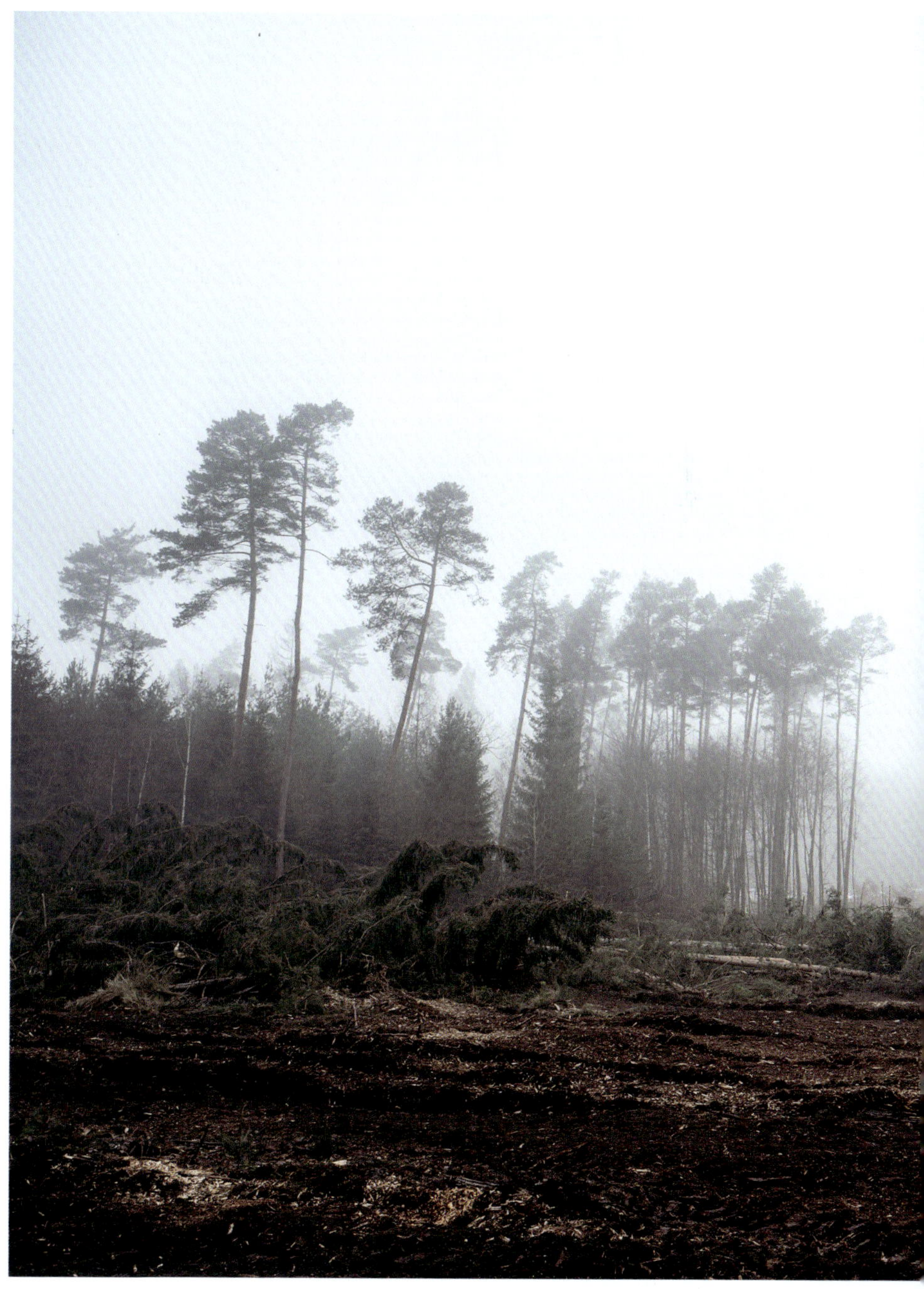

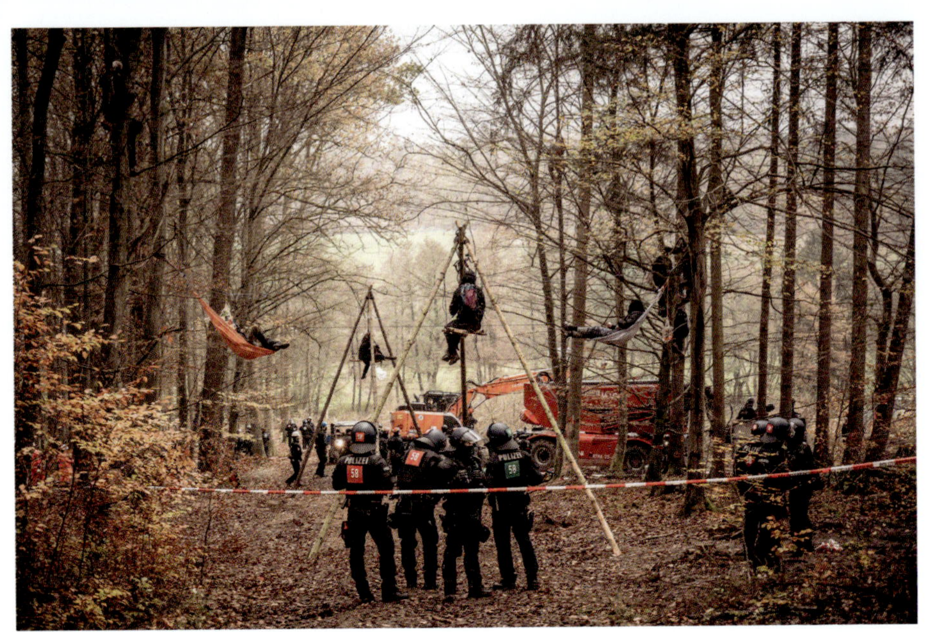
POLIZEI

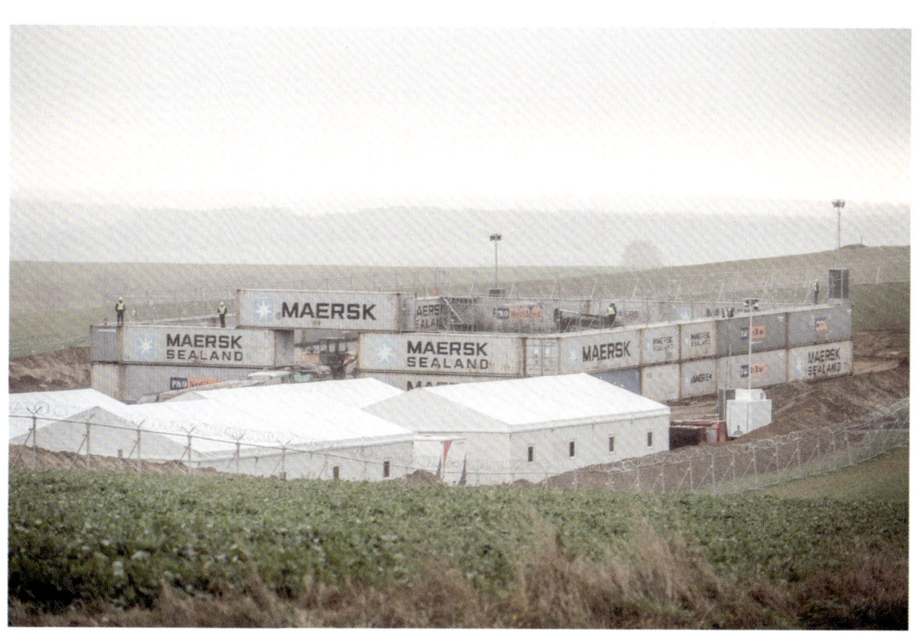
MAERSK
MAERSK
SEALAND
MAERSK
SEALAND
MAERSK
MAERSK
SEALAND

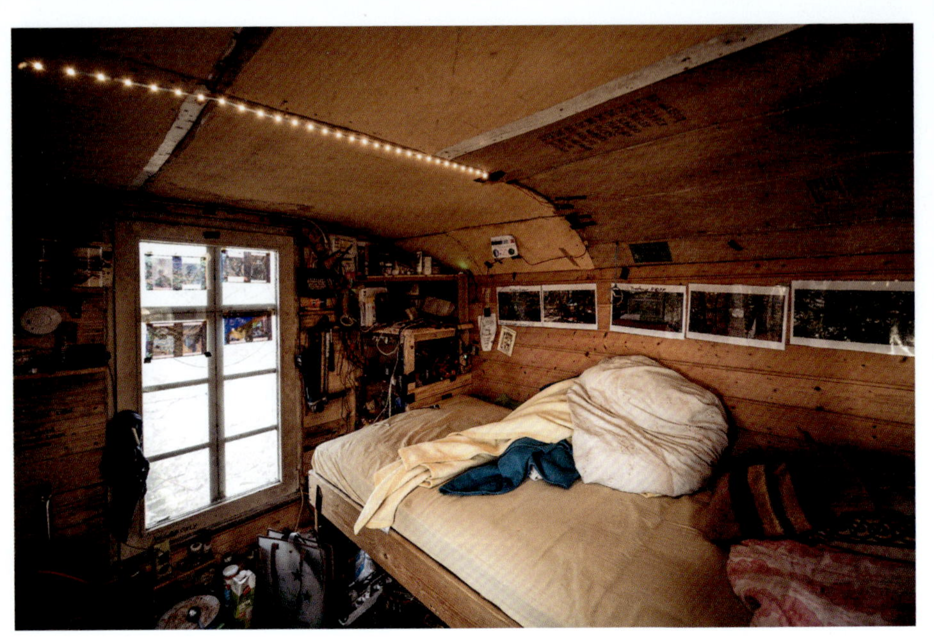

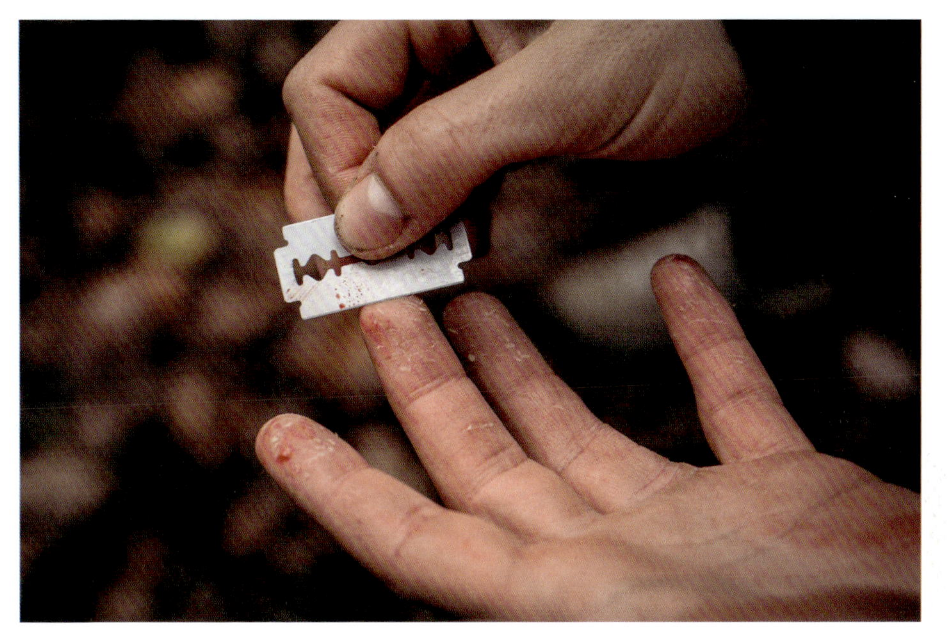

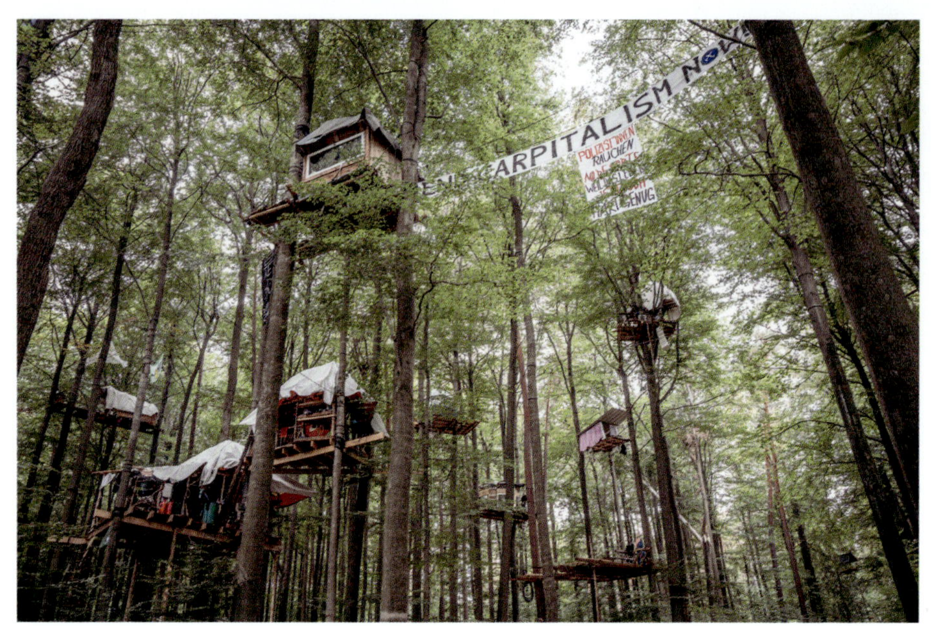
ARPITALISM
RAUCHEN
HART GENUG

The Dannenröder Forest is a 250-year-old mixed forest in Hessen, Germany, and the region‘s drinking water reservoir. For the construction of a highway planned in the 1970s, the forest was cleared in large parts at the end of 2020 –and with it, the police tore down the makeshift village from activists protesting the lack of environmental protection and the outdated, car-centred transport policies in Germany.

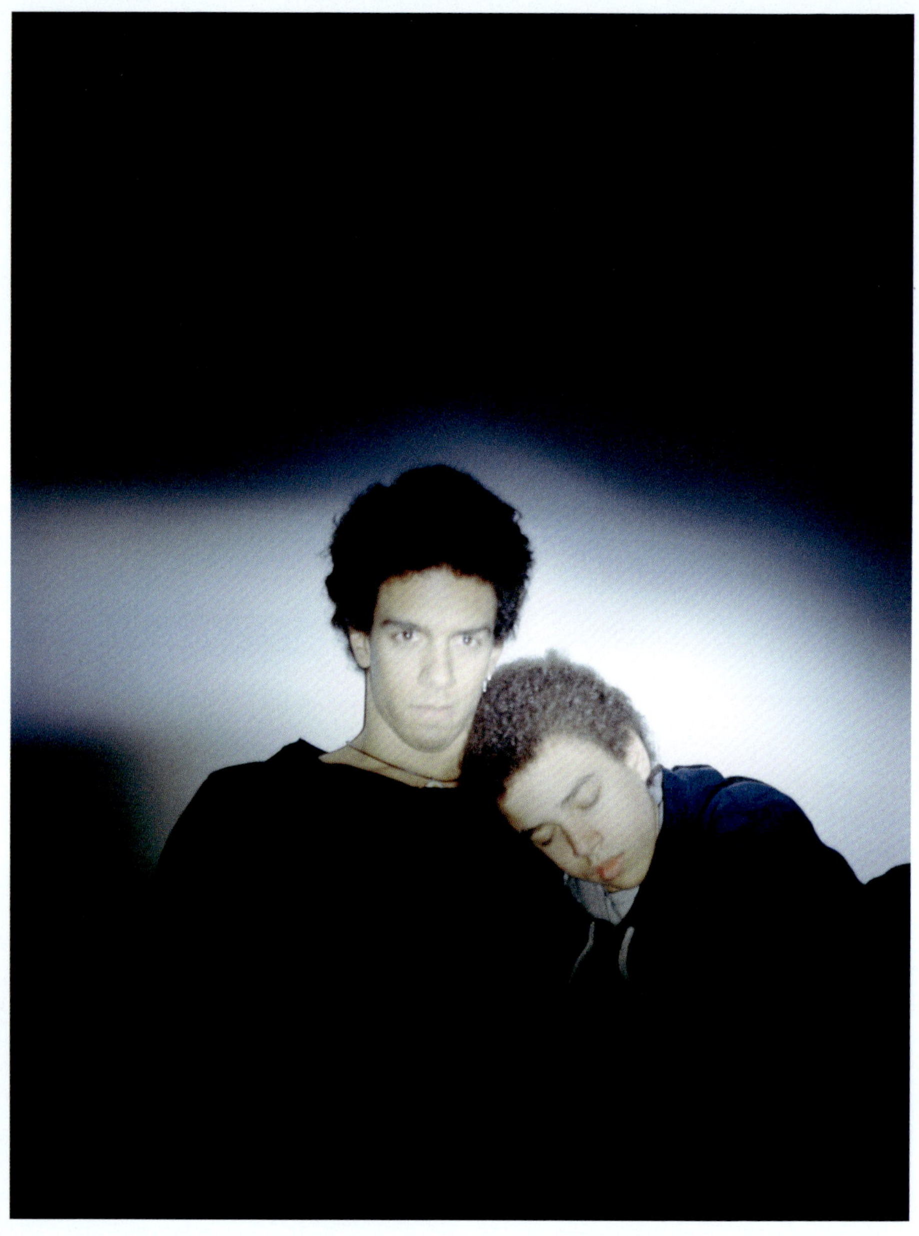

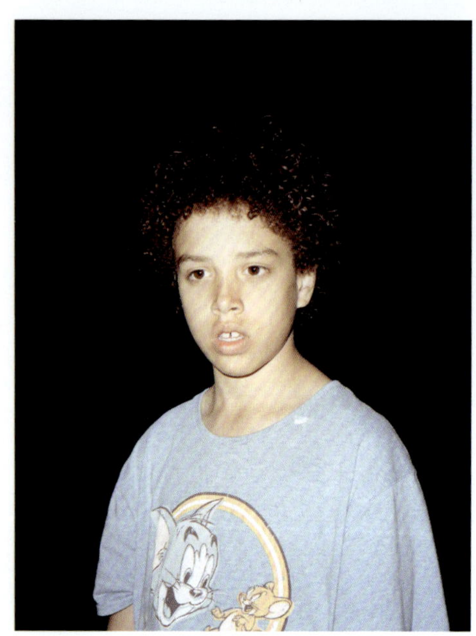

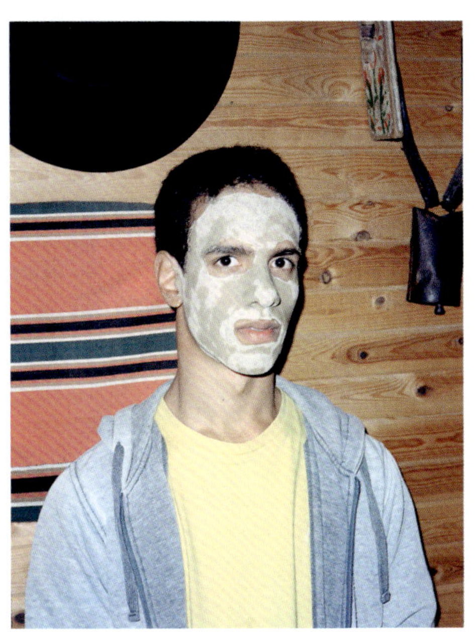

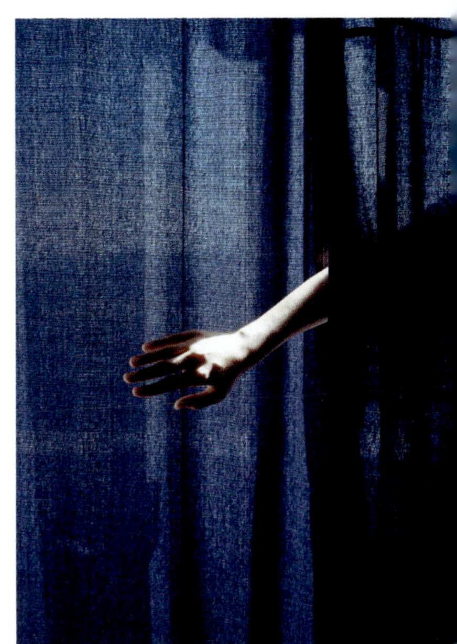

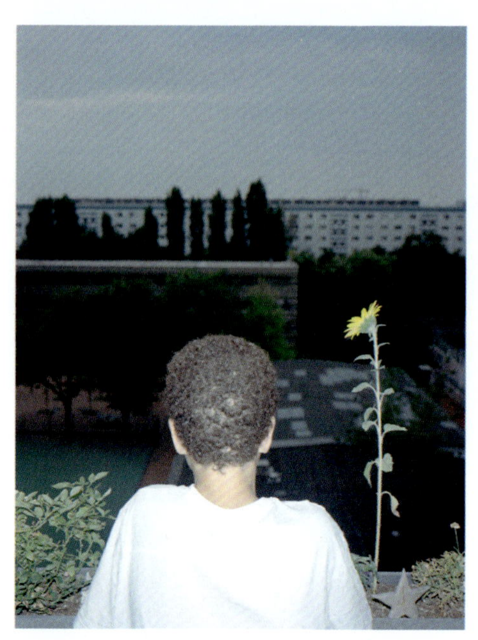

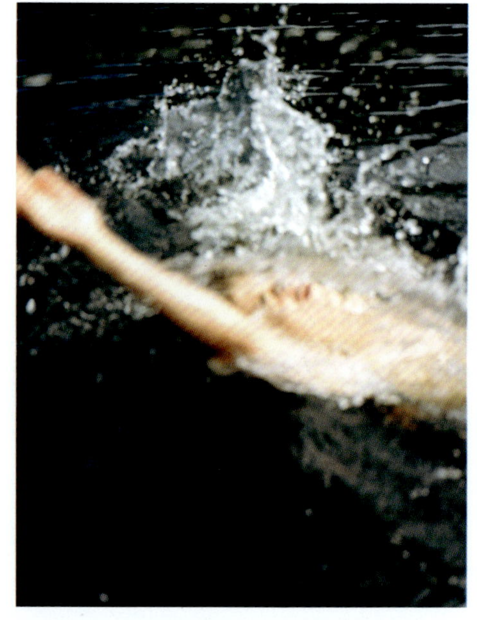

Ich mag Philosophie, weil man philosophische Gedanken nie ganz zuende denken kann. Es bleibt immer etwas, das unerklärlich ist und das niemand mit Sicherheit beantworten kann.
Das kann manchmal beunruhigend, manchmal aber auch sehr beruhigend sein.

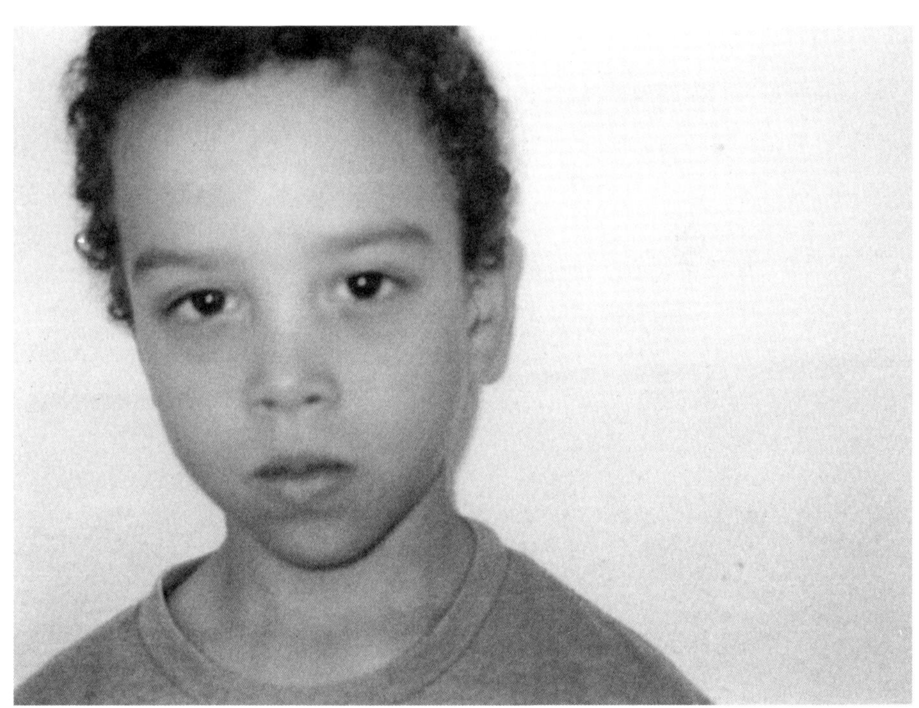

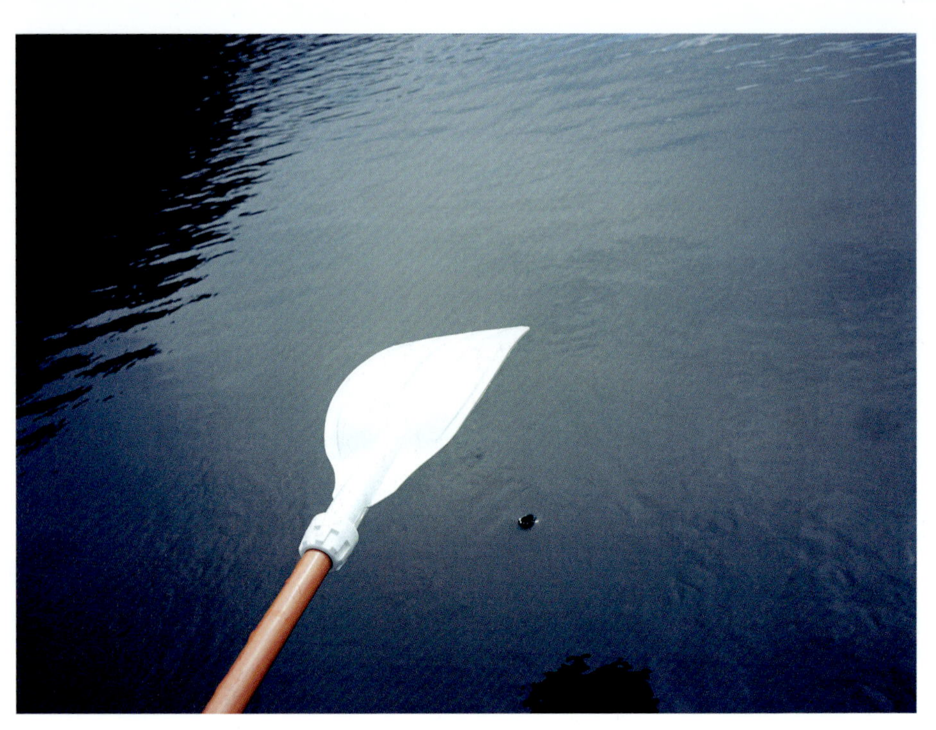

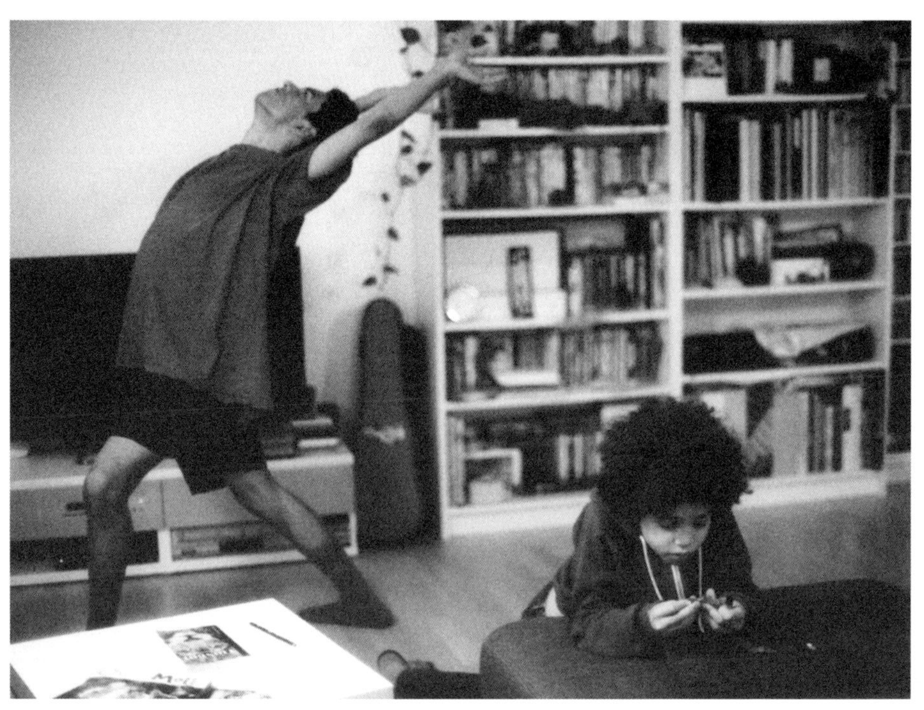

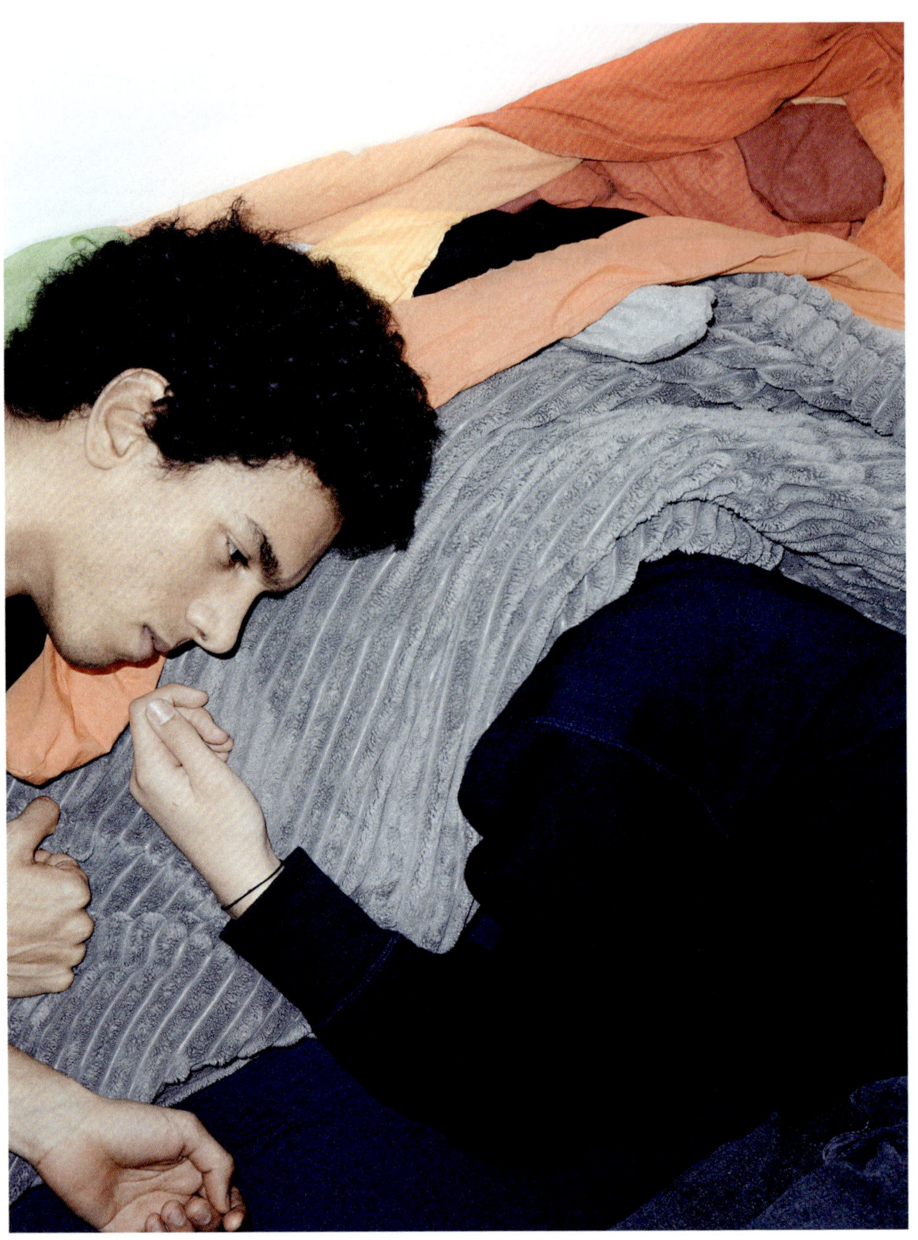

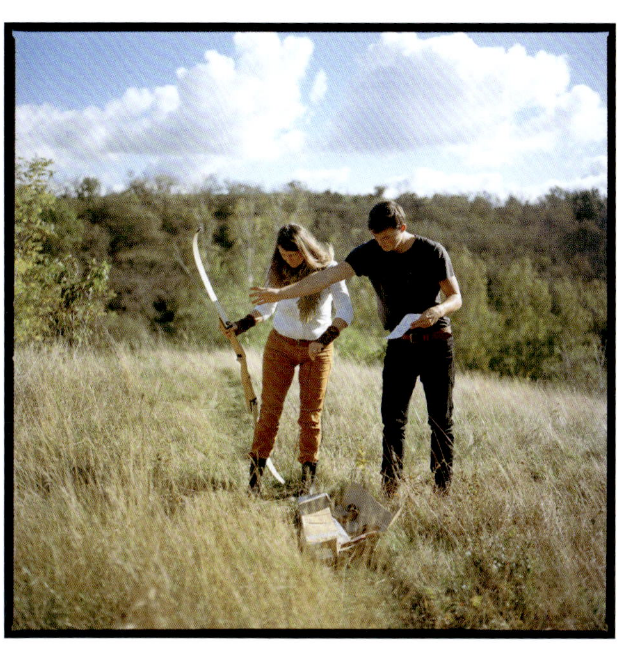

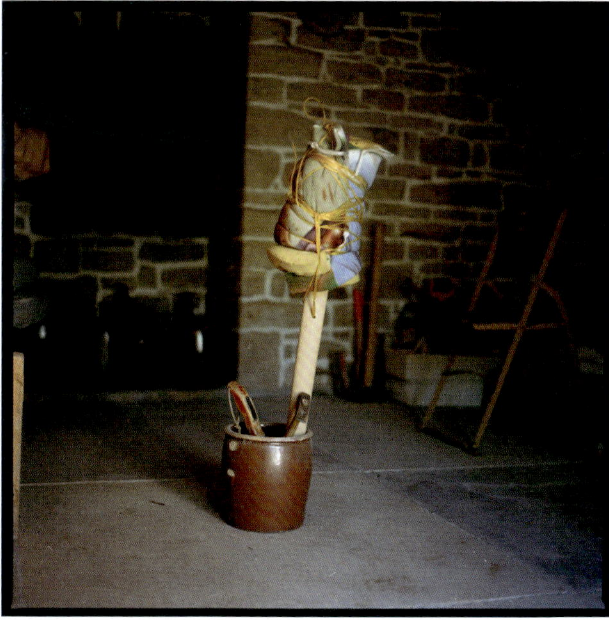

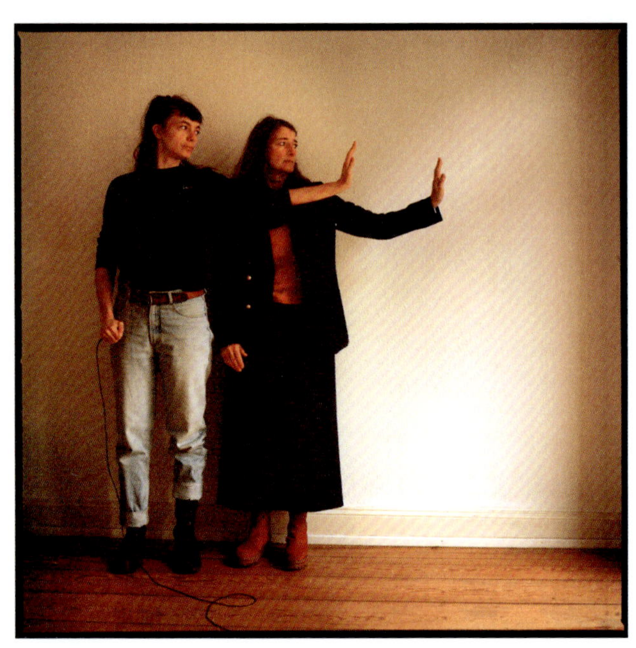

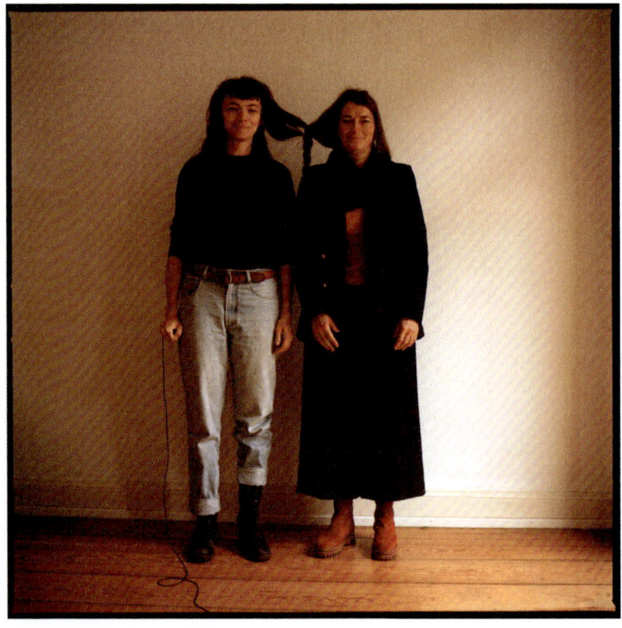

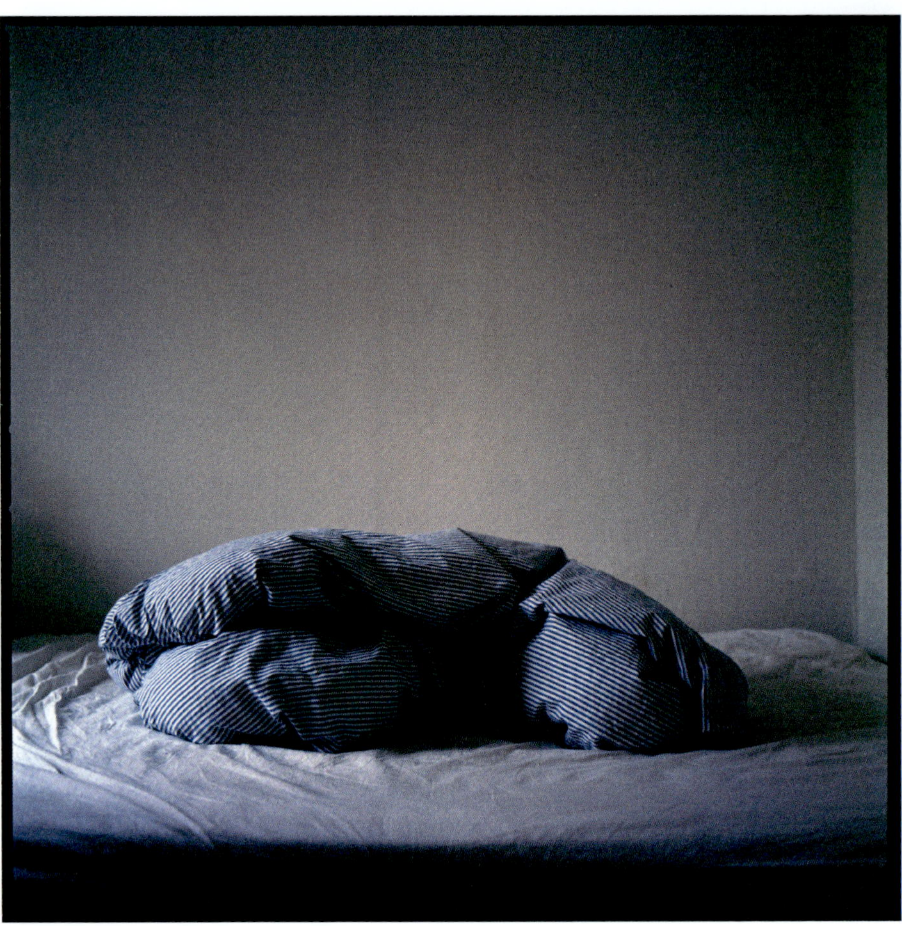

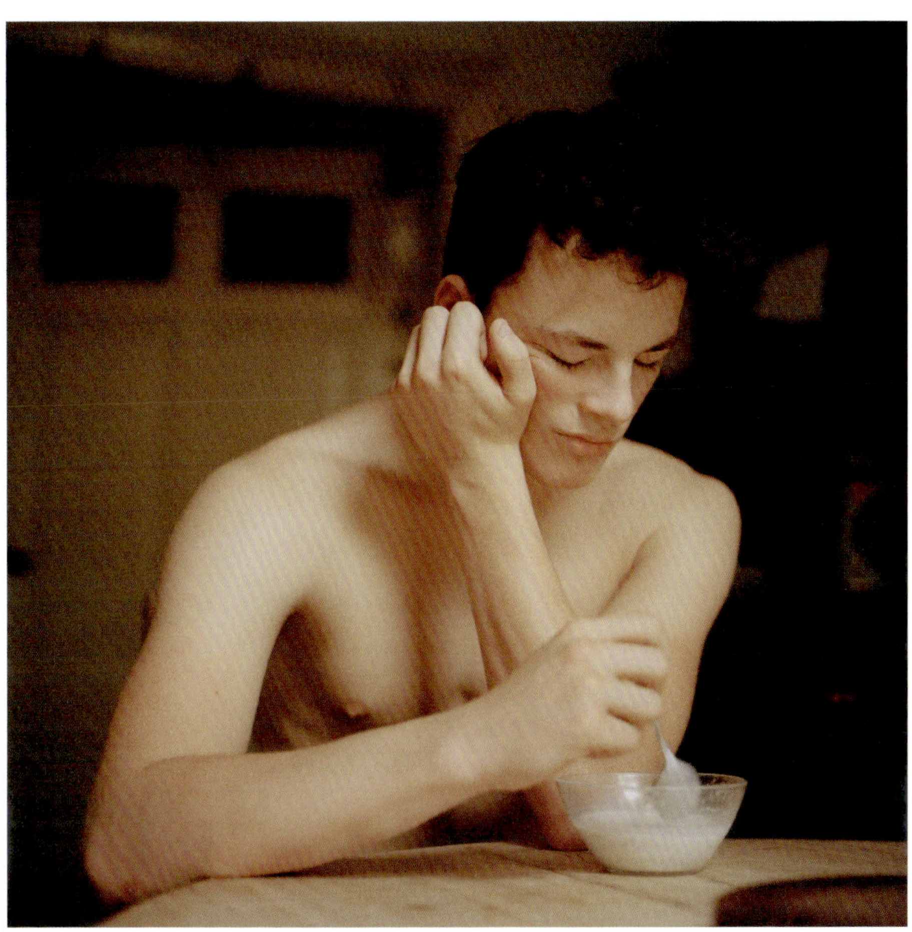

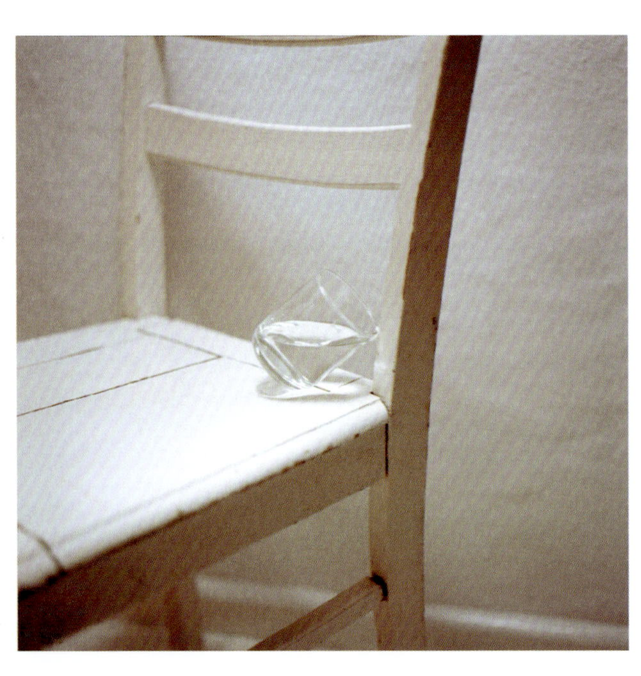

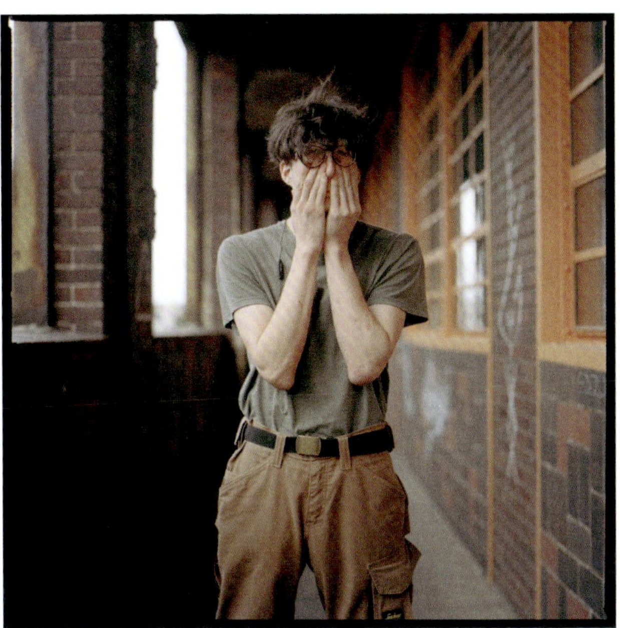

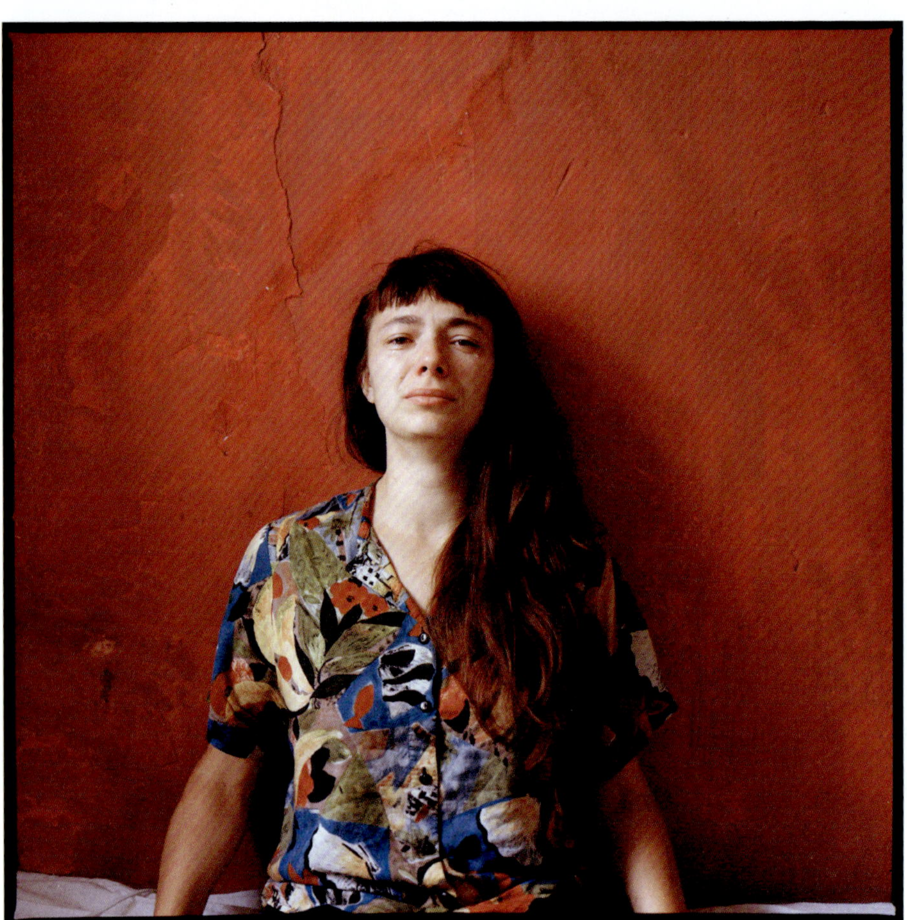

In her childhood, Lena was mentally abused by her parents. She ran away and lived in a protectory until she had to face the world on her own after turning 18. Loneliness and the haunting memories led to depression and also to her contacting her parents again. By accounting for the past and the experiences they shared, they realized that working on it together could lead to forgiveness and the processing of their family's trauma.

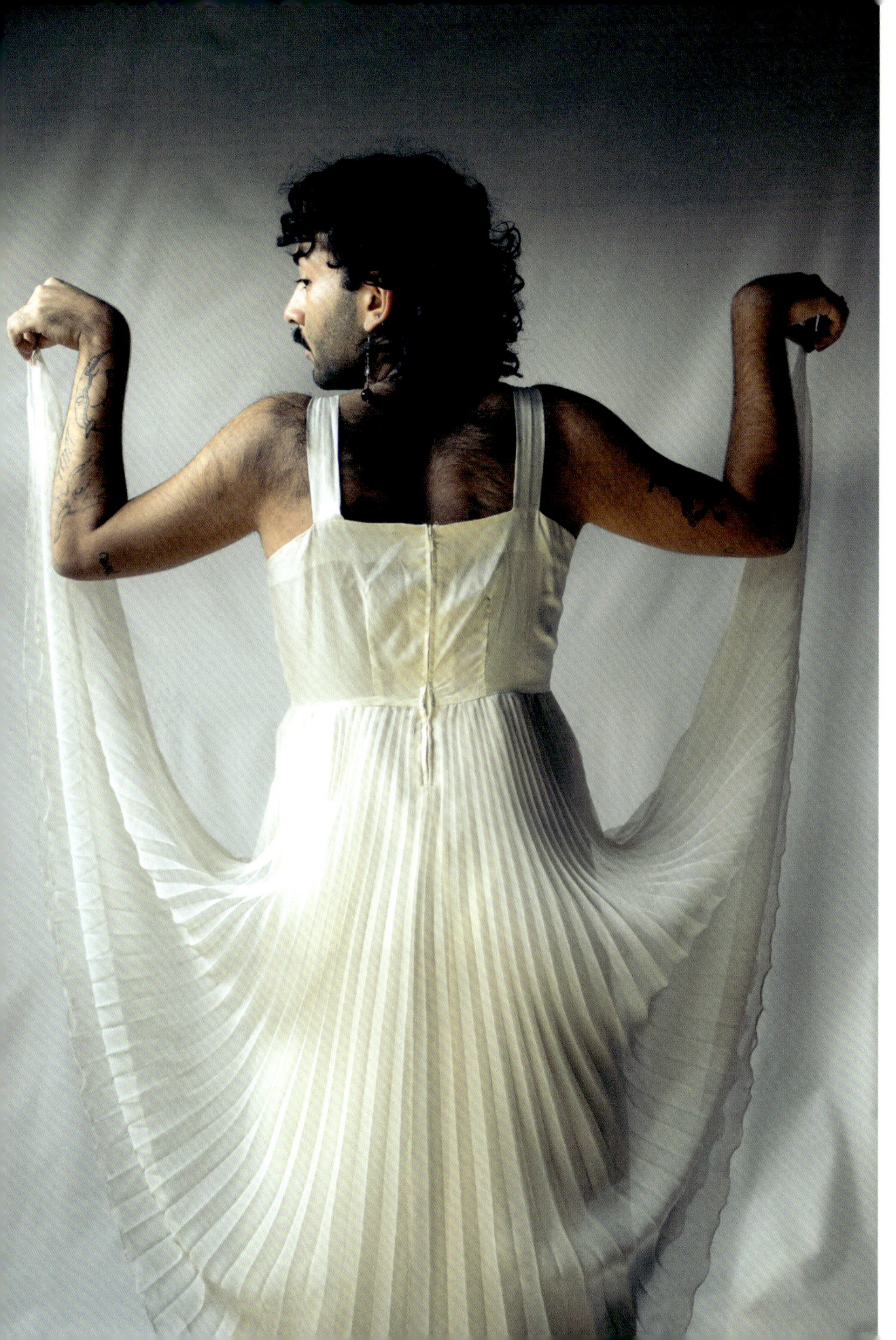

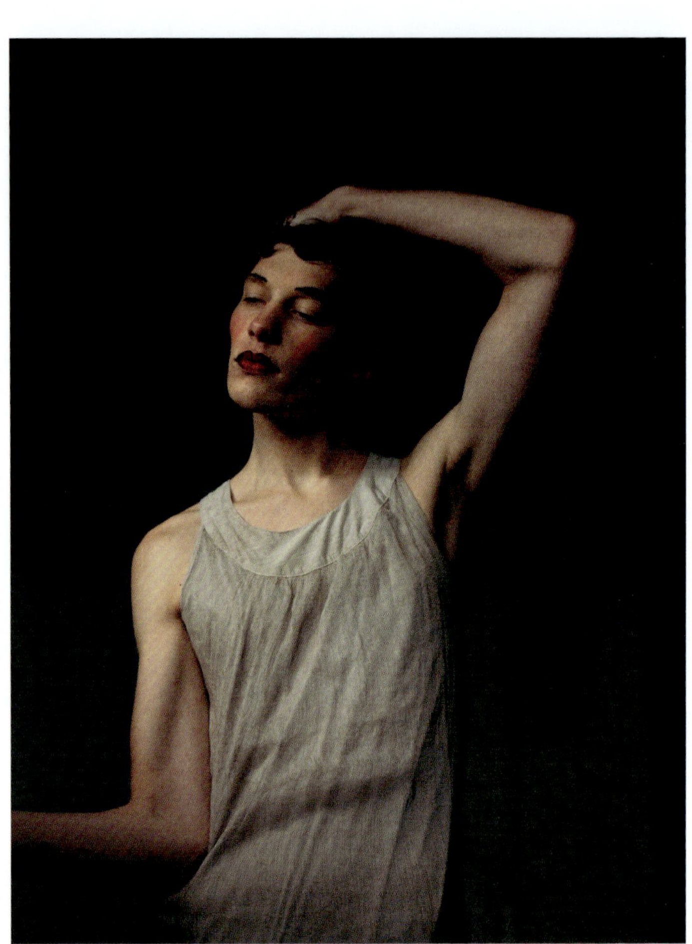

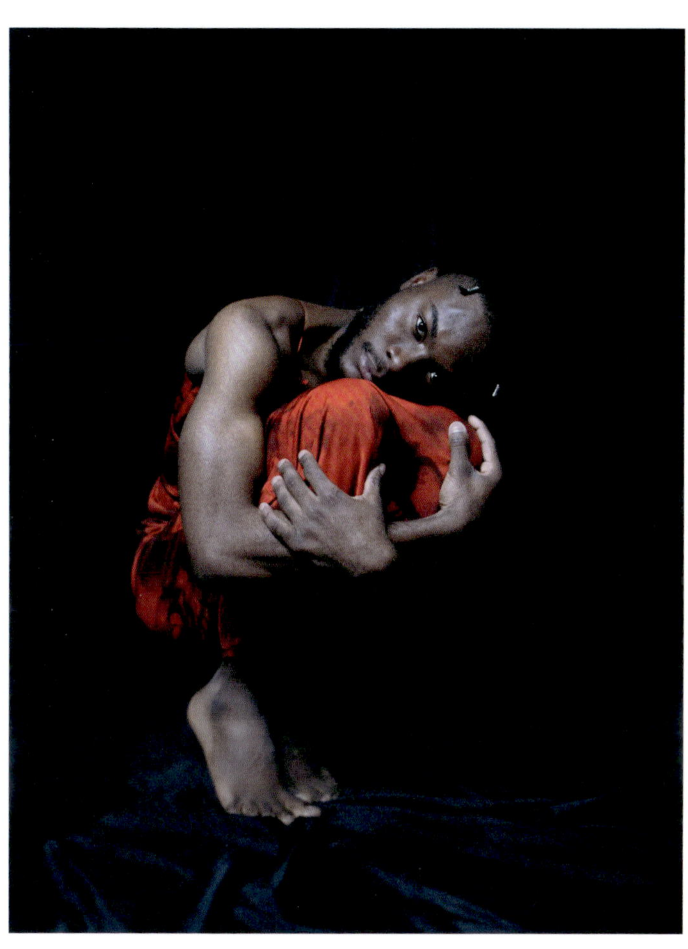

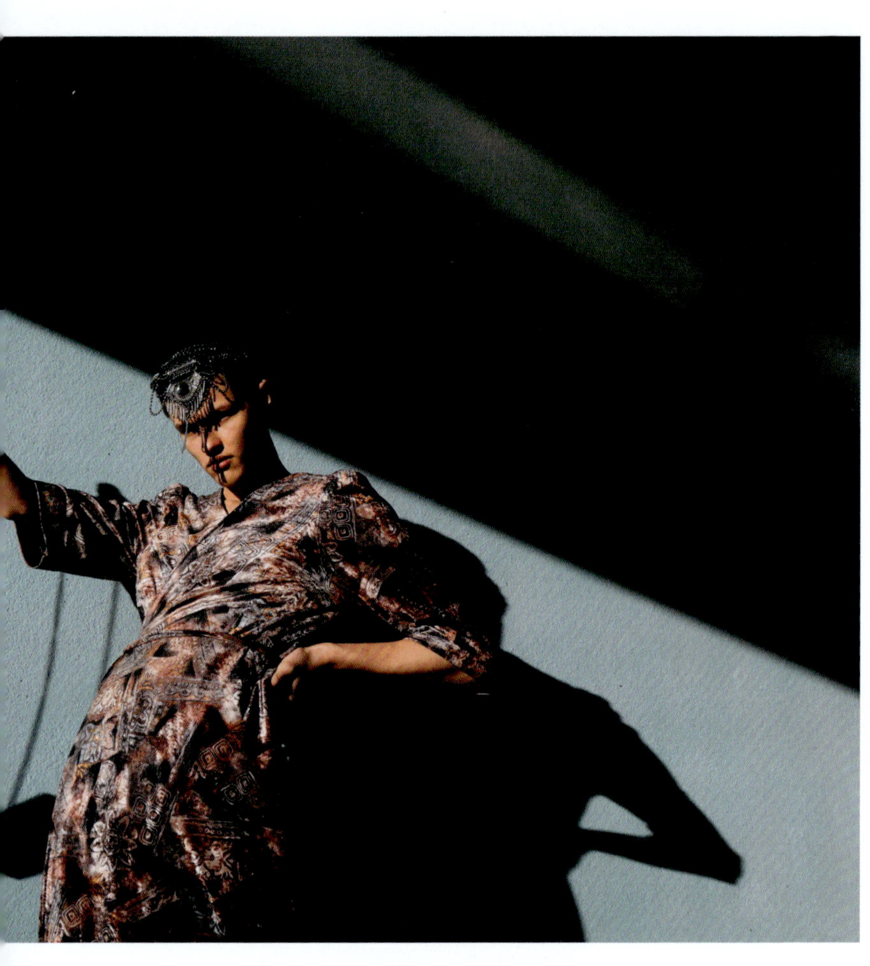

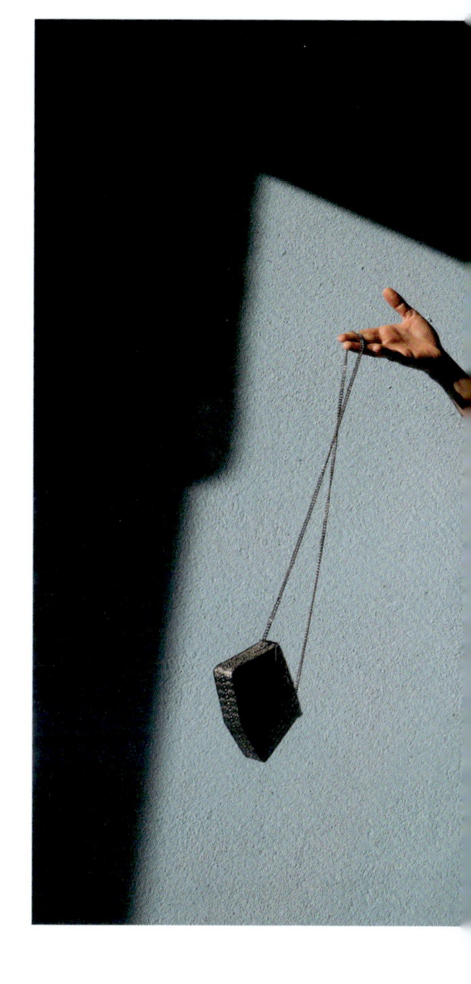

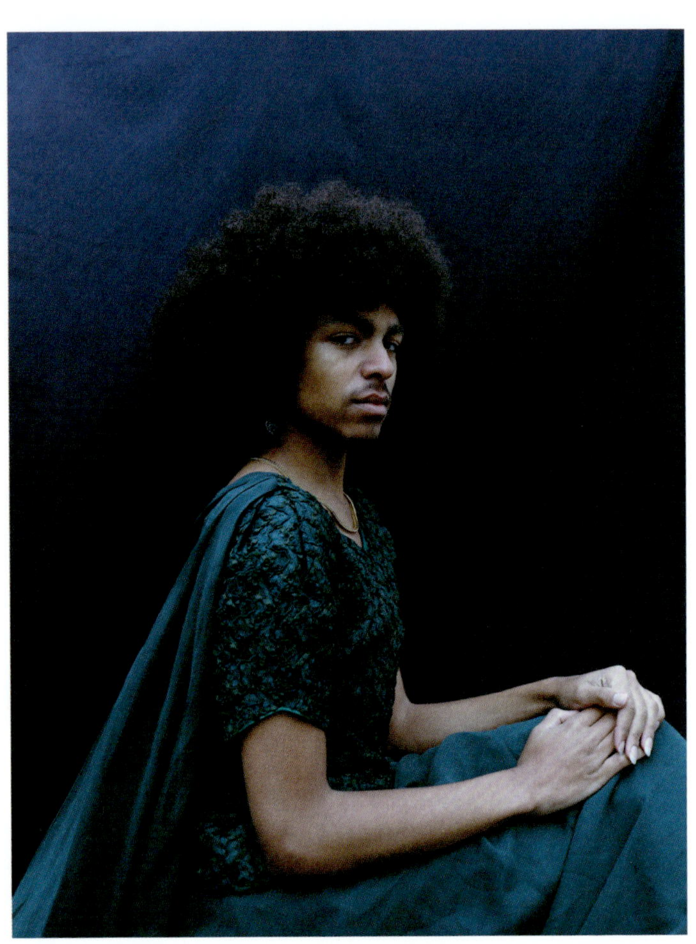

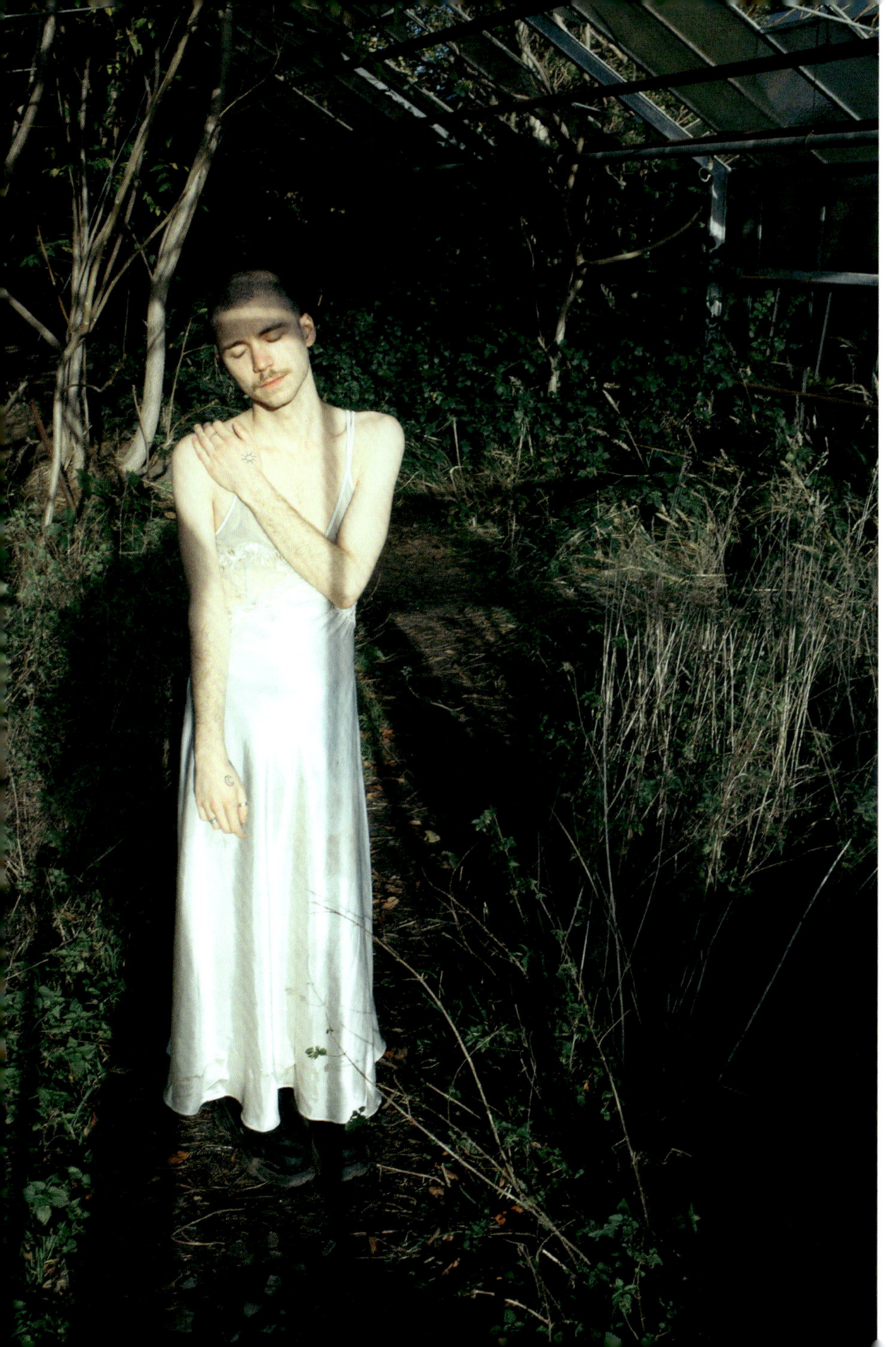

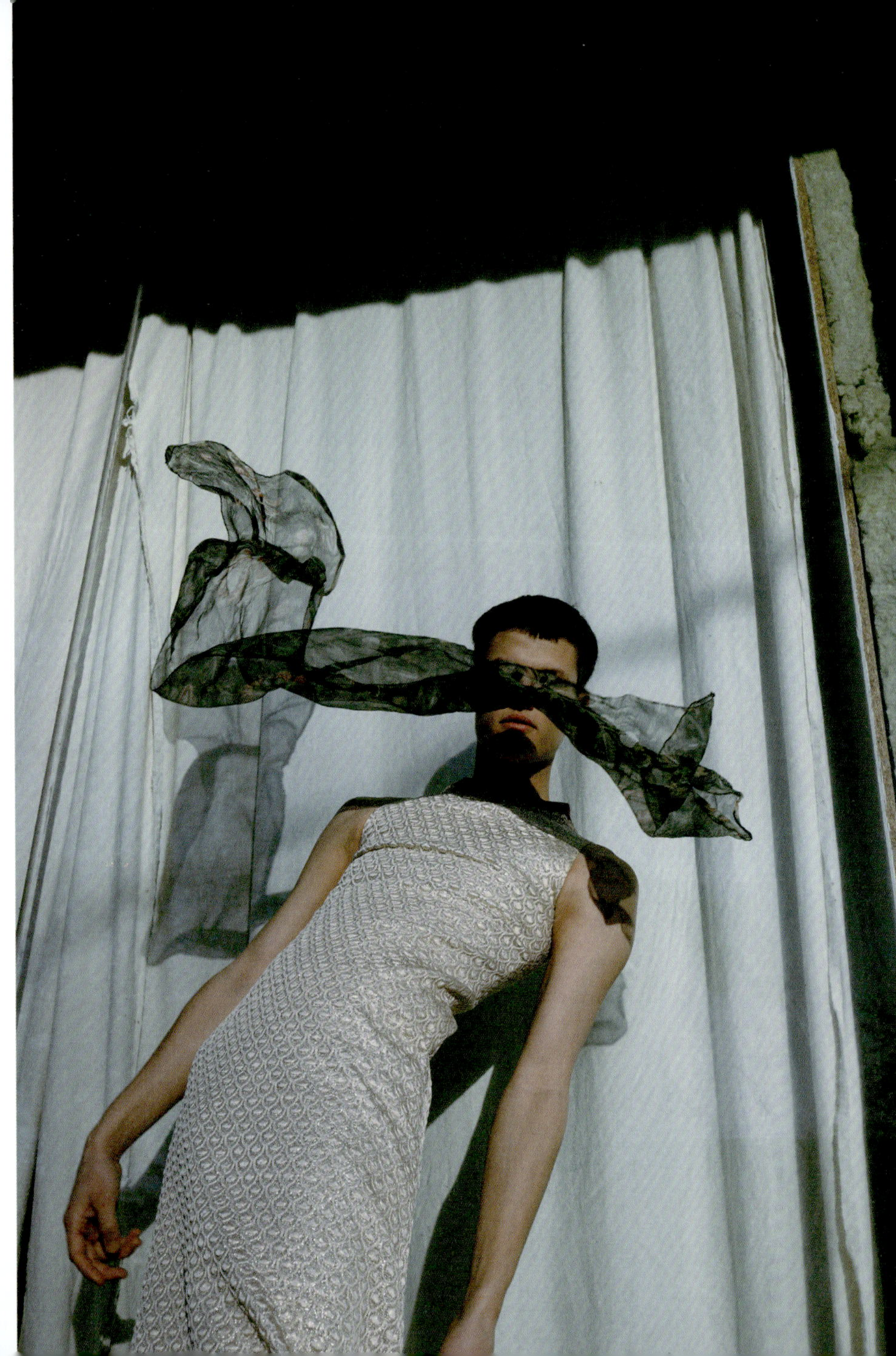

We as humans are sensitive beings, spiritual entities—determined dreamers. We imagine versions of reality and share intersubjective experiences about how we perceive the world, what things mean and how we classify them. Meanwhile, the things we cannot see are the most significant. We live trapped inside mental constructs that we ourselves built, imagined rules that have grown out of previous rules—thought processes that developed in secret. The shared dream of an entire culture. But, if we dream in a certain way, we can also dream differently.

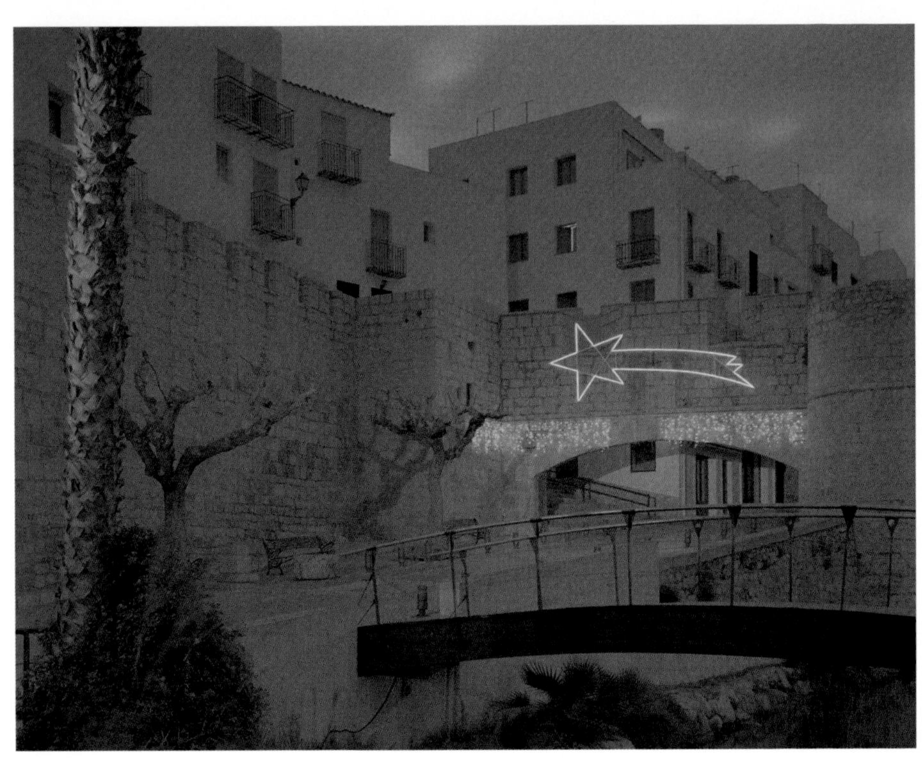

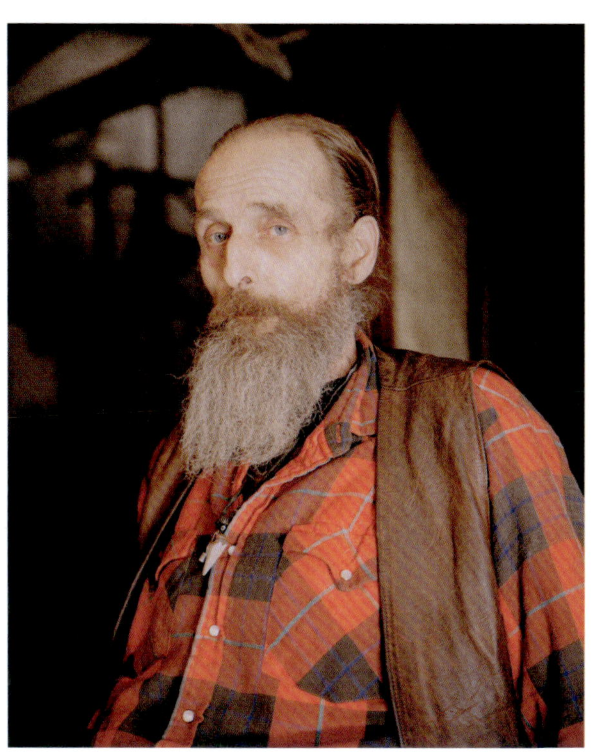

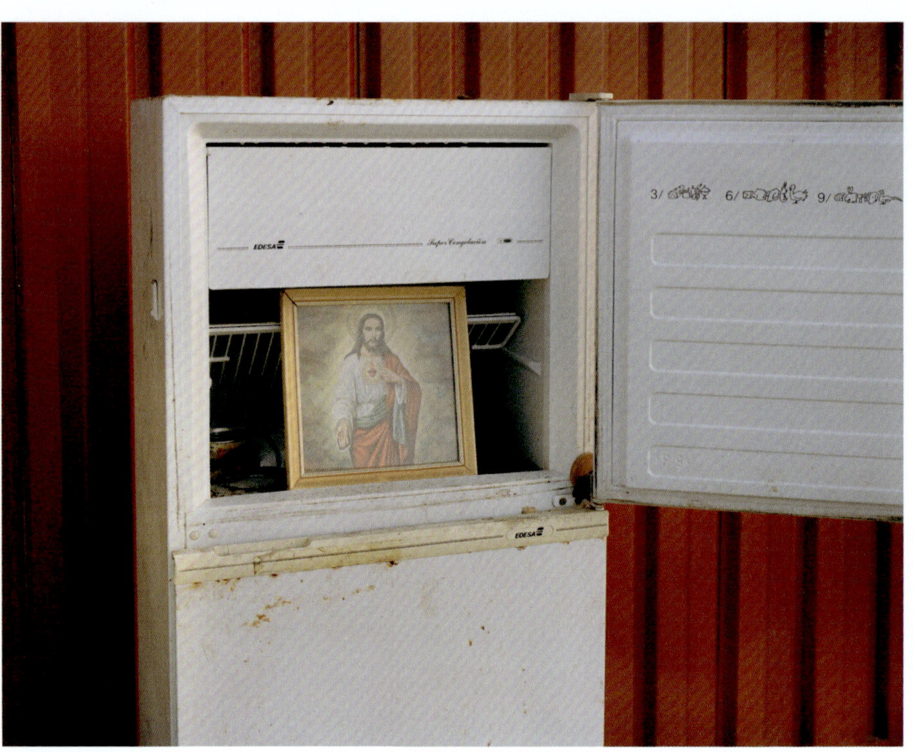
EDESA
Super Congelación
EDESA

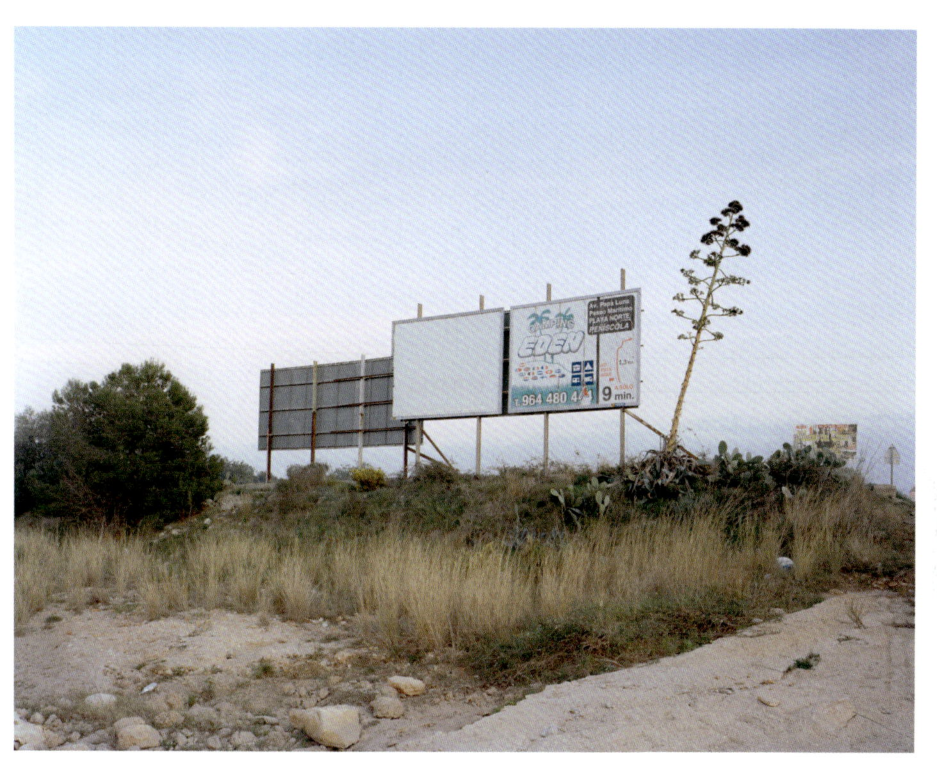
EDEN
PLAYA NORTE
PENISCOLA
T. 964 480 4
9 min.

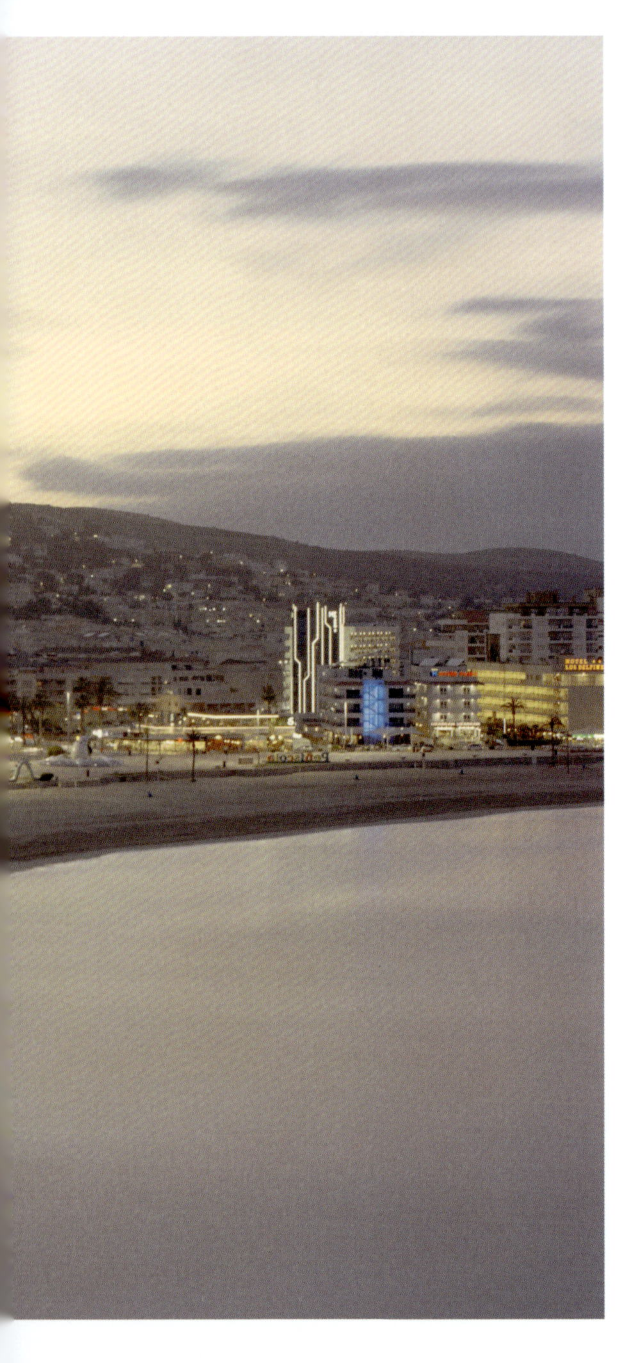

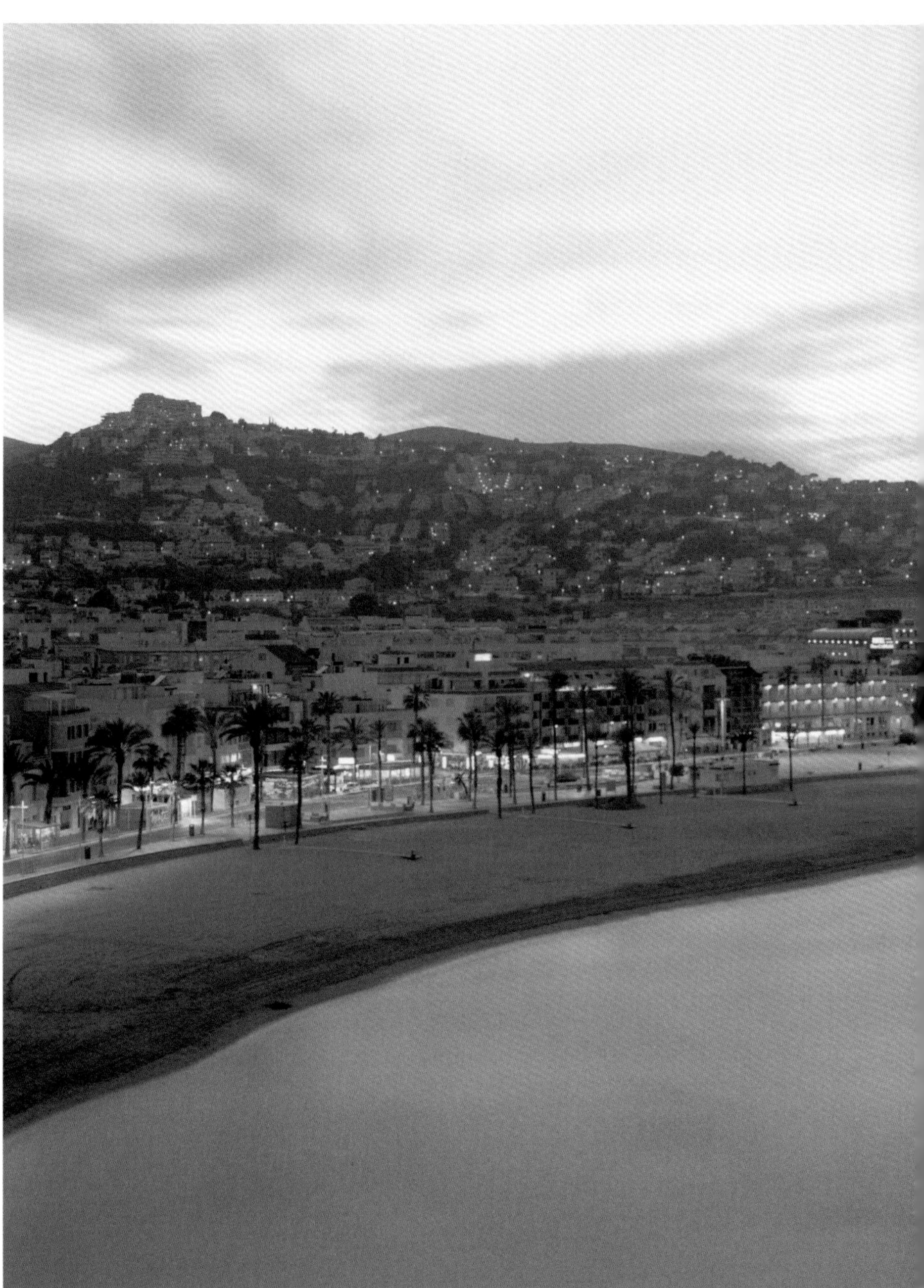

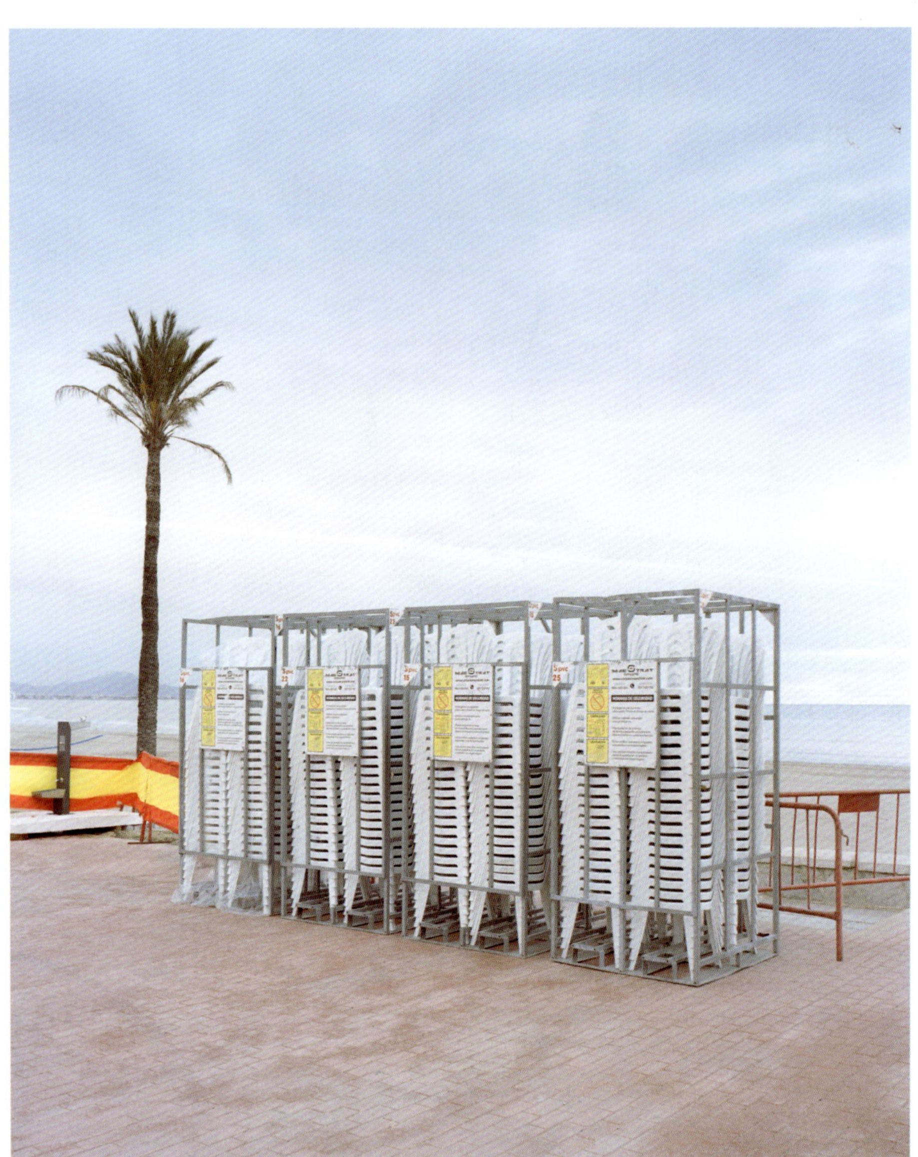

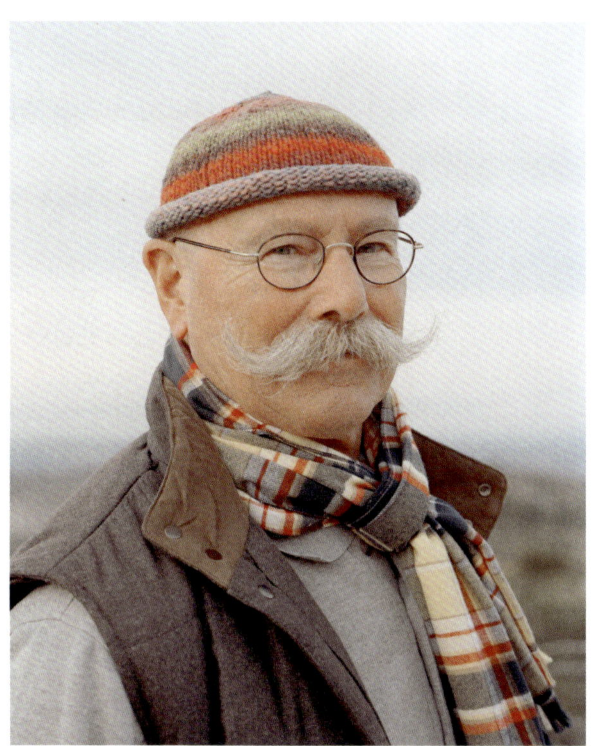

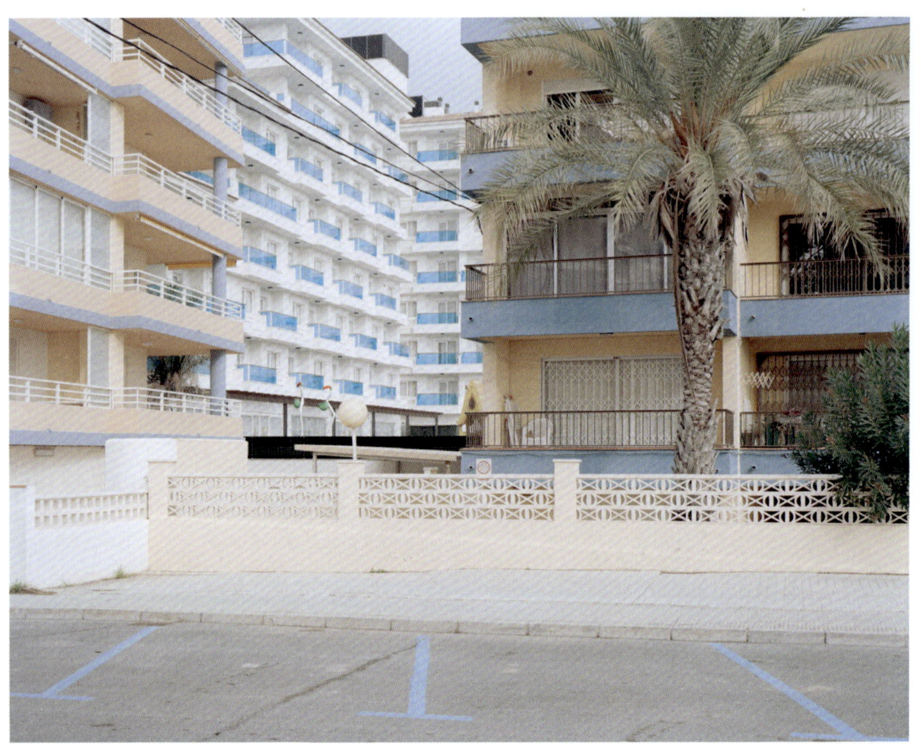

The emerging tourism in the 60s significantly changed the Spanish province Costa de Azahar. Farmers and fishermen became hoteliers, real estate agents and restaurateurs. Their land on the beach turned from an agricultural space into hotels and holiday resorts, attracting several hundred thousand guests each season. This project invites us to question the inherently dual effect caused by the touristic industry, which is both a blessing and a curse for the locals, forcing them to earn their annual income during the holiday season in summer and leaving them in a deserted and lonely infrastructure in winter.

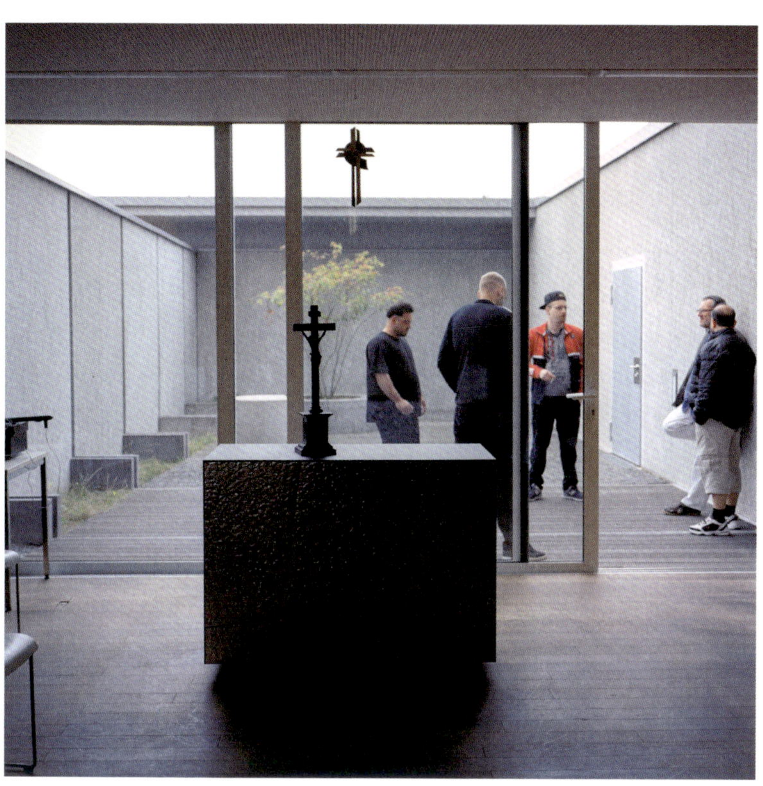

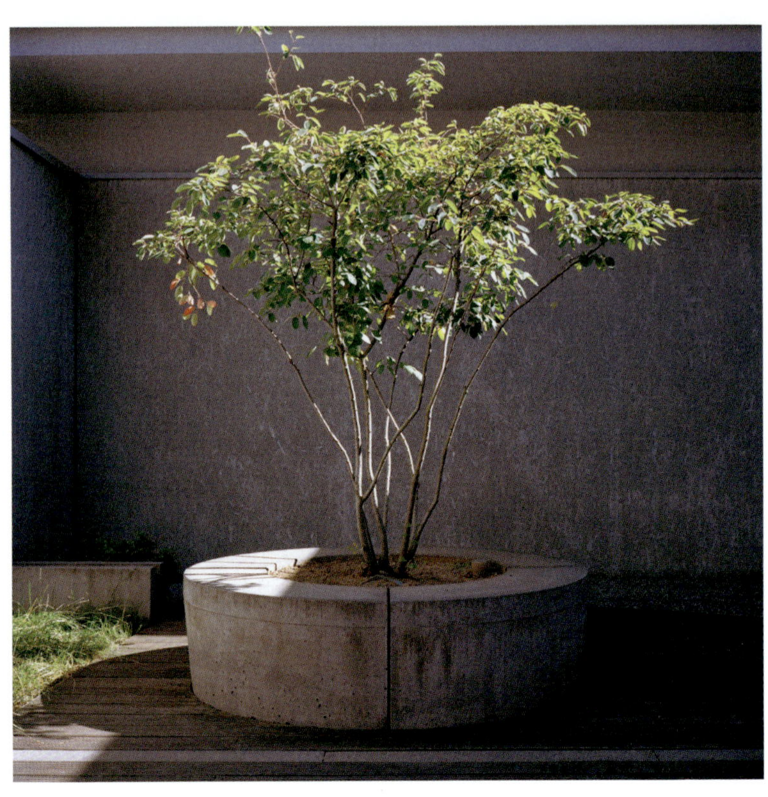

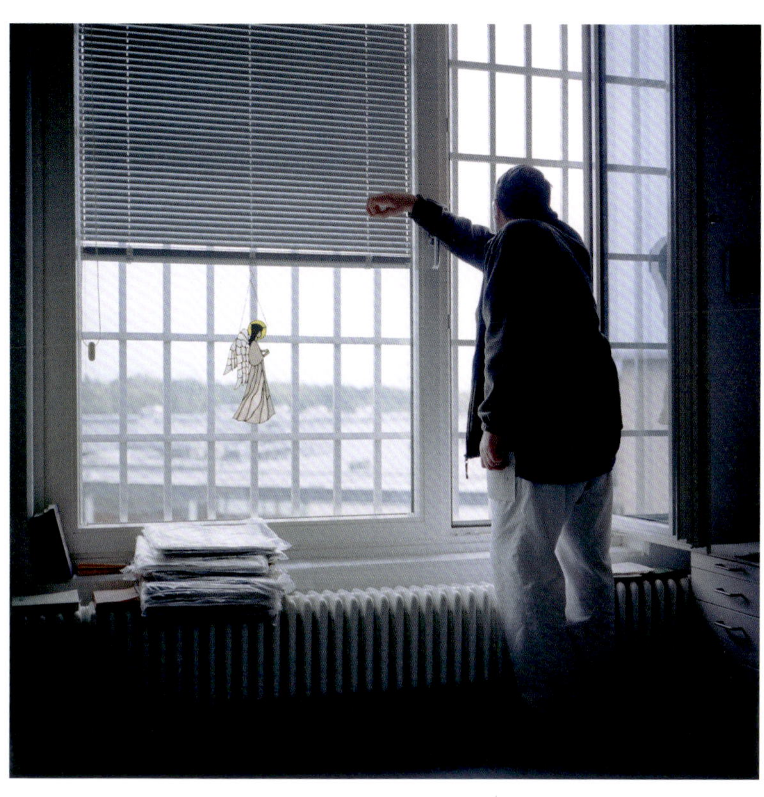

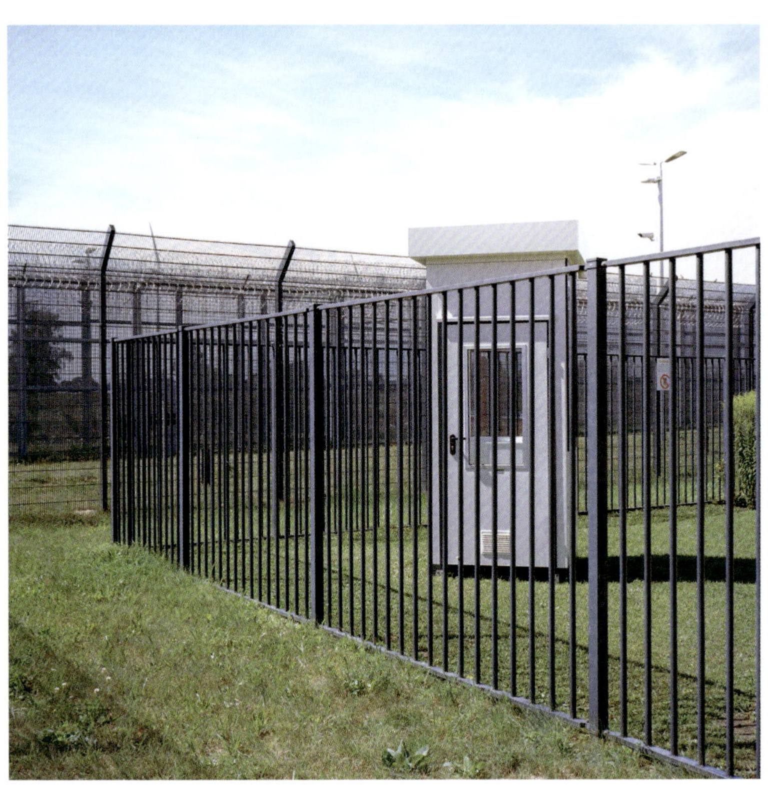

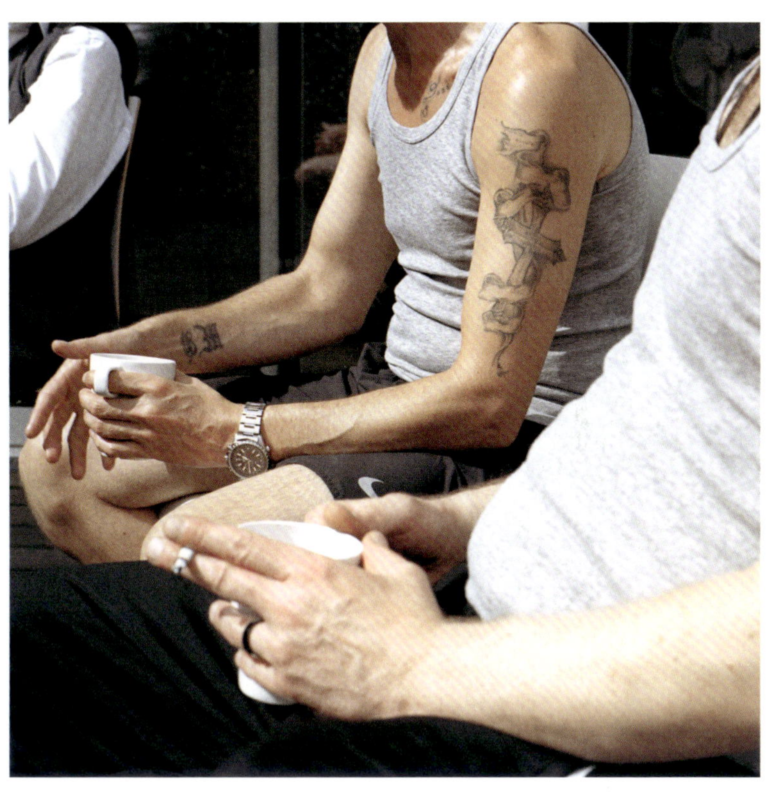

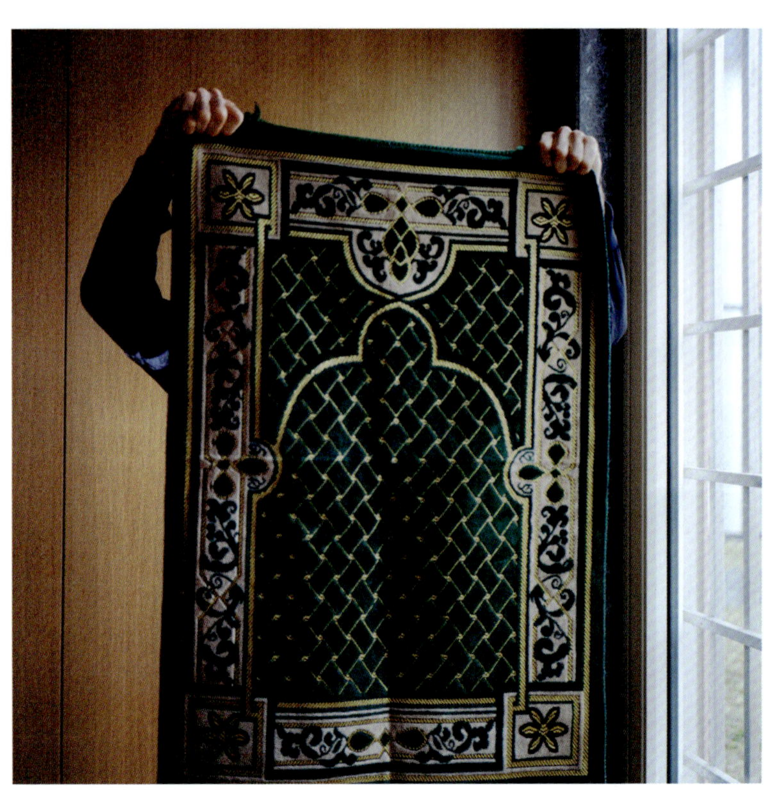

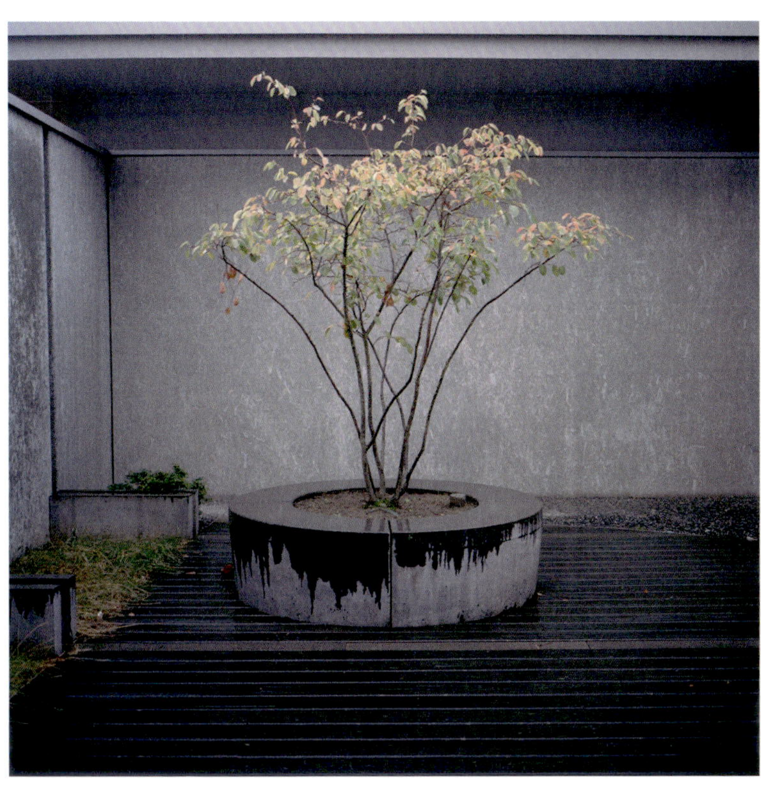

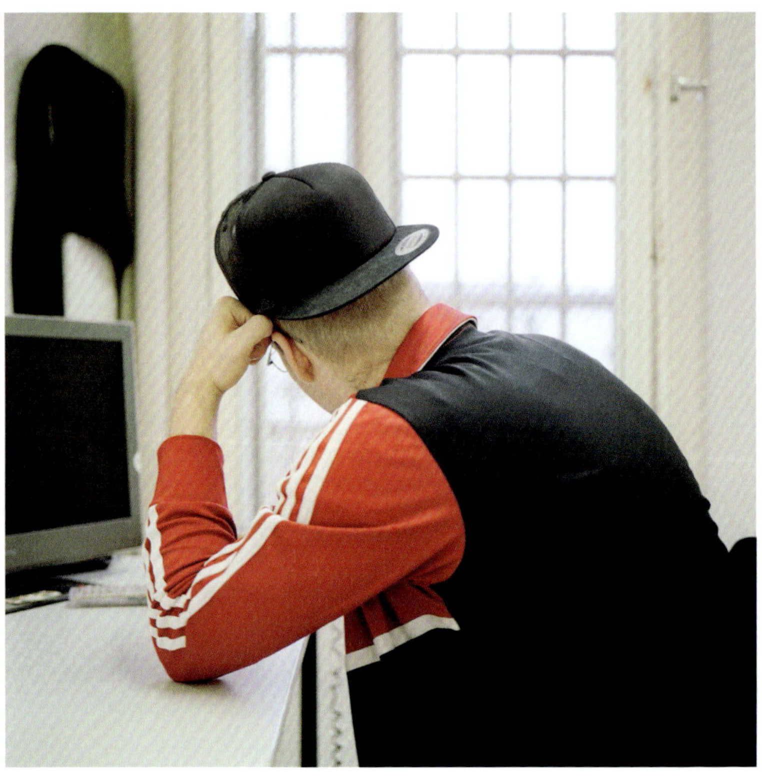

A prison is a place where people of different origins, social backgrounds, religions and ideologies come together. The loss of freedom and being alone without their loved ones leads some inmates to look for support. Chaplains of every religion offer discussion groups and individual support in German prisons. They offer exchange outside of the daily prison routine. Chiara photographed in Berlins prison JVA Heidering and accompanied the chaplain Axel Wiesbrock in his work.

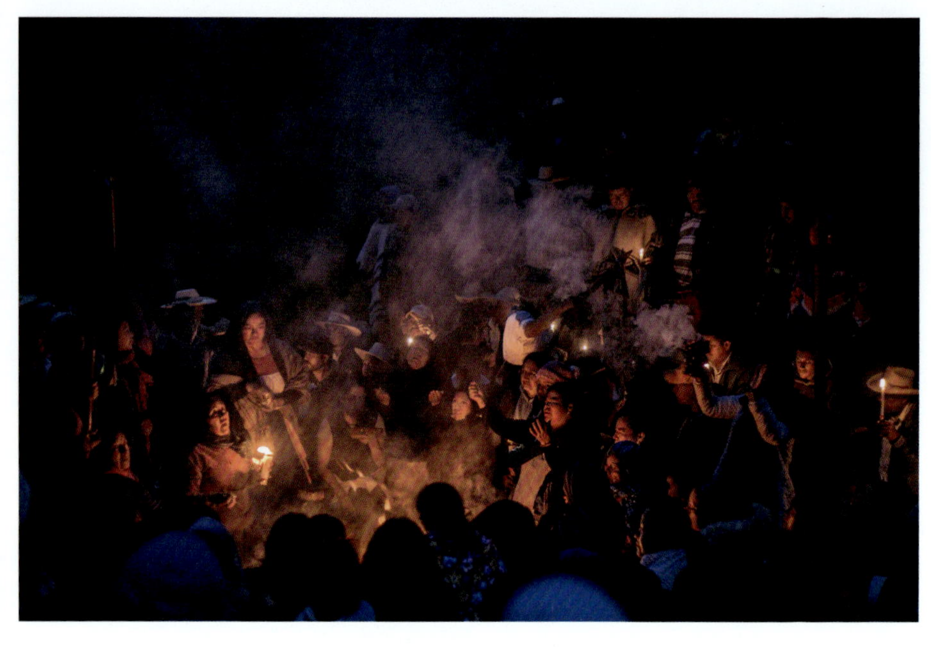

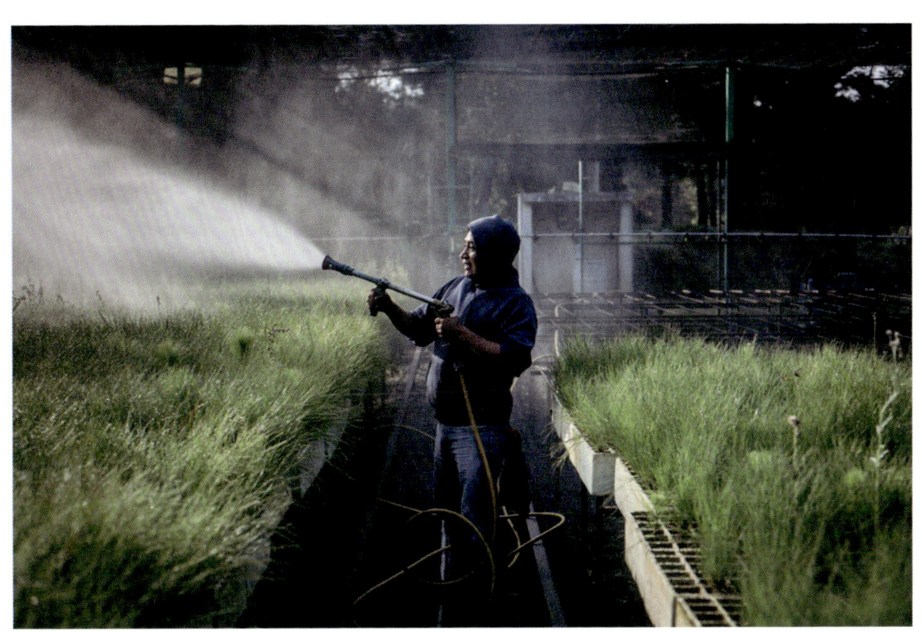

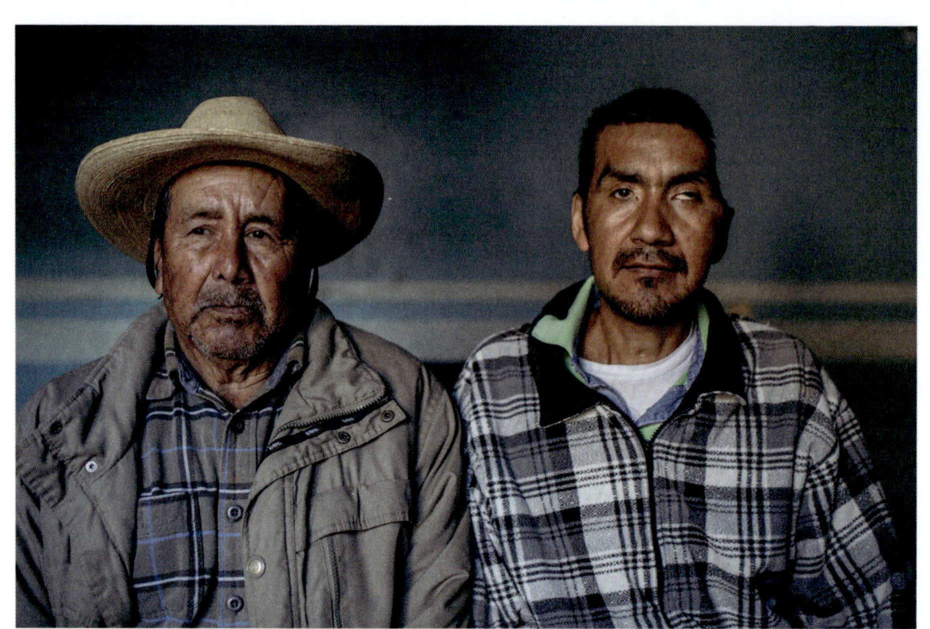

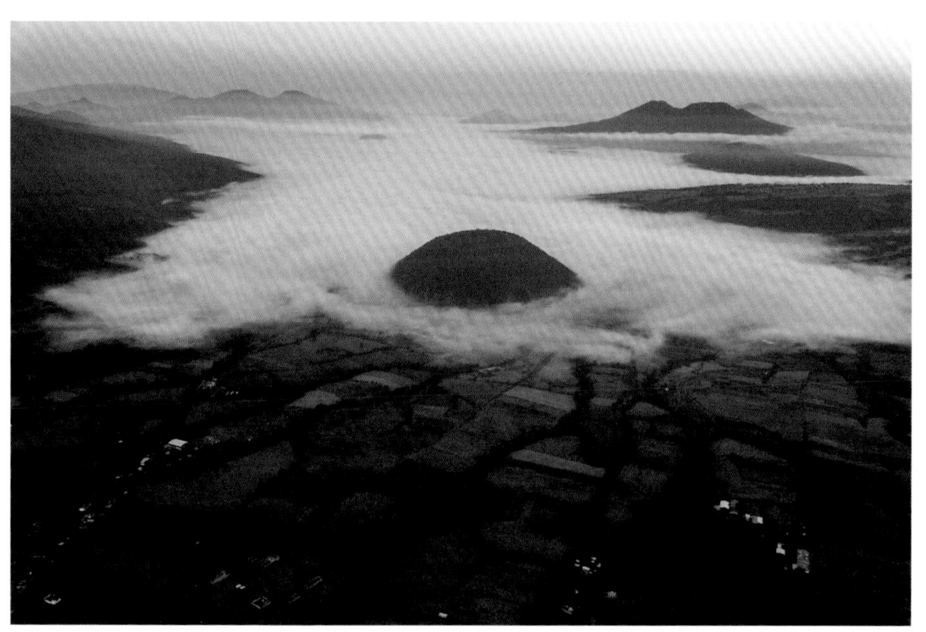

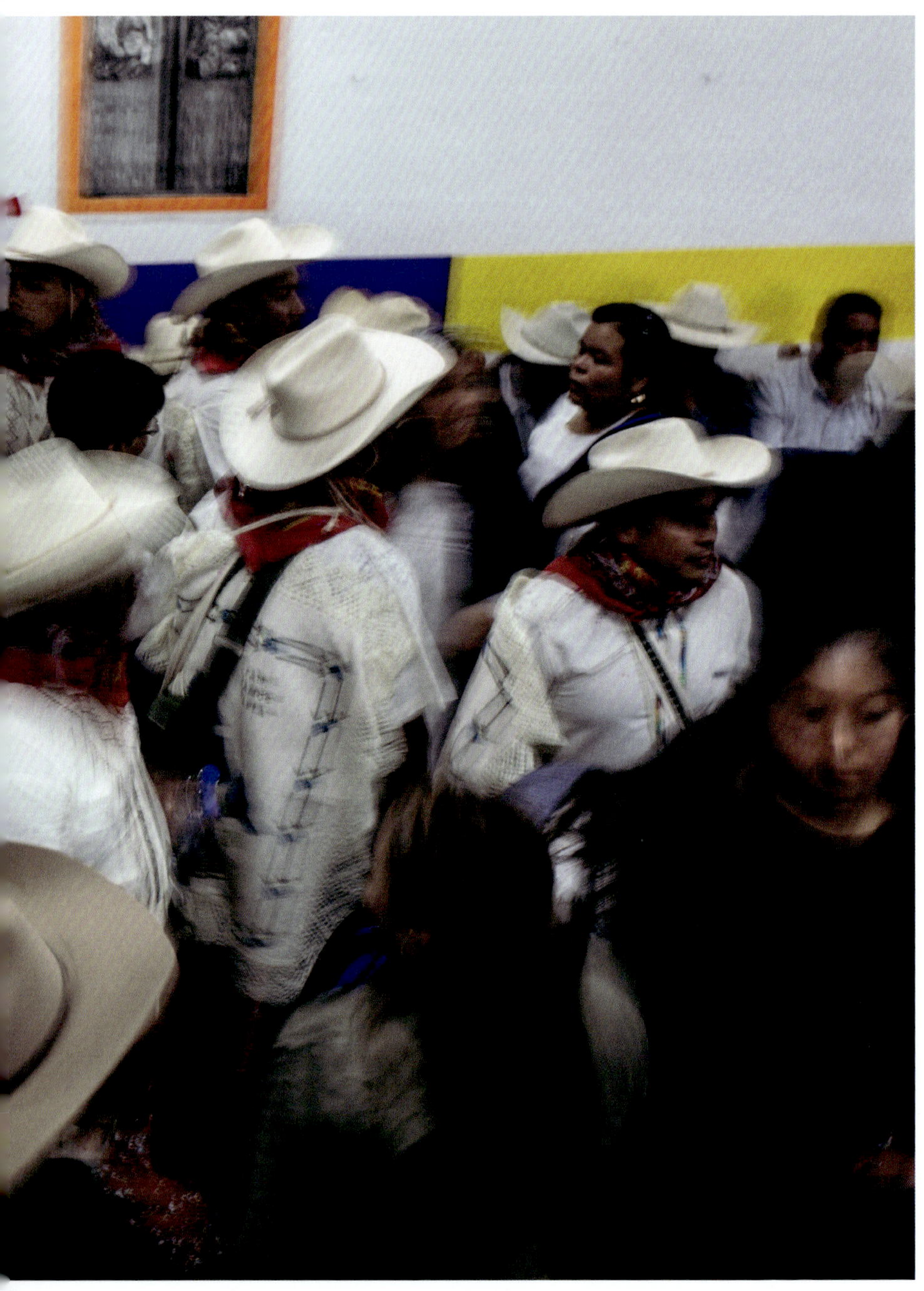

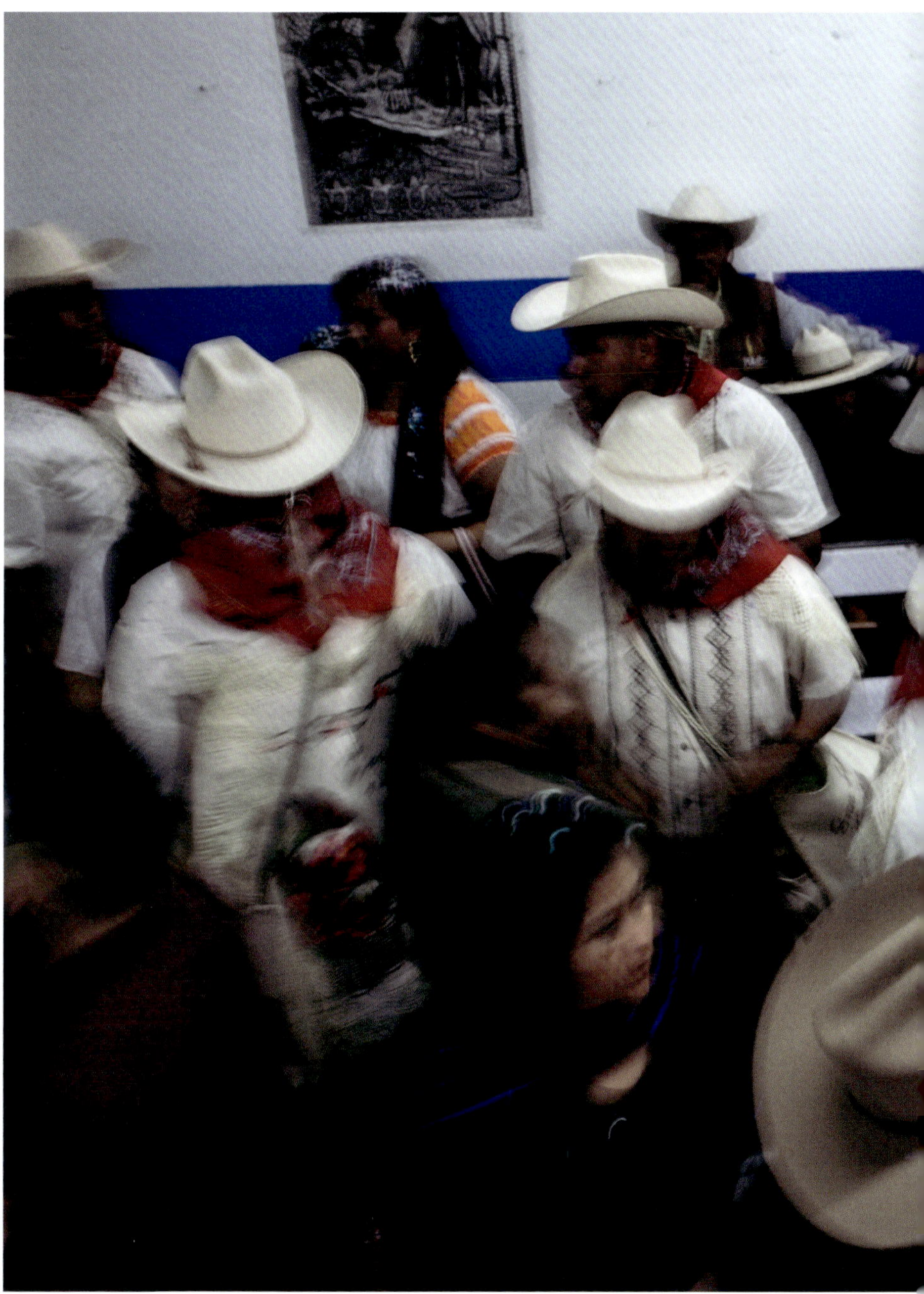

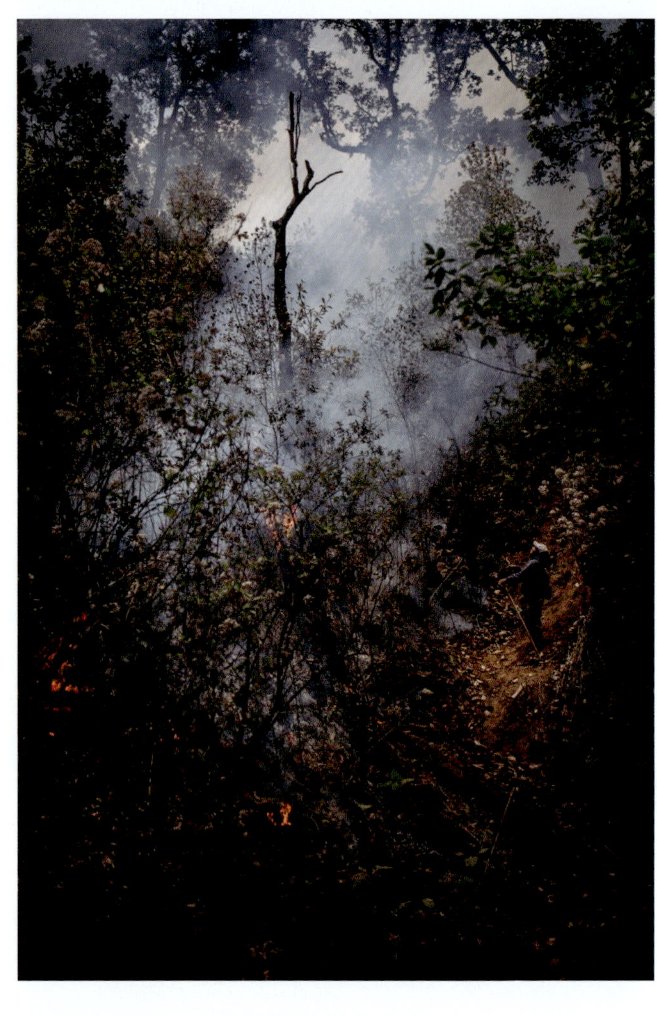

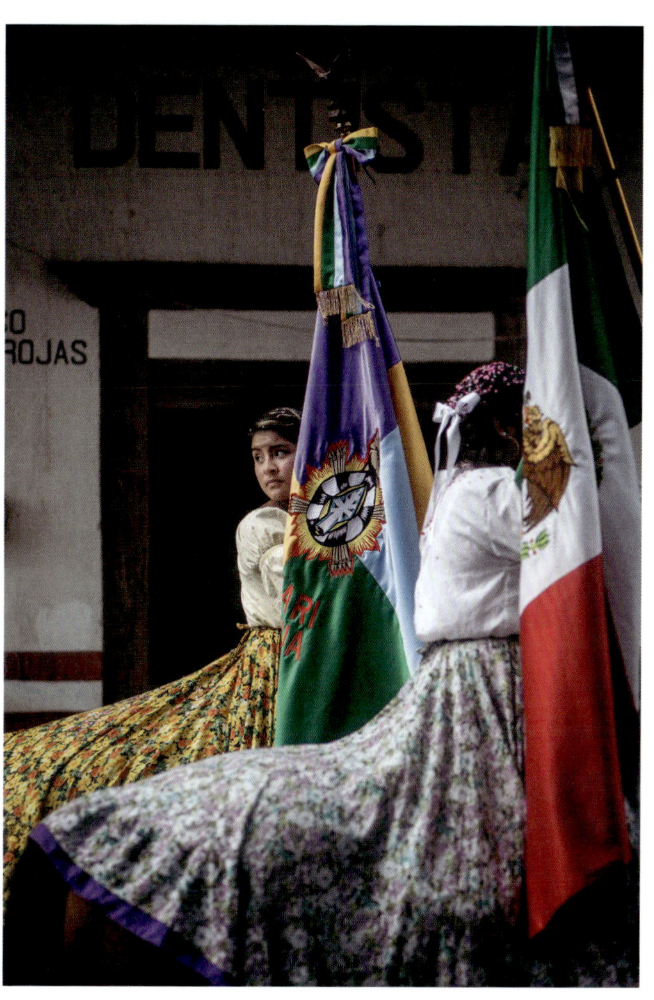
ROJAS

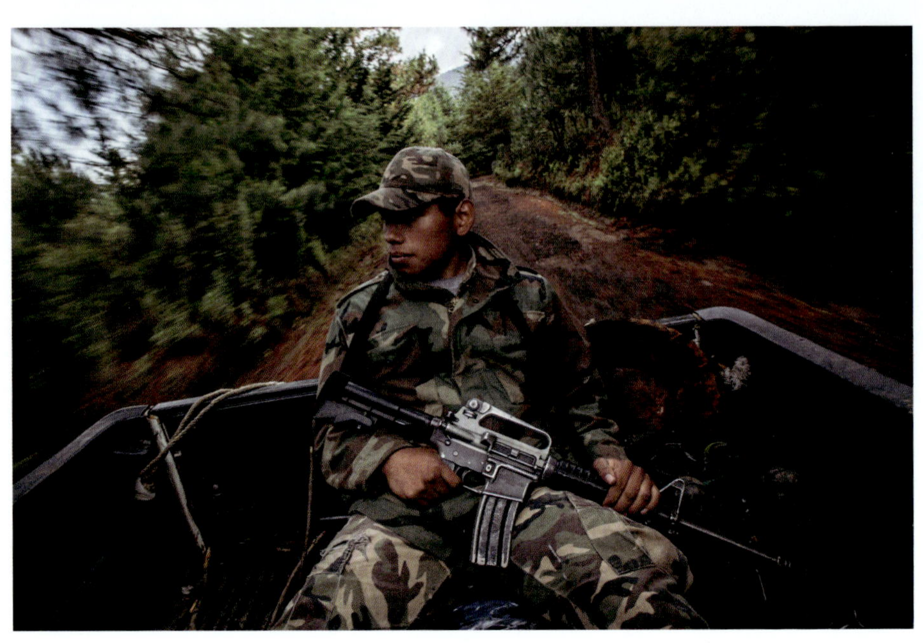

Organized crime has taken control of several regions of Mexico, bringing harm not only to the people, but also the flora and fauna. In Michoacan, large parts of what once were pinewood forests have been replaced by clean cut terrain and avocado mono populations. In 2011, not being able to endure this any longer, the indigenous Purepecha community rose up and revolted against the cartels and the corruption. After declaring autonomy, they started working on countering the damage done to both the environment and their community.

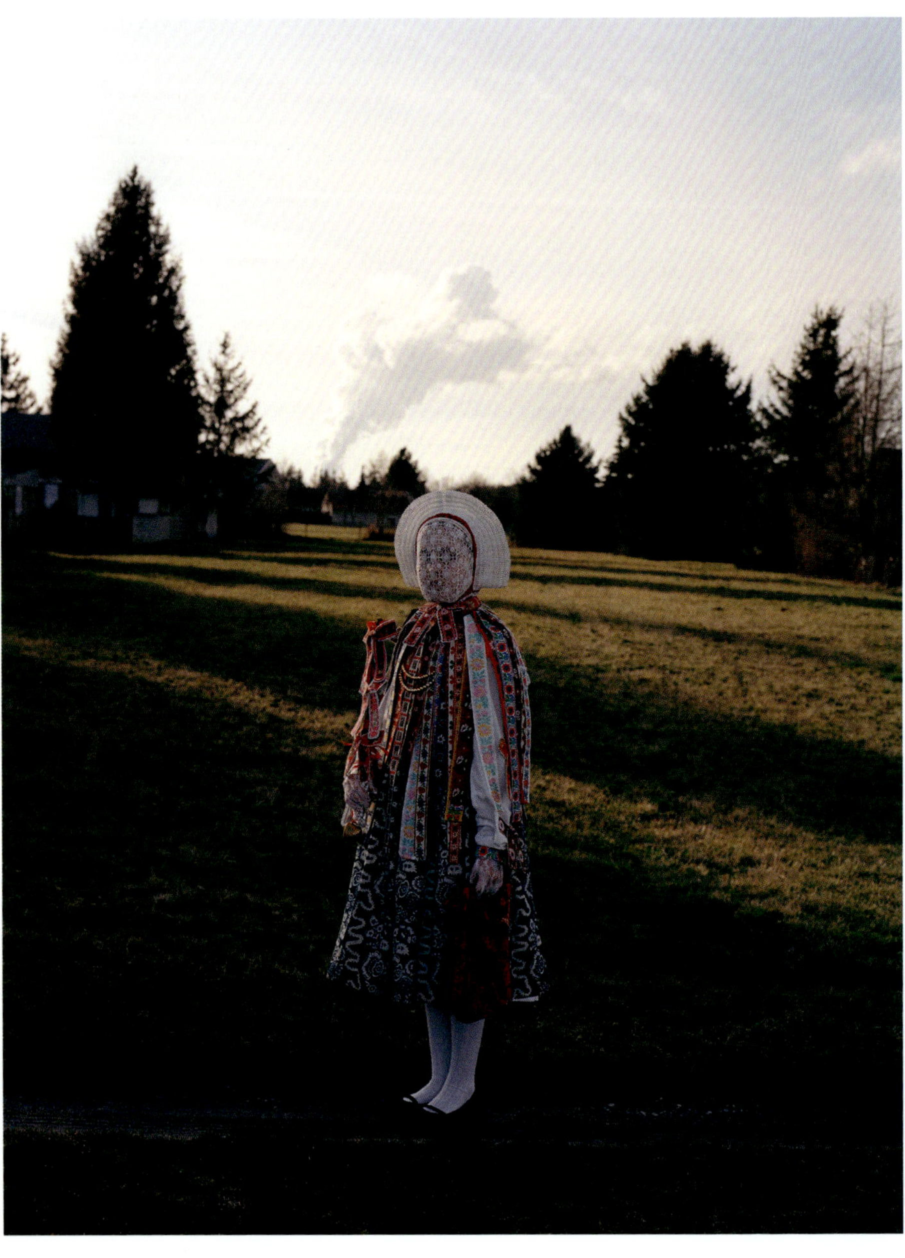

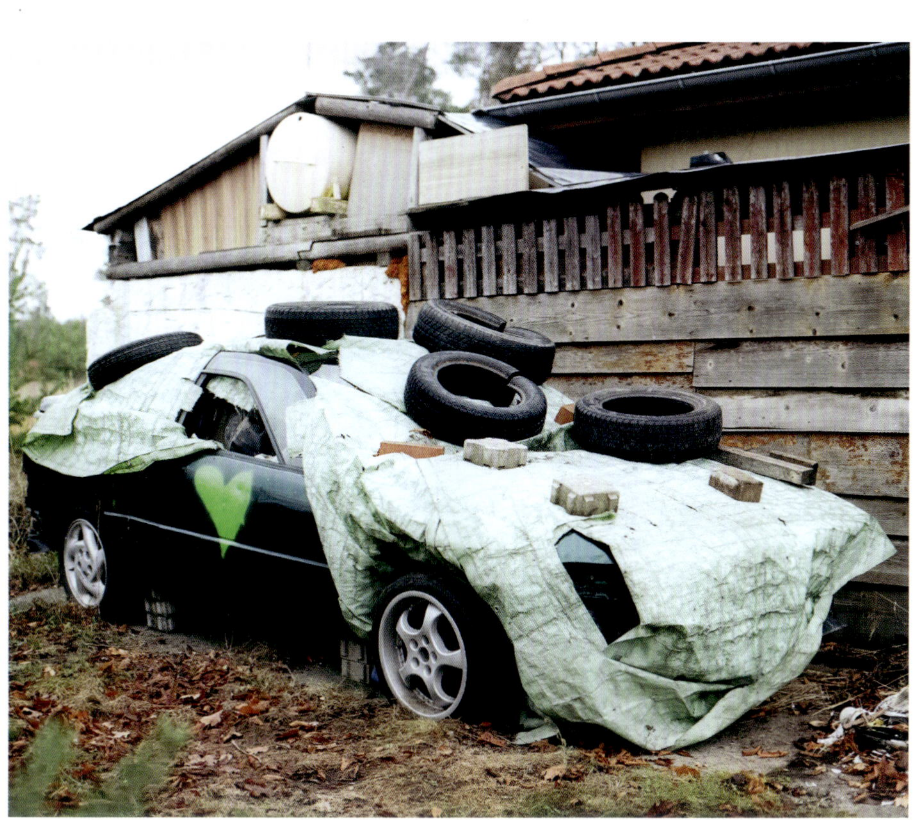

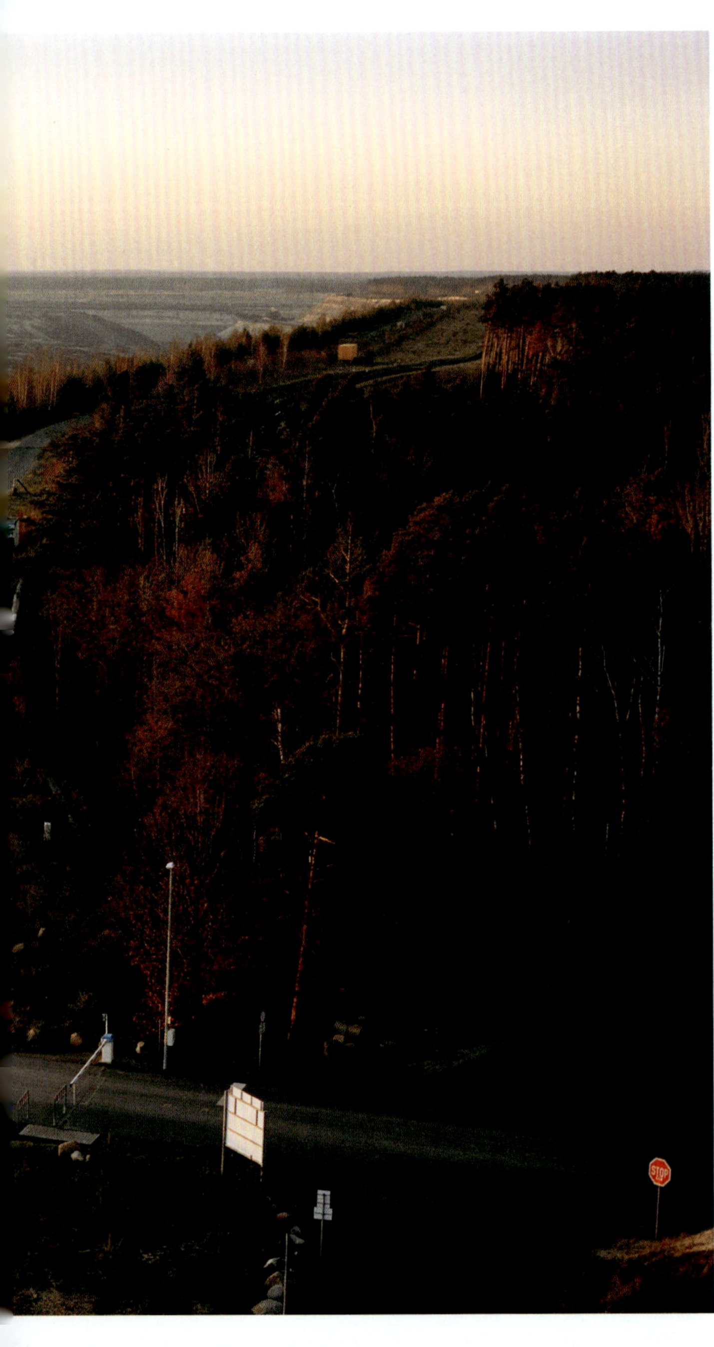
STOP

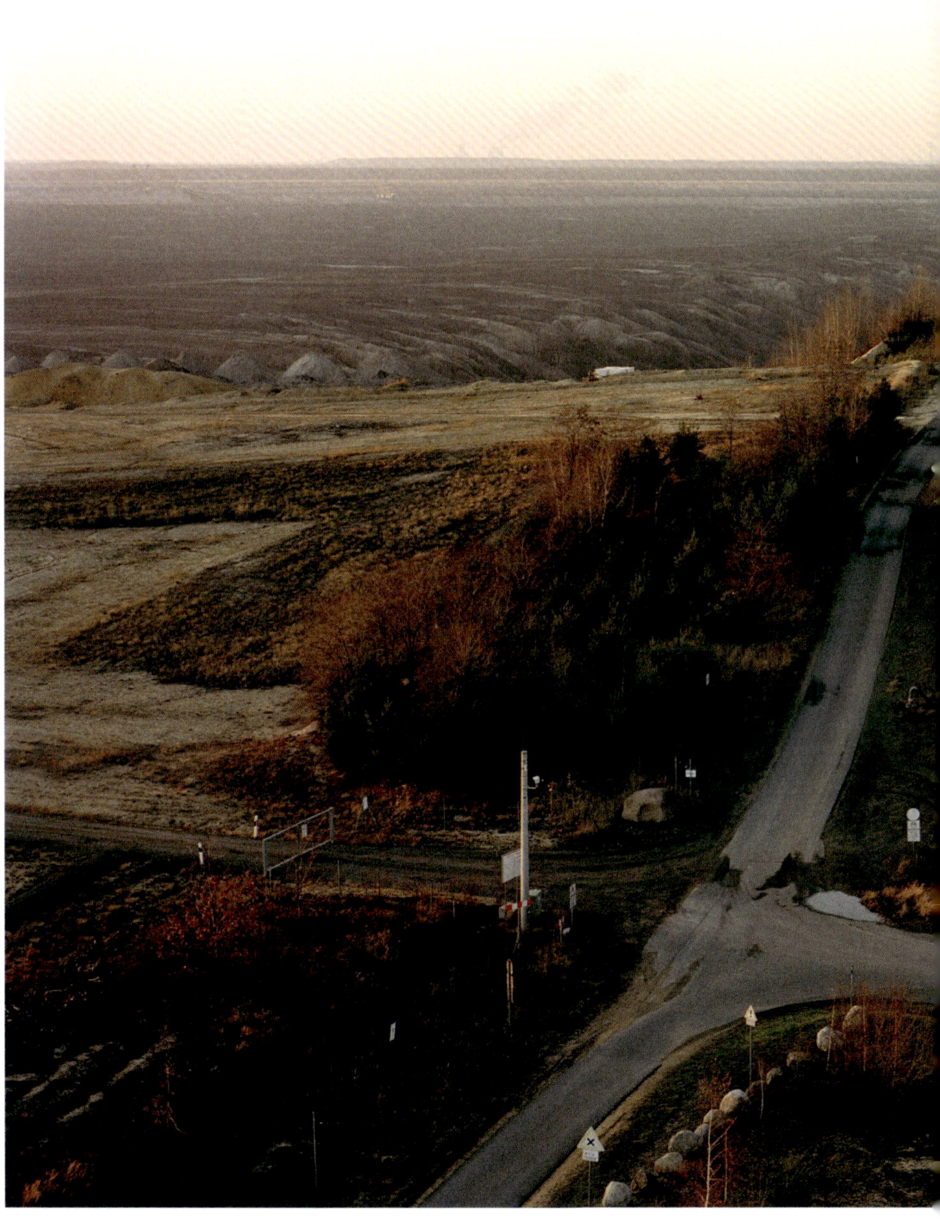

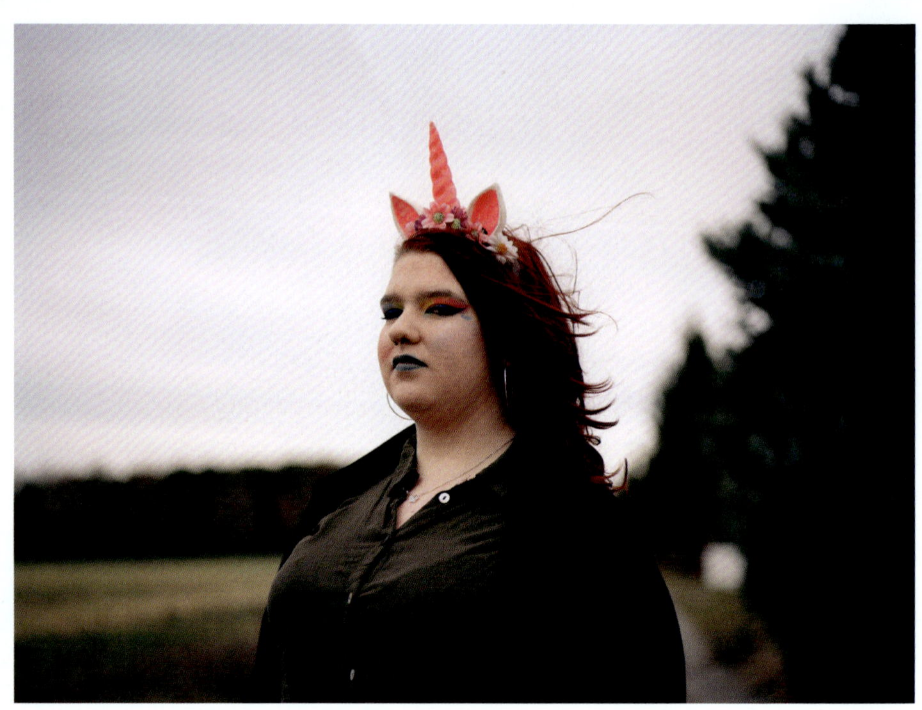

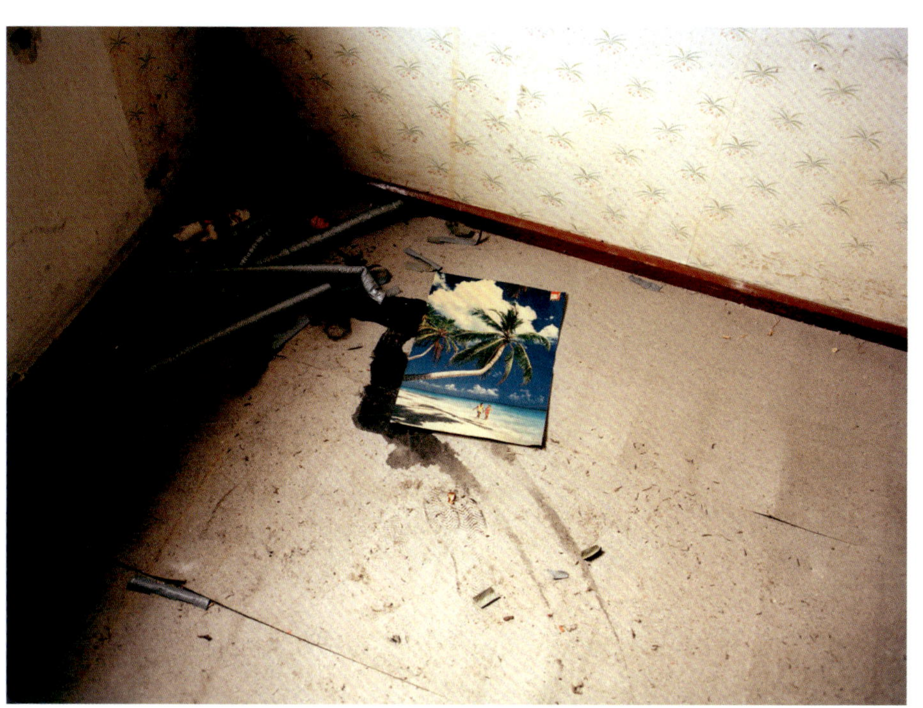

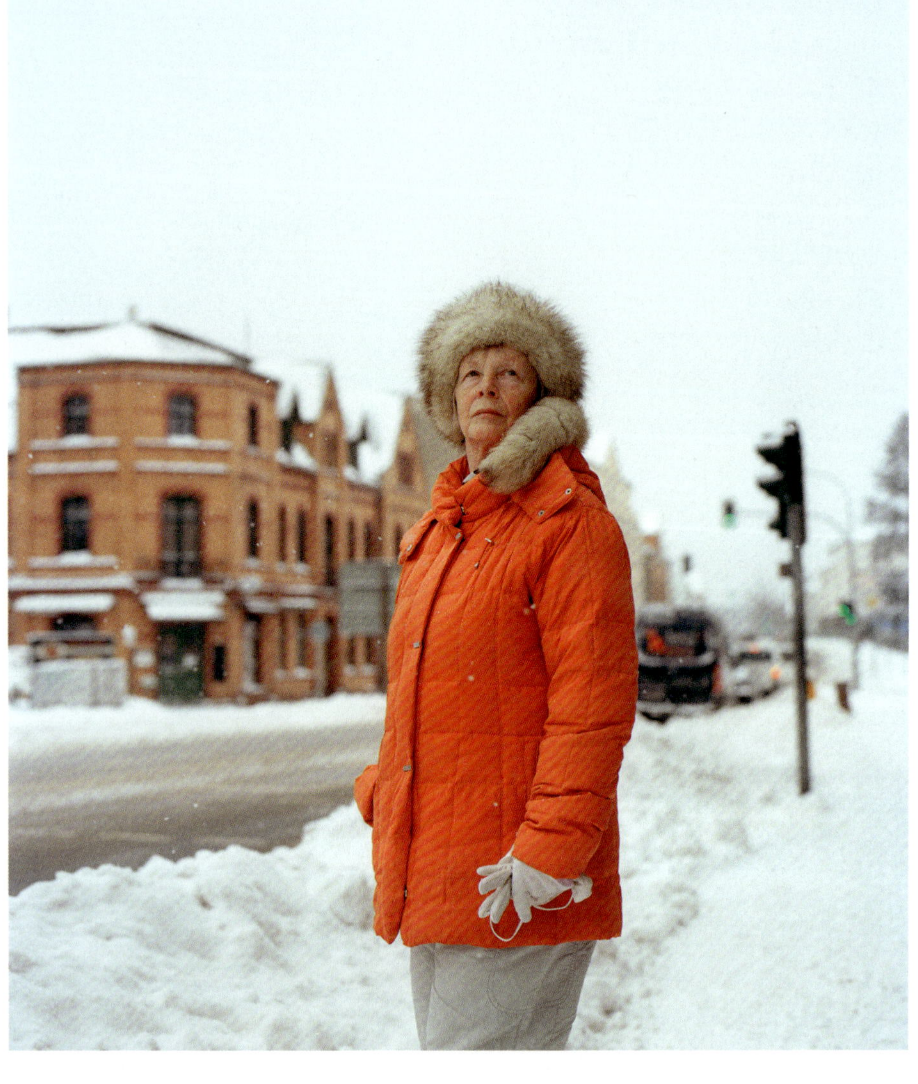

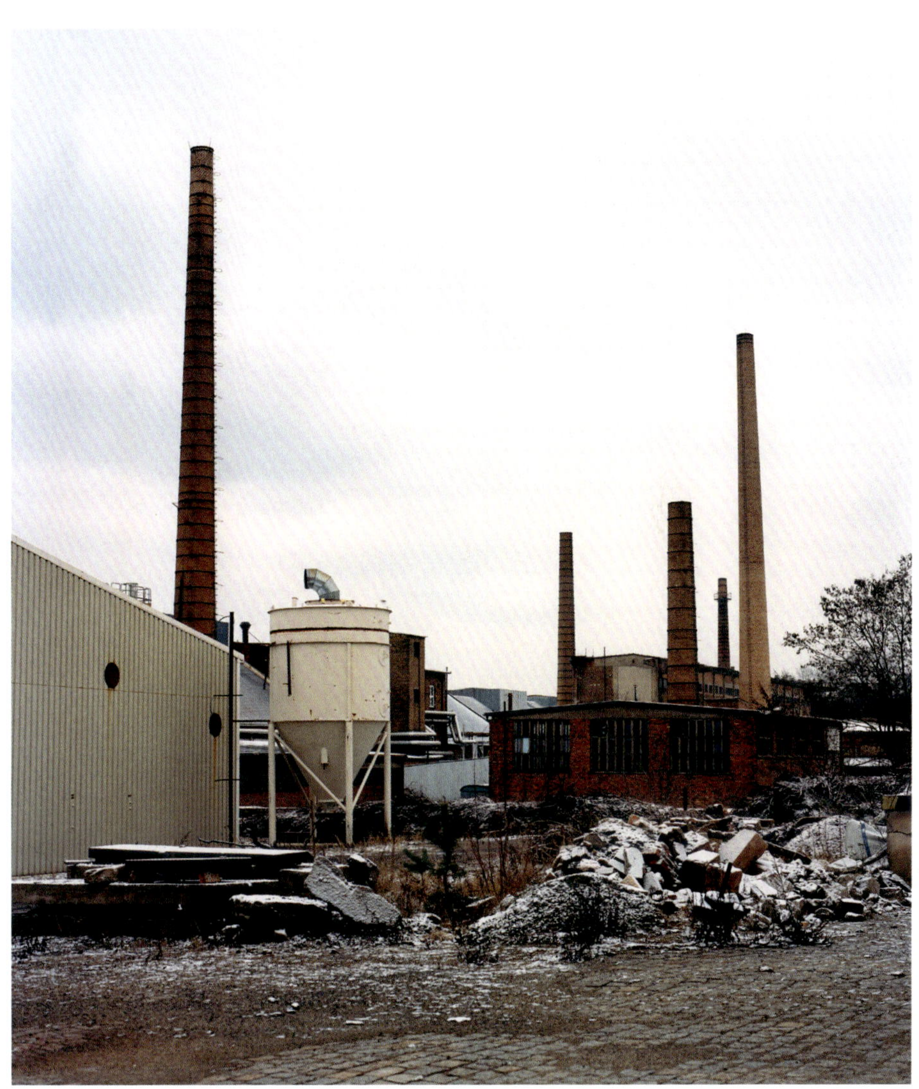

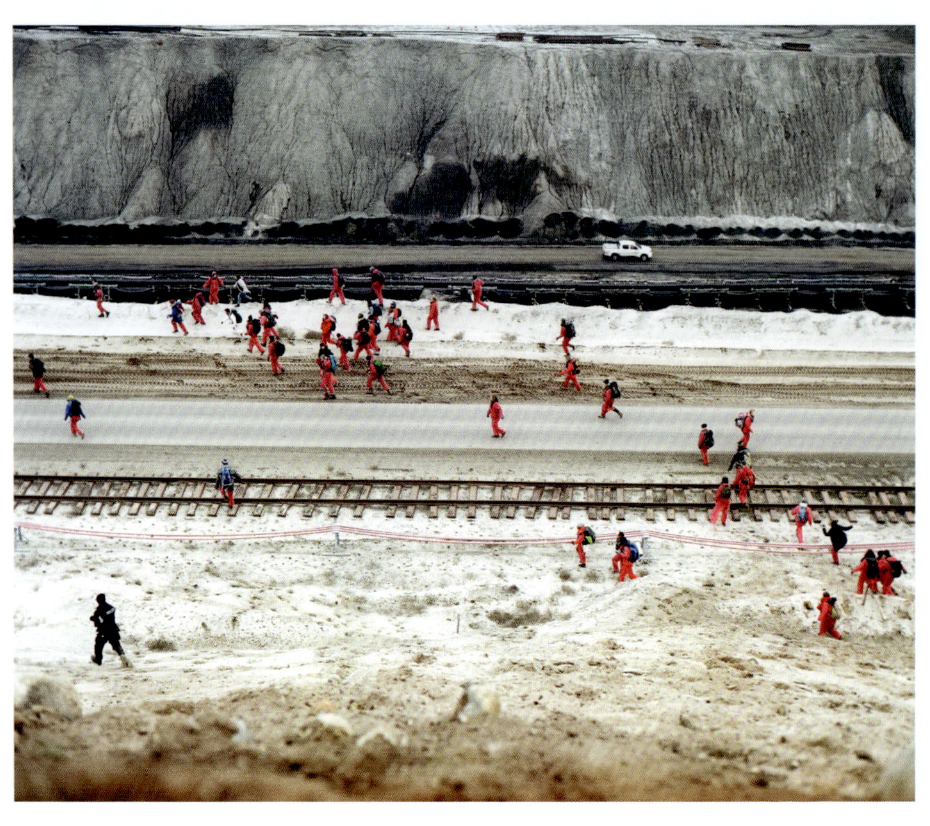

Like memorials of the glory days, the gigantic chimneys enthrone over the roofs of the town. The German reunification process let the fires of the old glassworks cool down. Deprived of their existence, half of the people left their homeland. Lignite Coal is still being mined here, yet. But in 2038 Lusatia is facing another historical turning point. The search for a new identity for the region and its people has begun.

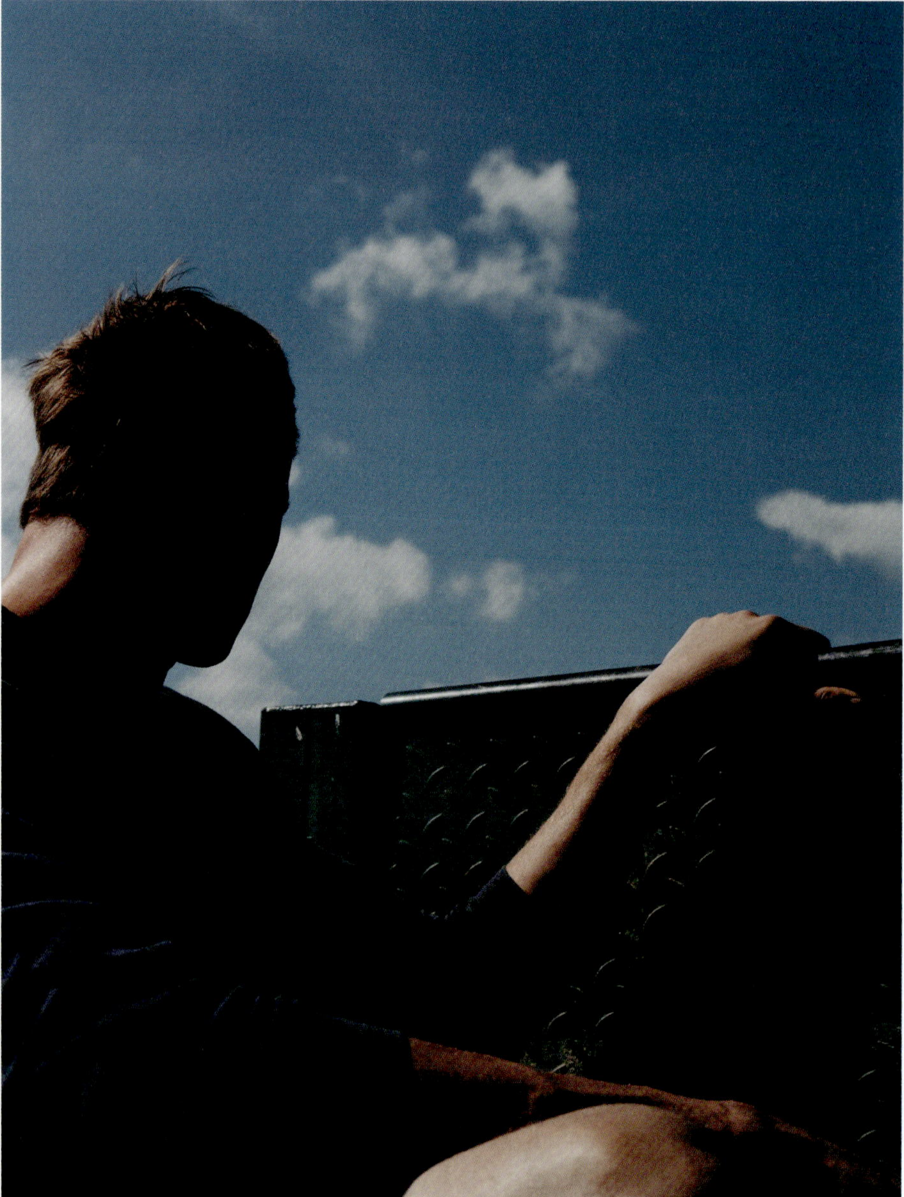

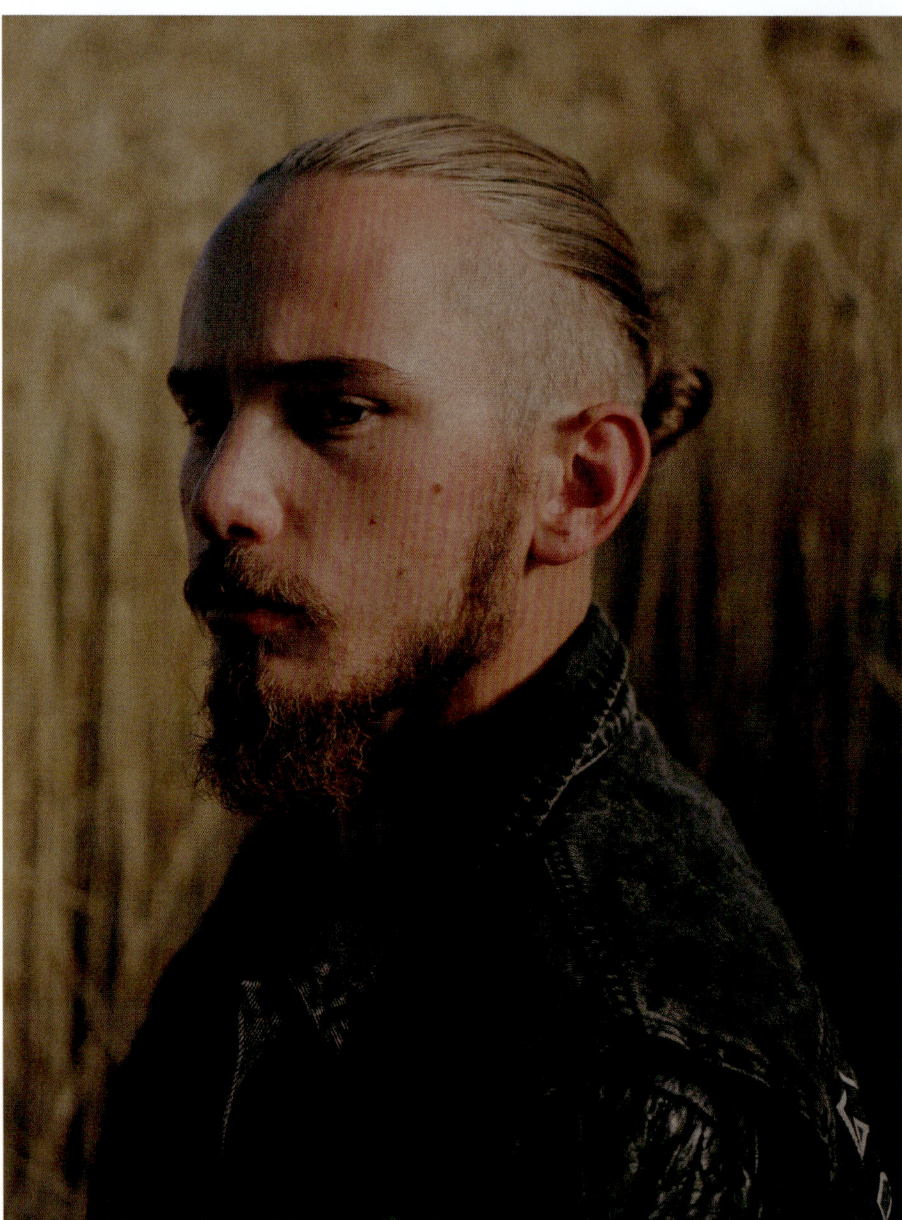

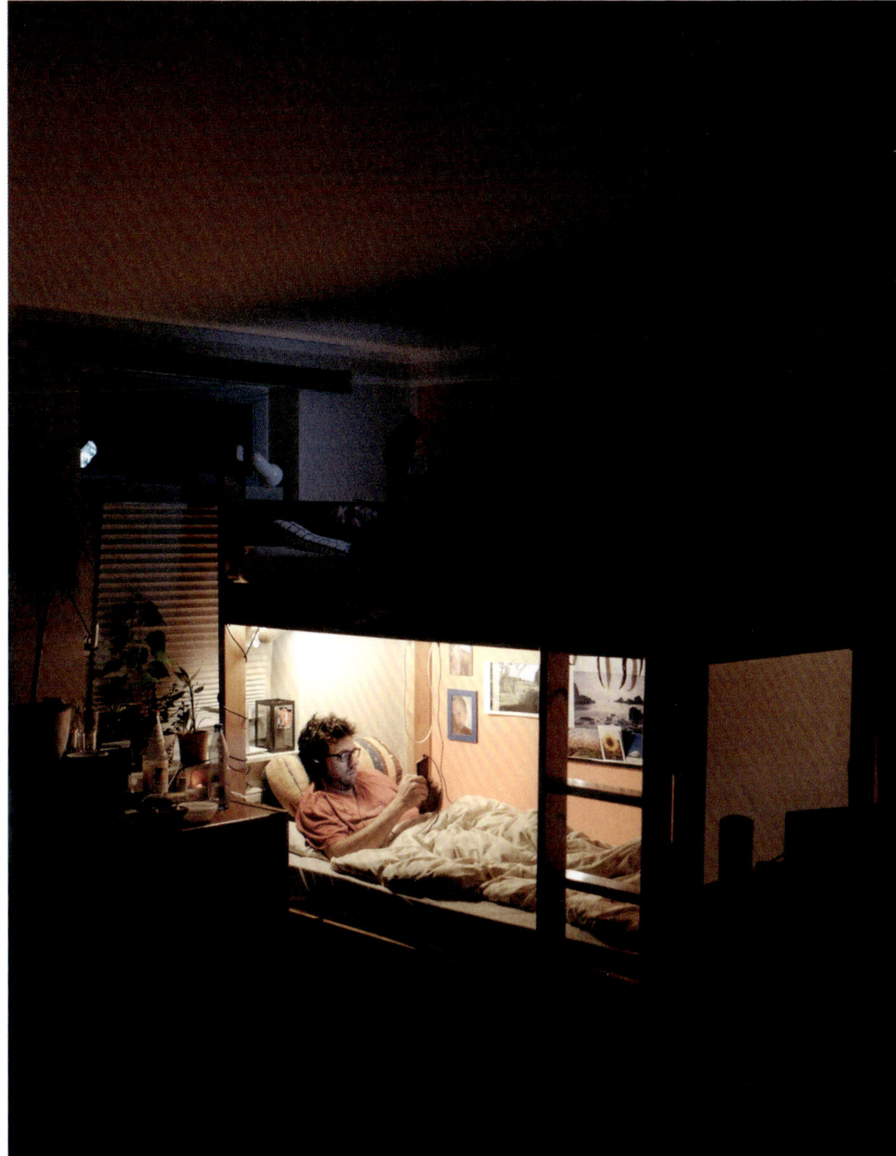

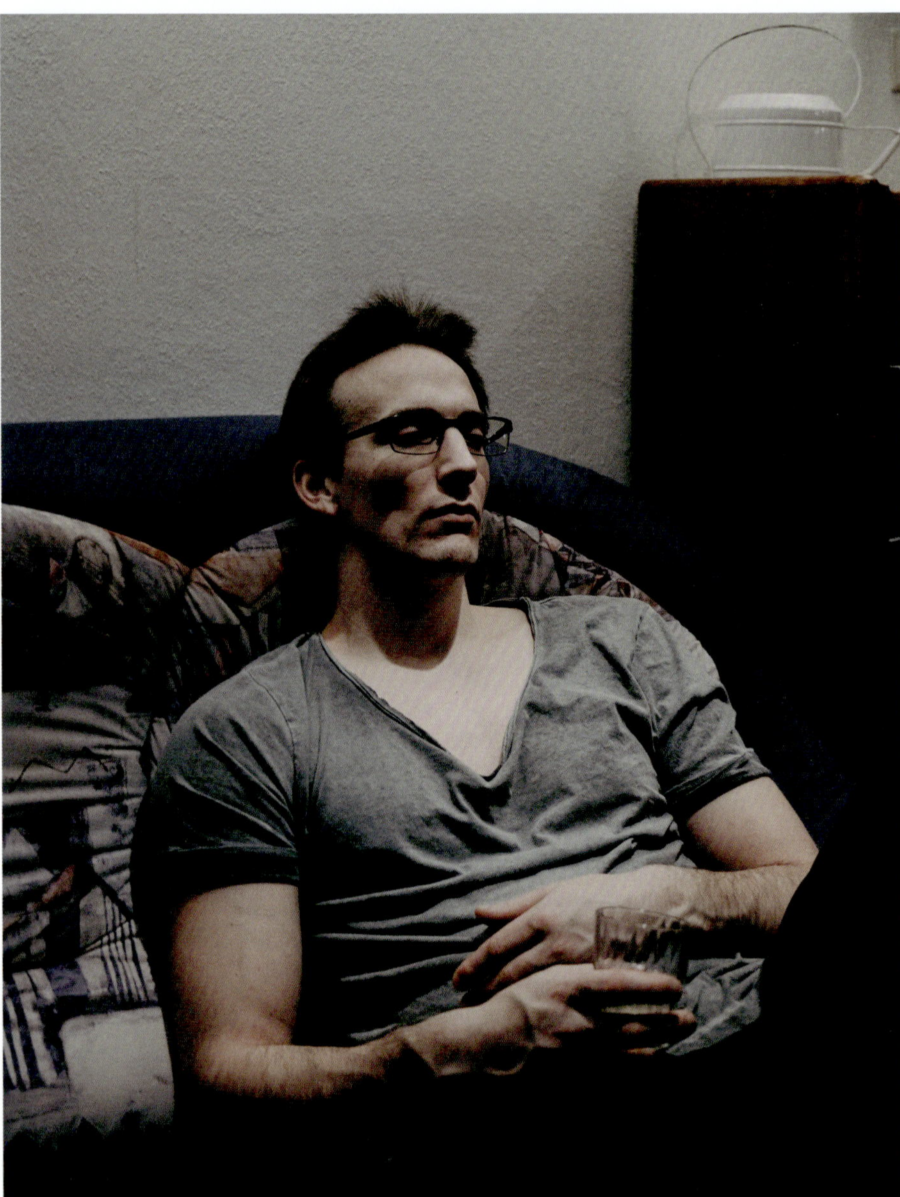

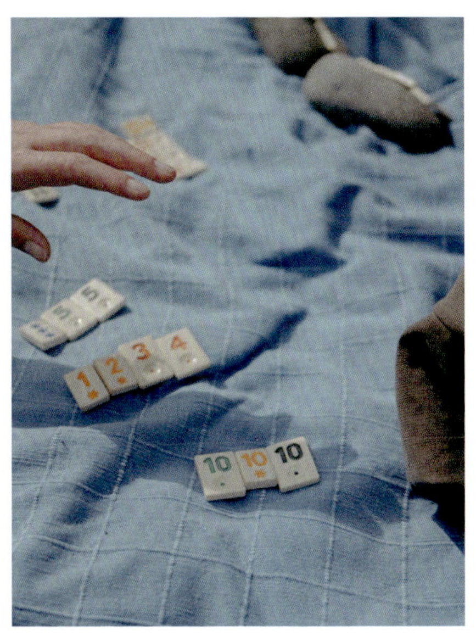
1 2 3 4
10 10 10

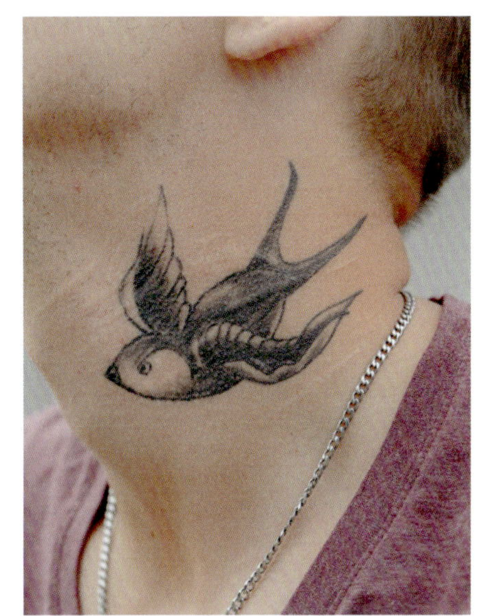

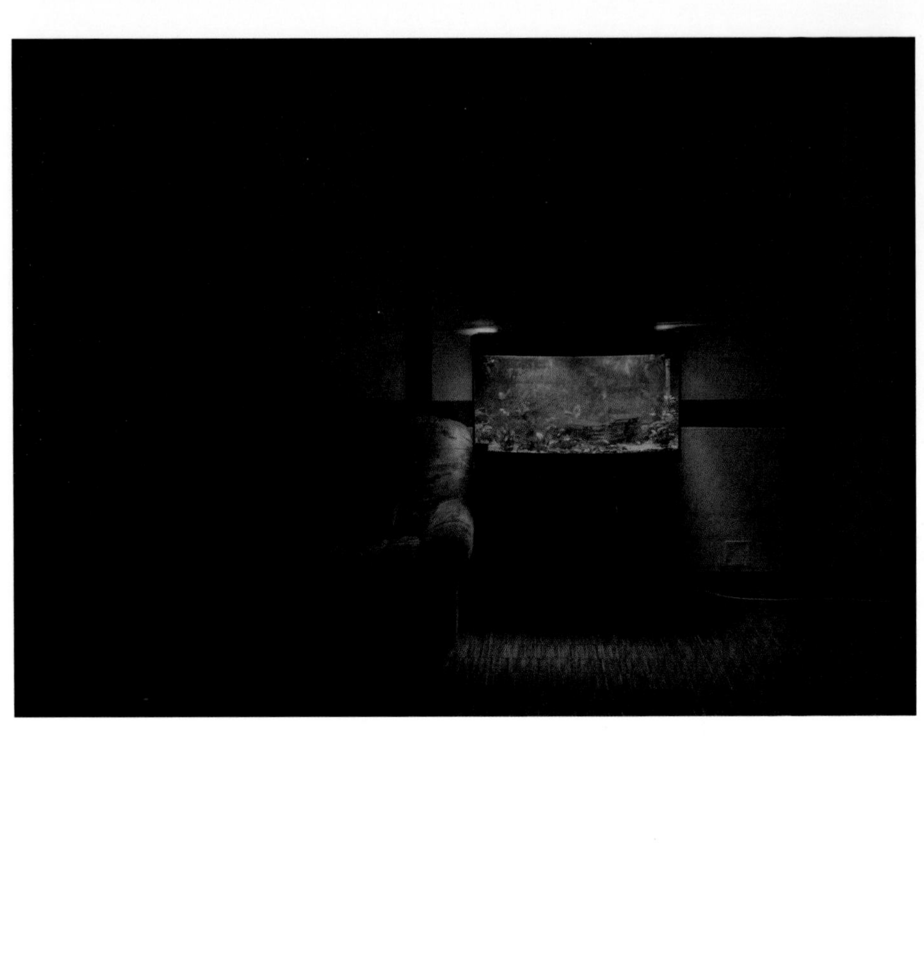

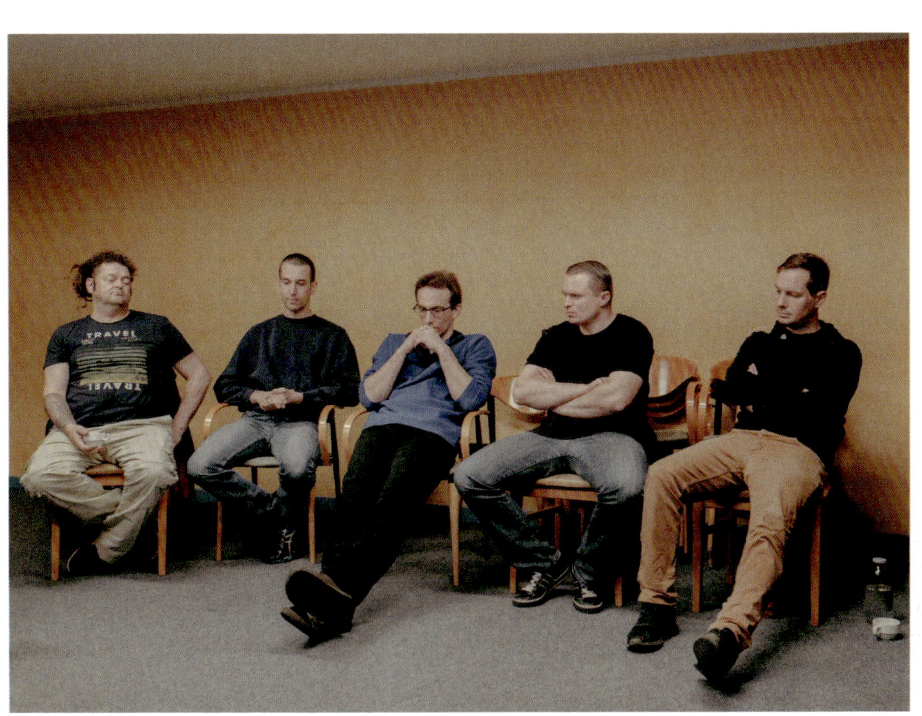
TRAVEL
TRAVEL

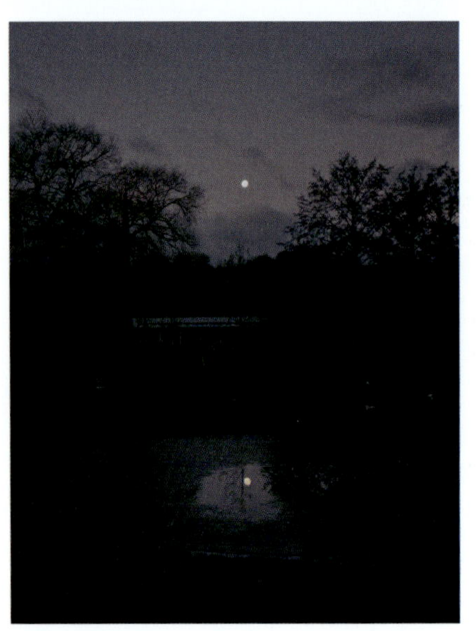

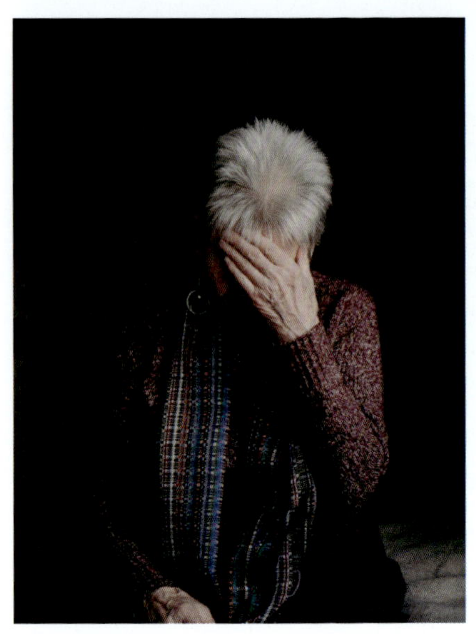

The Fleckenbühl farm, near Marburg in Germany, is home to over 100 drug addicts. They live together as a community and keep the farm running. Everyone can stay as long as they wish to, as long as they follow the rules: No contact with the outside world within the first six months; no drugs; no cigarettes; no violence.

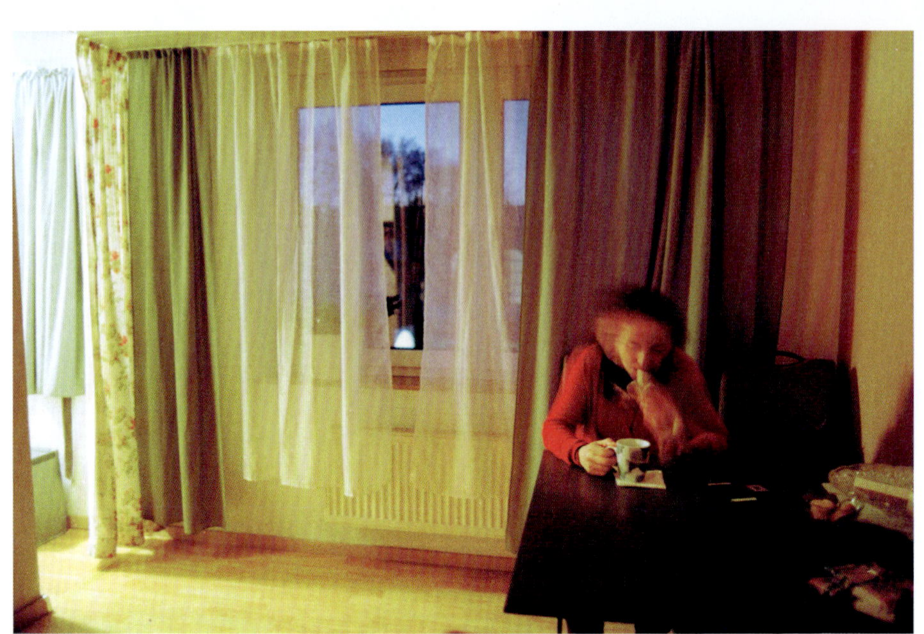

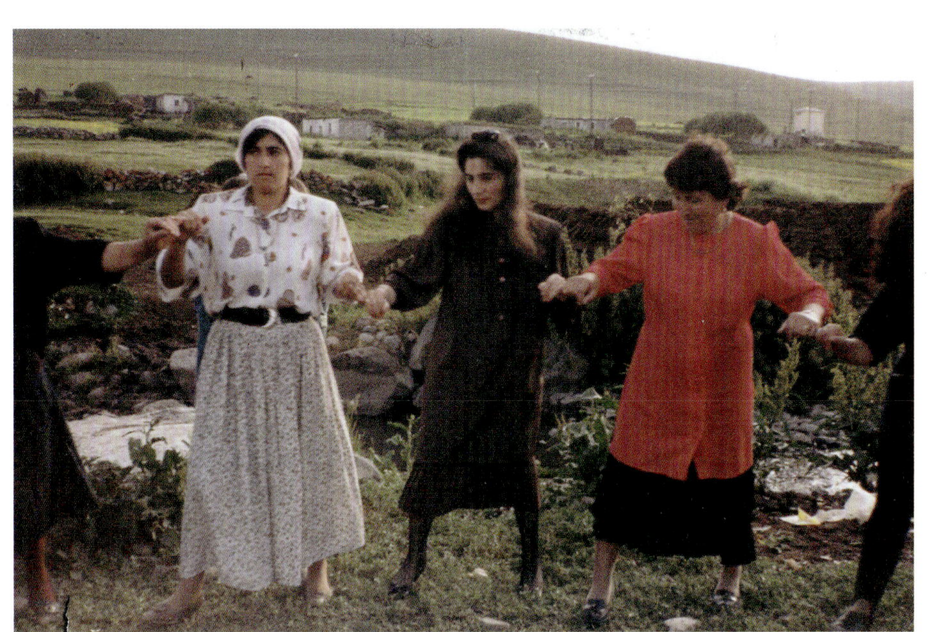

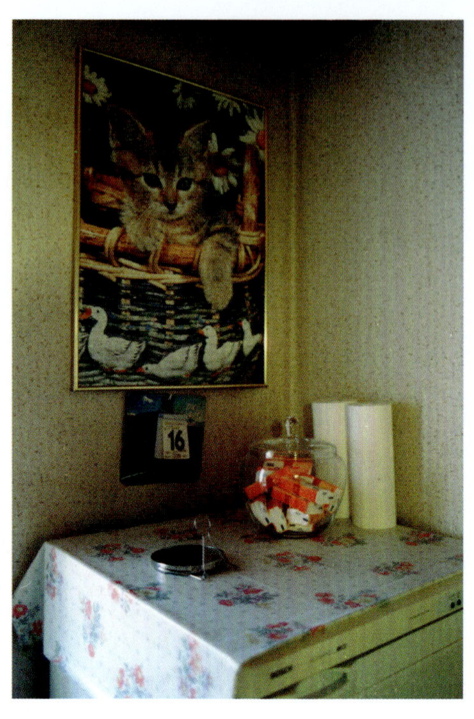

She says there is nothing else to say other than it was her wedding, taking place 3 months after she came to Germany and there were a bunch of people partying that she didn't know. Almost no one of her family was there because it was so hard for them to get a Visa and she danced with strangers.

There is no enthusiasm in her voice.

After two years she went back to her home town for holidays the first time.

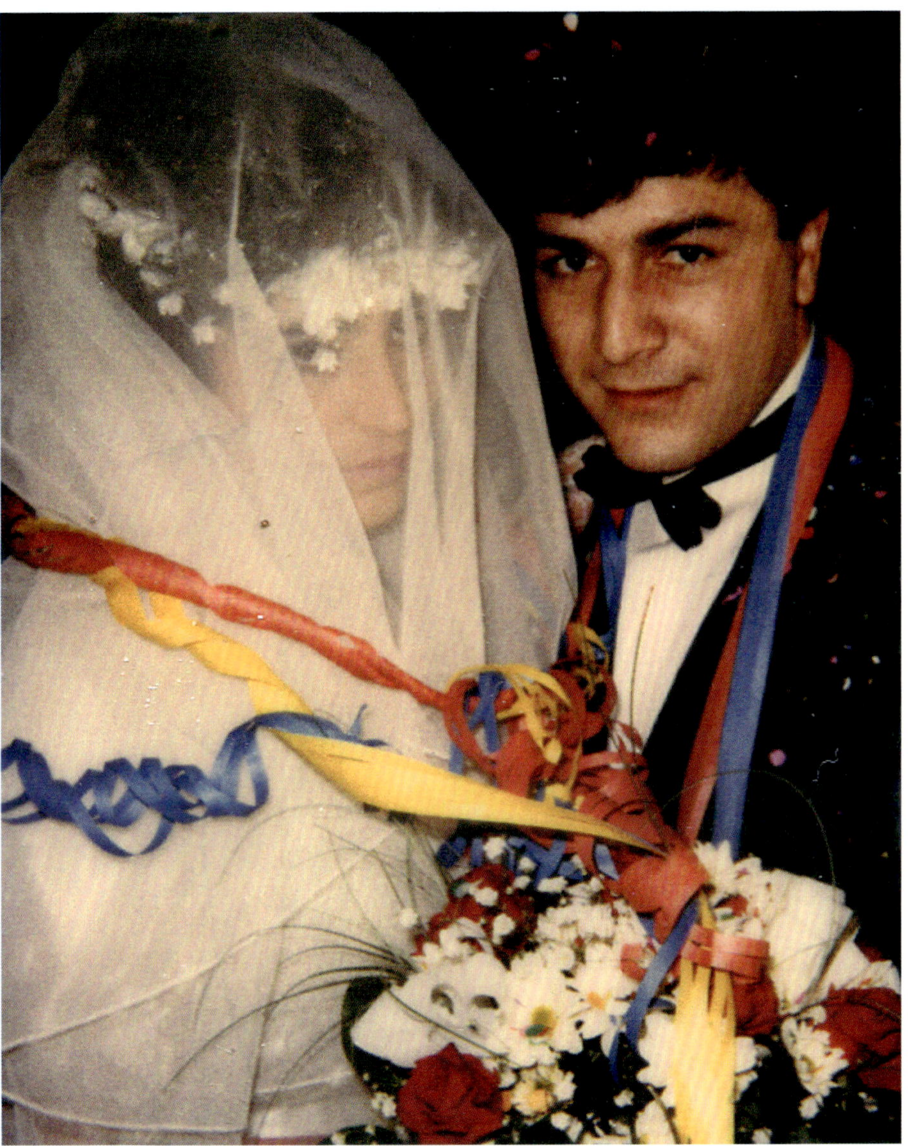

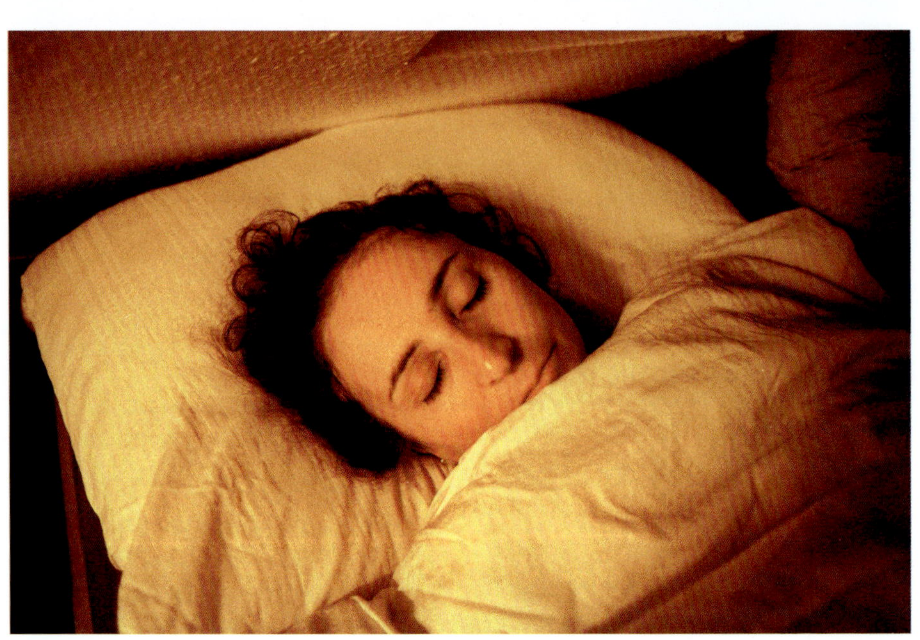

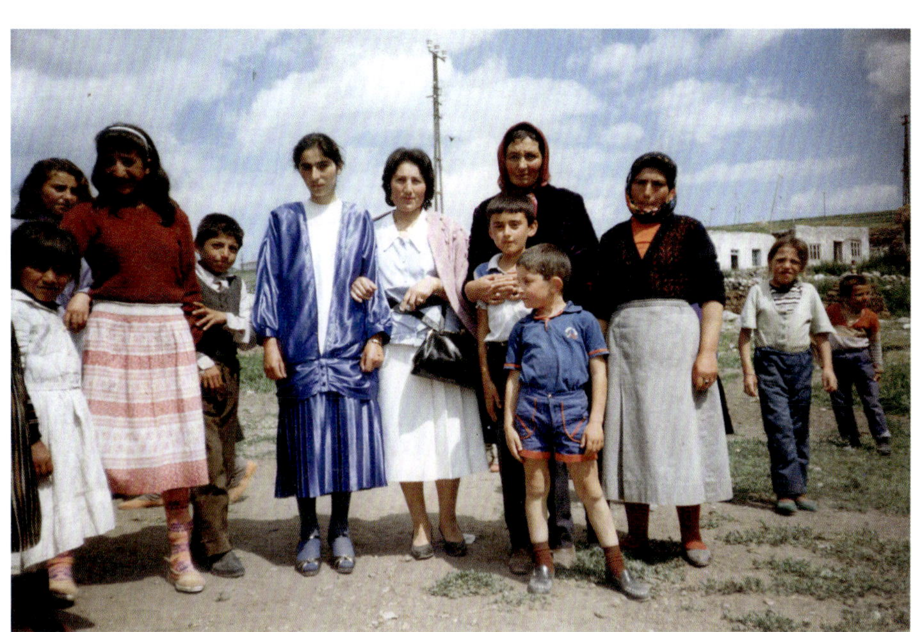

A lot of our conversations are about her current situation, about having money issues, searching for a job or an apartment, having debts and dealing with people that work in the job center. We repeat ourselves again and again. Sometimes we get some good news and feel some hope for a brief moment. I've seen her smile from ear to ear two times the past three weeks. We also have some good moments, we cook for each other and enjoy eating together a lot. Sometimes we watch a movie, after a long and exhausting day, when we both feel like we need a little closeness. Last week we had a pretty loud discussion and I called my brother, asking if he could talk to her because I was too exhausted. In the end she had to cry and said she always told him that he has to protect me and it makes her grateful and proud that she is now experiencing that he would even protect me from her. When I get out of the shower, I hear her saying "sıhhatler olsun" like for years ago when we still lived together. You say that in Turkey to basically wish someone health after the person takes a shower or gets a new haircut.

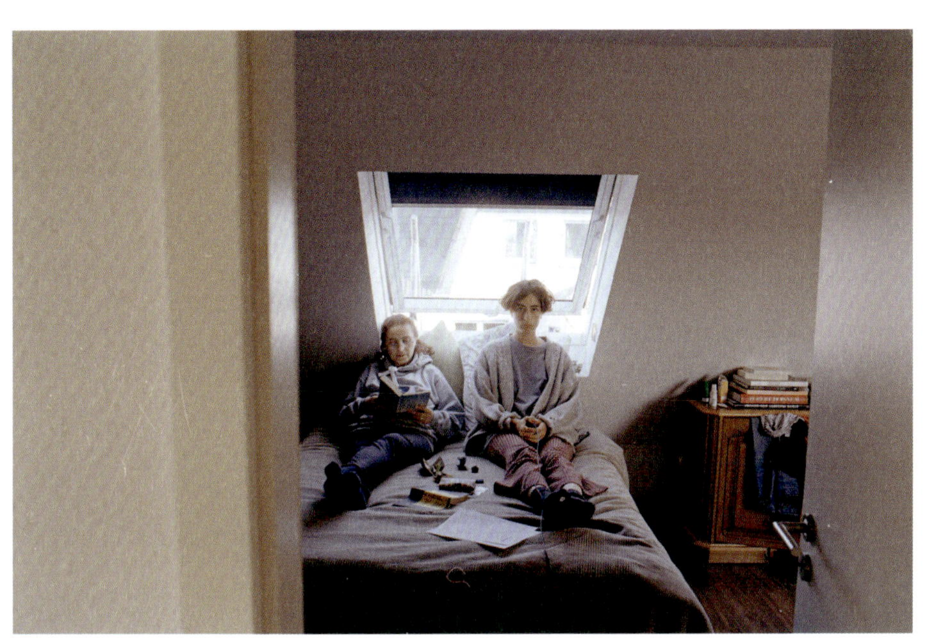

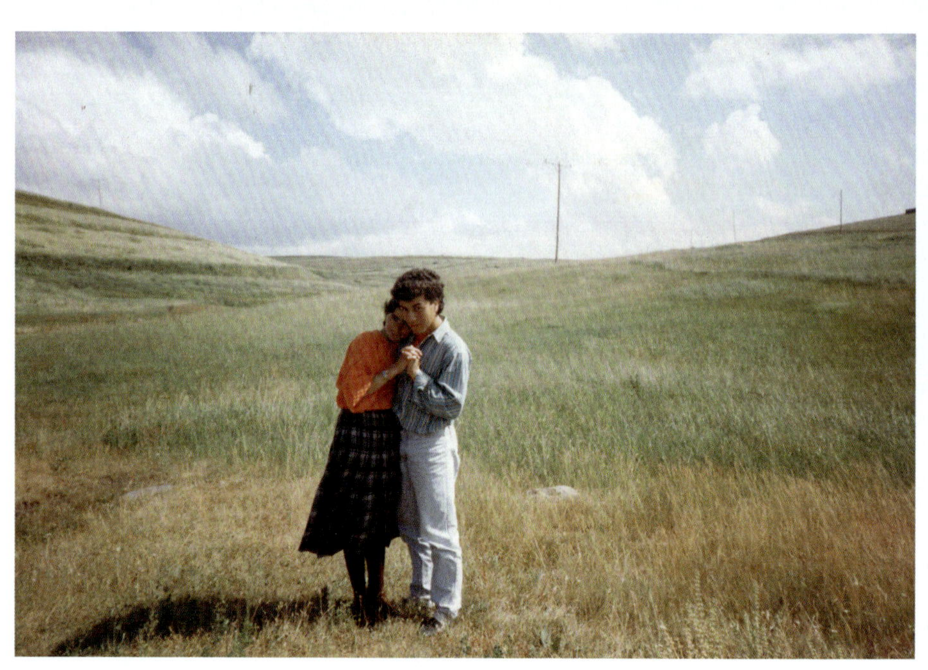

My mother grew up in Turkey and emigrated to Germany when she was 20 years old. In 2020, she had to leave her home once more: My father's debts forced them to leave their apartment. Suddenly, my mother had to rebuild her life again, faced by the difficult conditions in a country whose language she still speaks poorly. To gain a better understanding of her feelings, I started to catch up on her past.

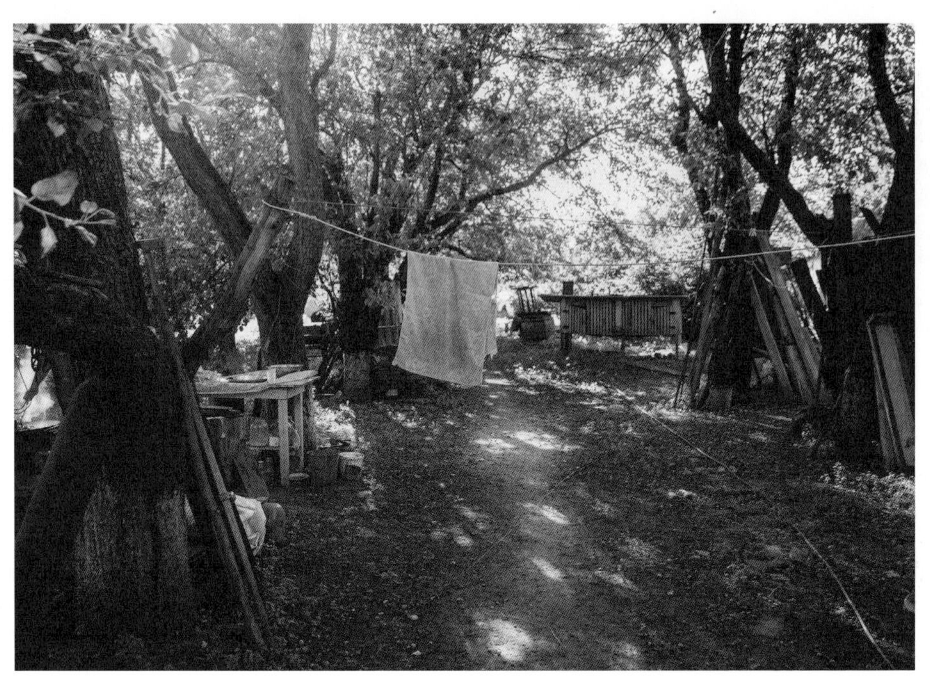

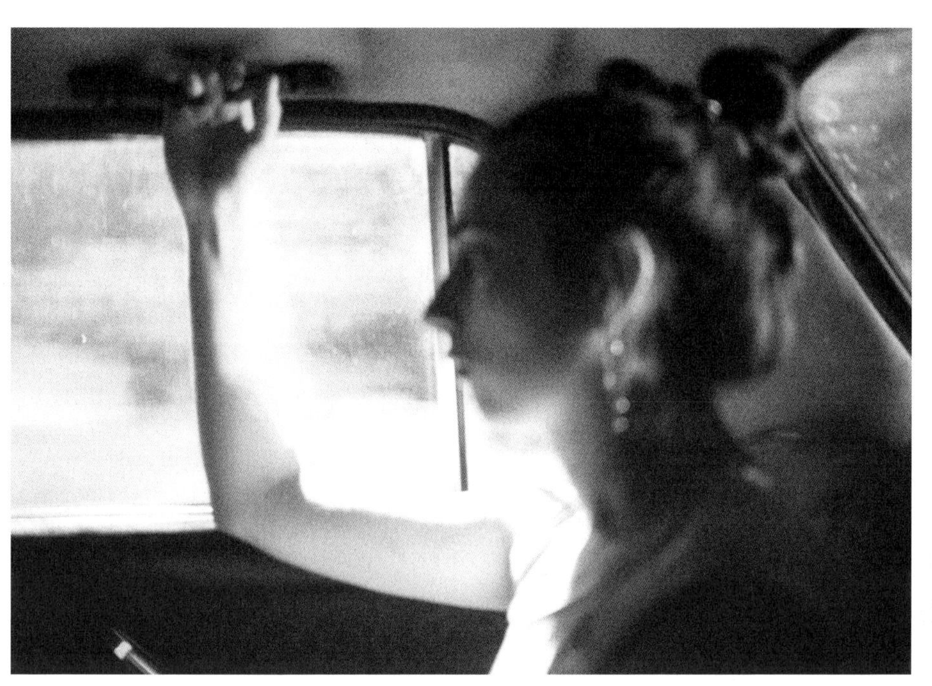

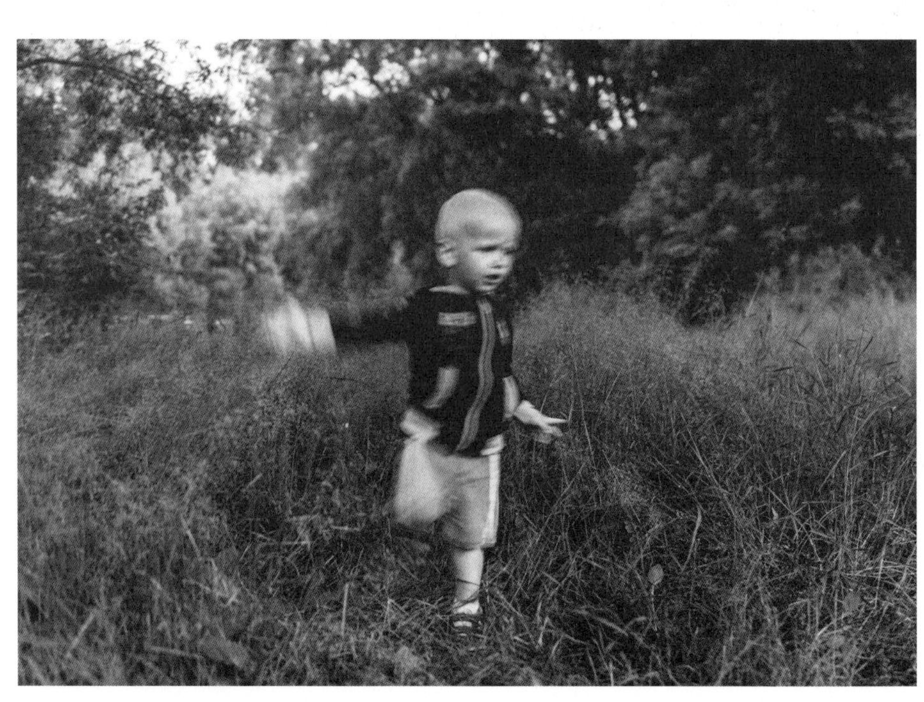

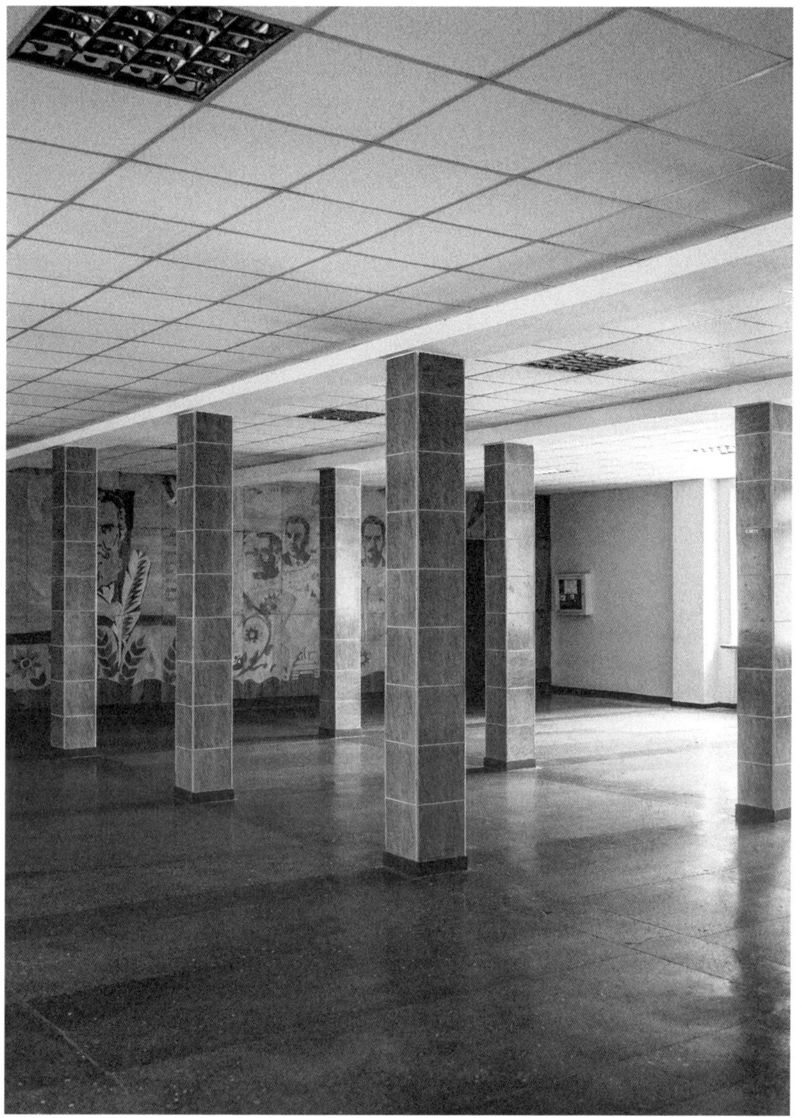

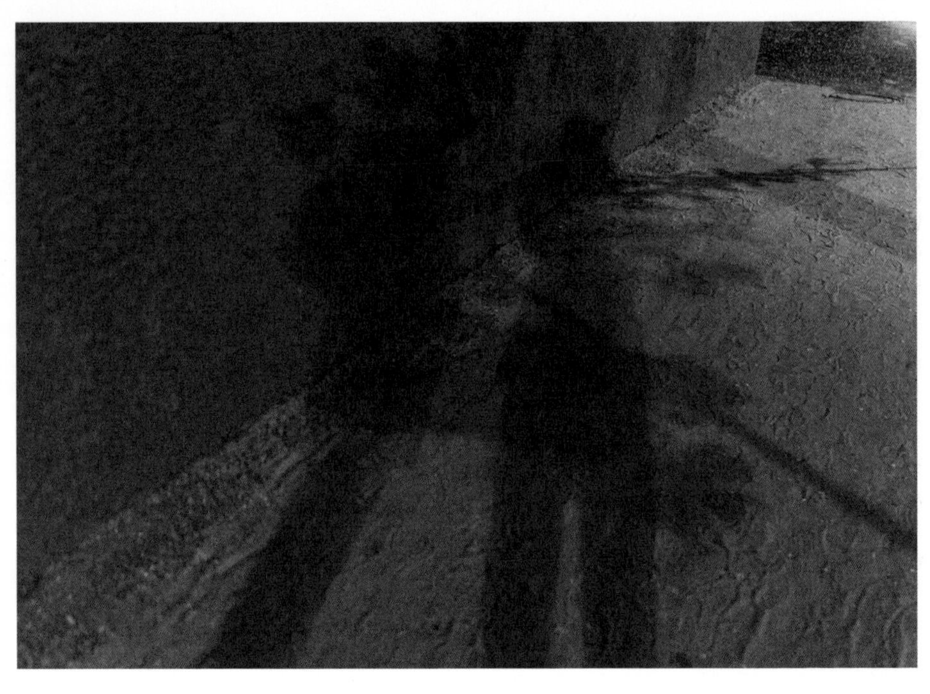

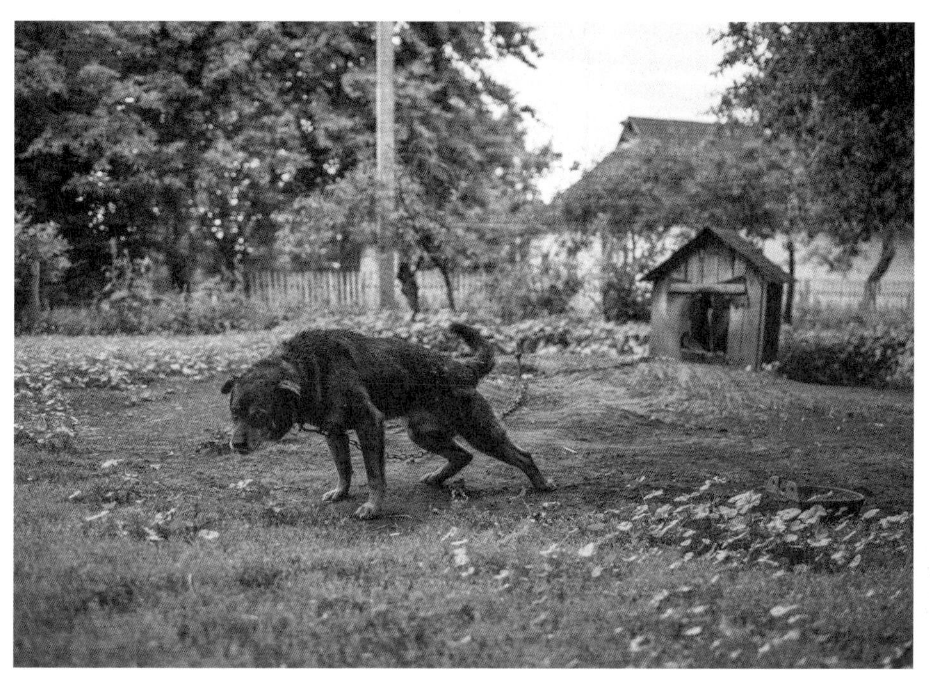

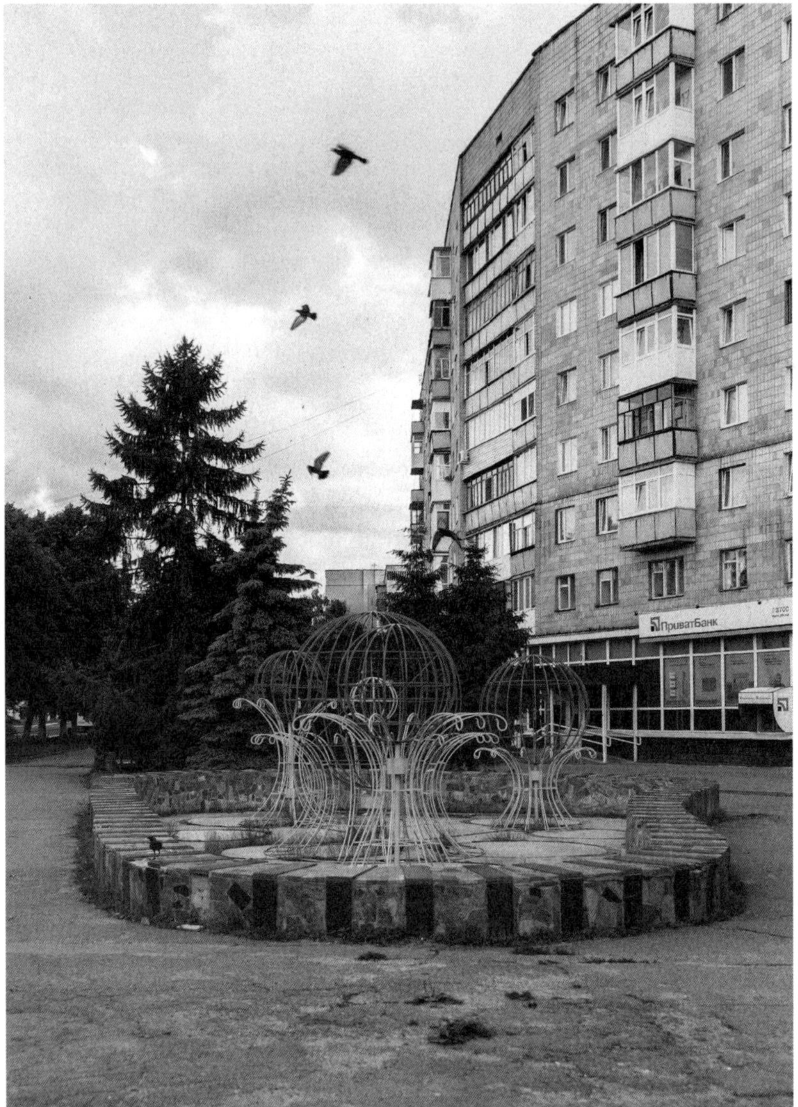
ПриватБанк
3700

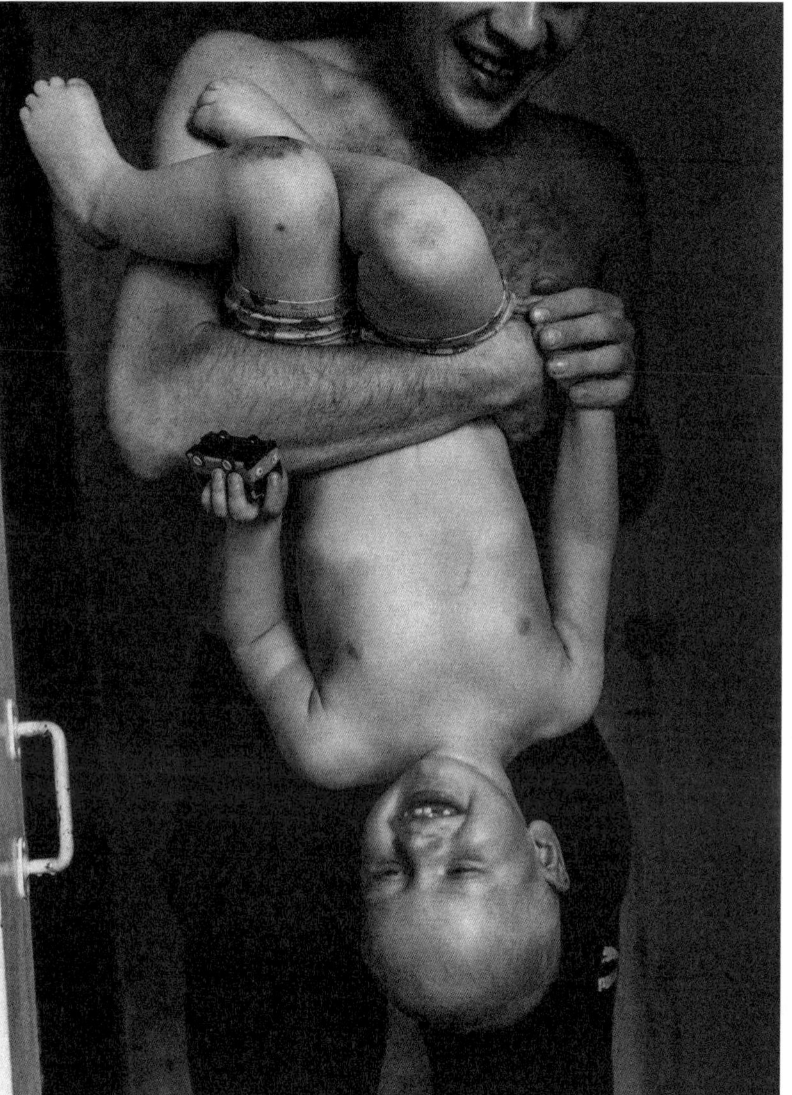

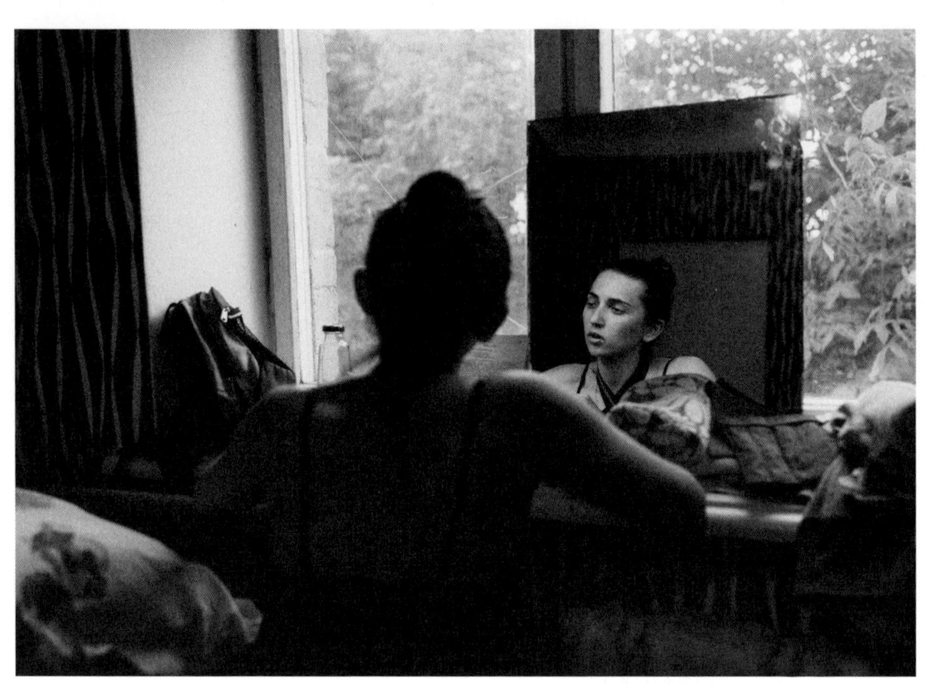

In June 2019, my girlfriend and I travelled together to Ukraine to meet her family for the first time. With questions in my head about her and her past, I documented our journey, trying to understand what I only knew from her stories.

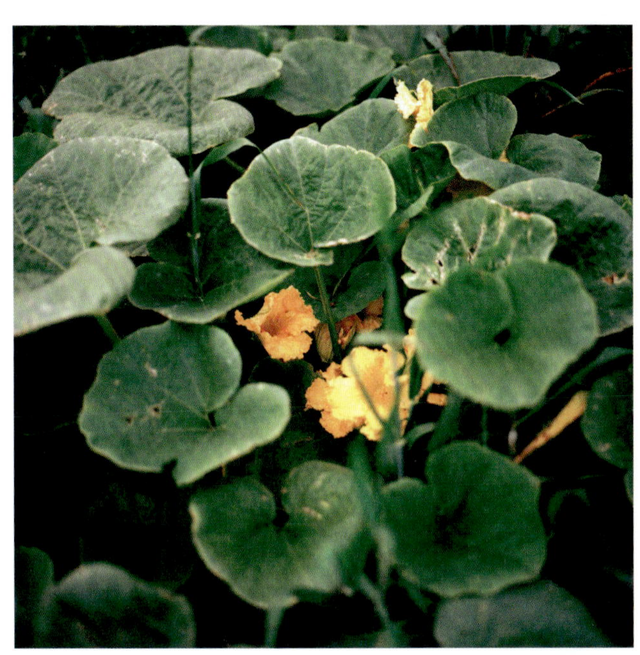

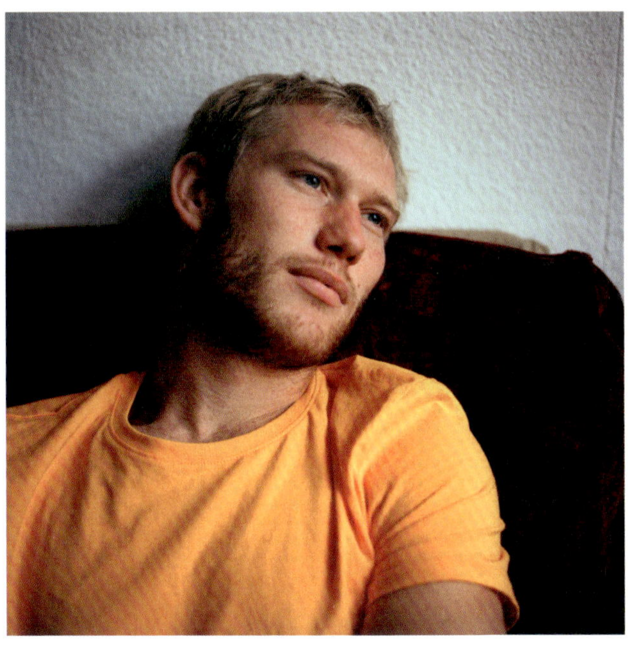

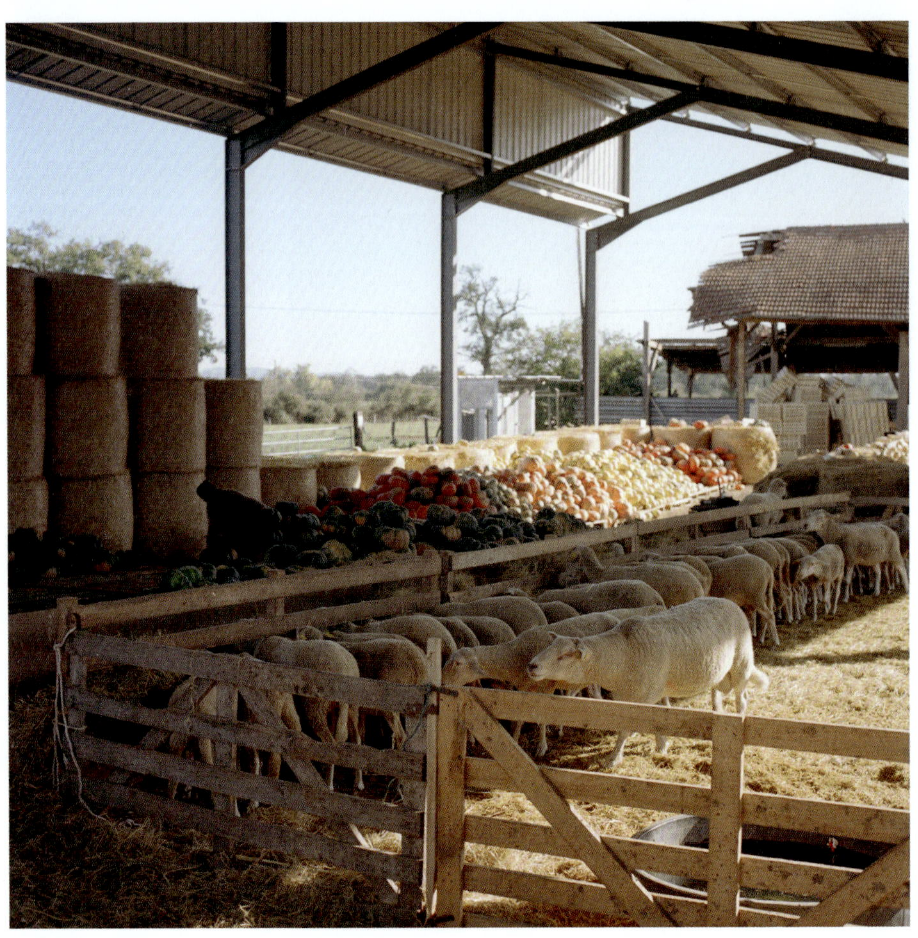

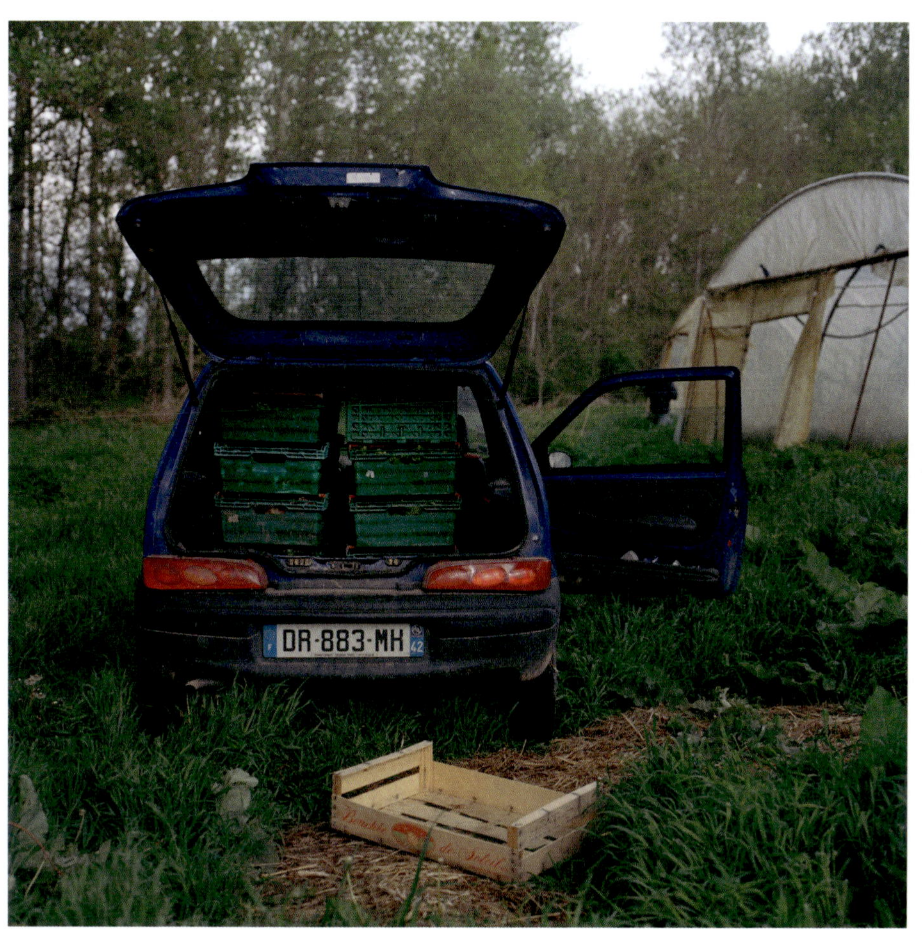
DR-883-MH
42

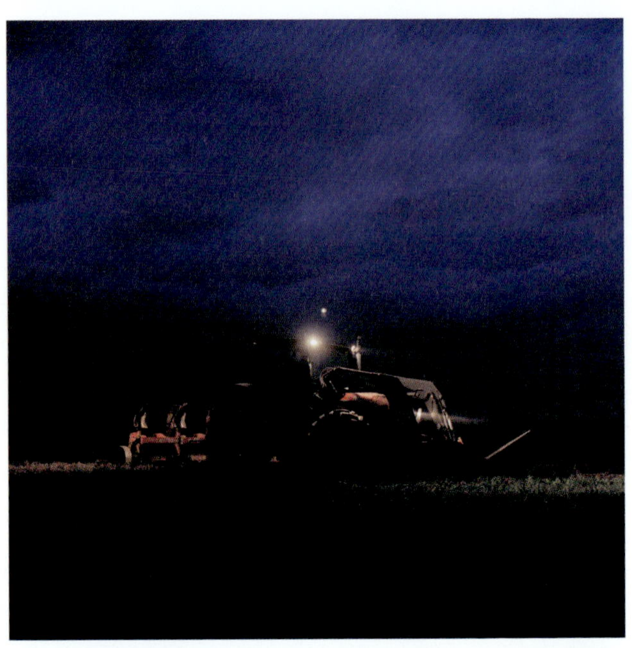

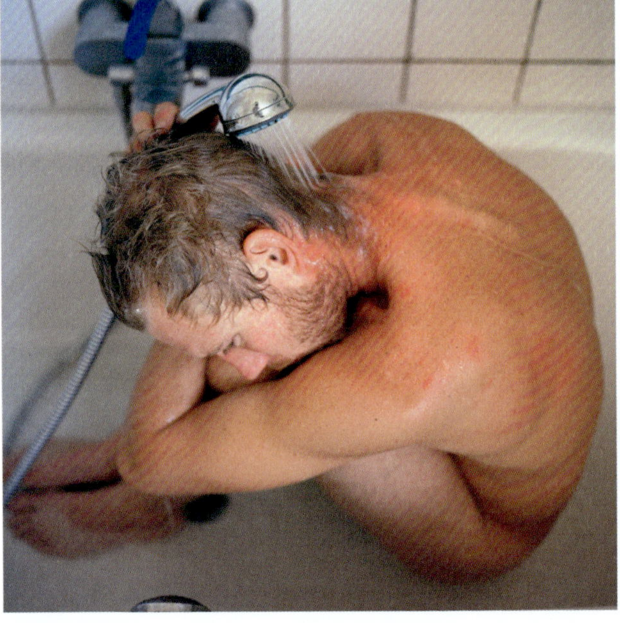

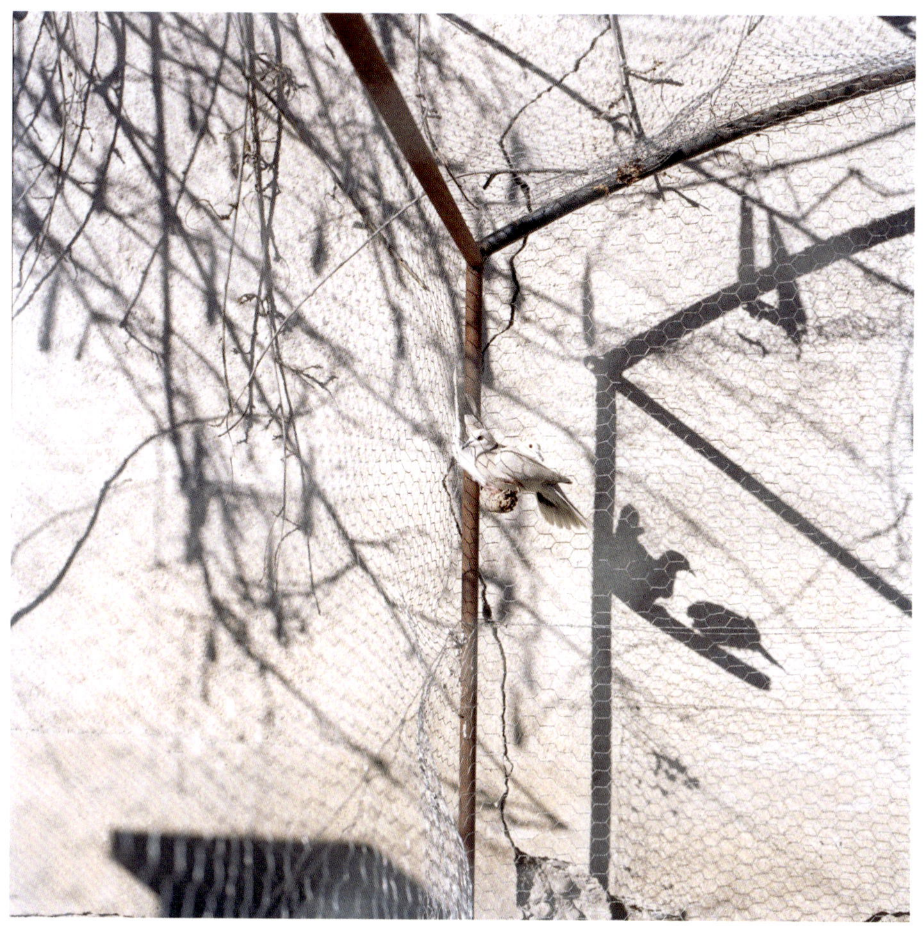

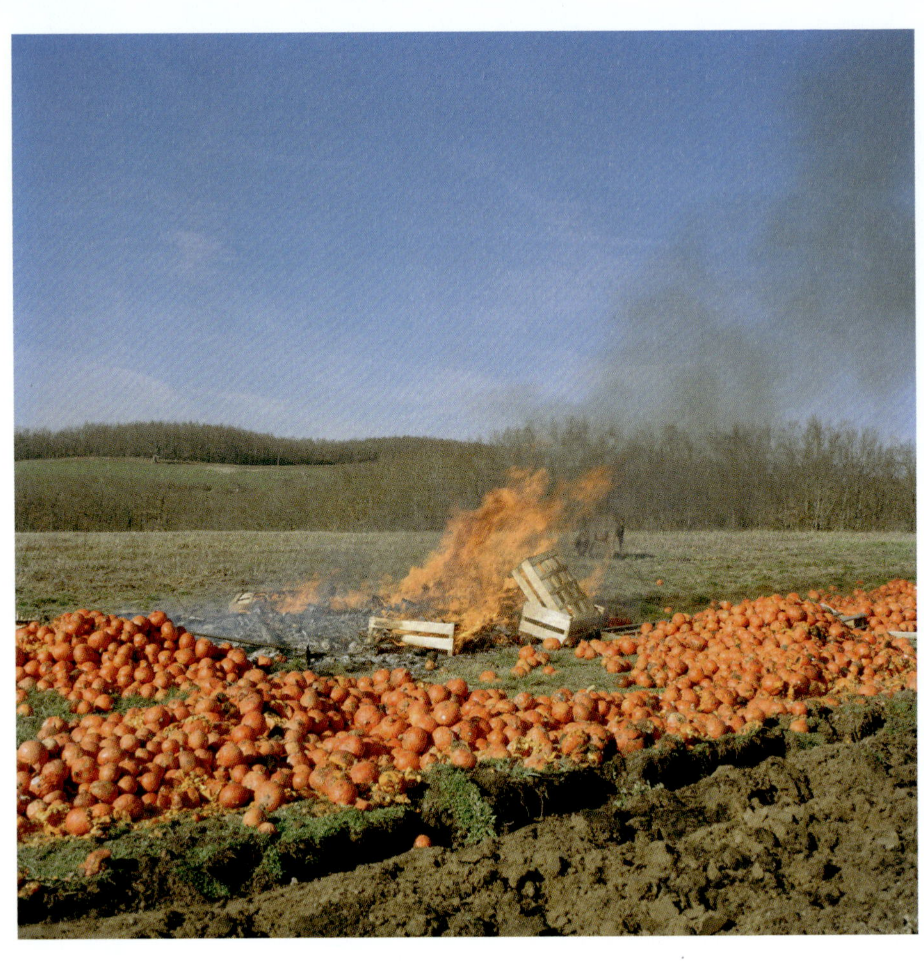

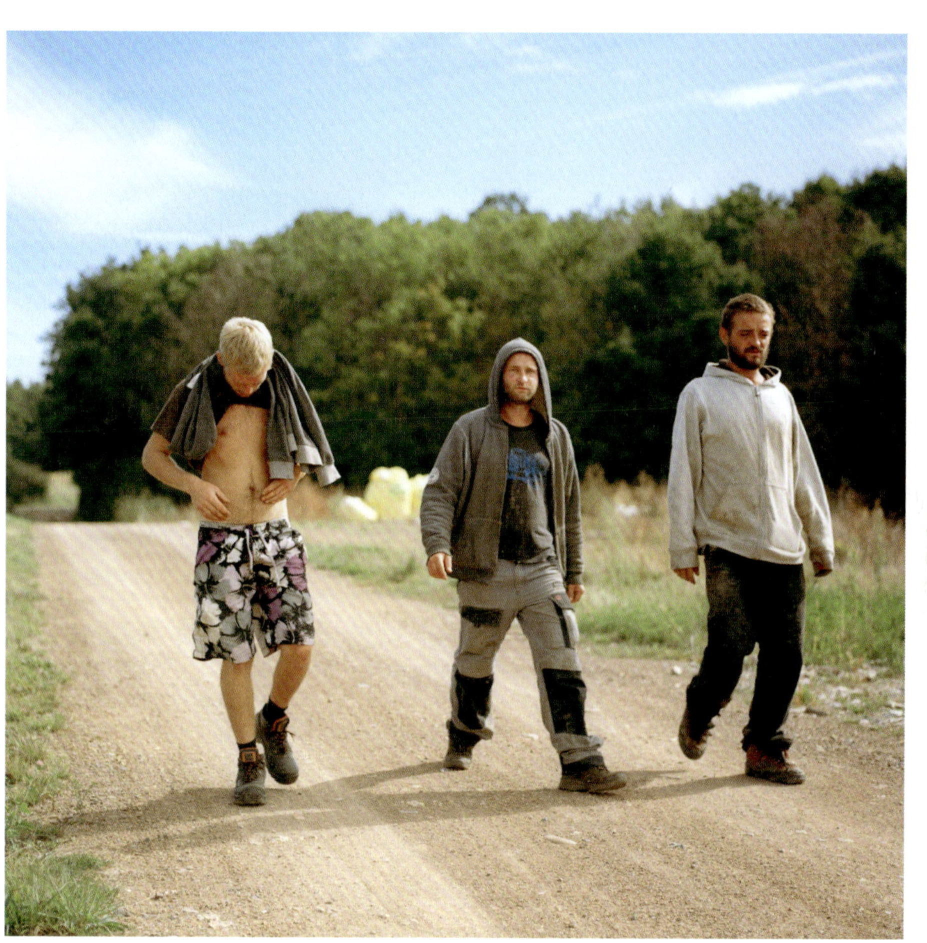

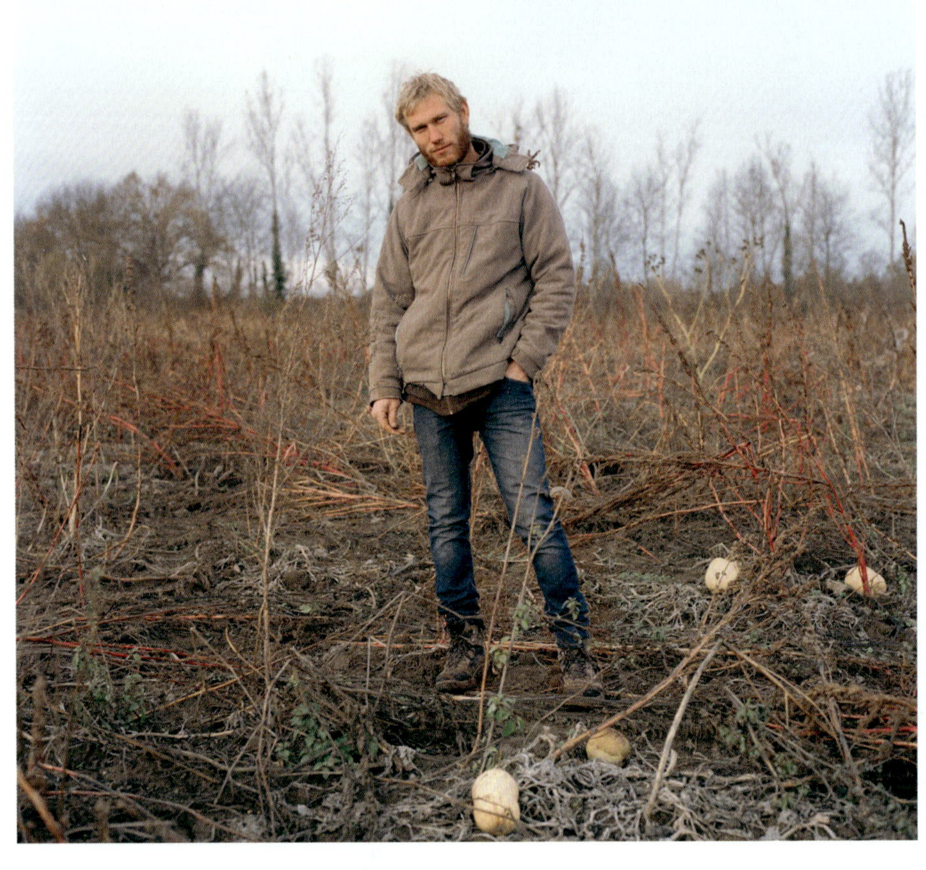

Antoine wanted to grow pumpkins ever since he was a child. With hard work, he has fulfilled his dream and now owns a 12 hectare farm next to Lyon in France. What might sound romantic at first turned into the daily struggle of agriculture very soon: Being entirely dependent on external factors, his livelihood is regularly getting challenged.

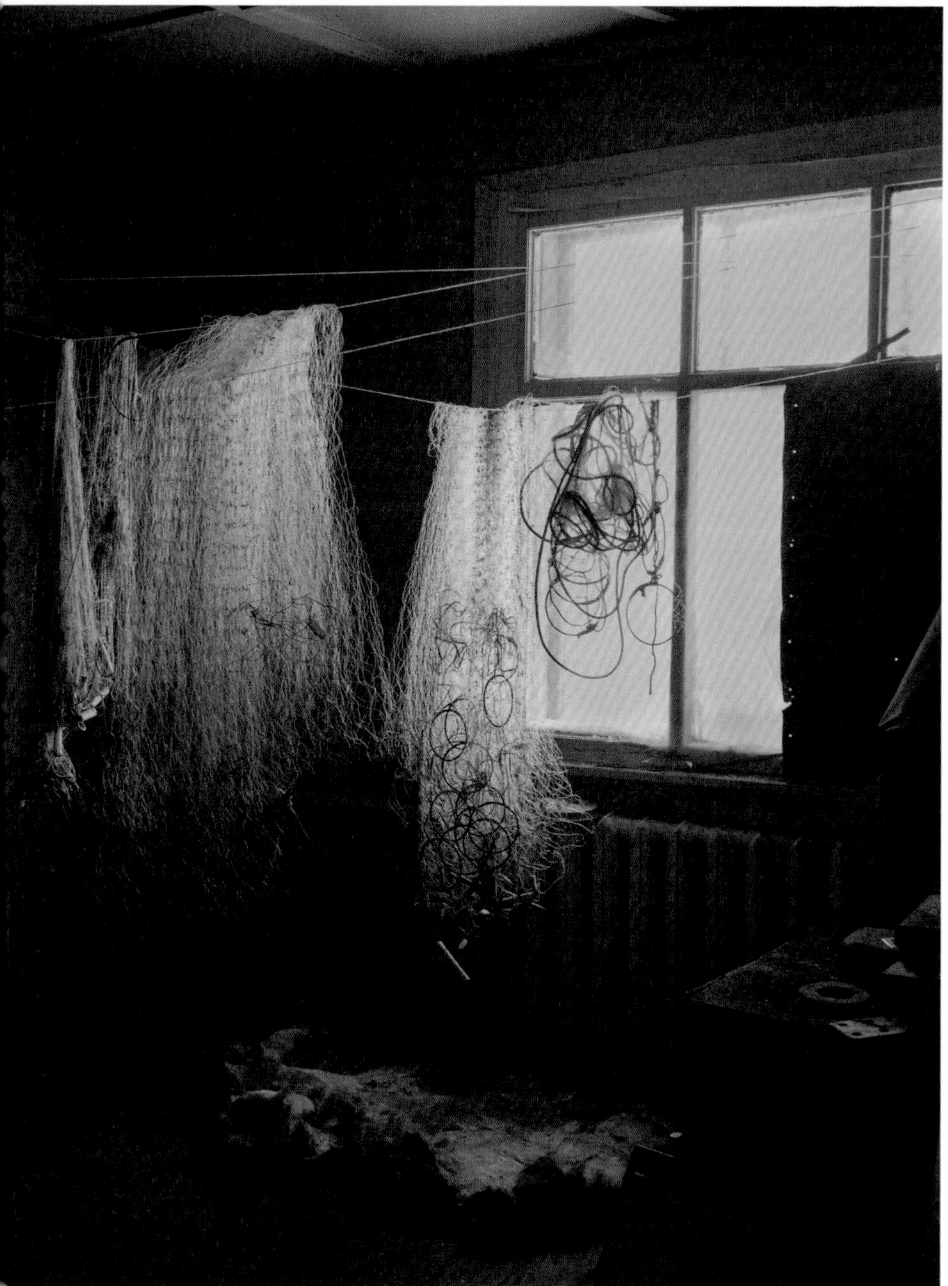

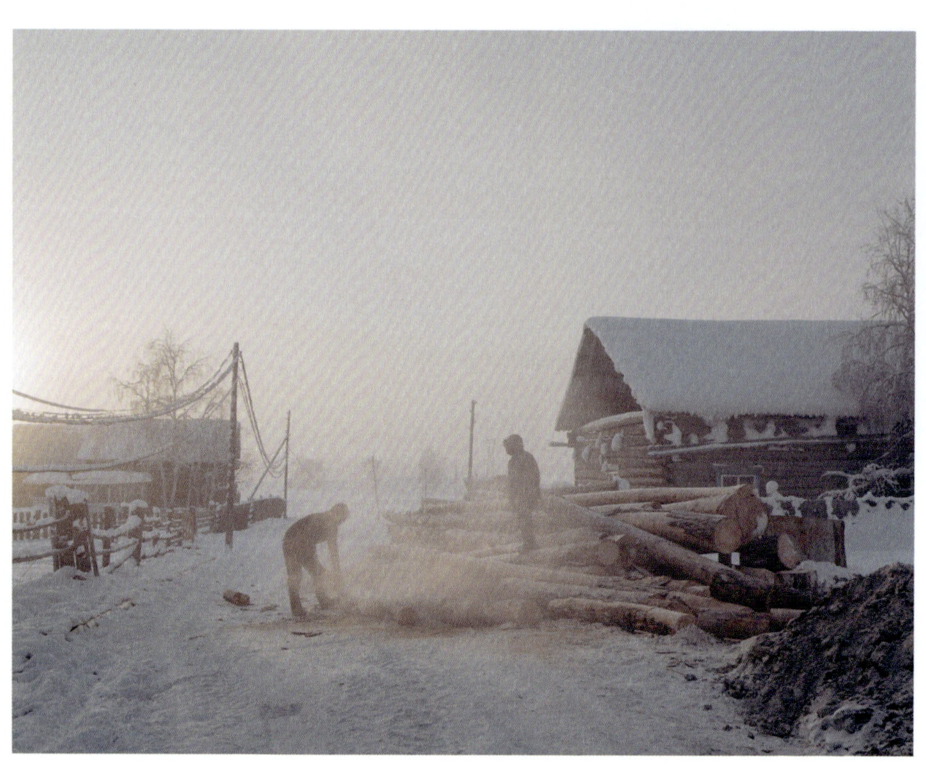

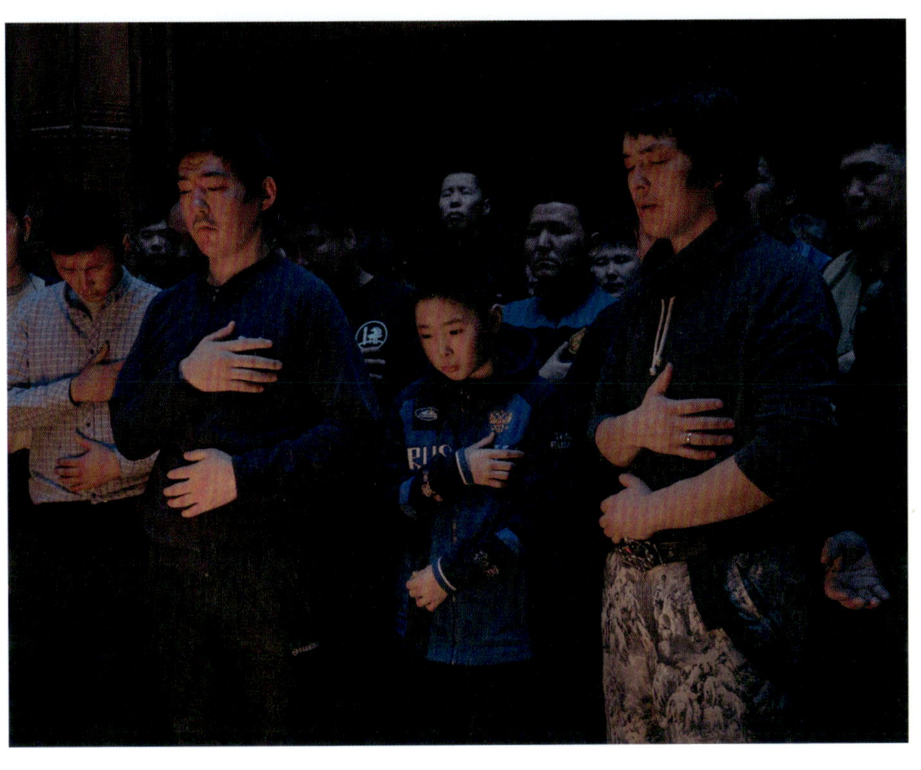

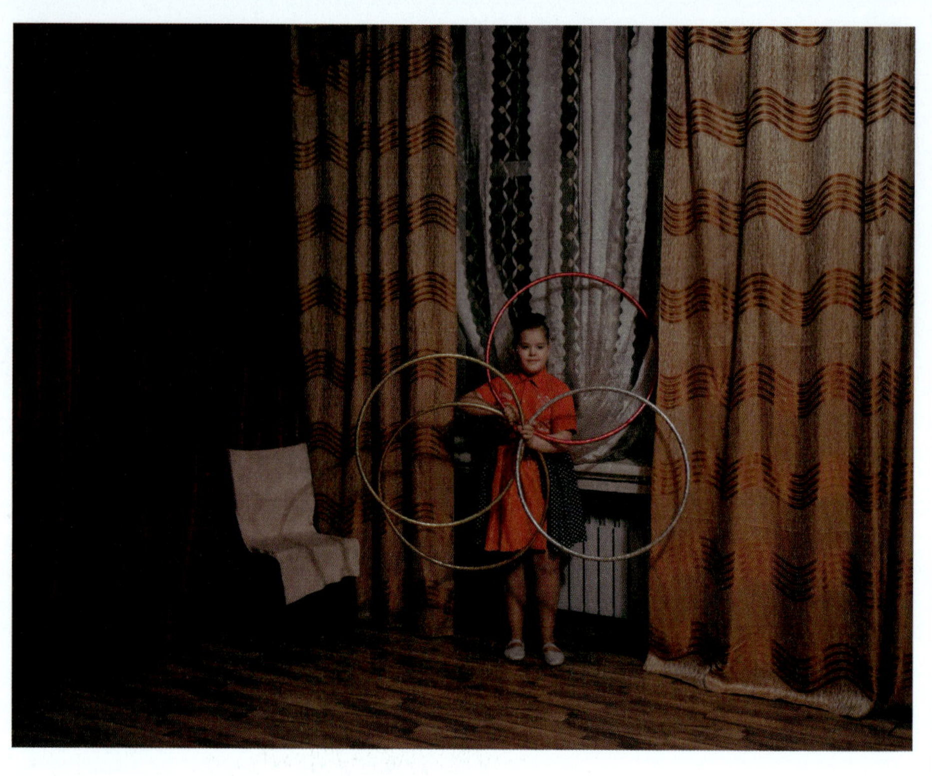

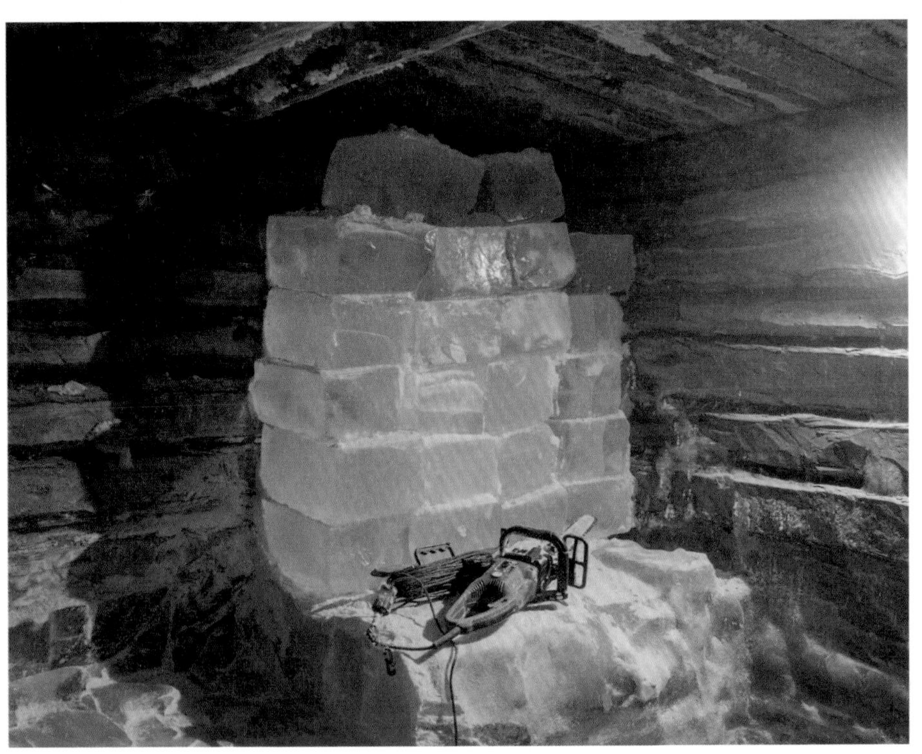

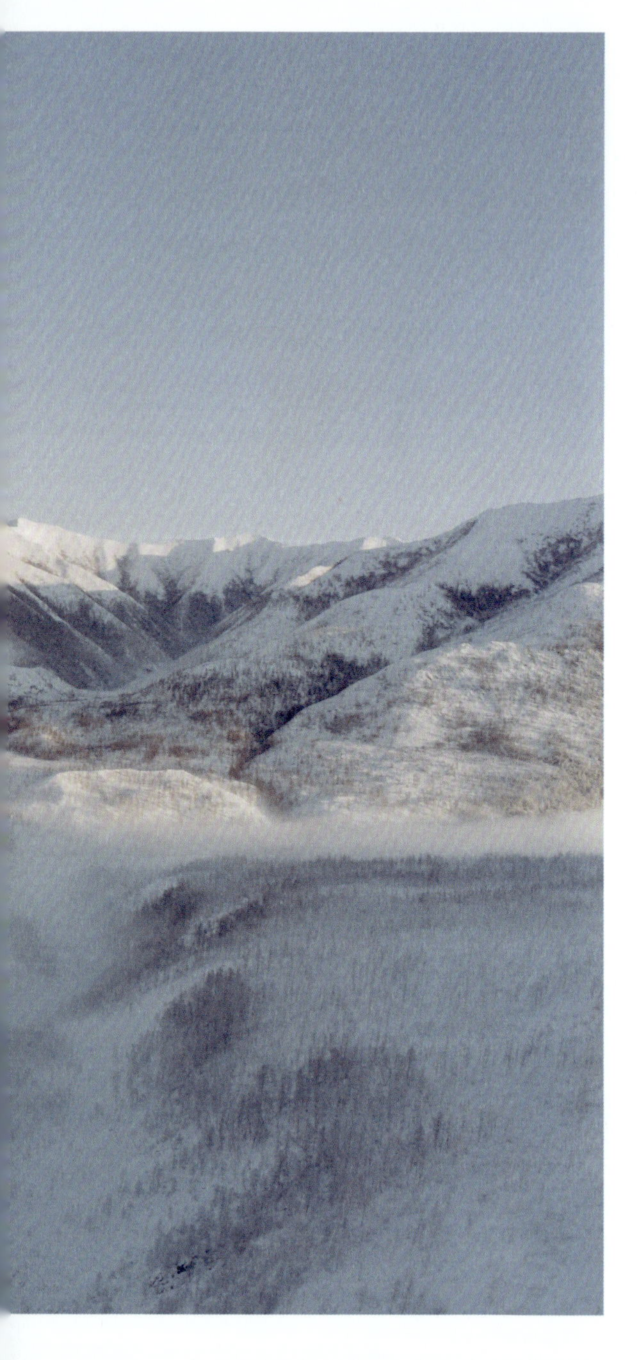

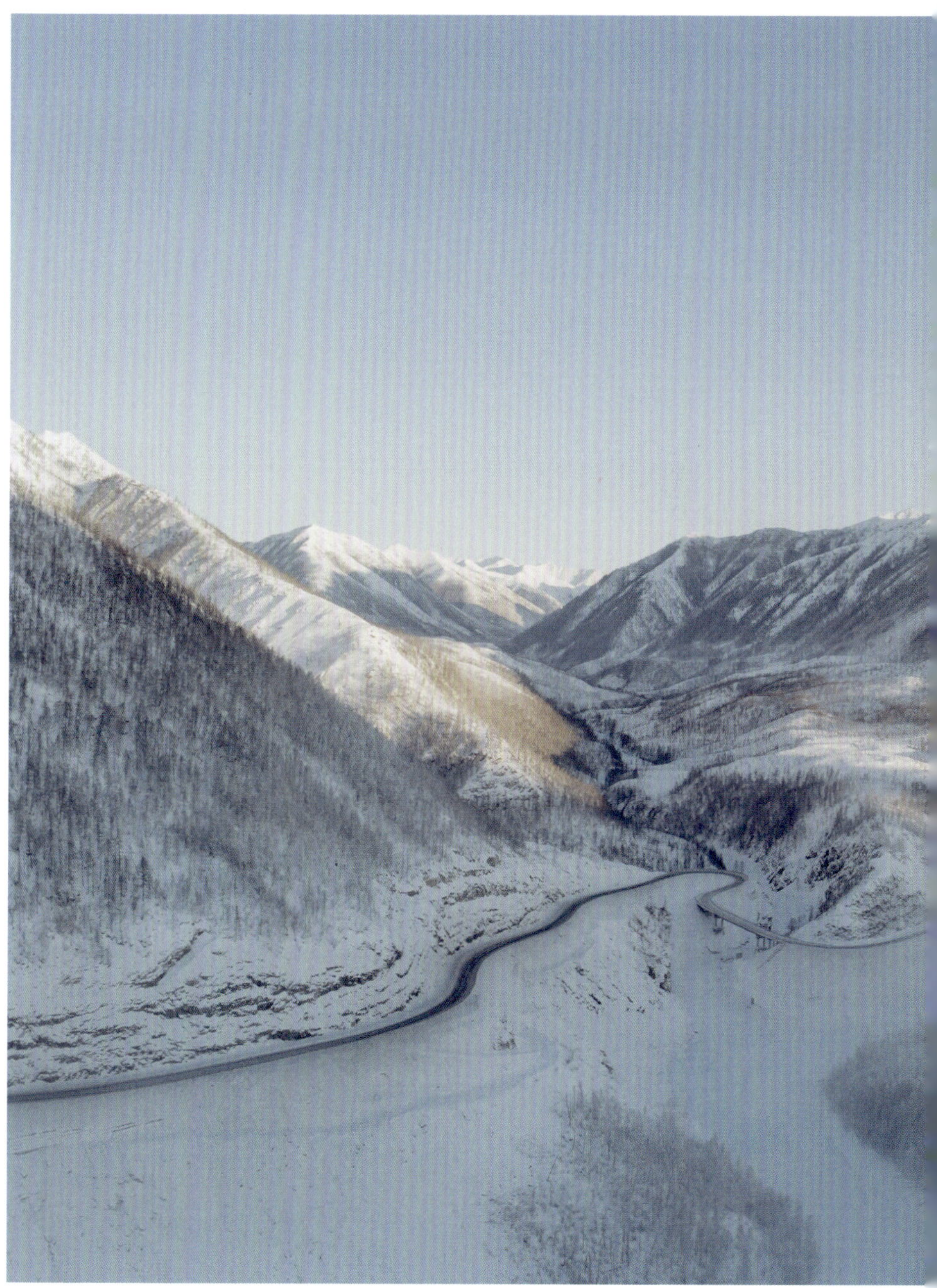

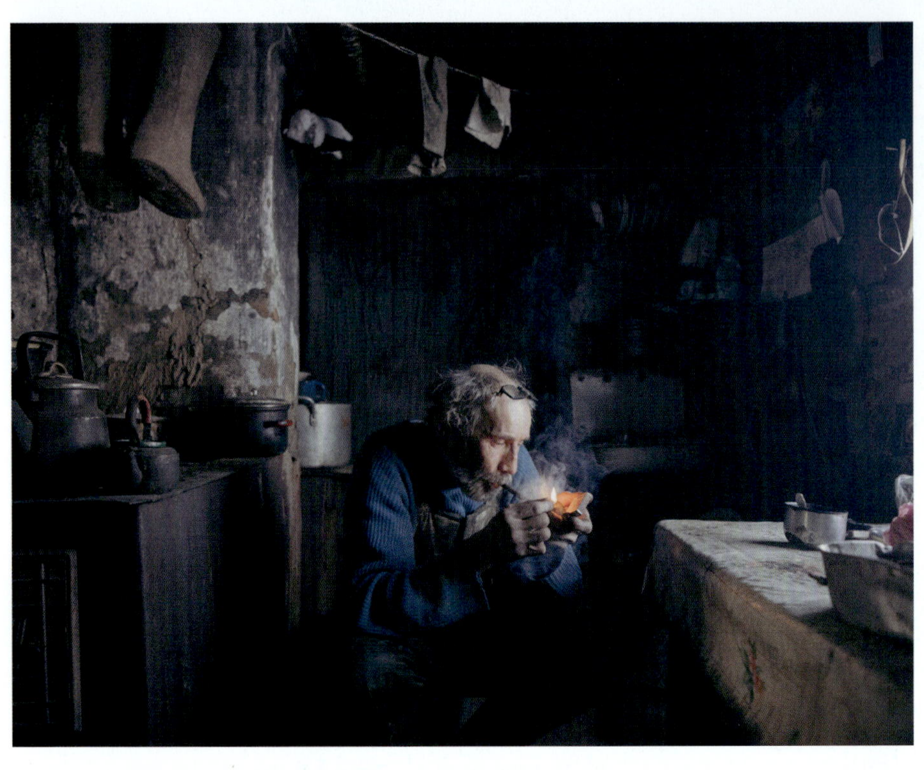

From 1932 to 1953, millions of prisoners were deported to remote labor camps in the course of the Stalinist repression. Political opponents, criminals and innocent people became inmates of the Siberian seclusion. Due to the extreme conditions there was no escape, in the 80 Gulag camps of the Kolyma region the prisoners found death at work. They also built the “Kolyma Highway“, one of the largest construction projects of the labour camps.

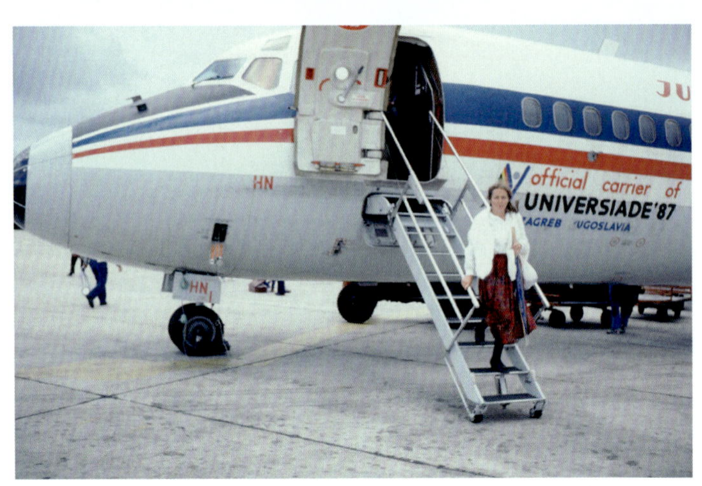
official carrier of
UNIVERSIADE'87

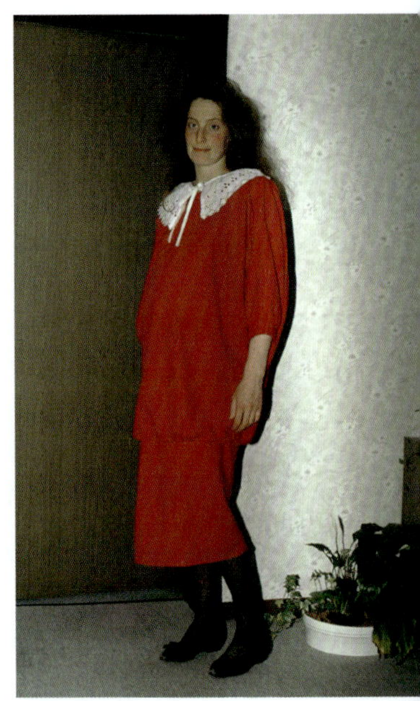

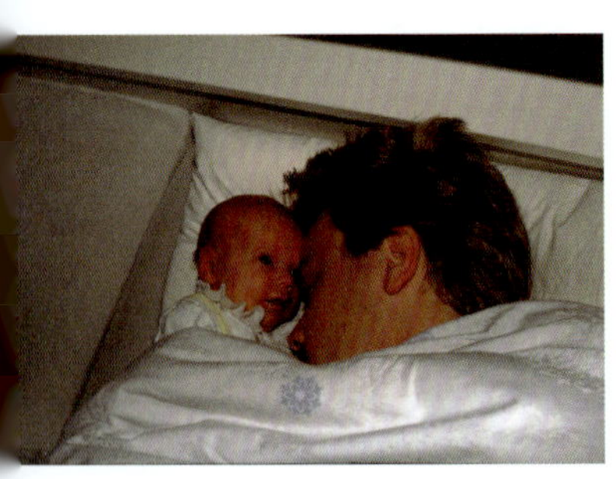

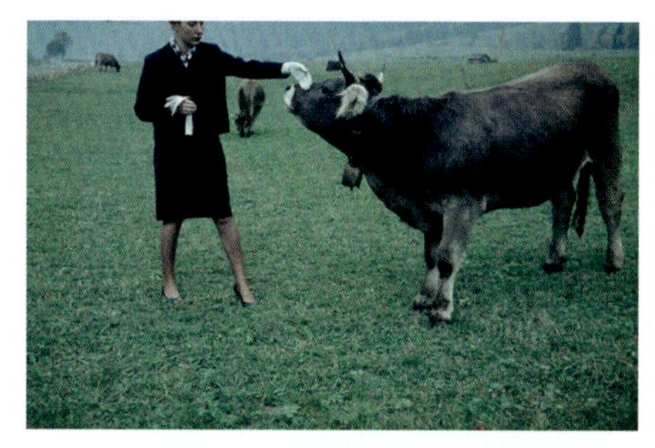

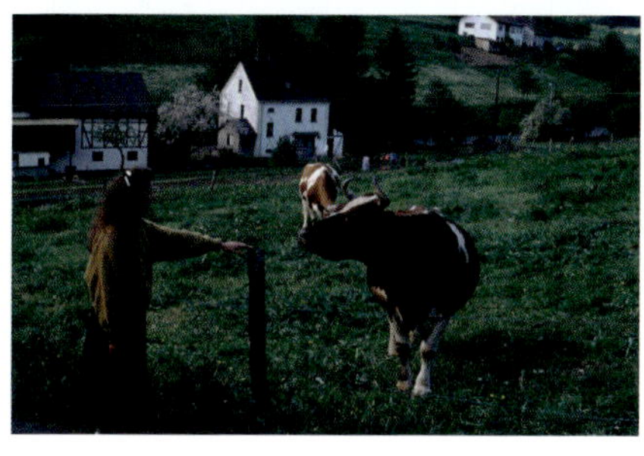

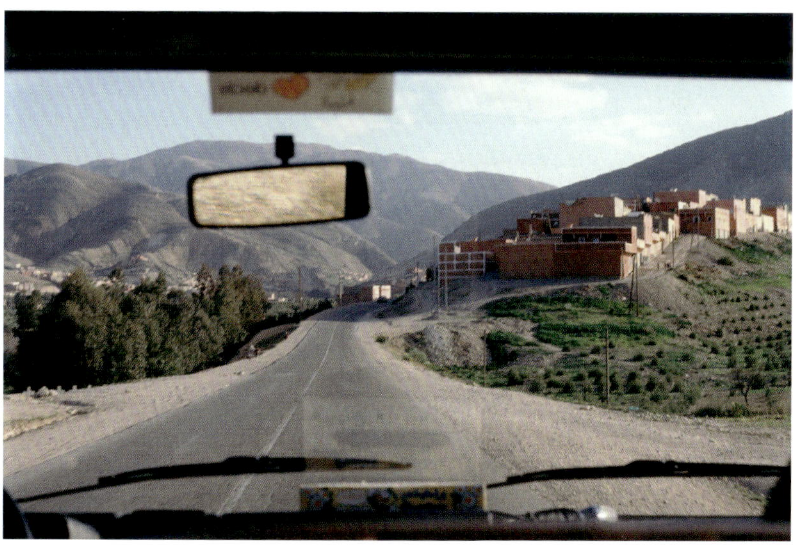

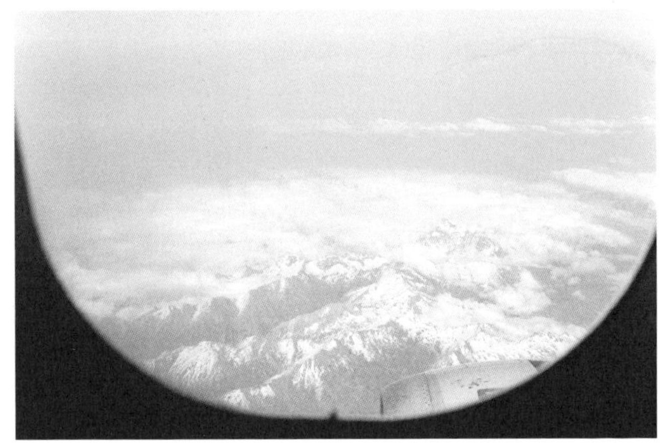

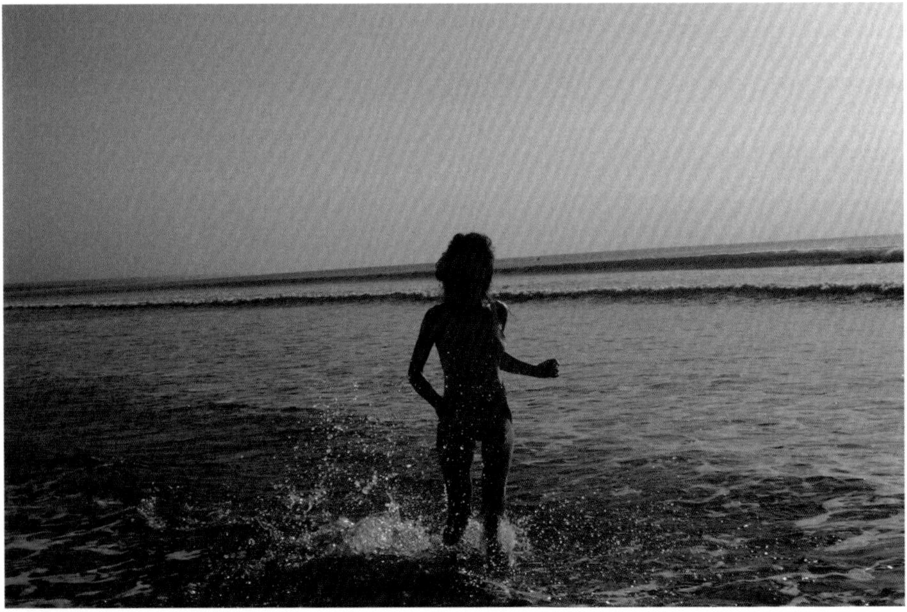

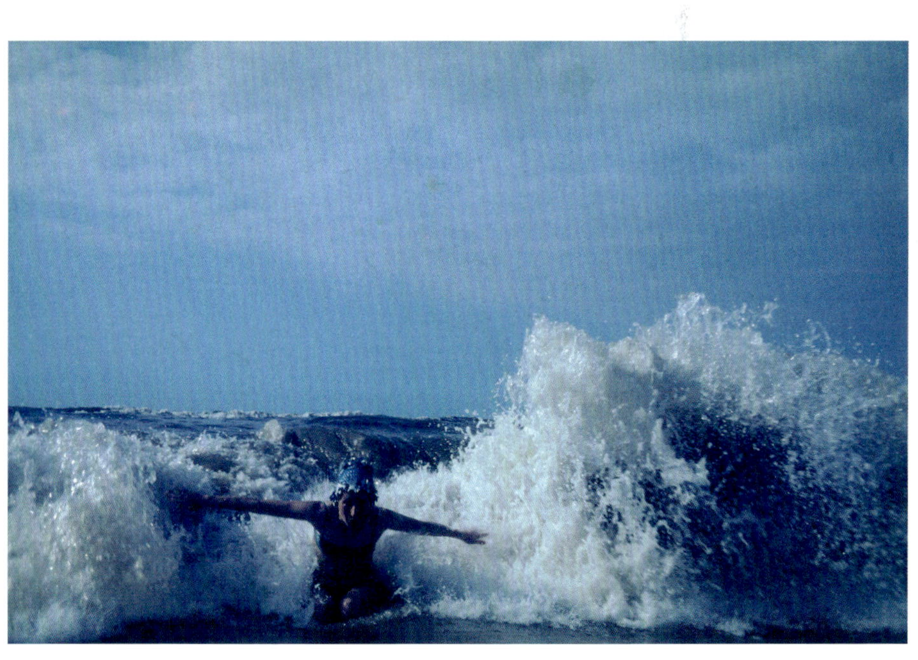

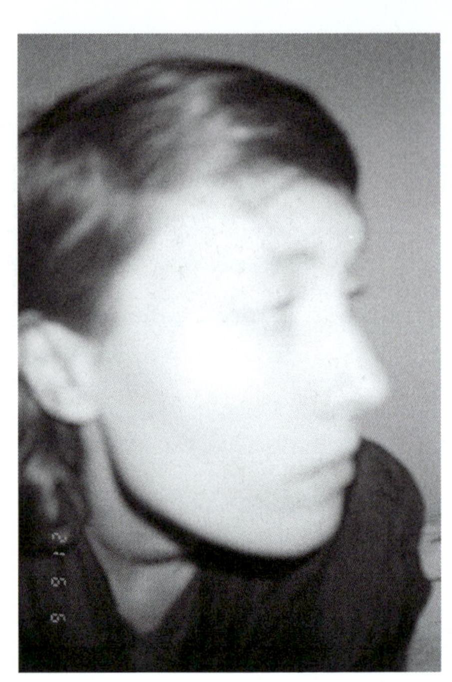

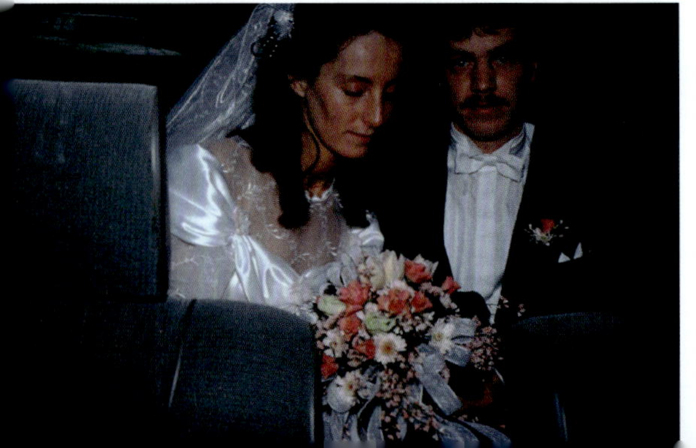

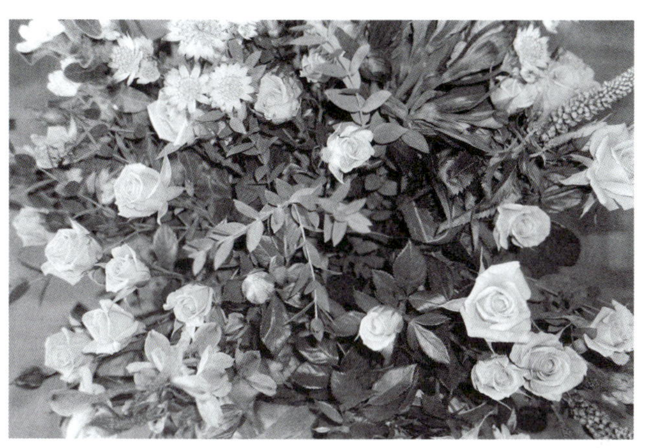

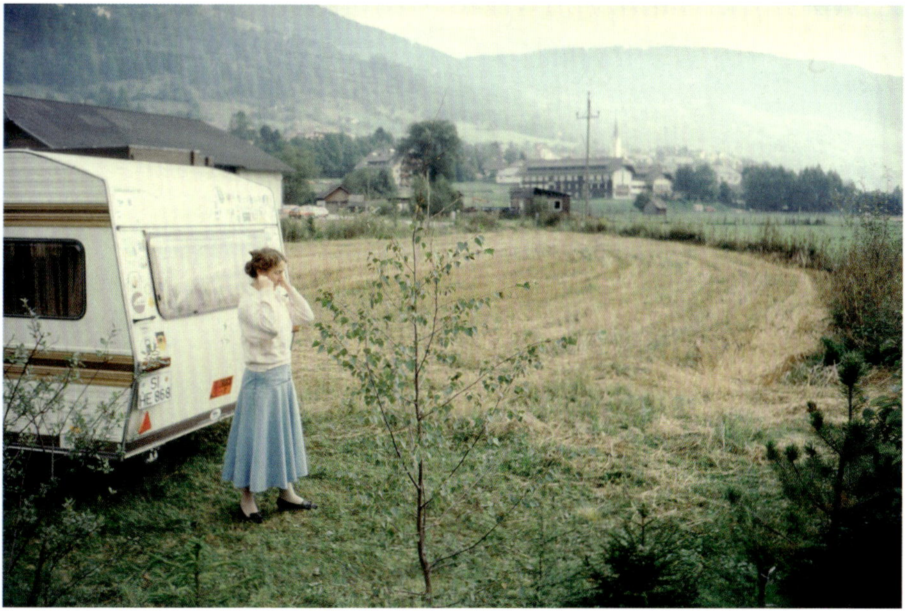

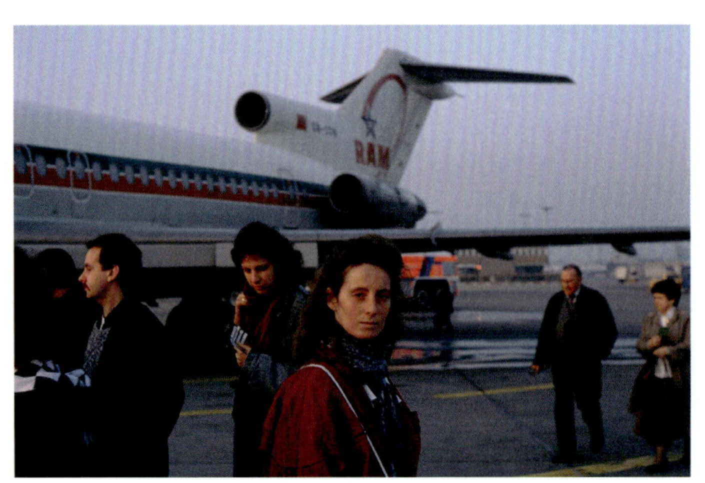
RAM

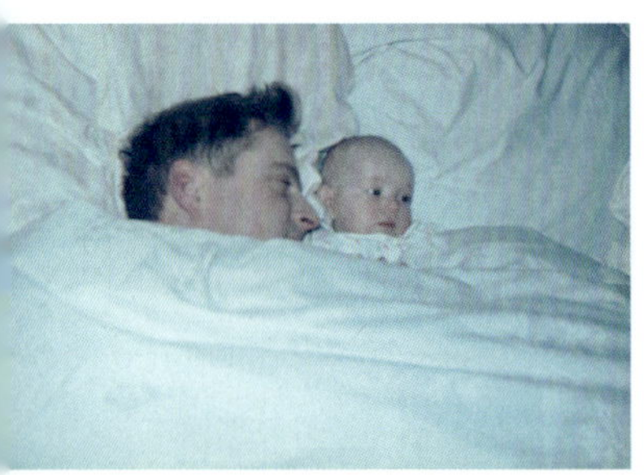

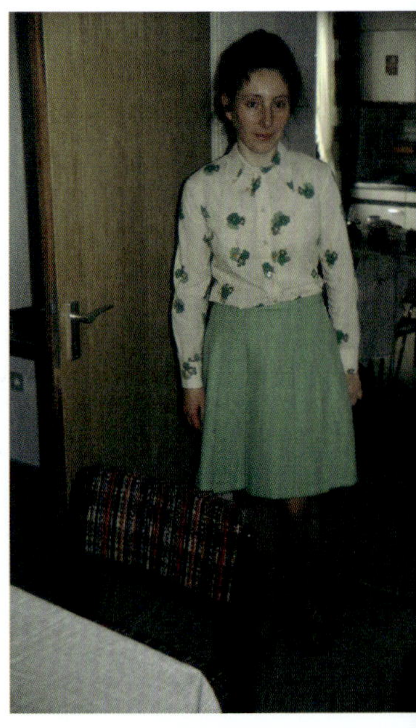

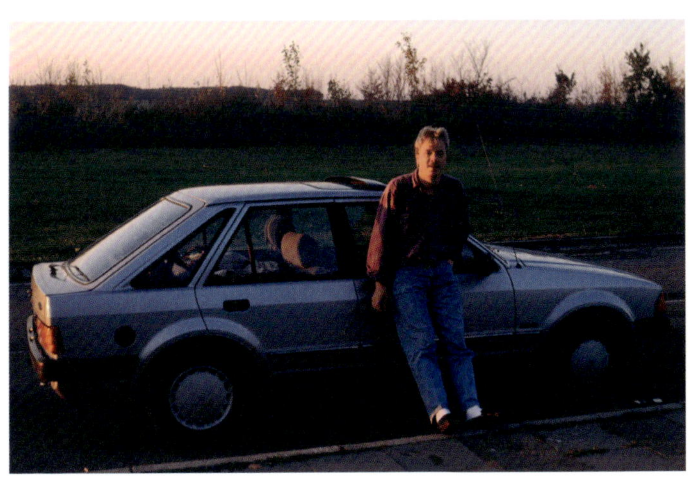

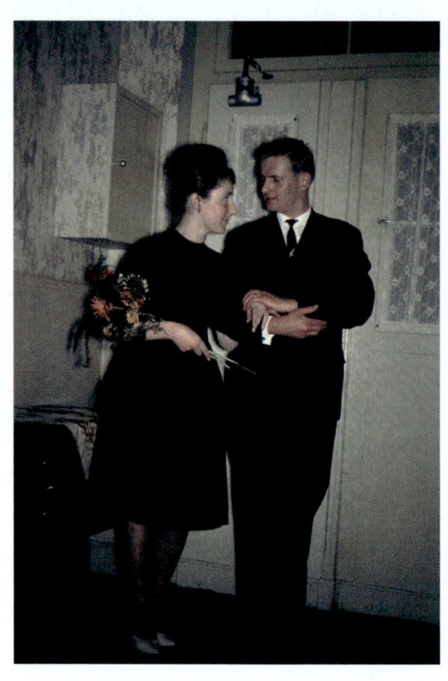

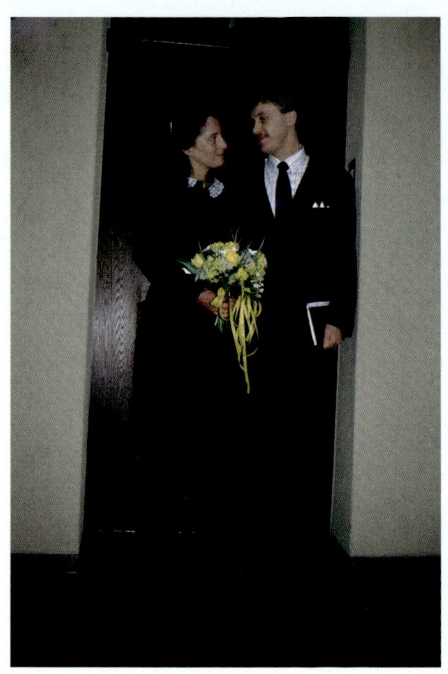

When Cathleen browsed through her family's picture archive, she noticed how similar the photographs of her parents and grandparents were. Decades apart, the captured experiences seem to repeat themselves. This prompted her to reflect not only on photography, but also on how her life is different and her role as an author next to the pictures her father and grandfather took.

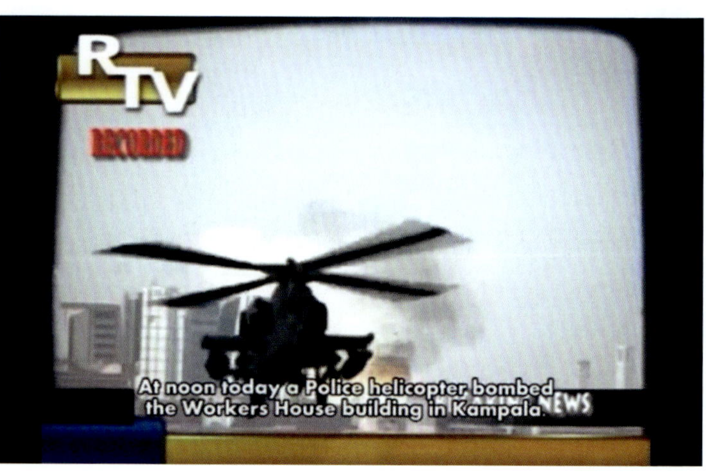
RTV
RECORDED
At noon today a Police helicopter bombed
the Workers House building in Kampala.
NEWS

RTV
RECORDED

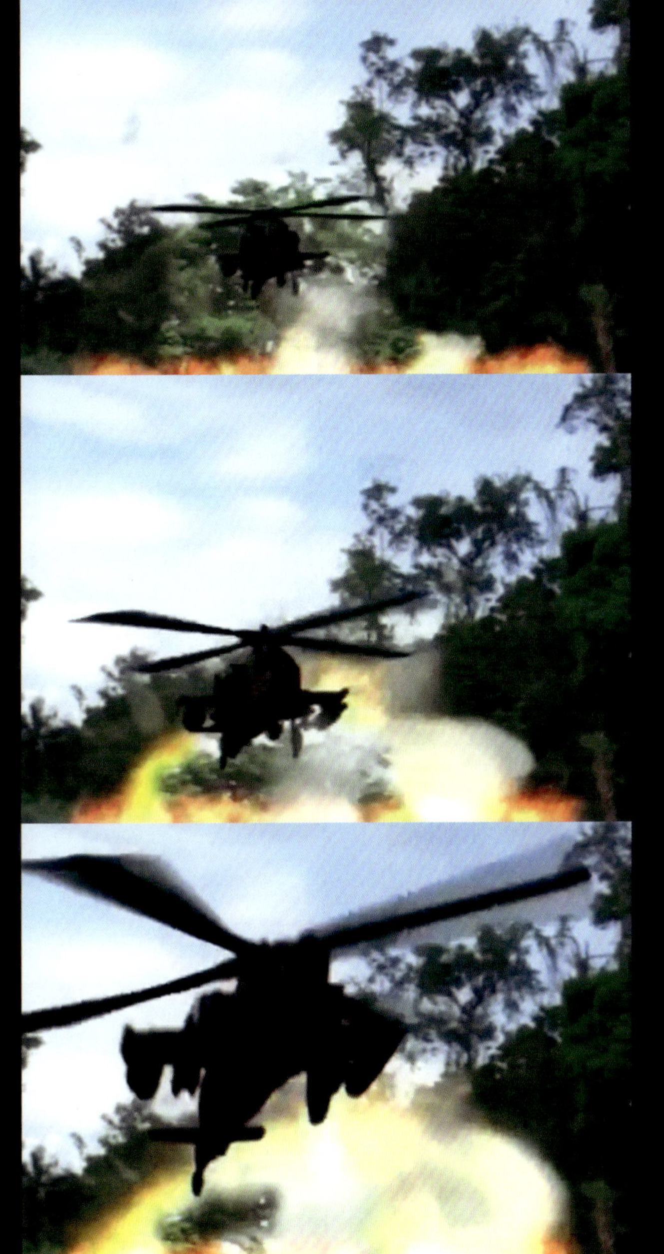

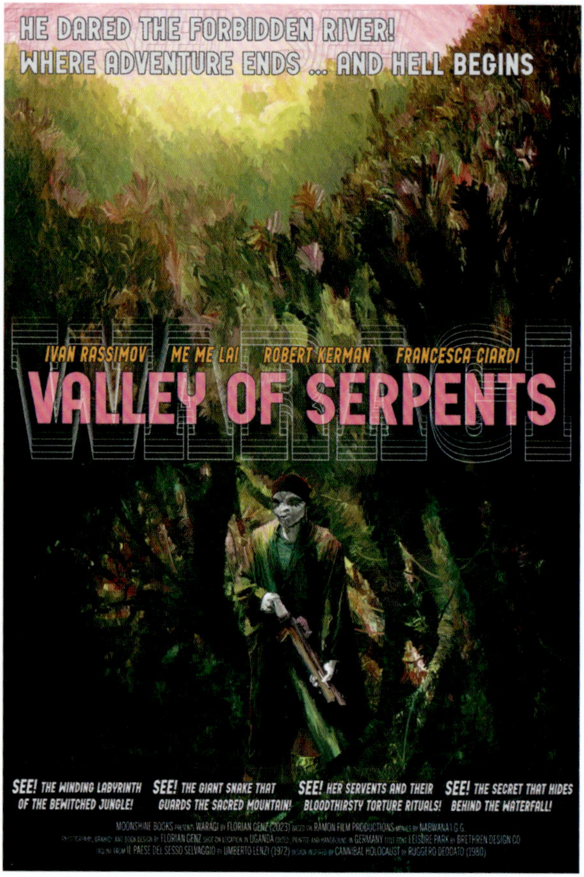

HE DARED THE FORBIDDEN RIVER!
WHERE ADVENTURE ENDS ... AND HELL BEGINS

IVAN RASSIMOV ME ME LAI ROBERT KERMAN FRANCESCA CIARDI

VALLEY OF SERPENTS

SEE! THE WINDING LABYRINTH OF THE BEWITCHED JUNGLE!

SEE! THE GIANT SNAKE THAT GUARDS THE SACRED MOUNTAIN!

SEE! HER SERVENTS AND THEIR BLOODTHIRSTY TORTURE RITUALS!

SEE! THE SECRET THAT HIDES BEHIND THE WATERFALL!

MOONSHINE BOOKS PRESENTS WARAGI BY FLORIAN GENZ (2023) BASED ON RAMON FILM PRODUCTIONS MOVIES BY NABWANA I.G.G.
PHOTOGRAPHY, GRAPHIC AND BOOK DESIGN BY FLORIAN GENZ SHOT ON LOCATION IN UGANDA EDITED, PRINTED AND HANDBOUND IN GERMANY TITLE FONT LEISURE PARK BY BRETHREN DESIGN CO
TAGLINE FROM IL PAESE DEL SESSO SELVAGGIO BY UMBERTO LENZI (1972) DESIGN INSPIRED BY CANNIBAL HOLOCAUST BY RUGGERO DEODATO (1980)

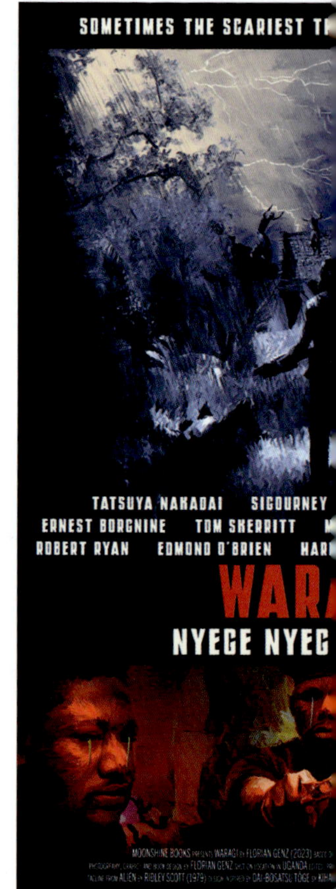

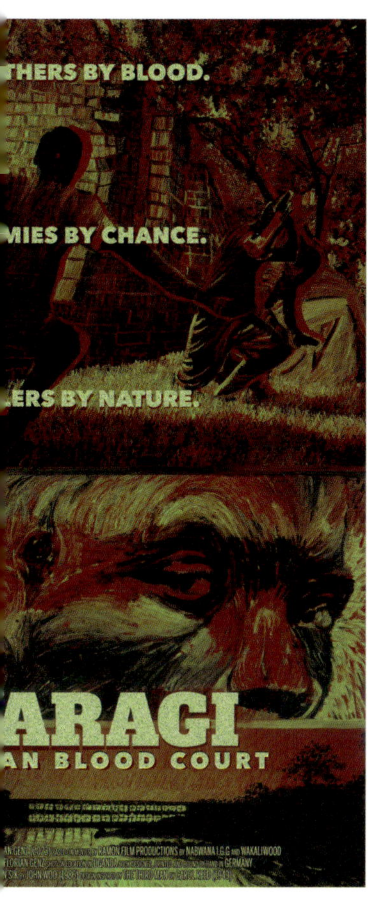
THERS BY BLOOD.
MIES BY CHANCE.
LERS BY NATURE.
ARAGI
AN BLOOD COURT

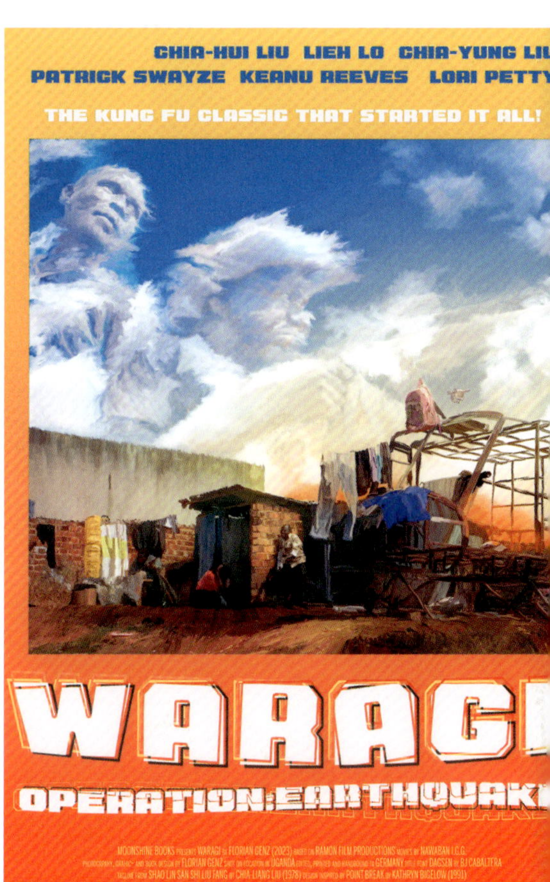
CHIA-HUI LIU LIEH LO CHIA-YUNG LIU
PATRICK SWAYZE KEANU REEVES LORI PETTY
THE KUNG FU CLASSIC THAT STARTED IT ALL!
WARAGI
OPERATION:EARTHQUAKE
MOONSHINE BOOKS PRESENTS WARAGI BY FLORIAN GENZ (2023) BASED ON RAMON FILM PRODUCTIONS MOVIES BY NAWABAN I.G.G.
PHOTOGRAPHY, GRAPHIC AND BOOK DESIGN BY FLORIAN GENZ SHOT ON LOCATION IN UGANDA EDITED, PRINTED AND HANDBOUND IN GERMANY TITLE FONT DAGSEN BY BJ CABALTERA
TAGLINE FROM SHAO LIN SAN SHI LIU FANG BY CHIA-LIANG LIU (1978) DESIGN INSPIRED BY POINT BREAK BY KATHRYN BIGELOW (1991)

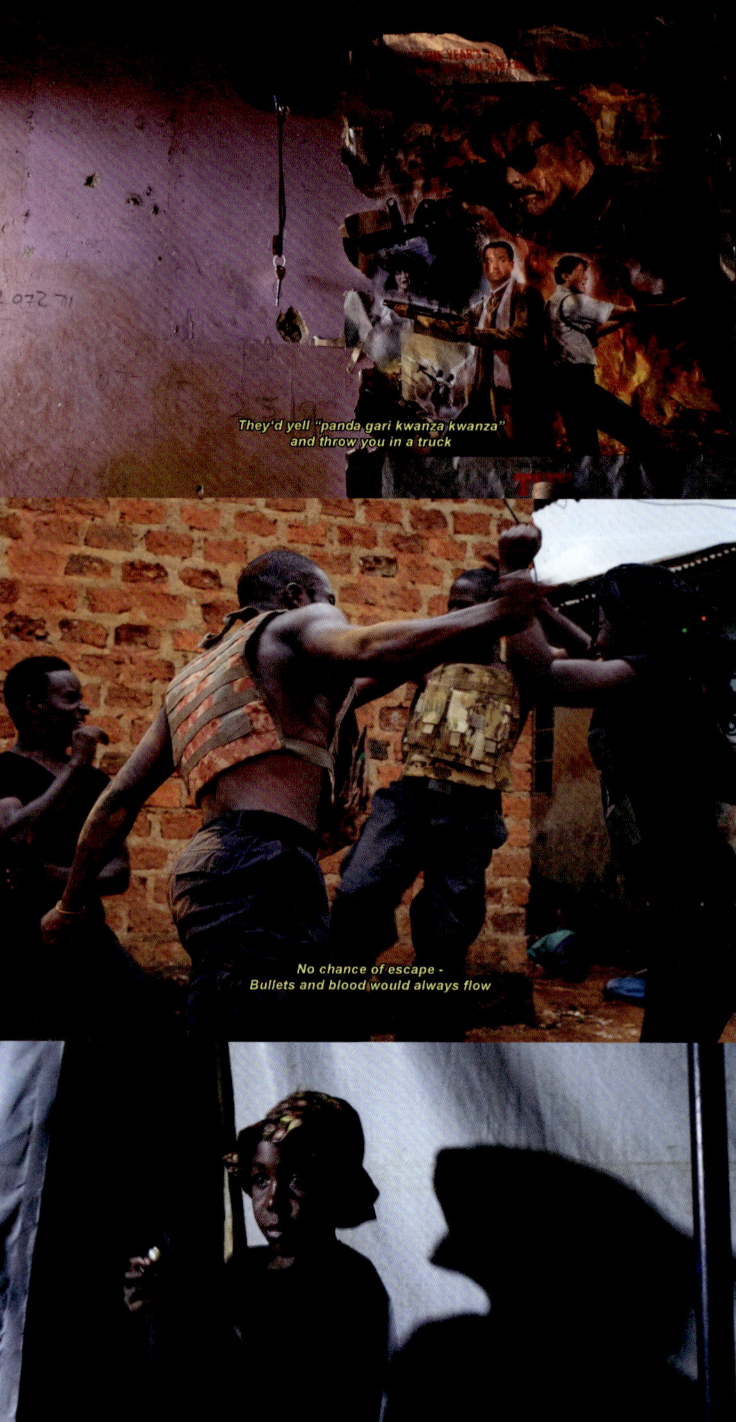
They'd yell "panda gari kwanza kwanza"
and throw you in a truck
No chance of escape -
Bullets and blood would always flow

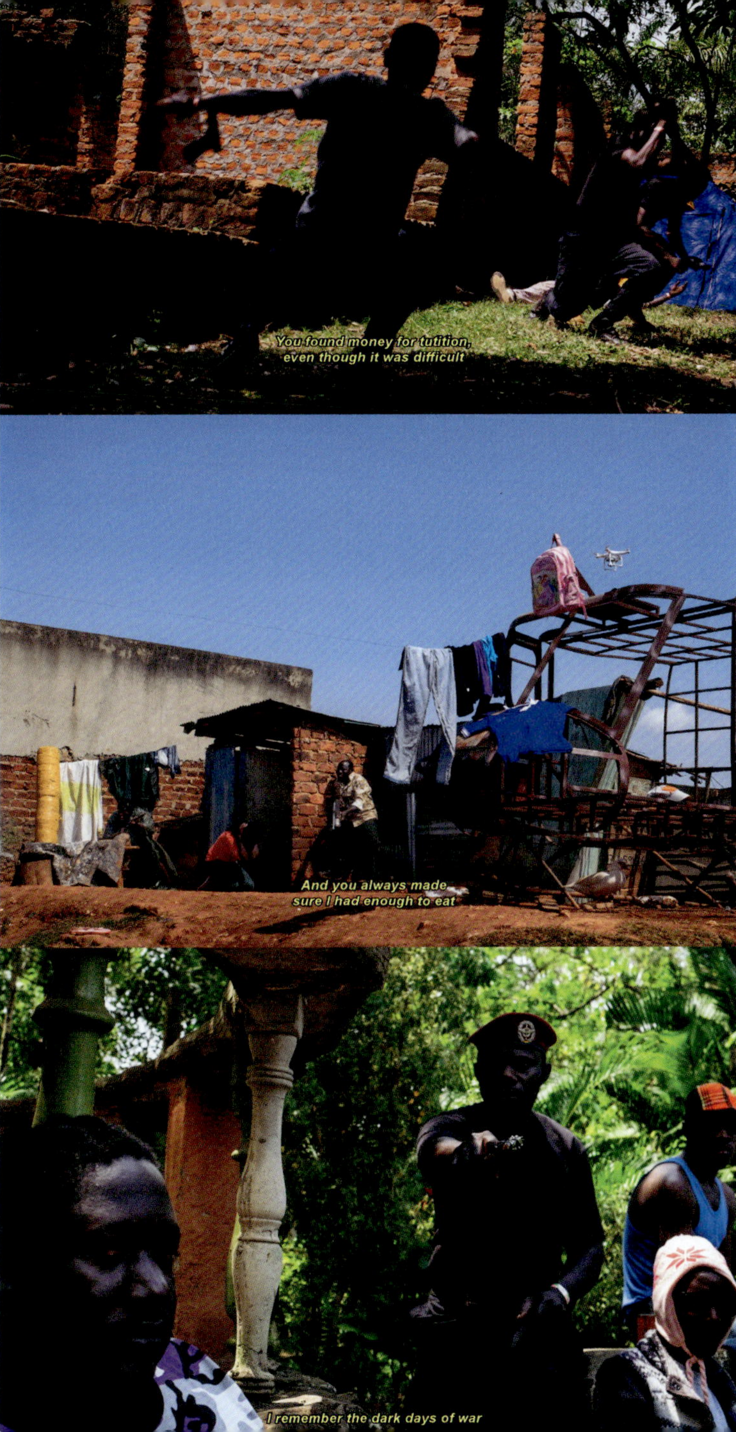
You found money for tutition,
even though it was difficult
And you always made
sure I had enough to eat
I remember the dark days of war

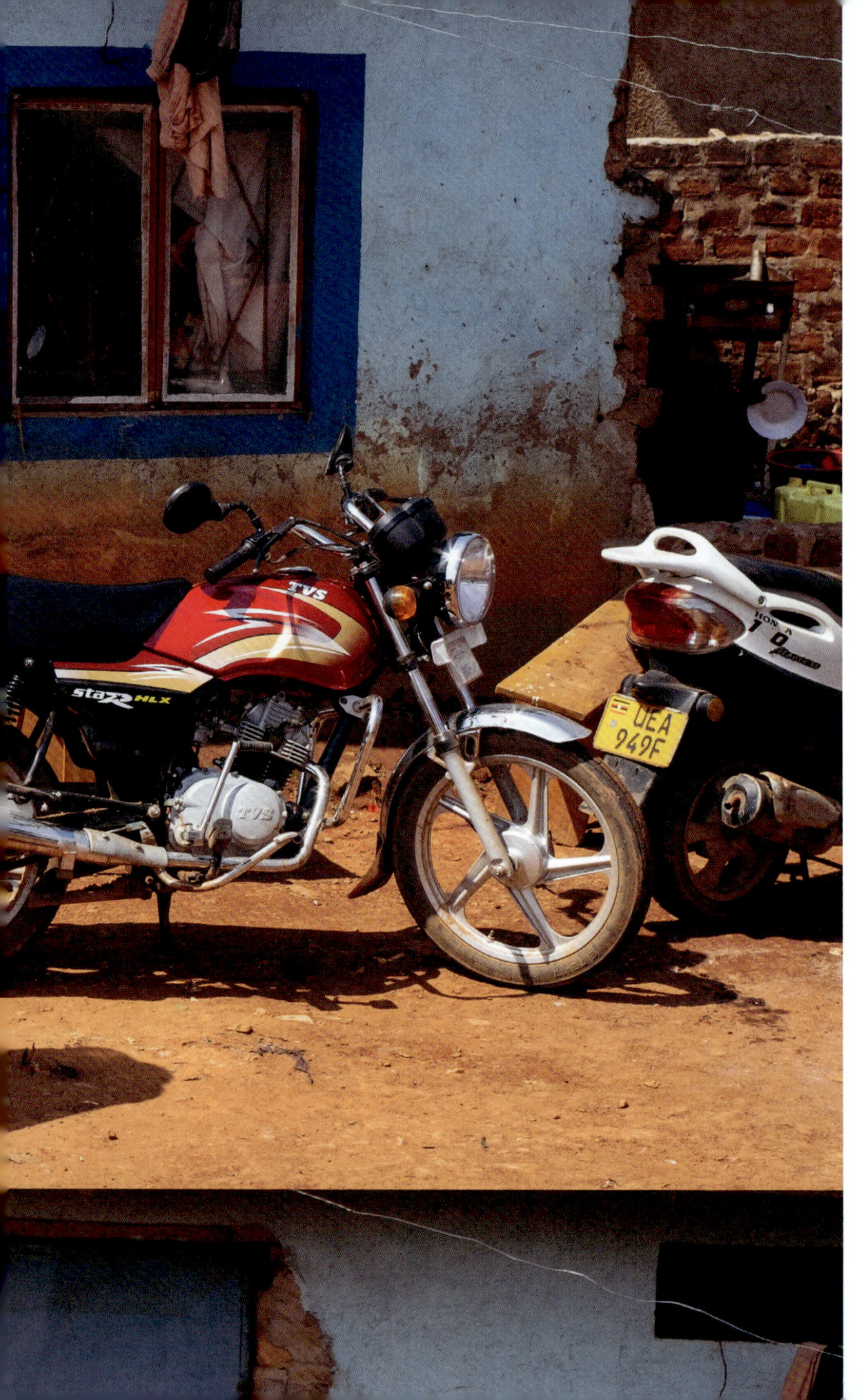
TVS
TVS
UEA
949F

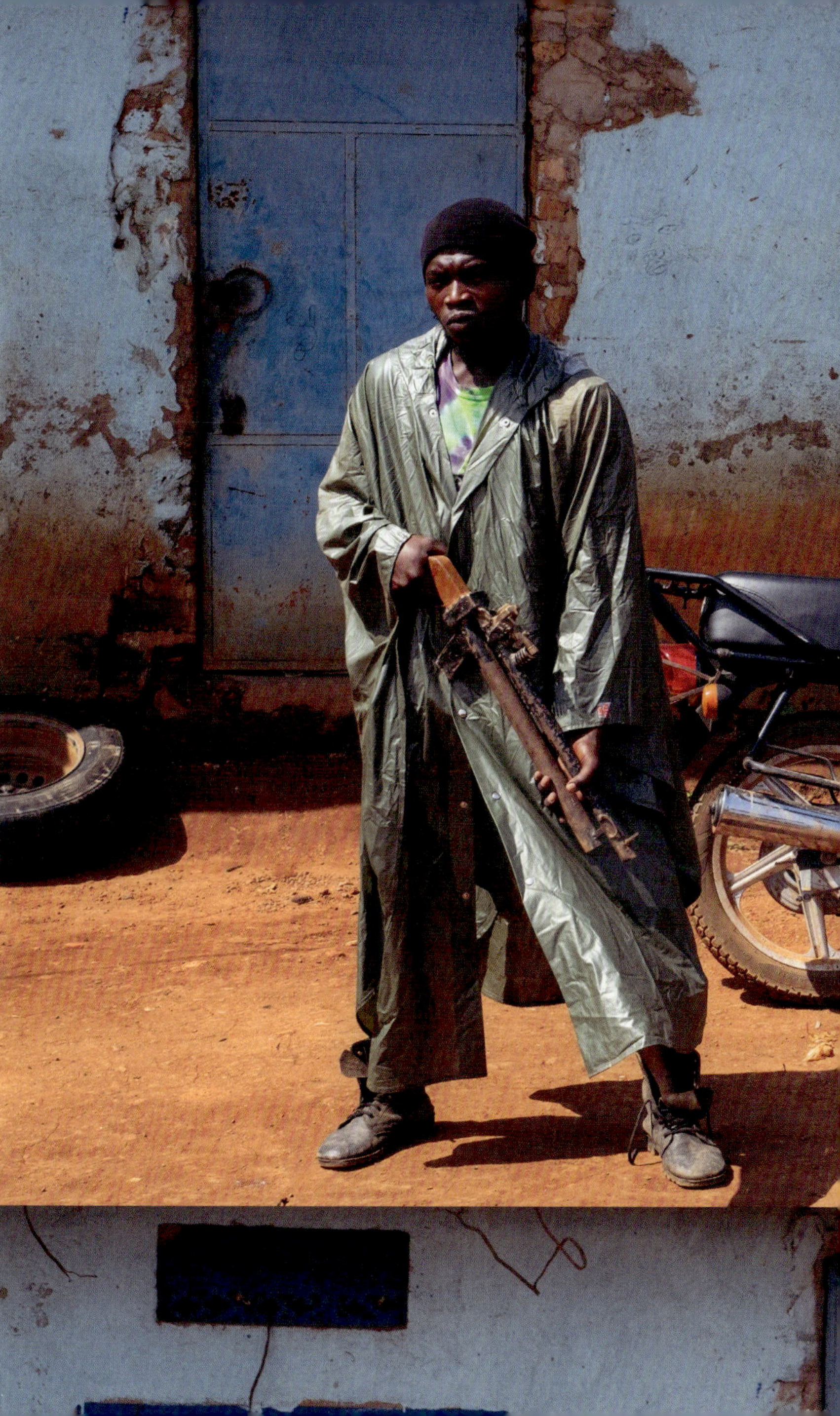

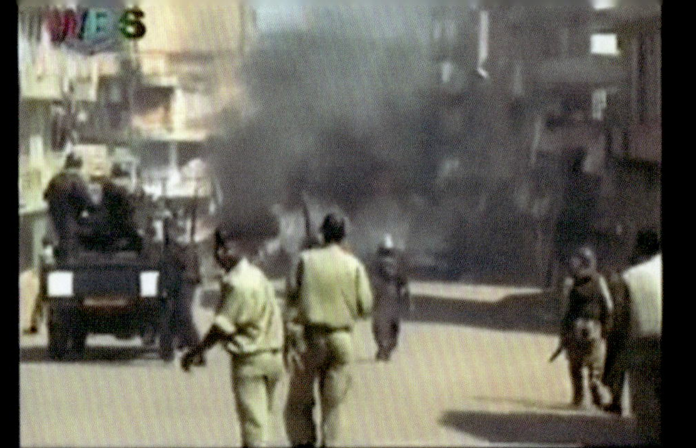
WBS

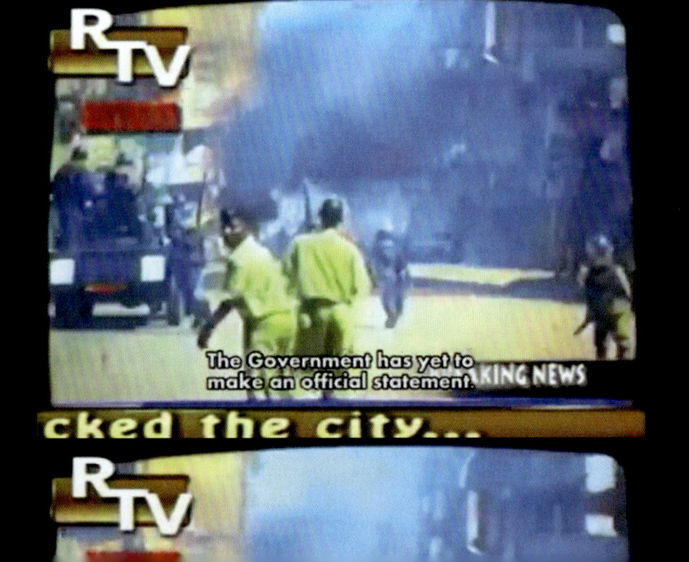
RTV
The Government has yet to
make an official statement.
AKING NEWS
cked the city...
RTV

Imagine war. What do you picture it to look like? Have you ever been involved in one—or is your idea based on the media you consume? There are countless representations of war; Some strive for authenticity, some were produced for entertainment. Others aim to deceive.

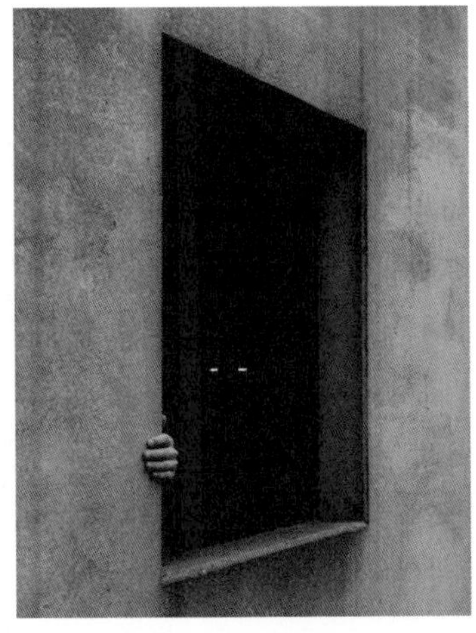

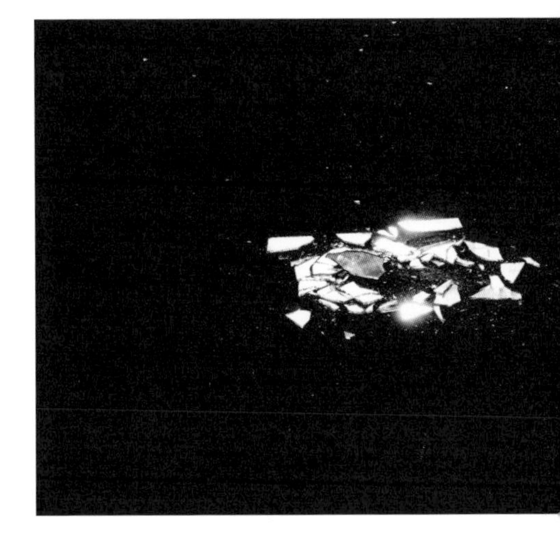

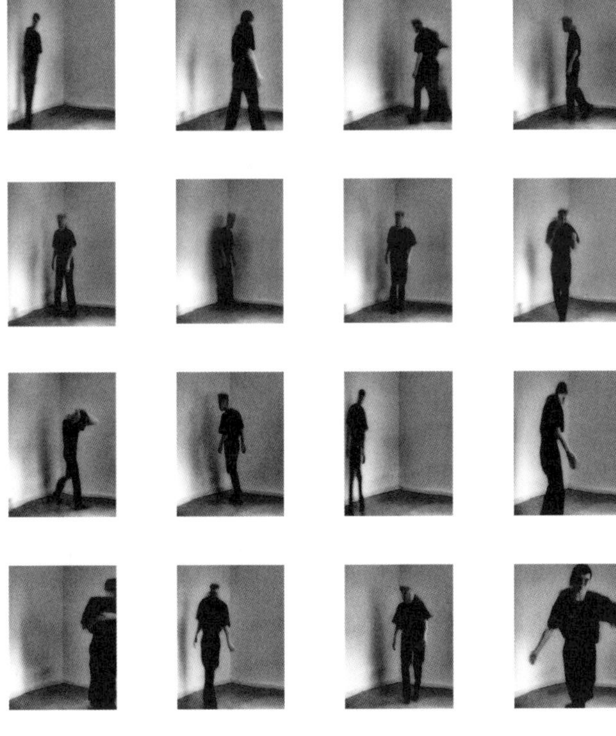

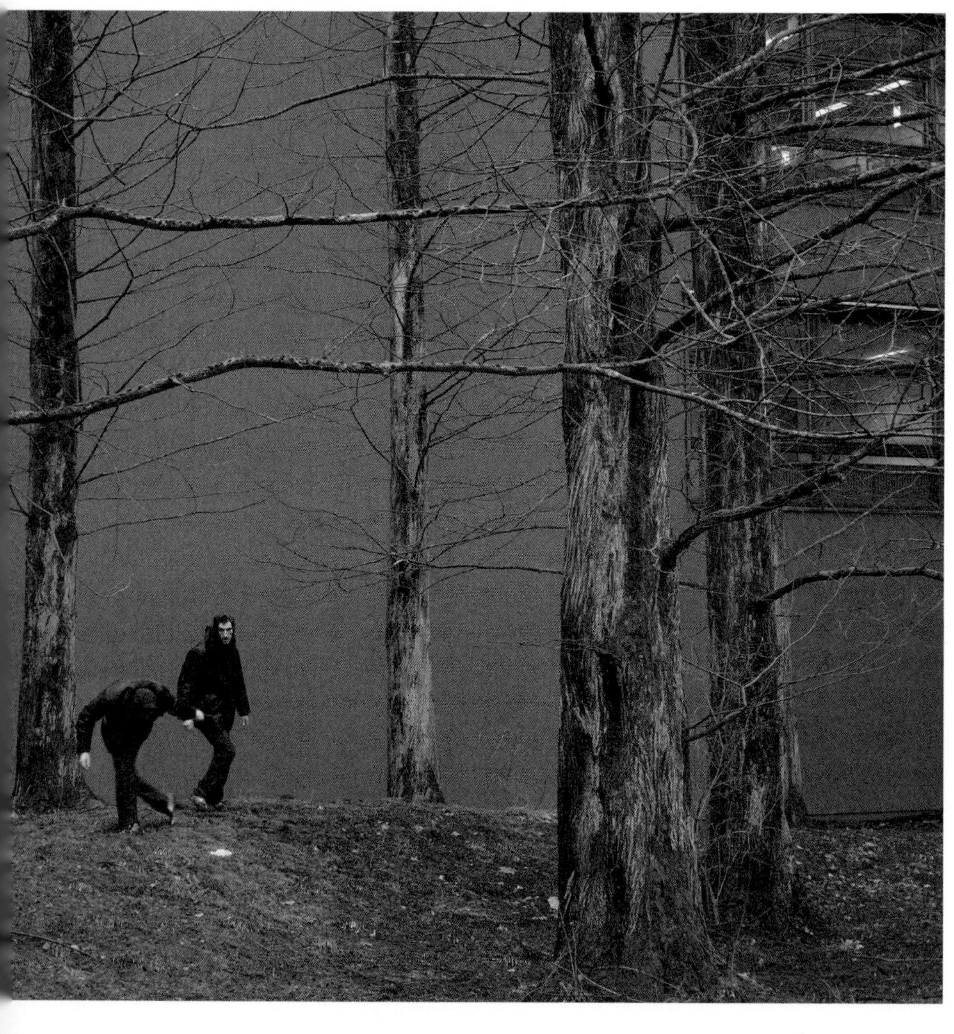

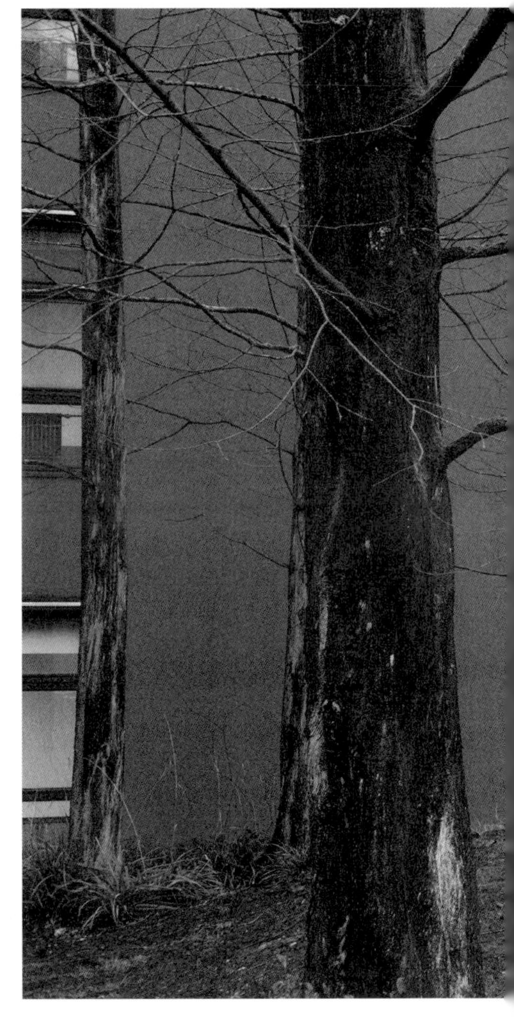

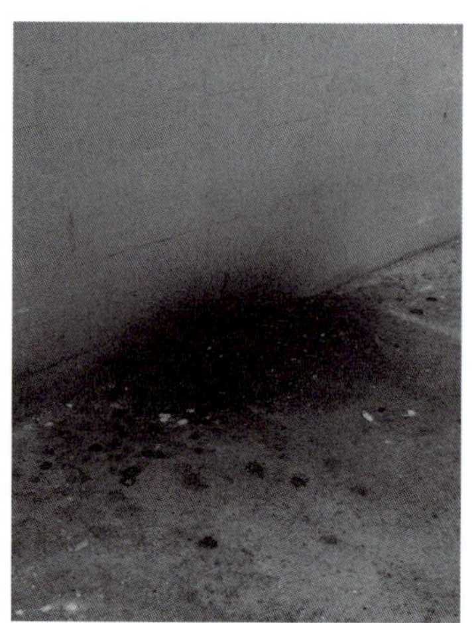

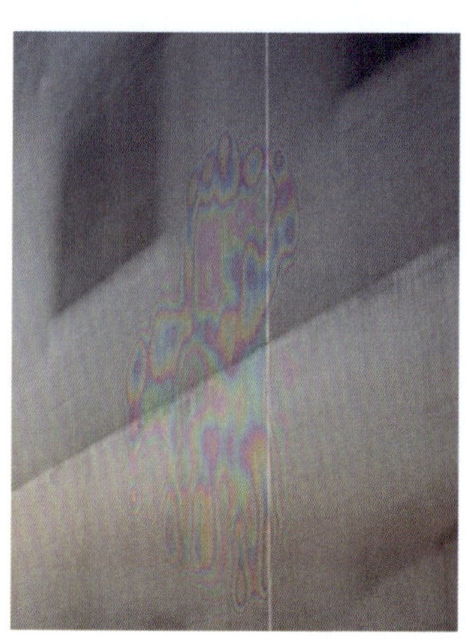

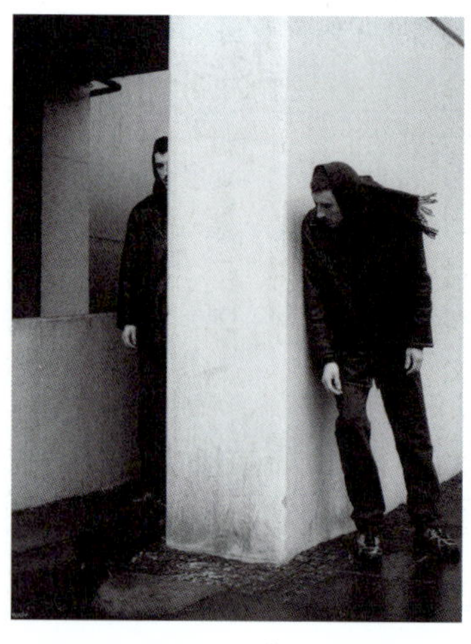

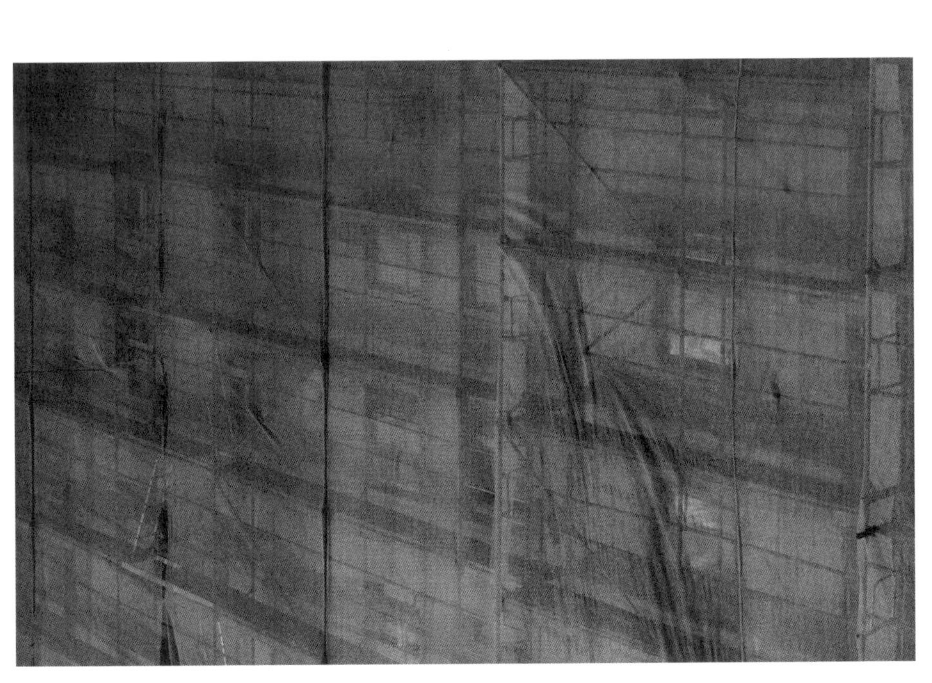

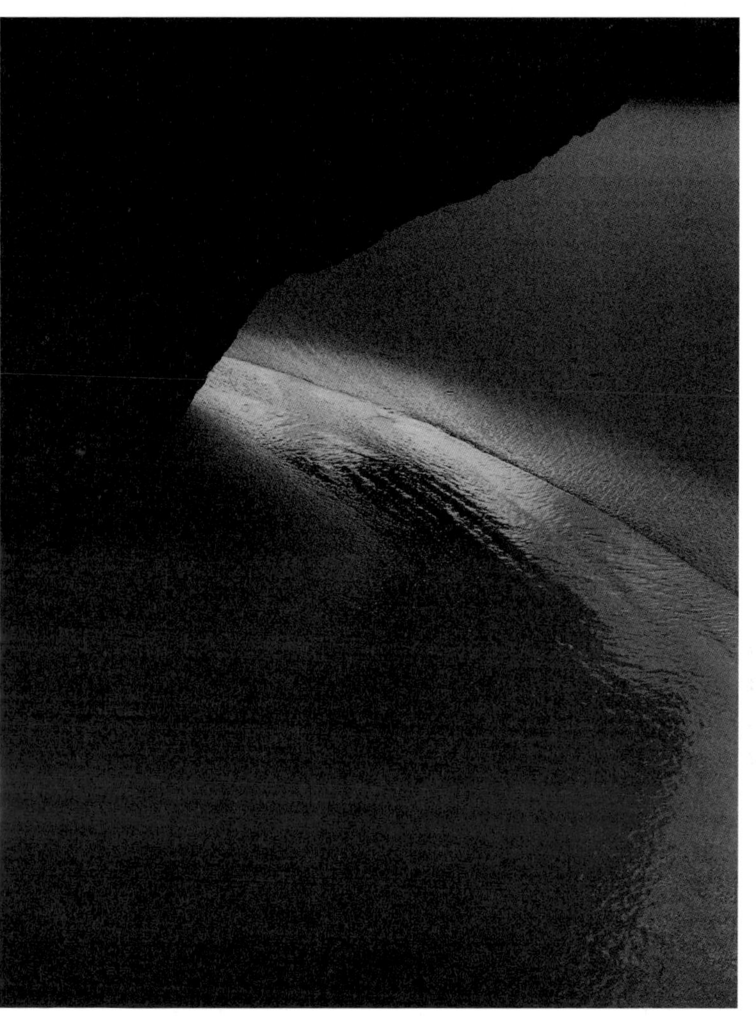

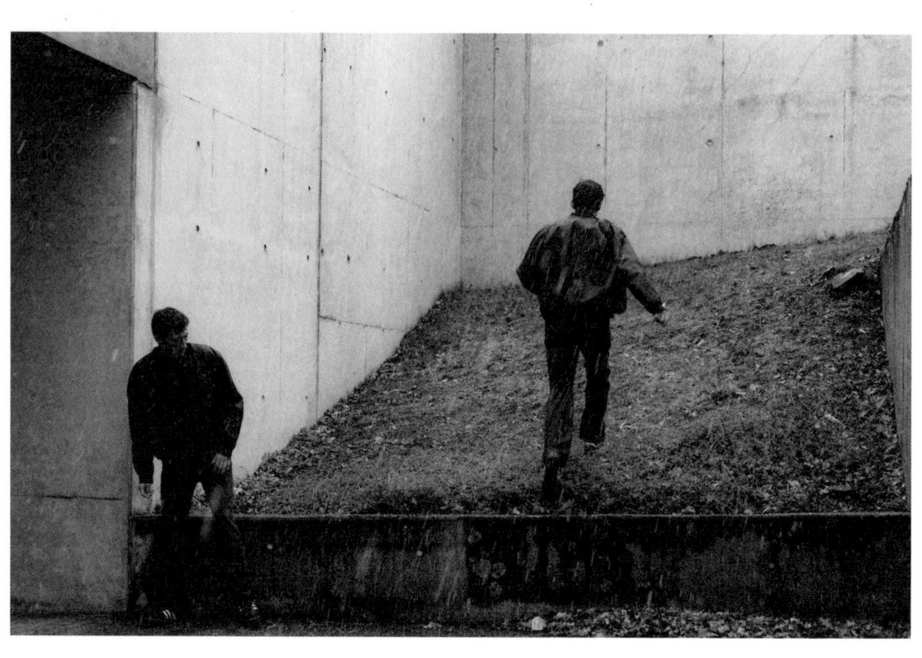

Facing what he feels is an ongoing narcissification of individuals and the resulting detachment from society, Yannis based his work on the philosopher Byung-Chul Han. In "Agony of Eros" he argues that, in a world of fetishized individualism and technologically mediated social interaction, it is the Other that is destroyed, not the self. Constantly comparing ourself with the Other and developing the need to take what we see in and make it our own, we risk our perception of love and desire.

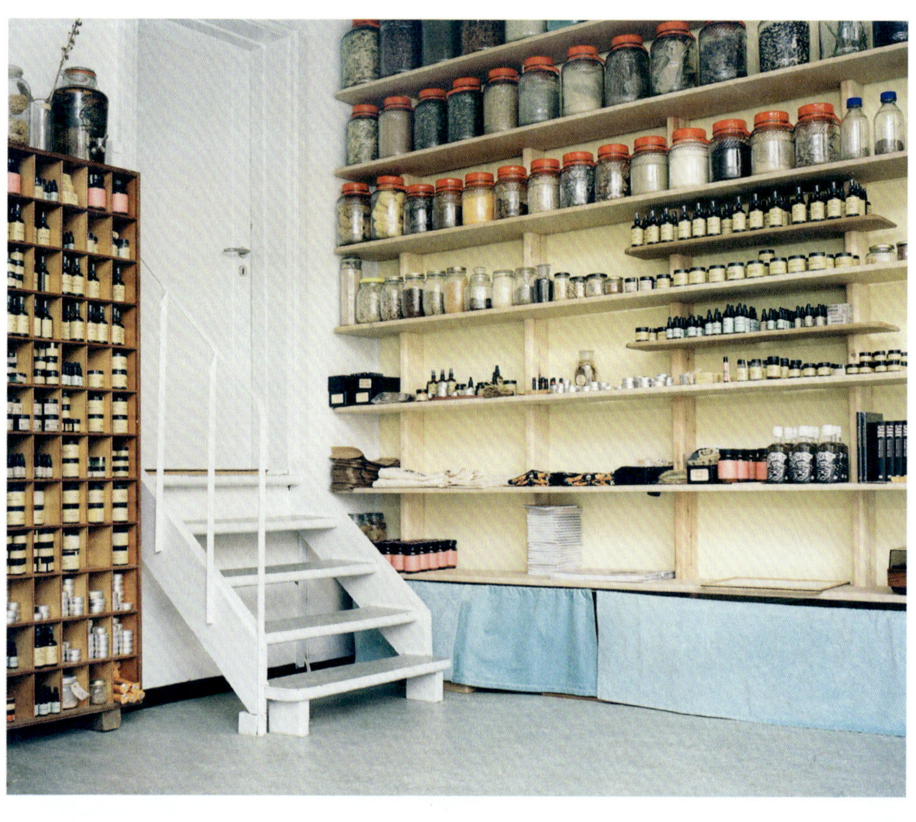

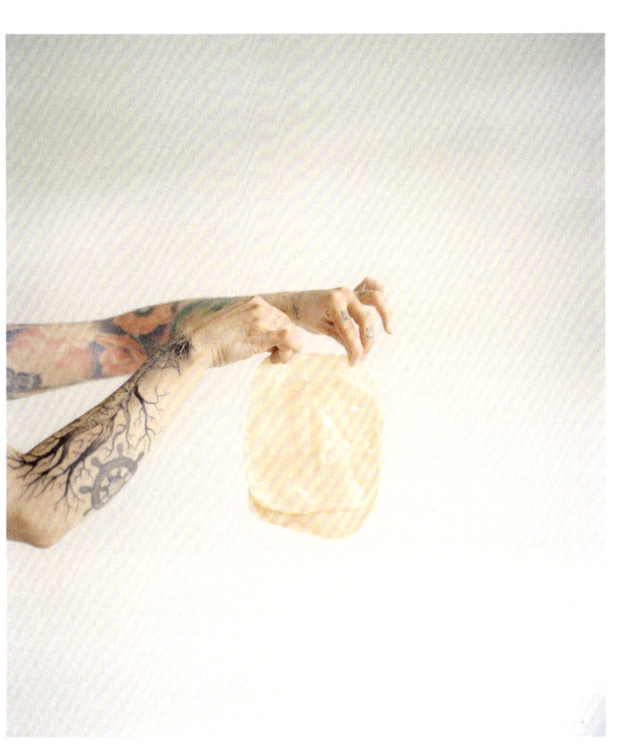

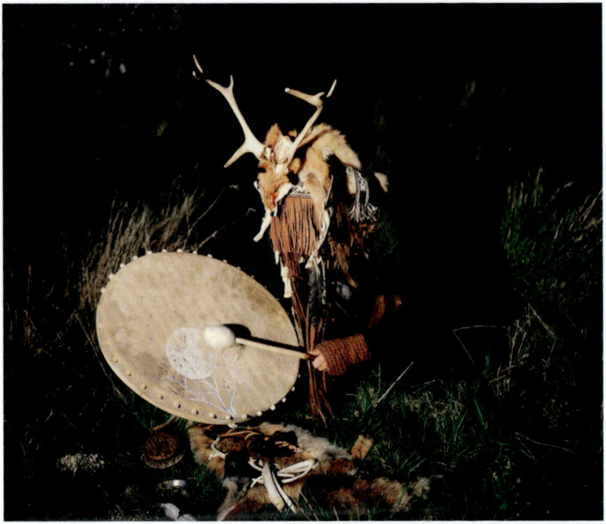

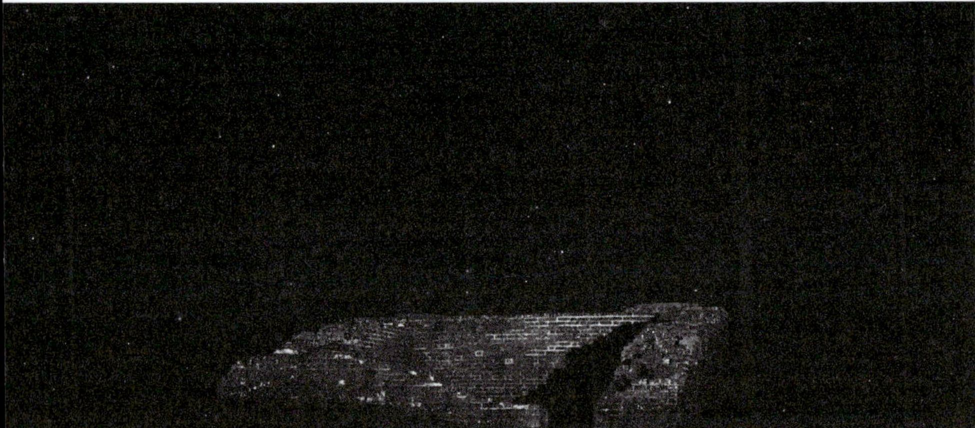

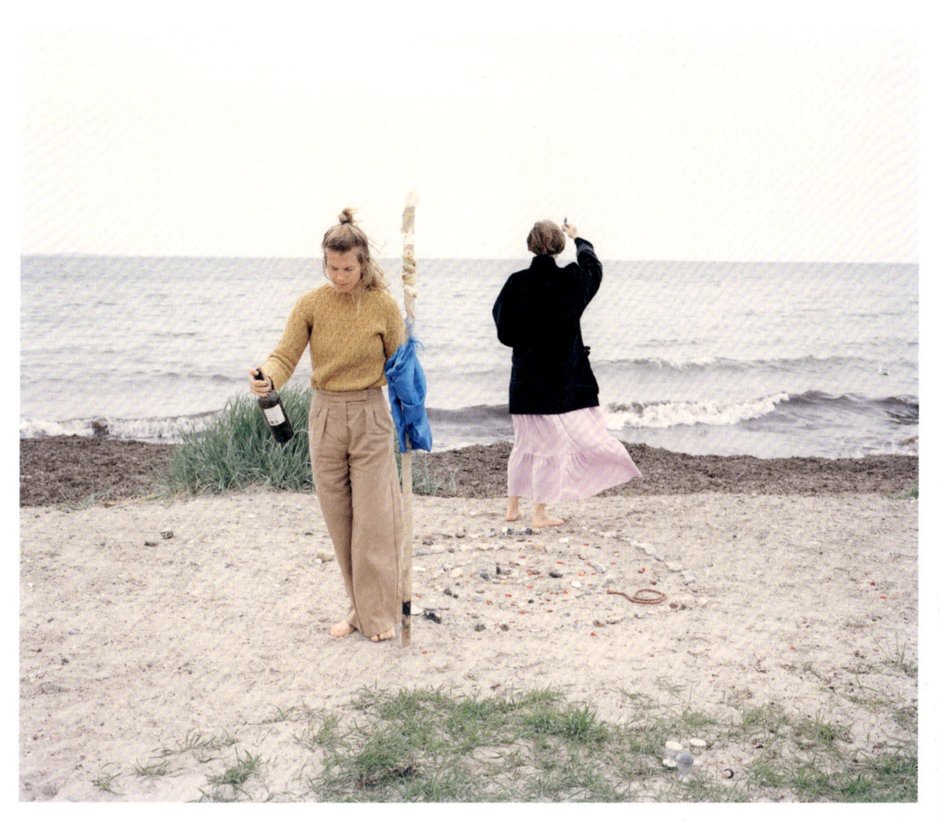

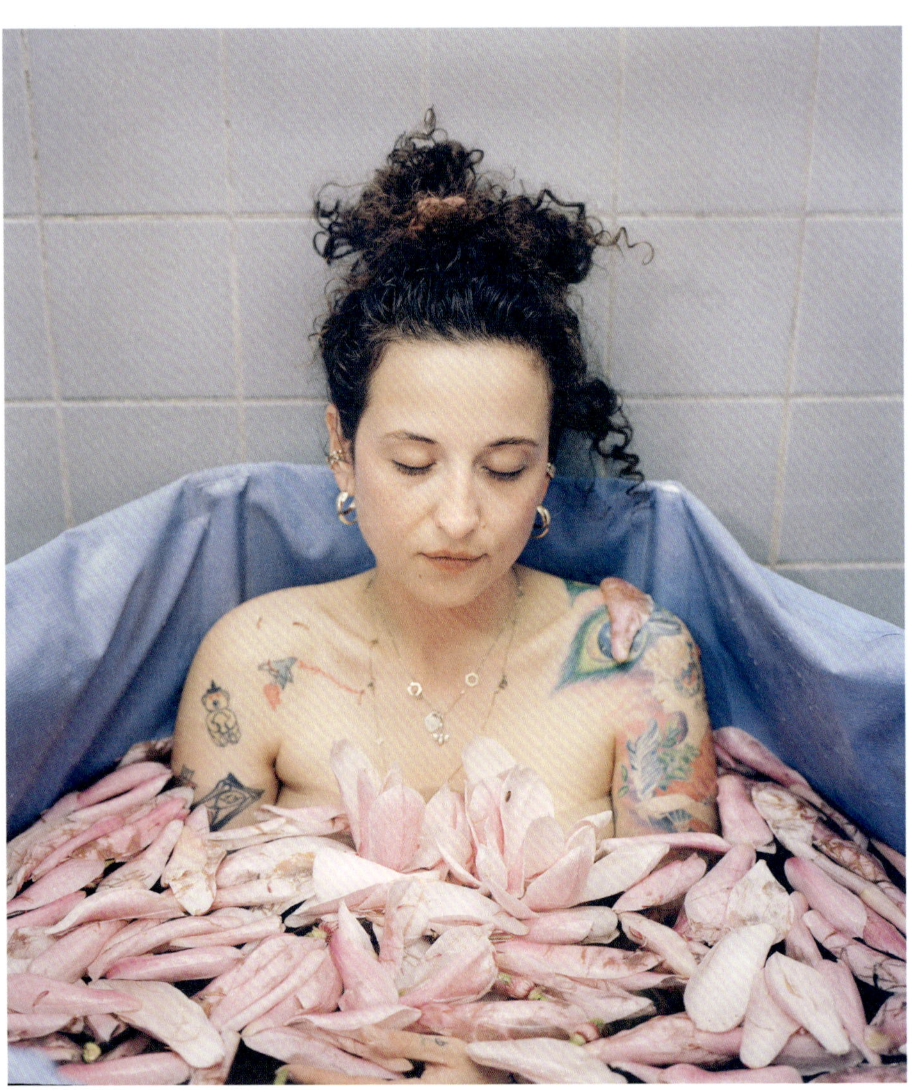

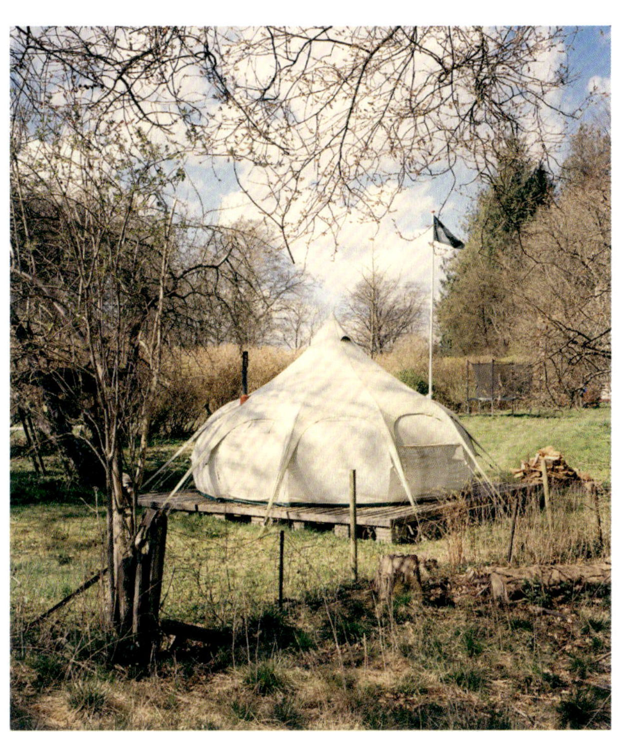

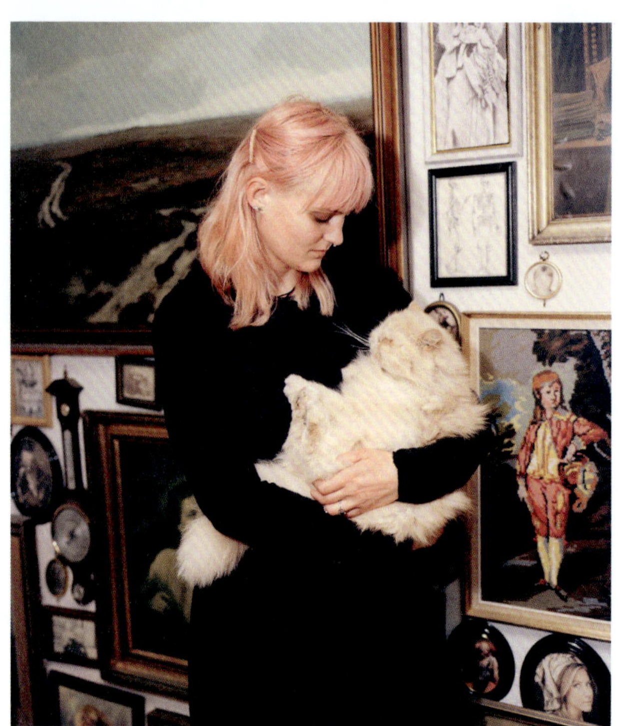

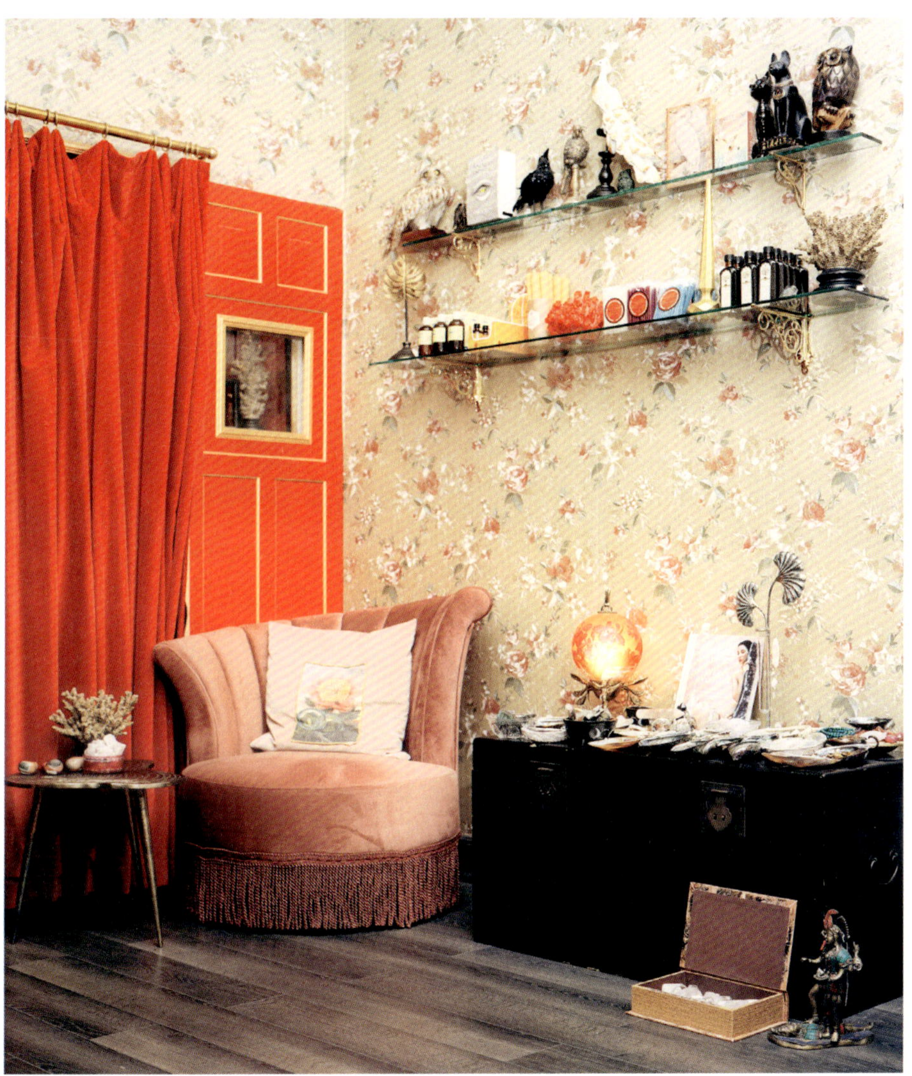

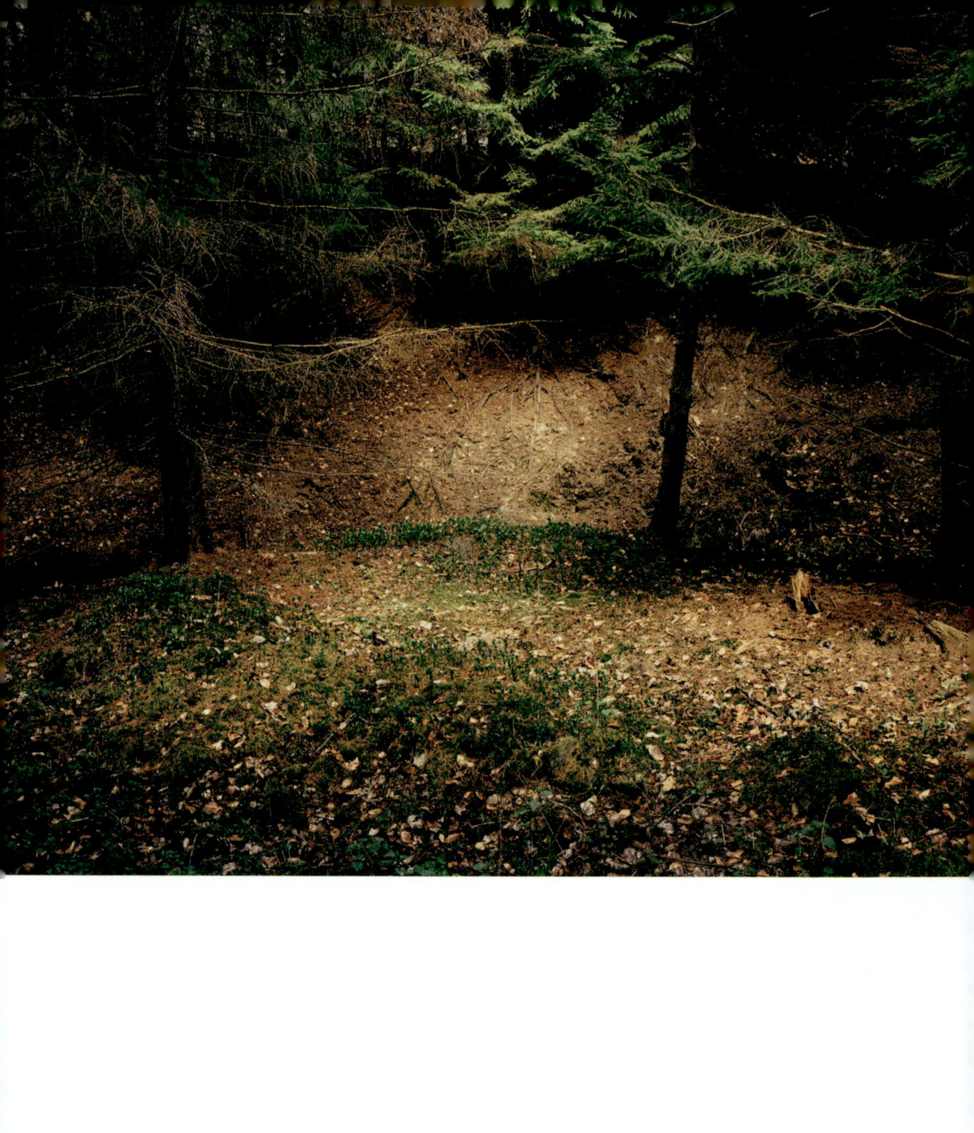

The witch huntings of the Early Modern Age are some of the darkest chapters in Europe's history. Denmark, in proportion to the country's population, was one of the most significant regions of these persecutions. Driven by the mostly negative image of the witch as an unmarried, childless, old woman, Amelie went out to search for contemporary perspectives on witchcraft among women who reclaim the term for themselves.

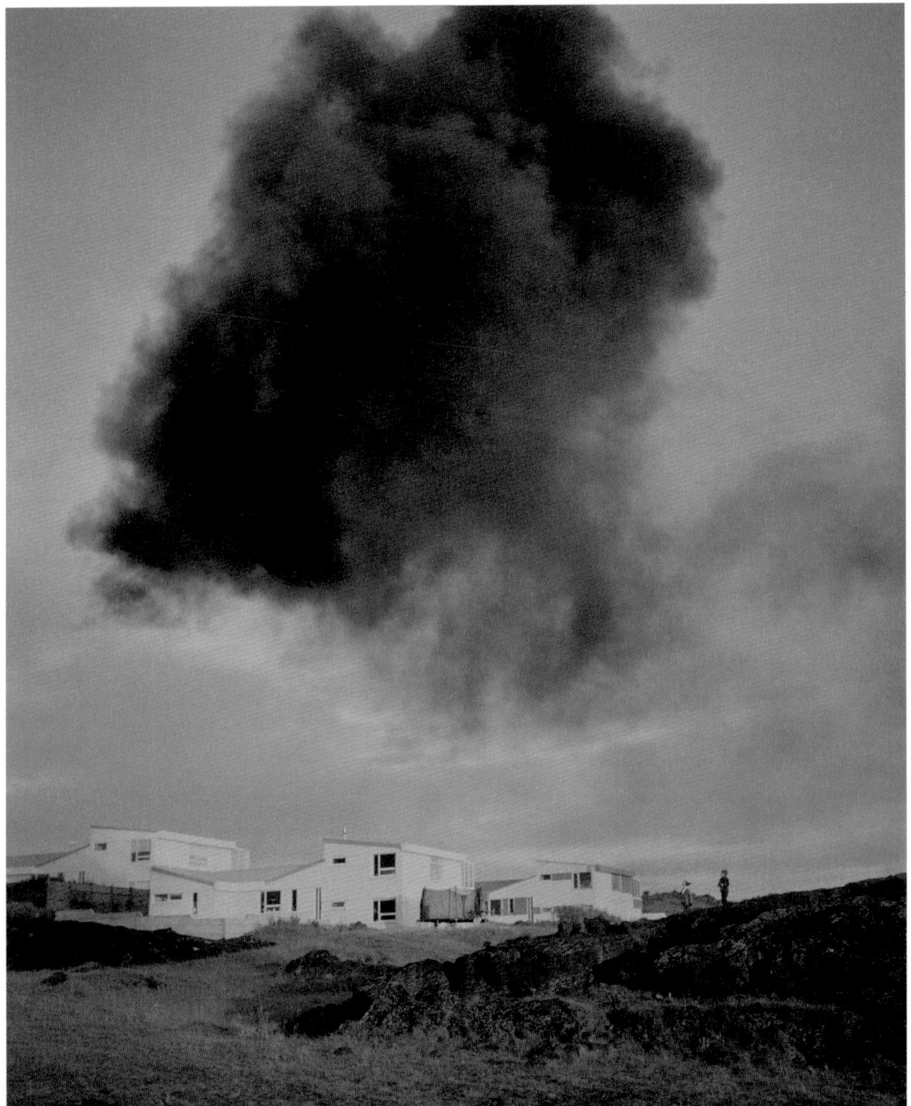

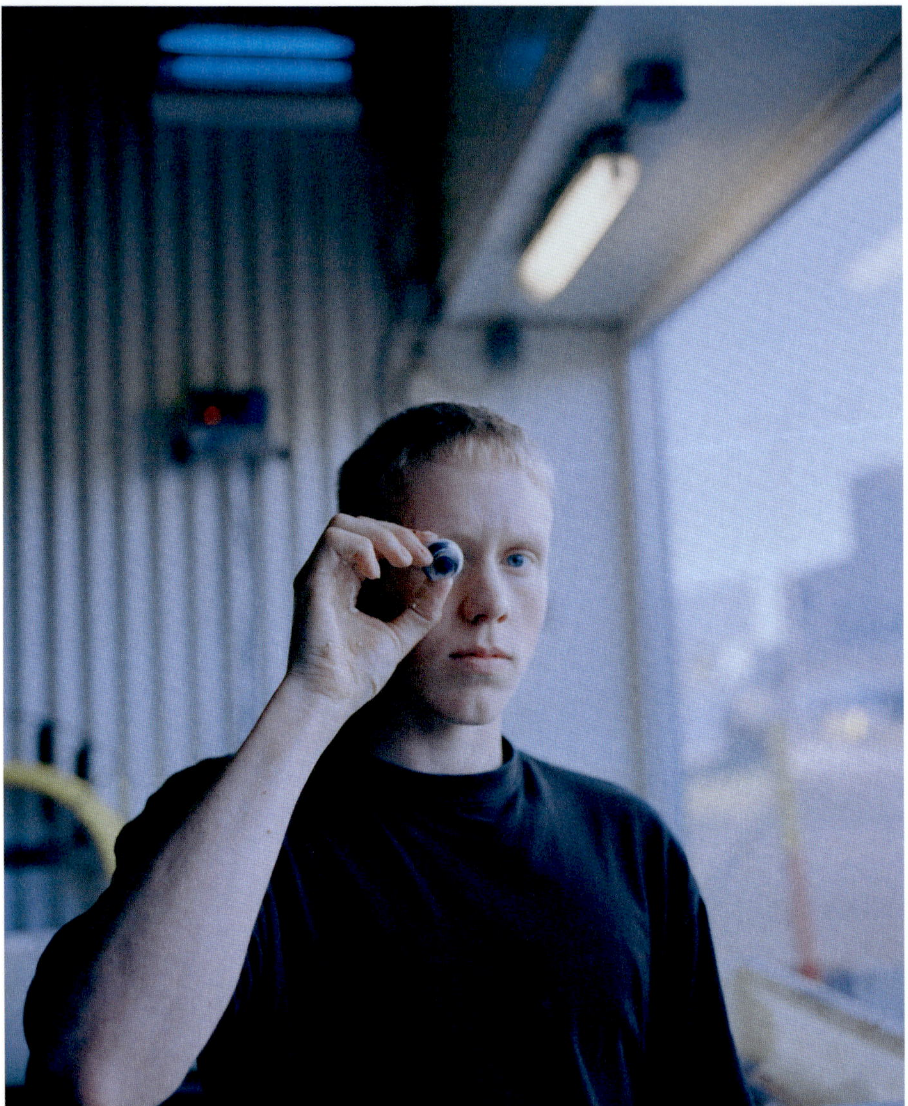

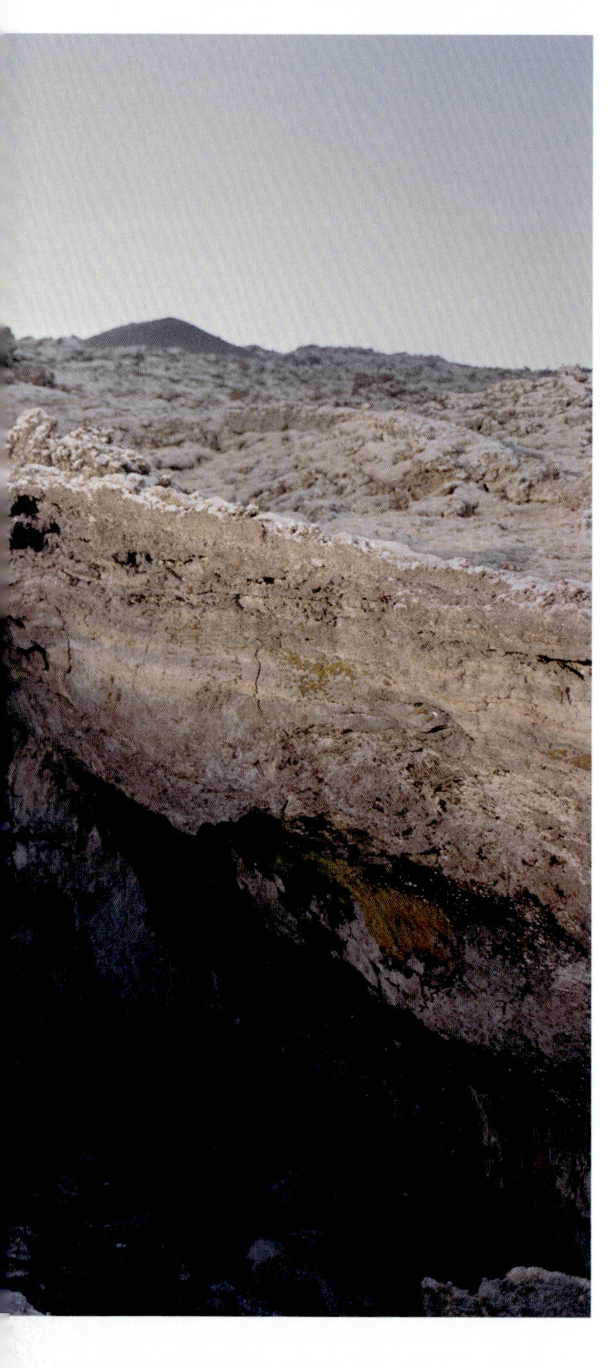

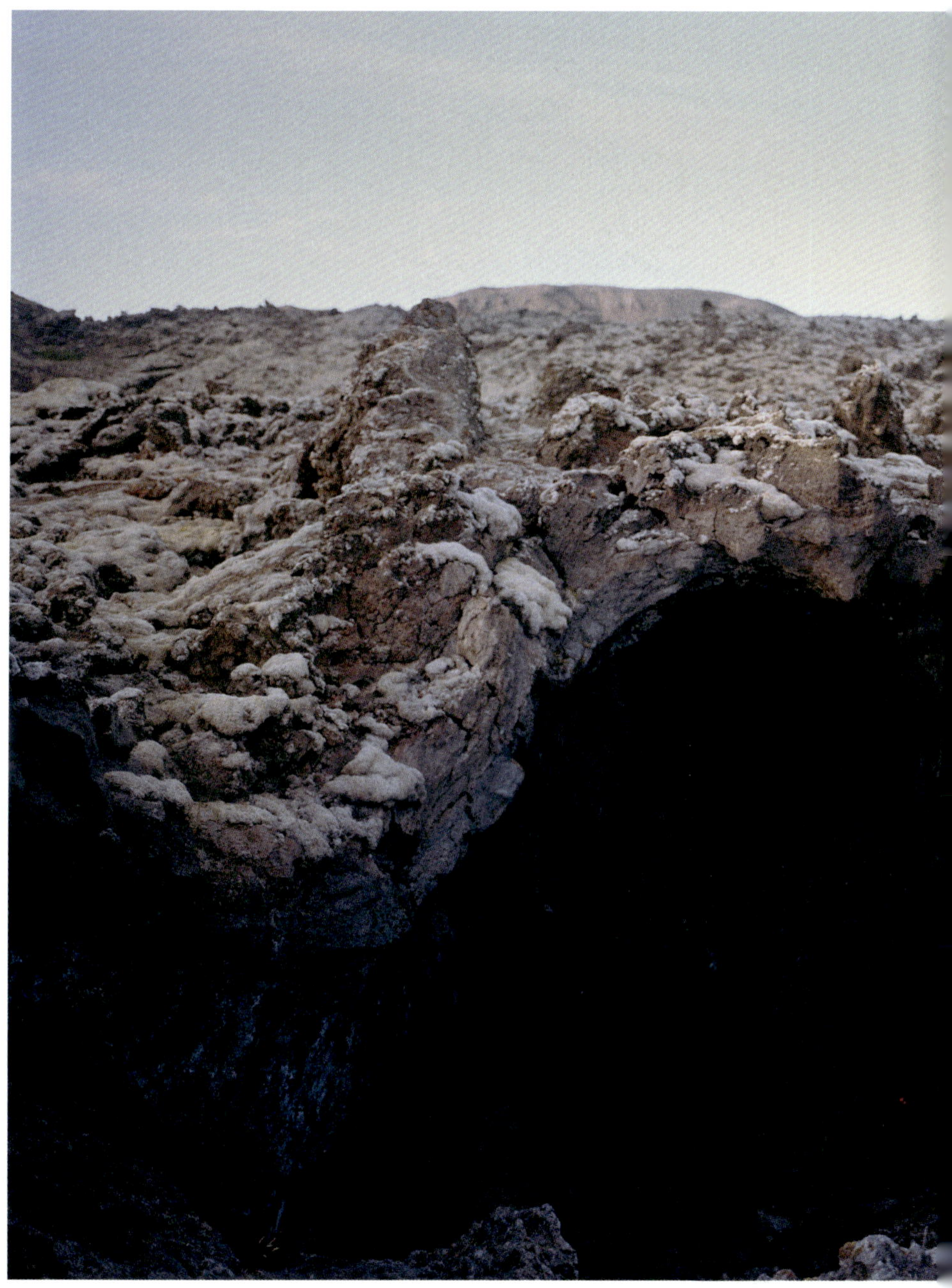

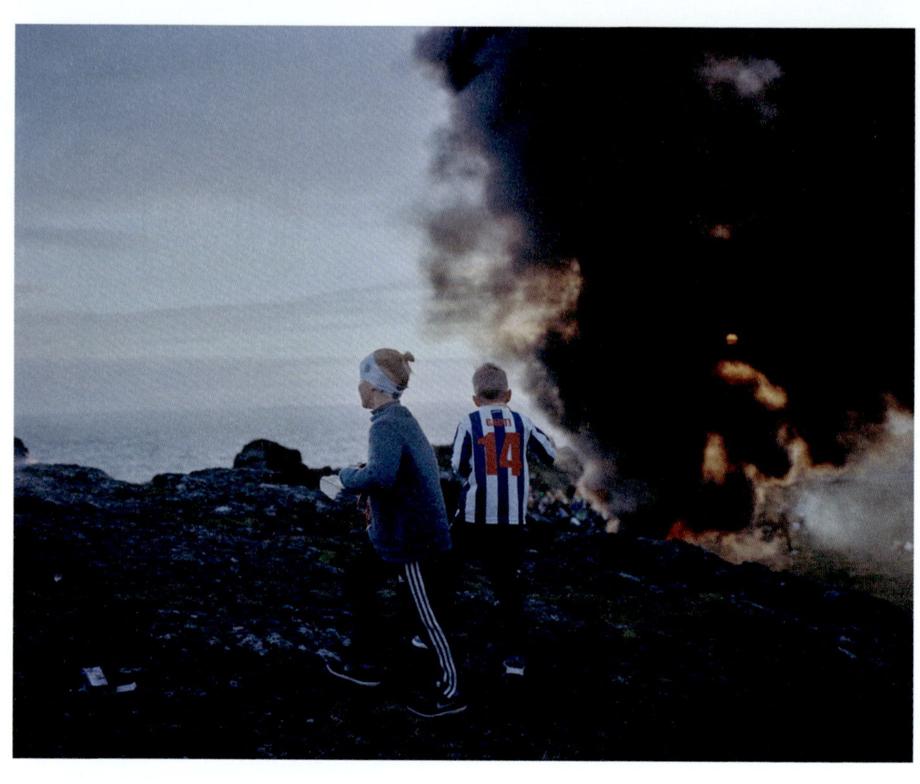
14

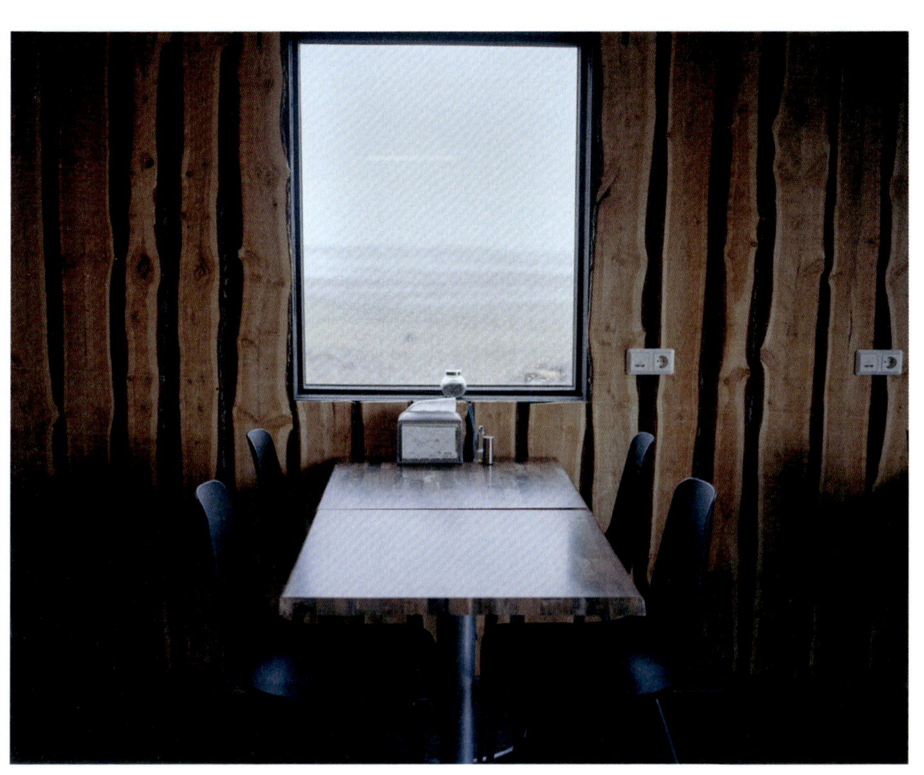

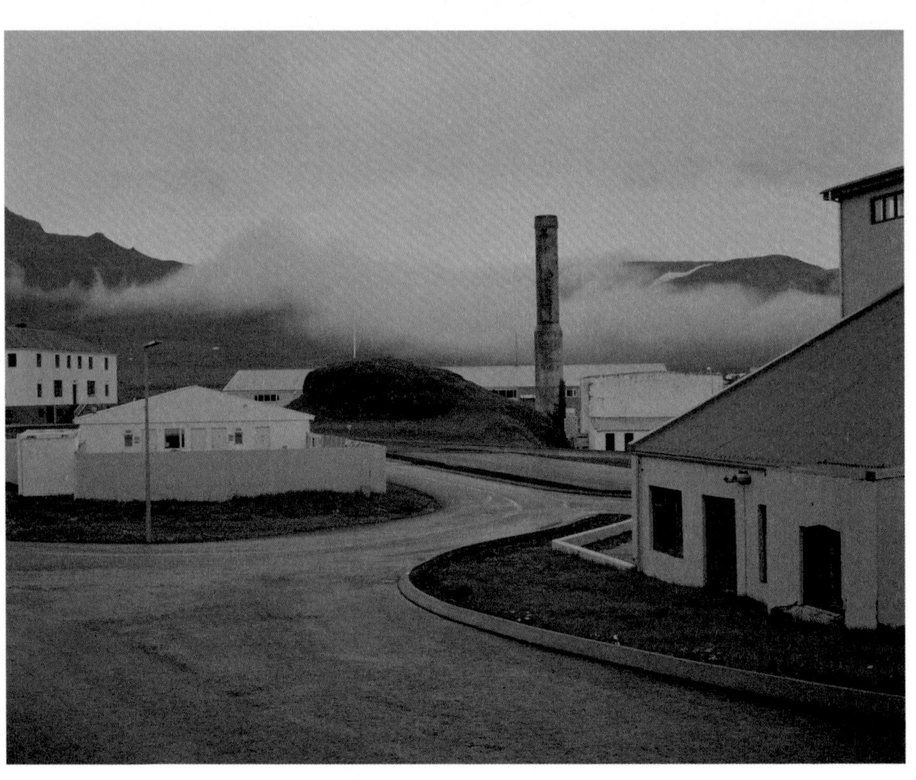

Shot in remote communities in Ice- land, Ludwig ref- lects on isolation, perception and memory. He mixes his conceptual approach with autobiographical elements—while avoiding a strict narrative, inviting the viewer to make their own inter- pretations and find resonance.

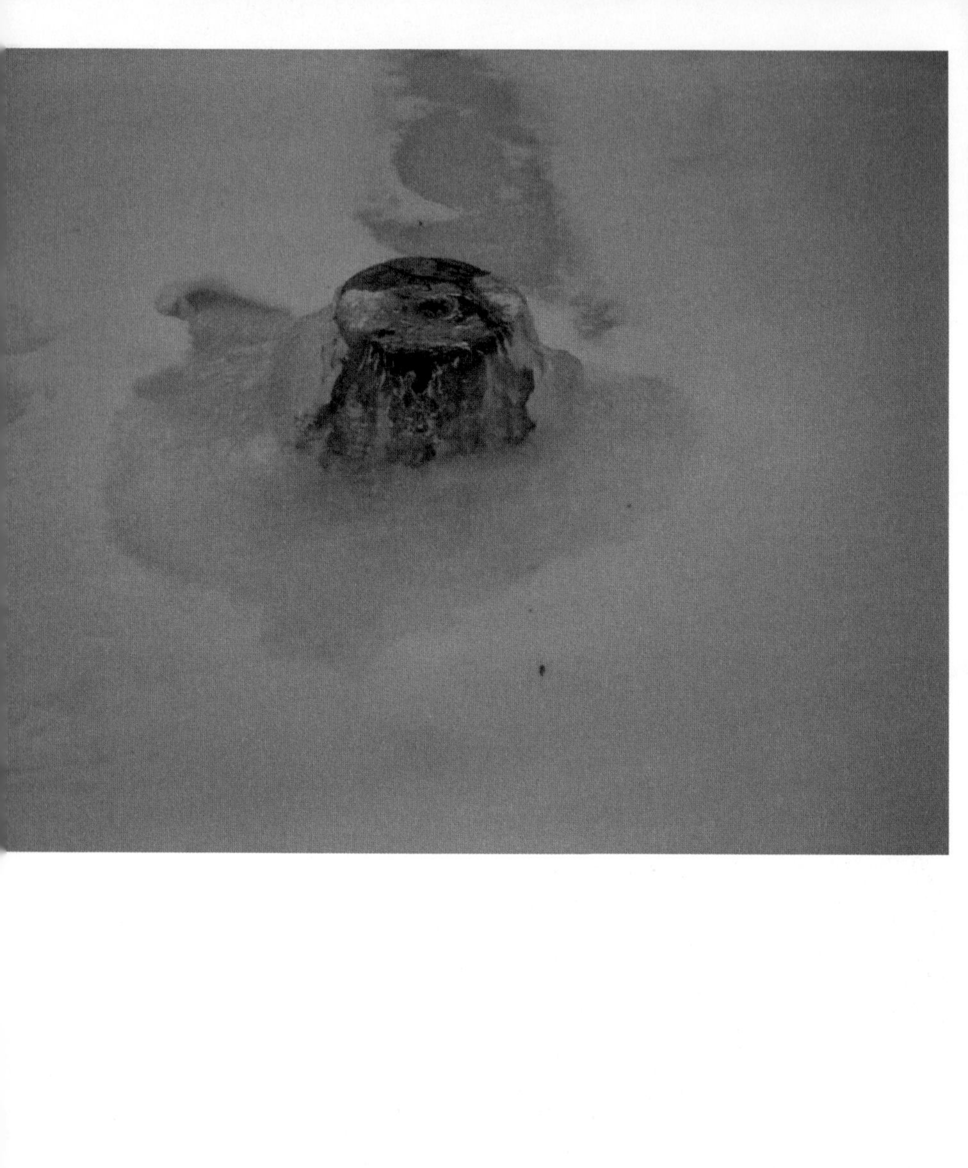

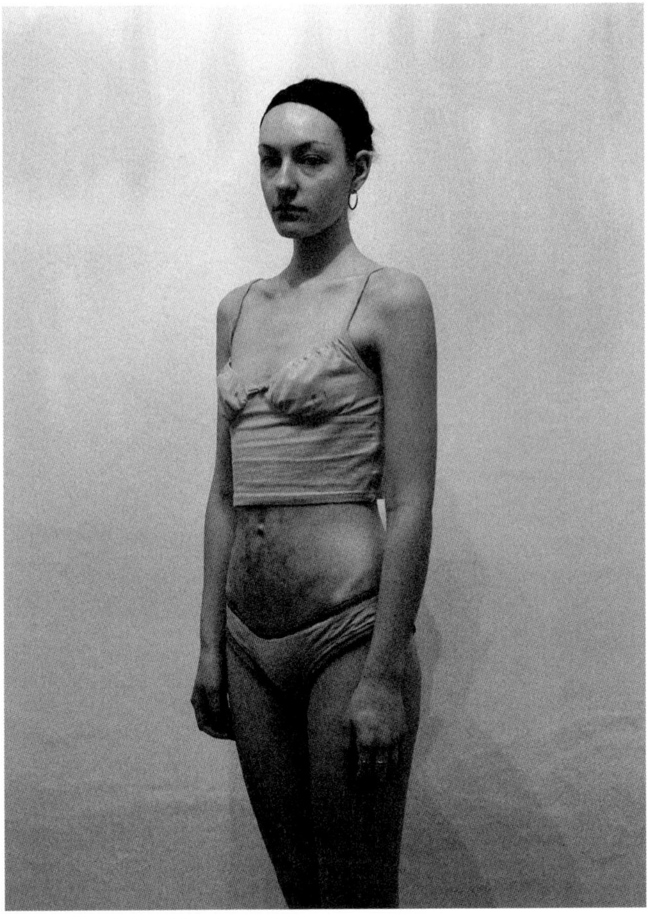

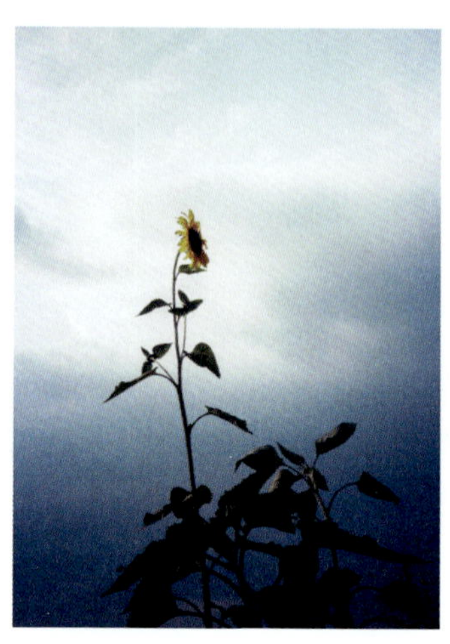

Tag 1

Fleisch mit Panade und Käse, wenig Gemüse, danach Kaffee. Starke Verzweiflung nach Mahlzeit, Ständiges verharren an auf 5 aufgedrehter Heizung. Knochen reiben schrecklich am Boden, ~~was~~ Ständiges Frieren und Schmerzen, gut zum Kalorienverbrennen. Abends im Gruppenraum „der Bachelor", nie wieder. Kurz vorm Schlafen 30 min unter heißem Wasser, Körperpflege mit Rasierer und Öl, zum ersten Mal seit langem, starkes Ekelgefühl beim Berühren des Körpers, Verzweiflung weil ich ~~mich~~ so fett bin, die Beine viel zu dick und sie wollen dass ich zunehme.

Schlechtes Einschlafen, durch die Wand kommen Zeichentrickseriengeräusche.

Tag 2

Urinprobe und Wiegen (51,2), starke Verzweiflung, beim Frühstück mit Aufstrichtöpfchen getrickst, Zucker geht gar nicht (Marmelade)

Tablette vergessen und Einsamkeit, viel Schnee aus dem Fenster, Buch „der letzte Satz" angefangen. Stimmung nicht gut, wegen Körpergewicht Angst, dass Wärmflaschenverbrennung verschwindet. Die Anorexen sehen echt scheiße aus.

Halben Nachtisch gegessen (Apfelkuchen) werde ich in Zukunft bleiben lassen. Alle Anorexen haben ihn stehen lassen.

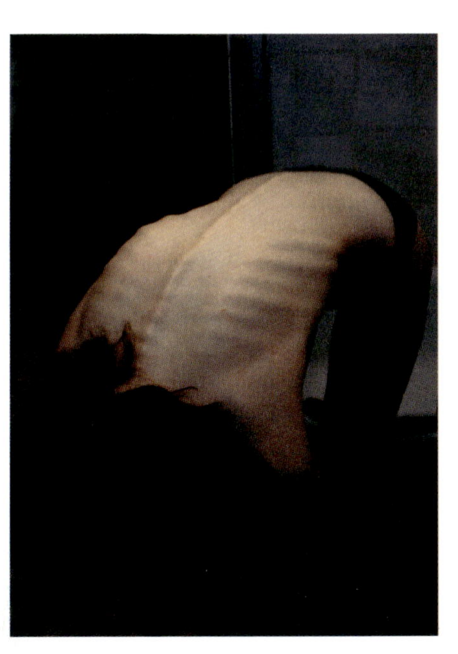

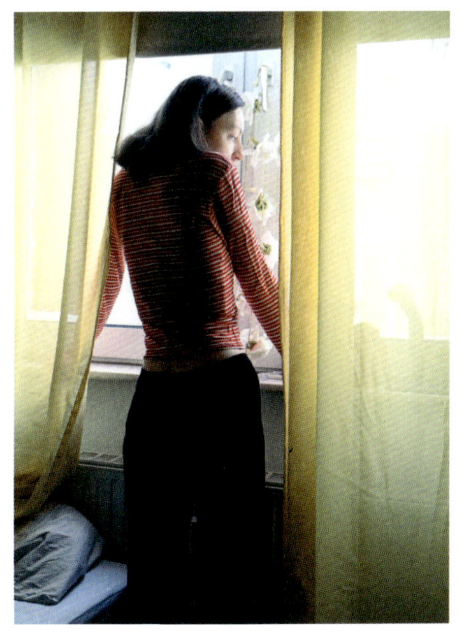

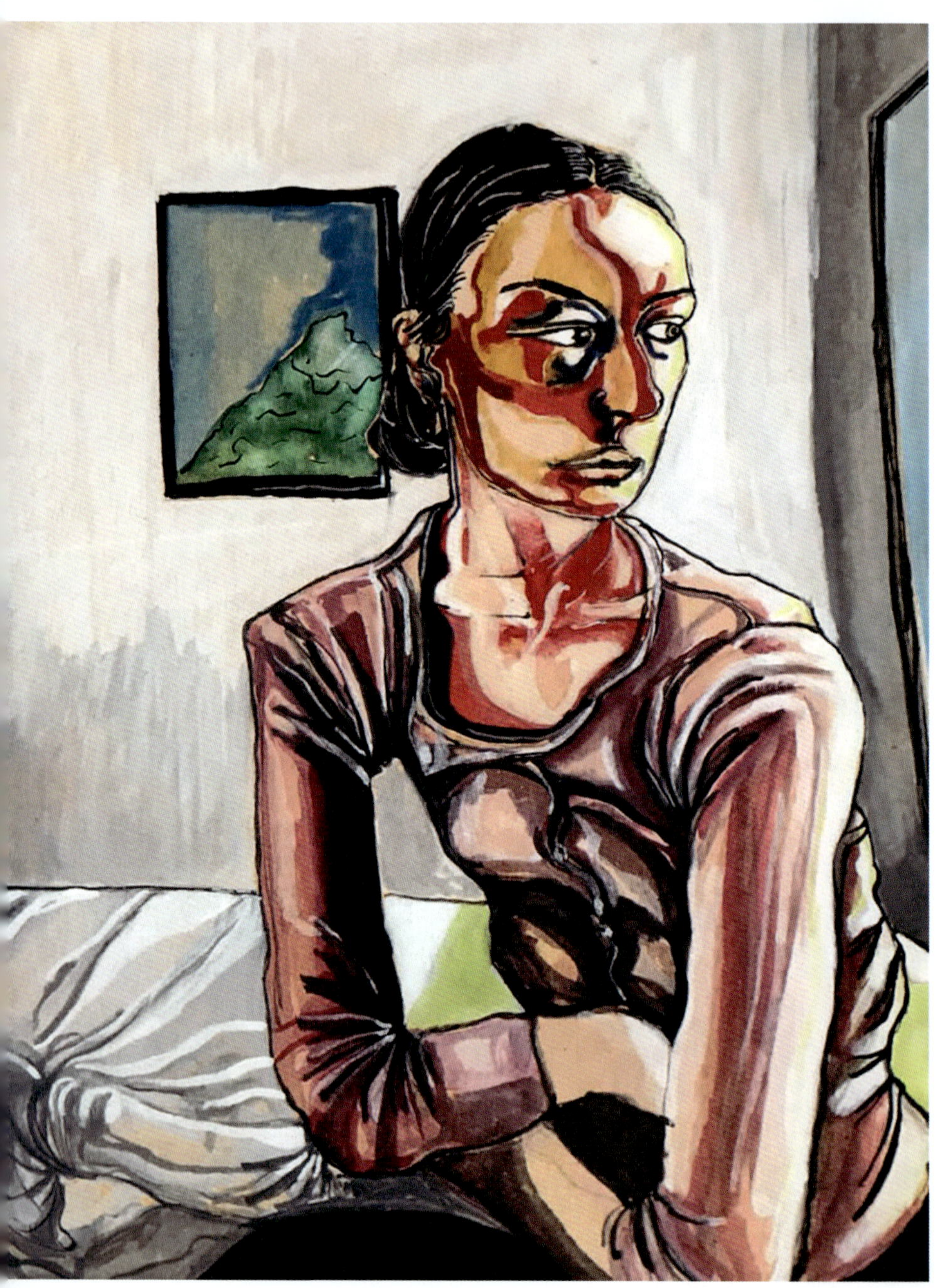

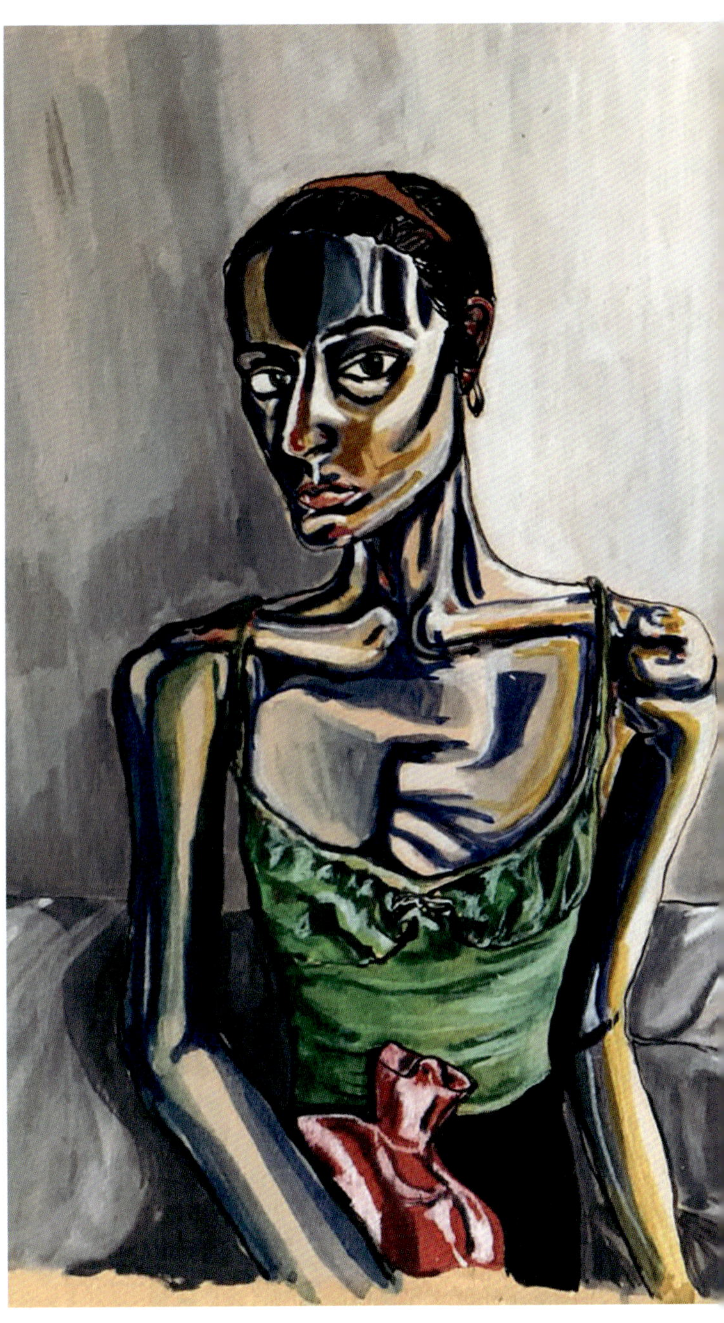

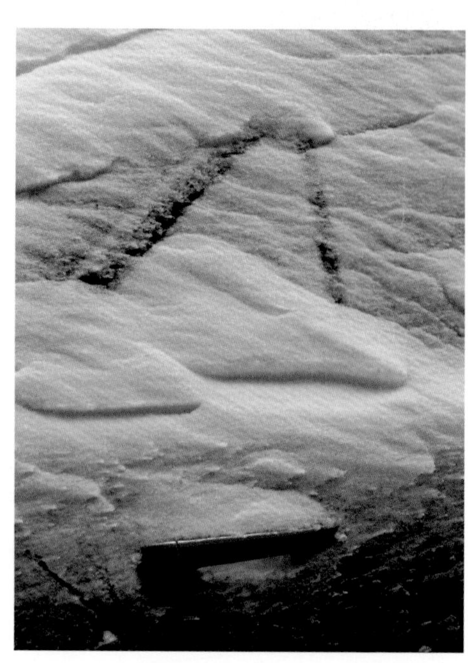

was ich essen würde

- Spargel 1 Scheibe VK-Brot
- alle Gewürzgurken + Zwiebelchen
- Kräuterquark
- Deko aus Petersilie, Tomate
- Radieschen
- halbes Ei

schlimme Angst vor

- weißem Toastbrot (Angst vor nicht verdauen können -> Darmverschluss (dumm aber ohne Scheiß ich hab echt Angst davor)
- Fleisch weil fettig und arme Tiere
- Chips -> direkt Zunahme -> leere Kalorien
- Teigtaste, Kohlenhydrate, selbst beim Angucken merke ich, wie meine Beine dicker werden -> Bewegungsdrang jetzt!
- Säfte = purer Zucker! soviele Orangen kann ich gar nicht essen
- Kuchen Sahne niemals

unangenehm, will weglaufen, ~~et~~ habe den Geruch in der Nase!'

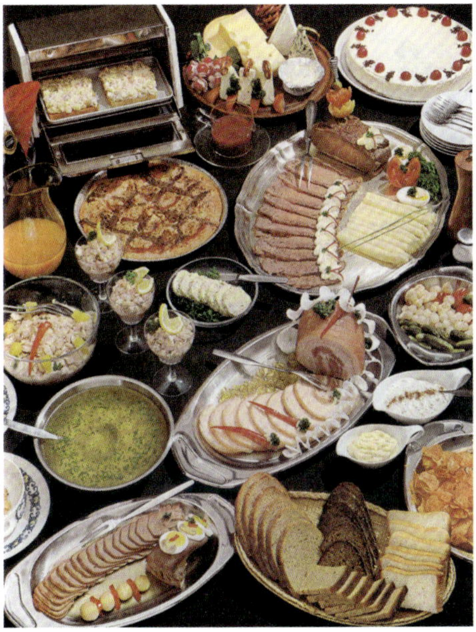

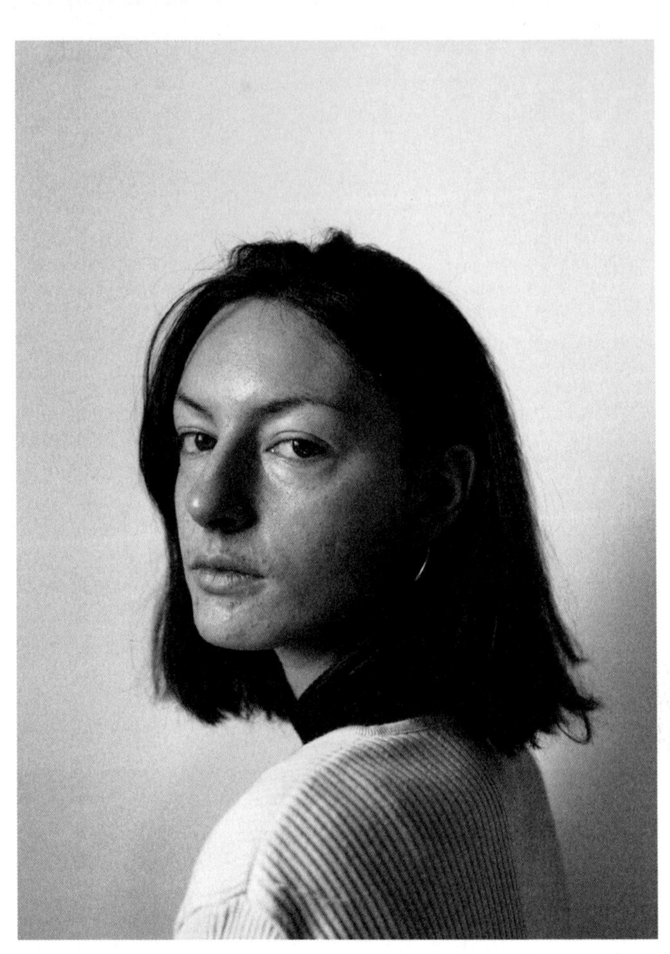